International Political Economy Series

Series Editor: **Timothy M. Shaw**, Visiting Professor, University of Massachusetts Boston, USA and Emeritus Professor, University of London, UK

The global political economy is in flux as a series of cumulative crises impacts its organization and governance. The IPE series has tracked its development in both analysis and structure over the last three decades. It has always had a concentration on the global South. Now the South increasingly challenges the North as the centre of development, also reflected in a growing number of submissions and publications on indebted Eurozone economies in Southern Europe.

An indispensable resource for scholars and researchers, the series examines a variety of capitalisms and connections by focusing on emerging economies, companies and sectors, debates and policies. It informs diverse policy communities as the established trans-Atlantic North declines and 'the rest', especially the BRICS, rise.

Titles include:

Yıldız Atasoy (*editor*)
GLOBAL ECONOMIC CRISIS AND THE POLITICS OF DIVERSITY

Gabriel Siles-Brügge
CONSTRUCTING EUROPEAN UNION TRADE POLICY A Global Idea of Europe

Jewellord Singh and France Bourgouin (*editors*)
RESOURCE GOVERNANCE AND DEVELOPMENTAL STATES IN THE GLOBAL SOUTH
Critical International Political Economy Perspectives

Tan Tai Yong and Md Mizanur Rahman (*editors*)
DIASPORA ENGAGEMENT AND DEVELOPMENT IN SOUTH ASIA

Leila Simona Talani, Alexander Clarkson and Ramon Pacheco Pardo (*editors*)
DIRTY CITIES
Towards a Political Economy of the Underground in Global Cities

Matthew Louis Bishop
THE POLITICAL ECONOMY OF CARIBBEAN DEVELOPMENT

Xiaoming Huang (*editor*)
MODERN ECONOMIC DEVELOPMENT IN JAPAN AND CHINA
Developmentalism, Capitalism and the World Economic System

Bonnie K. Campbell (*editor*)
MODES OF GOVERNANCE AND REVENUE FLOWS OF AFRICAN MINING

Gopinath Pillai (*editor*)
THE POLITICAL ECONOMY OF SOUTH ASIAN DIASPORA
Patterns of Socio-Economic Influence

Rachel K. Brickner (*editor*)
MIGRATION, GLOBALIZATION AND THE STATE

Juanita Elias and Samanthi Gunawardana (*editors*)
THE GLOBAL POLITICAL ECONOMY OF THE HOUSEHOLD IN ASIA

Tony Heron
PATHWAYS FROM PREFERENTIAL TRADE
The Politics of Trade Adjustment in Africa, the Caribbean and Pacific

David J. Hornsby
RISK REGULATION, SCIENCE AND INTERESTS IN TRANSATLANTIC TRADE CONFLICTS

Yang Jiang
CHINA'S POLICYMAKING FOR REGIONAL ECONOMIC COOPERATION

Martin Geiger and Antoine Pécoud (*editors*)
DISCIPLINING THE TRANSNATIONAL MOBILITY OF PEOPLE

Michael Breen
THE POLITICS OF IMF LENDING

Laura Carsten Mahrenbach
THE TRADE POLICY OF EMERGING POWERS
Strategic Choices of Brazil and India

Vassilis K. Fouskas and Constantine Dimoulas
GREECE, FINANCIALIZATION AND THE EU
The Political Economy of Debt and Destruction

Hany Besada and Shannon Kindornay (*editors*)
MULTILATERAL DEVELOPMENT COOPERATION IN A CHANGING GLOBAL ORDER

Caroline Kuzemko
THE ENERGY SECURITY-CLIMATE NEXUS
Institutional Change in Britain and Beyond

Hans Löfgren and Owain David Williams (*editors*)
THE NEW POLITICAL ECONOMY OF PHARMACEUTICALS
Production, Innovation and TRIPS in the Global South

Timothy Cadman (*editor*)
CLIMATE CHANGE AND GLOBAL POLICY REGIMES
Towards Institutional Legitimacy

Mark Hudson, Ian Hudson and Mara Fridell
FAIR TRADE, SUSTAINABILITY, AND SOCIAL CHANGE

Andrés Rivarola Puntigliano and José Briceño-Ruiz (*editors*)
RESILIENCE OF REGIONALISM IN LATIN AMERICA AND THE CARIBBEAN
Development and Autonomy

Godfrey Baldacchino (*editor*)
THE POLITICAL ECONOMY OF DIVIDED ISLANDS
Unified Geographies, Multiple Polities

Mark Findlay
CONTEMPORARY CHALLENGES IN REGULATING GLOBAL CRISES

Helen Hawthorne
LEAST DEVELOPED COUNTRIES AND THE WTO
Special Treatment in Trade

Nir Kshetri
CYBERCRIME AND CYBERSECURITY IN THE GLOBAL SOUTH

Kristian Stokke and Olle Törnquist (*editors*)
DEMOCRATIZATION IN THE GLOBAL SOUTH
The Importance of Transformative Politics

Jeffrey D. Wilson
GOVERNING GLOBAL PRODUCTION
Resource Networks in the Asia-Pacific Steel Industry

International Political Economy Series
Series Standing Order ISBN 978–0–333–71708–0 hardcover
Series Standing Order ISBN 978–0–333–71110–1 paperback
(*outside North America only*)

You can receive future titles in this series as they are published by placing a standing order. Please contact your bookseller or, in case of difficulty, write to us at the address below with your name and address, the title of the series and one of the ISBNs quoted above.

Customer Services Department, Macmillan Distribution Ltd, Houndmills, Basingstoke, Hampshire RG21 6XS, England

---

Global Economic Crisis and the Politics of Diversity

Edited by

Yıldız Atasoy
Professor of Sociology, Simon Fraser University, Canada

palgrave
macmillan

First published 2014 by
PALGRAVE MACMILLAN

Palgrave Macmillan in the UK is an imprint of Macmillan Publishers Limited, registered in England, company number 785998, of Houndmills, Basingstoke, Hampshire RG21 6XS.

Palgrave Macmillan in the US is a division of St Martin's Press LLC, 175 Fifth Avenue, New York, NY 10010.

Palgrave Macmillan is the global academic imprint of the above companies and has companies and representatives throughout the world.

Palgrave® and Macmillan® are registered trademarks in the United States, the United Kingdom, Europe and other countries.

ISBN 978–1–137–29367–1

This book is printed on paper suitable for recycling and made from fully managed and sustained forest sources. Logging, pulping and manufacturing processes are expected to conform to the environmental regulations of the country of origin.

A catalogue record for this book is available from the British Library.

A catalog record for this book is available from the Library of Congress.

Transferred to Digital Printing in 2014

Contents

Part III State Restructuring and Economic Development

Part IV Alternative Forms of Politics

Figures and Tables

Figures

Tables

Acknowledgements

This volume has been created through the collective effort of scholars who participated in an international workshop in early September 2011. The workshop took place at Simon Fraser University (SFU) in Vancouver, Canada, under the auspices of SFU's Department of Sociology and Anthropology. I was Chair of the organizing committee. The intensive two-day workshop brought together an interdisciplinary group of scholars from six countries: Brazil, China, India, Mexico, Turkey, and Canada. It generated interdisciplinary dialogue across empirical cases and theoretical perspectives, allowing us to explore the different realities and multifaceted forms of global crisis that accompany historical and geographical variations among countries in the global proliferation of a market model. The participants of the workshop wrote their initial papers in early 2011. The completed papers were distributed to participants and read by them before the workshop began. Because the workshop was closed and invitational, and the papers were read prior to the meeting, participants were provided ample opportunity for extensive feedback on, and critique of, papers presented for publication.

There were 23 papers initially presented at the workshop, from which I selected 13 for inclusion in the workshop proceedings. Each paper was then sent to independent academic reviewers and revised, based on comments from external reviewers, in addition to several rounds of my own reviews and editorial revisions. Following this extensive process, ten papers were selected to become chapters for the book. I would like to take this opportunity to acknowledge and thank the 22 anonymous peer reviewers for their insightful comments on these chapters.

The volume includes contributions from an interdisciplinary group of scholars from five countries: Brazil, Canada, China, Mexico, and Turkey. With such diverse geographical and cultural backgrounds, these scholars have brought forward a uniquely 'global' representation of the different realities of market-oriented economic growth models based on four distinct regions of the world (North and Latin America, East Asia, and the Middle East). Contributors were encouraged to express their own diverse views, rather than conform to a single all-embracing argument or perspective. They were also encouraged to refer to, and engage with, each other's papers. As a result, there is extensive cross-referencing of chapters throughout the book.

The volume is also global in its genesis. The intellectual shaping of the project began in 2009 when I was a Visiting Research Fellow in the Department of International Studies at Middle East Technical University (METU) in Ankara, Turkey. While at METU, I managed to bring together a small group of five scholars from the Department of International Studies and Political

Science to work towards establishing an international research collaboration between SFU and METU. In fact, the topic for the workshop emerged from those meetings in Turkey. I would like to thank the participants in those early meetings: Meliha Altunışık, Pınar Bedirhanoğlu, Ayşegül Kibaroğlu, Aylin Topal, and Galip Yalman. After my return to Canada, I spoke about this idea of an international research collaboration with Steven McBride, then Director of the Centre for Global Political Economy at SFU. We thought it best to organize a workshop first, and then work towards the major international collaborative research project. The initial step taken towards this collaborative project was the international workshop. This volume is directly based on the workshop proceedings.

I must express my deep gratitude to a number of organizations which made this all possible through their generosity and support. The Social Sciences and Humanities Research Counsel of Canada (SSHRC) provided me with a very generous workshop grant. Without this support, the workshop would not have materialized. I must thank Beverly Neufield, Director of Research and Communications in SFU's Faculty of Arts, who read various versions of my grant application and provided valuable comments. A number of institutions within SFU provided their generous support. They include the Office of the Dean of the Faculty of Arts and Social Sciences, Office of Vice President-Research, Office of Vice-President-Academic Conference Fund, Arts Research Incentive Grant, Department of Political Science, School of International Studies, Centre for the Comparative Study of Muslim Societies and Cultures, Centre for Global Political Economy, Department of History, Department of Geography, Latin American Studies Program, and Labour Studies. My own department of Sociology and Anthropology (SA) has been very generous. I would like to thank Dr. Dany Lacombe, then Acting Chair, and Dr. Jane Pulkingham, then Chair of the SA Department, for this generosity.

There are a number of colleagues from SFU and the University of British Columbia (UBC) who were involved in various stages of organizing the workshop. My warmest thanks go to all members of the conference organizing committee. The committee included Marjorie Cohen (SFU's Departments of Political Science and Gender Relations), Leila Harris (UBC's Institute for Resources, Environment, and Sustainability, and the Women's and Gender Studies Department), Stephen McBride (McMaster University's Department of Political Science), Gerardo Otero (SFU's Department of Sociology and Anthropology), Jamie Peck (UBC's Department of Geography), Jane Pulkingham (SFU's Department of Sociology and Anthropology), Hannah Wittman (SFU's Department of Sociology and Anthropology), Jie Yang (SFU's Department of Sociology and Anthropology), and Efe Peker (a graduate student from SFU's Department of Sociology and Anthropology). Geoff Mann (SFU's Department of Geography) was also involved in the initial planning stage of the workshop. I would like to thank Esin Gözükara, Justin Rawlins,

Efe Can Gürcan, and Brad Hornick, graduate students in Sociology at SFU, for kindly assisting me with the last-minute arrangements for the workshop. Special thanks also go to Jeanne Persoon, Secretary to the Department Chair in Sociology and Anthropology, for the design of the workshop programme and for many other tasks. She has been wonderfully helpful and dedicated.

All chapters are original contributions, written specifically for the book. Two chapters include sections from previously published work. Therefore, I would like to acknowledge Routledge for giving permission to Xinying Hu to reproduce extensively revised excerpts from pages 63–79 of her book, *China's New Underclass: Paid Domestic Labour* (2011). I would also like to thank Taylor & Francis Ltd. (http://www.tandfonline.com) for giving permission to Paul Bowles, on behalf of the Canadian Association for the Study of Development, to reprint a revised version of his 2012 article, 'Re-balancing China's Growth: Some Unsettled Questions', *Canadian Journal of Development Studies* 33(1): 1–13.

I am indebted to Christina Brian, Publisher; Tim Shaw, Editor of the International Political Economy Series; and Amanda McGrath, Assistant Editor, at Palgrave Macmillan, for their support and excellent editorial work. Tim deserves a very special thank you for his outstanding generosity and diligence. I also thank Ken Jalowica, Instructor of Sociology at Kwantlen Polytechnic University in Vancouver, who made numerous insightful comments on the development of the workshop and the manuscript.

Contributors

Fikret Adaman is Professor of Economics at Boğaziçi University. His articles have appeared in *Cambridge Journal of Economics, Development and Change, Ecological Economics, Energy Policy, Environment and Behavior, Environment and Planning C, European Journal of History of Economic Thought, Journal of Economic Issues, Journal of European Social Policy,* and *New Left Review*. He currently serves (with Burcay Erus) as an expert on social inclusion to the European Commission. He co-edited *Rethinking Structural Reform in Turkish Agriculture* (2010, with B. Karapınar and G. Özertan), *Environmentalism in Turkey* (2005, with M. Arsel), and *Integrating and Articulating Environments* (2003, with O. Seippel, F. Gökşen, M. O'Brien, Ü. Zenginobuz, and J. Grolin). His research focuses on the political economy of the environment.

Yıldız Atasoy is Professor of Sociology at Simon Fraser University. Her books include *Islam's Marriage with Neoliberalism: State Transformation in Turkey* (2009); *Hegemonic Transitions, the State and Crisis in Neoliberal Capitalism* (2009, editor); *Turkey, Islamists and Democracy: Transition and Globalization in a Muslim State* (2005); and *Global Shaping and Its Alternatives* (2003, co-edited with William K. Carroll). Her most recent book, *Supermarkets and Global Agrifood Systems: Shifting Relations of Food Provisioning in Turkey and Brazil,* will be published in 2014 by Routledge. Her areas of research include the political economy of agrifood systems and the supermarketization of agriculture, neoliberal capitalism and state restructuring, genealogies of citizenship, Islamic politics, and gender relations. Her work has appeared in *Journal of Agrarian Change, European Journal of Cultural Studies, Studies in Political Economy, Socialist Register, International Journal of Politics, Culture, and Society, Sociological Focus,* and *Social Compass*.

Paul Bowles is Professor of Economics and International Studies at the University of Northern British Columbia. His recent books include *National Currencies and Globalization: Endangered Species?* (2008) and *Globalization and Labour in China and India: Impacts and Responses* (2010, co-edited with John Harriss). His research interests are globalization and the political economy of China's development. With respect to the latter, he has published in the areas of financial reform, labour reform, and privatization. He is currently working on China's currency policy.

James M. Cypher is Professor of Economics in the Doctoral Program in Development Studies, Universidad Autónoma de Zacatecas, Mexico. His (co-authored) books include *México a la deriva* (2012); *Mexico's Economic*

Dilemma (2010); and *The Process of Economic Development* (2009). His areas of research include political economy, technology, and development in Latin America, state-led development policies, and the theory of the state. His work has appeared in *Canadian Journal of Development Studies, Journal of Economic Issues, Problemas del Desarrollo, New Labor Forum, Annals of the American Academy of Political and Social Science,* and *Forum for Social Economics.*

William K. Carroll is Professor of Sociology at the University of Victoria and a founding participant in the Graduate Program in Cultural, Social, and Political Thought. He served as founding director of UVic's Interdisciplinary Program in Social Justice Studies (2008–12). He is President of Economy and Society, Research Committee 2 of the International Sociological Association (2010–14). His books include *The Making of a Transnational Capitalist Class* (2010); *Corporate Power in a Globalizing World* (revised edition, 2010); *Remaking Media* (2006, with Bob Hackett); and *Organizing Dissent* (1997). His research interests are in the areas of social movements and social change, the political economy of corporate capitalism, and critical social theory and method. His work has appeared in *International Sociology, Capital & Class, Global Networks, Critical Sociology, Journal of World-System Research, Antipode, Sociological Review, Media, Culture & Society, Studies in Social Justice,* and *Socialist Studies.*

Leila M. Harris is Associate Professor with the Institute for Resources, Environment and Sustainability and the Institute for Gender, Race, Sexuality and Social Justice at the University of British Columbia. Her publications include *Water Governance in the Global South: Scarcity, Marketization, Participation* (2013, co-edited with J. A. Goldin and C. Sneddon) as well as a range of journal articles appearing in such journals as *Political Geography, World Development, Geoforum,* and *Environment and Planning D.* Her areas of interest include water governance and politics, gender and inequality with respect to environmental and developmental change, environmental citizenship, and linked debates in political ecology and nature-society studies. She has worked extensively in Turkey and the Middle East. Her recent work focuses on Ghana, South Africa, and North America.

Xinying Hu is a sessional lecturer in the Labour Studies Program at Simon Fraser University. She is the author of *China's New Underclass: Paid Domestic Labour* (2011). Her areas of research include globalization and labour, social policy for women, and gender and economic restructuring in China. Her work has appeared in Chinese in the journal *Collection of Women's Studies.*

Noela Invernizzi is Professor of Education and Public Policy at the Federal University of Paraná, Brazil. Her books include *The Brazilian Labor-force After Industrial Restructuring* (2004) and two volumes on *Nanotechnology in Latin*

America (2008 and 2011, co-edited with Guillermo Foladori). Her areas of research include the implications of industrial innovation for workers' skills and employment conditions, science and technology policy, and the implications of nanotechnology for developing countries. Her work has appeared in *Science, Technology and Society*, *NanoEthics*, *Nanotechnology, Law and Business*, *Latin American Perspectives*, and several journals published in Latin America.

Mine Işlar is a doctoral candidate at Lund University Centre for Sustainability Studies in Sweden. Her thesis on private rivers is a study of the contested processes whereby usage rights to water are privatized for electricity production. She focuses on renewable energy development, resource rights struggles, and shifting patterns of ownership. Beyond her thesis, her general area of research is on community well-being in relation to 'sustainability' oriented projects, water politics, securitization, social movements, and environmental justice. Recent publications include 'Struggles for Recognition: Privatization of Water Use Rights of Turkish Rivers', *Local Environment: The International Journal of Justice and Sustainability* (2012) and 'Privatised Hydropower Development in Turkey: A Case of Water Grabbing?' *Water Alternatives* (2012). She has also published in edited volumes.

Yahya M. Madra studied economics in İstanbul and Amherst, Massachusetts. He has taught at the universities of Massachusetts and Boğaziçi, and at Skidmore and Gettysburg Colleges. He is currently an associate professor of economics at Boğaziçi University where he also conducts research in the history of modern economics with the support of TÜBITAK-BIDEB Scholarship. His work has appeared in *Journal of Economic Issues*, *Rethinking Marxism*, *The European Journal of History of Economic Thought*, *Psychoanalysis, Society, Culture and Subjectivity* as well as edited volumes. He served as an associate editor of *Rethinking Marxism* between 2009 and 2012 and continues to be a member of the editorial collective of the journal. His current research is on the role of subjectivity in political economy of capitalism and post-capitalism.

Hepzibah Muñoz Martínez is Assistant Professor in the Department of History and Politics at the University of New Brunswick, Saint John campus. Her areas of research include the study of export processing zones, finance, and drug-related violence in Mexico. Recent publications include 'Competitiveness vs. Sustainability: Canadian Regulations on Hazardous Waste', *Revista Vetas* (2009); 'Neoliberal Reforms and Currency Pegs in Mexico and Argentina', *Policy and Society* (2008) (co-authored with Ruth Felder); and 'State, Second Nature and Reterritorialization of Capital in the Plan Puebla Panama', *Capitalism Nature Socialism* (2004).

Heather Whiteside is a postdoctoral fellow in the Department of Geography, the University of British Columbia, studying the design, mobility, and mutation of P3 policies. Her books include *Private Affluence, Public Austerity* (2011, co-authored with Stephen McBride). Her doctoral research focuses on public–private partnership (P3) policy and the track record of P3 hospitals in the Canadian public health care system. Beyond P3s and privatization, her areas of research include fiscal austerity, capitalist crises, and neoliberal restructuring. Her work has appeared in *Studies in Political Economy, Health Sociology Review,* and *Alternate Routes,* among other journals.

Jun Zhang is Assistant Professor in the Department of Geography and Program in Planning at the University of Toronto. His areas of research include urban and regional development, geography of innovation and technological development, variegated capitalism, Internet industry development, venture capital, and China. His work has appeared in *Journal of Economic Geography, Regional Studies, Urban Studies, Environment and Planning A,* and *China Review.*

1

Introduction: Global Economic Crisis and the Politics of Diversity

Yıldız Atasoy

The current global economic crisis has led countries in Europe and the United States to adopt various austerity measures, following an initial emergency policy response of monetary and fiscal stimuli and a series of government bailouts of banks and other financial institutions (Boyer 2012; Callinicos 2012; King et al. 2012). However, this is not a general trend in the global economy, as there is great variation among countries in terms of the impact of the crisis and policy responses to it. While economic growth in Canada, for example, has been slow, many countries from the global South continue to experience higher levels of economic growth. These divergent patterns and context-bound particularities require critical reflection in regard to the intensification of a market-oriented path of development and the tensions and uncertainties associated with an increasingly precarious mode of living for many in the world. This book analyses the deep structural issues, fundamental ontological insecurities, and ecological consequences that express uneven processes in the global proliferation of a market model. The authors in this collection concretize these processes across geographically varied contextual conditions, yet do so within the general global conjuncture of the economic crisis.

The book does not debate with various explanations as to the causes, consequences, and impact of the economic crisis, for which there is a now a significant body of literature (e.g. Callinicos 2010; Crotty 2009; Reinhart and Rogoff 2009), nor does it treat 'diversities' and/or geo-historical differences observed across cases as national/regional instances of a global project of restructuring capitalism. The study of such a project is undoubtedly worthwhile in its own right. Certainly, growing commercial and financial ties can be expected to create interesting and novel forms of global

---

I would like to express my gratitude to Fikret Adaman, Yahya Madra, James Cypher, and William K. Carroll for their constructive comments on a previous draft of the chapter.

interconnectedness (cf. Arrighi 2007; 1994; Panitch and Gindin 2012), but this is beyond the scope of the present book. Our book avoids a conceptual leap from the empirical observation of a diversity of specific cases to theoretical conclusions which insinuate an 'enclosed' outcome as to the fundamental nature of the restructuring of capitalism occurring in response to economic crisis. Rather, the book observes that a complicated political process is currently underway in deepening a market-oriented model of development that is directed towards buoying economic growth. In describing and interpreting this process, the book brings together an interdisciplinary group of scholars from five countries: Brazil, China, Mexico, Turkey, and Canada. Our goal is to generate interdisciplinary dialogue across empirical cases and theoretical perspectives in order to critically explore the various forms of social polarization, ontological insecurity, and ecological consequences that have accompanied the historical and geographical variation among cases in the global intensification of market-driven solutions. This approach is useful for *rethinking* the global restructuring of the capitalist economy – not as a coherent and unified system but as a phenomenon which is entirely historical (cf. Block 2000) and deeply *messy*. The contributors to this volume investigate the localized meanings, dynamics, and consequences of market intensification. We do not engage in a macro-historical comparison of cases. Our cases are different from one another in regard to their domestic politics, specific trajectories, and geo-historical complexities, even though we observe that they also reveal reasonable similarities in regard to their placement in the global economy and their policy choice of a market-oriented economic-growth model. While it seems that a policy commitment to a market model persists in the name of economic development, our analysis of various forms of socio-economic insecurity, exclusionary practices, and ecological consequences helps us expose the different realities of market models which express multifaceted forms of global crisis. In short, the book interprets the varied experiences of Brazil, China, Mexico, Turkey, and Canada with a market model. These countries are geographical representatives of four distinct regions of the world: North America, Latin America, East Asia, and the Middle East. All reveal different aspects of global processes that have resulted in the consolidation and reformulation of – as well as critique of – a market form of development.

The market form of development has often been defined in the literature as characterizing the 'neoliberal' phase of the capitalist economy. Since its emergence in the 1970s and the 1980s, this phase has been expressed through trade liberalization, the privatization of various forms of public property, services and policy/norm-making, welfare retrenchment, public austerity measures, and new contractual and managerial arrangements (e.g. Atasoy 2009a: 7; Short 2012: 47). Beyond this 'general' understanding, however, there are different meanings attributed to neoliberalism. Harvey (2005: 19), for example, sees it as a 'political project' closely associated with the restoration of the power of economic elites and the revitalization of global capital accumulation. For Callinicos (2012: 67), neoliberalism is best understood as 'an economic policy regime whose objective is to secure monetary and fiscal stability, and is legitimised by an ideology which holds that markets are best treated as self-regulating' entities. Callinicos' definition draws attention not only to the 'restoration of class power' argued by Harvey, but to a much broader process of 'financialization',[1] which represents a significant change in the structure and dynamics of capitalism (Callinicos 2012: 67–9; 2010: 24–34). On the other hand, McMichael (2012) and Gill (2012) regard neoliberalism as something more than an economic project and a set of policy measures that emphasize market-based mechanisms designed to bolster business and economic growth. They view it as an intellectual, normative project which justifies the elevation of market principles to the status of an organizing principle of society. As an intellectual project of market rule which 'brings an economic calculus to cultural and social relationships' (McMichael and Morarji 2010: 235), neoliberalism rests on certain normative assumptions about the nature of lived reality. For Gill (2000: 49), these assumptions constitute 'the knowledge structures of political economy'. In this volume, Adaman and Madra propose that the knowledge structure of neoliberalism is best understood as a drive towards the 'economization' of the social. This entails more than market rule; *economization* as a form of governmentality institutes the ideational dominance of a calculative episteme in a plethora of social, cultural, and ecological relationships. It does so based on the assumption that all social agents are calculatively rational and calculably responsive towards economic incentives. On the whole, and particularly since the 1980s, neoliberalism has gained prominence in regard to its role in the intensification of market-driven development projects, continuing a process of commodification across the globe, and an epistemic drive towards economization of the ensemble of social, cultural, and ecological relations.

In explaining why the ongoing economic crisis has not resulted in a shift away from neoliberalism, and why it persists despite resistance and crisis, Peck, Theodore, and Brenner (2010) point to the tremendous adaptive capacity of neoliberalism. These authors (2010: 95) describe neoliberalism as a 'flexibly mutating regime of "market rule"'. It is continuously contested as a variety of different social groups across the world struggle for power and make demands for social inclusion and justice (e.g. Atasoy 2009b; Lindblom and Zuquete 2010; McMichael 2010; McNally 2006). It is through, and in response to, this contestation that neoliberalism is simultaneously restructured as an adaptive, regulatory regime of 'market rule' in the management of the economy. According to Peck, Theodore, and Brenner (2010: 104–5), neoliberalism should therefore be conceptualized as a '*restructuring ethos*', a dominant pattern of regulatory transformation, politically reshaped in the process of regulatory political struggles. For King et al. (2012) and Callinicos

(2012), the evolving political and economic responses to the crisis, which they observe in relation to a policy reversal from fiscal stimuli and bank bailouts to austerity measures, make sense if considered as part of the market-oriented reorganization of capitalism and balance of class power designed to roll back the welfare state. This explanation may be true for EU-member countries and the United States, as well as Canada, which indeed instituted a welfare-state structure during the mid-twentieth century international political economy (e.g. Harvey 1989). However, it is not a useful explanation for other countries from the global South which have experienced greater inequality, poverty, inadequate social-welfare programmes, debt, and serious environmental damage as they implemented 'developmentalist projects' (Crow and Lodha 2011; McMichael 2012; Rist 1997). Similarly, although economic-crisis management through austerity measures has been a signifier of neoliberal policy restructuring since the 1970s, neoliberalism has not taken hold to the same degree nor have its effects been uniform across all countries (Brady et al. 2005).

Without doubt, there is significant geo-historical diversity across places and cultures, and context-specificity always matters in any meaningful analysis of social change. In their recent book, *The Making of Global Capitalism: The Political Economy of American Empire* (2012: 1), Panitch and Gindin present an analytical approach which shows that global capitalism has now 'truly encompassed the world', mainly through an exceptional role played by the American state 'in managing and superintending capitalism on a worldwide plane', in addition to its 'restructuring other states to these ends'. They further argue that the global extension of capitalism has been intimately related to the development of new mechanisms of international coordination and cooperation with the American state for the management of the global capitalist system. For Panitch and Gindin, then, the political fault-lines of global capitalism do not seem to be running between states but *within* them. However, they do not focus on what actually happens within states. In their analysis, the significance of diversity and context-dependency across states is secondary. Thus, we may conclude that it is necessary to direct attention to an examination of specific features and particularities of cases, but without neglecting general, world-historical circumstances. Our book forwards distinct, context-bound, social, economic, and environmental relations observed across cases. And these relations are increasingly marked by the pursuit of an economic calculus and political reworking of a market-economy model with long-held views, ideological commitments, and varying degrees of compliance from a variety of actors.

Recently, the concept of 'post-neoliberalism' has come to figure in debates on policy modification and transformation in neoliberalism (e.g. Grugel and Riggirozzi 2012; Macdonald and Ruckert 2009). Specifically, it has been advanced to address the policy shifts in neoliberalism experienced across

Latin America since the late 1990s, following the 1998 presidential election of Hugo Chavez in Venezuela. Post-neoliberalism expresses the legitimacy crisis of neoliberal austerity and draws inspiration from widespread deepening poverty, inequality, and diminished social rights (McMichael 2012: 228). It captures an attempt to refocus the direction of the economy through greater state involvement, both in ensuring economic growth and attending to the challenges of poverty, unemployment, and inequality (Panizza 2009). The recent and ongoing wave of rebellion across the Middle East and North Africa known as the 'Arab Spring' also reflects neoliberalism's crisis, drawing on high levels of unemployment, poverty, and inadequate social-welfare programmes, combined with the political repression of old authoritarian regimes, to mobilize support. The current global economic crisis has played an important role in the outbreak of these rebellions, often expressed through the slogan 'bread and freedom' (e.g. McNally 2012; Messkoub 2011). Those participating in the Arab Spring are demanding the restoration of citizenship rights by combining economic and social issues with pleas for democracy.

Interestingly, according to Grugel and Riggirozzi (2012: 6), 'post-neoliberalism' does not undermine the normative dominance of market-based economic growth. Hence, it does not signal a new way of rebuilding the economy and society by unravelling neoliberalism, nor does it portend a 'paradigm shift' away from market-oriented growth strategies. It combines market-oriented growth-restoration strategies with government attentiveness to citizen demands and social-redistributive issues (Macdonald and Ruckert 2009: 6–10). This approach is also in line with the characterization of poverty advanced by various policy-oriented international agencies – through a 'rights-based approach' (as seen with UNICEF – the United Nations Children's Fund), through 'social exclusion' (the EU and ILO – the European Union and the International Labour Organization), and through 'human security' (the UN – the United Nations) (e.g. R. Bush 2007). Moreover, the World Bank's *World Development Report*: *Attacking Poverty* (2001) and the UN Millennium Project have framed their approach to poverty management using the strategies of redistribution and asset building in human capital via education and skill attainment. Therefore, post-neoliberalism 'is best understood as a call for a "new form of social contract between the state and people"' (Wylde 2011: 436 quoted in Grugel and Riggirozzi 2012: 4), which is more inclusive, rather than 'the dawning of a post-neoliberal era in which the tyranny of market rule is vanquished' (Peck, Theodore, and Brenner 2010: 109). Post-neoliberalism indicates a modality of economic growth reshaped through regulatory struggles in the context of the crisis conjuncture, but it continues to value the normative primacy of market rule. This may seem to be business-as-usual *within* neoliberalism, but it also helps direct our attention to the importance of specificity of context in an analysis of social change.

The contributors to this volume maintain a context-bound focus in their examination of market-oriented restructuring by situating their analysis within the commonly experienced material and discursive relations of global capitalism, as well as the associated social tensions of livelihood and ecology. They point to significant diversity across places and cultures in the intensification of market-based development models. The contributors are well aware that the historical conditions for re*thinking* restructuring and the possibilities for *conceiving* ways to combine social–ecological tensions into a coherent politics of contention might be best described as *muddy*. Thus, they avoid using the term 'post-neoliberalism' altogether as it generates more confusion than clarity in regard to what it actually refers to in relation to creating new choices for restructuring. Post-neoliberalism as formulated in the context of Latin America does not refer to building social forms beyond market capitalism but to a process of restructuring a twenty-first century capitalism which remains *within* neoliberalism, assigning a stronger role to the state and its attentiveness to citizen demands (e.g. Altvater 2009; Brand and Sekler 2009; Sader 2009). In this volume, we approach capitalist restructuring *historically* in terms of the complicated relations at play in the intensification of a market-economy model, the process of commodification, and the normative principles of neoliberalism. Emphasis is given to exploring geo-historical differences, rather than formulating some type of conceptual aggregation into a unified understanding of change.

The current economic crisis has not affected the countries studied in this book in a significant and enduring way. Even Mexico, which suffered an economic downturn in 2007–10 (Cypher 2011; 2010), has largely recovered and is now recording economic growth. However, the centrality of economic crisis is undeniable as a crucial factor in policies which are being implemented in the United States and the EU. Recent collections published in the *Socialist Register* (2011), for example, describe the crisis as an 'interruption of accumulation' in the United States and European economies. While the US economy appears to have registered recent improvements, it remains fragile. Crisis in the Eurozone remains very volatile as many countries continue to struggle with massive debt, fiscal discipline and stability in banking, and the widespread promotion of austerity policies. The European response to the economic crisis has included a new 'fiscal compact', involving a joint effort by France and Germany to rebuild trust in finances and between governments (O' Riain 2012).[2] The fiscal compact links bailout programmes and austerity measures to competitiveness enhancement, emphasizing cost cutting, and weakened social protection. It offers a clear political project in managing European crisis by imposing 'fiscal rules' formulated by technocratic cadres to discipline governments and citizens. The recent bailout plan offered by the EU to the Republic of Cyprus, which included a 'tax' of up to 10 per cent of savings held in the country's banks, offers a dramatic and telling example. The proposal was eventually rejected by the parliament of

Cyprus (*The Guardian* 20 March 2013). In McNally's (2012) assessment, the possibility of instituting a new cycle of accumulation through these measures is precarious. Nevertheless, according to O' Riain (2012), the present market-oriented restructuring places the 'European model' itself in crisis – a model historically based on strong social protection and productive investments manifested in a social-democratic political vision. As countries within the EU are required to improve competitiveness by making labour cheaper and more flexible, Europe is confronted with a challenge in maintaining an enduring social model and can be expected to experience generalized social unrest (King et al. 2012: 7).

Given that the countries studied here have not experienced lasting interruptions of accumulation, our book does not strive to examine the impact of the global financial crisis on their economies. Rather, we observe that the structural changes which have occurred reveal an increasing normative conformity with a market-oriented model that contributes to the reconstitution of the ontology of the social. These changes are taking place in a manner that is virtually identical to that described by Walt W. Rostow (1960) as 'catch-up developmentalism'. As these countries increasingly adopt a 'developmentalist' perspective on the road to competitive growth, a market-oriented perspective is further deepened as a vehicle that institutionalizes the global restructuring of capitalism. Our book provides a critical assessment of this turn towards 'developmentalism'. It sheds light on the meaning and consequences of this turn for a multidimensional understanding of *crises*, which include vital, existential inequalities, and insecurities (cf. Therborn 2006; Tilly 1998).

Although our book does not focus on the so-called BRIC countries, it is worth noting their impressive growth rate. Brazil, Russia, India, and China, which make up this group, have contributed more than 50 per cent of recent world economic growth and account for about 15 per cent of the world economy (Rozhnov 2010 quoted in McMichael 2012: 229). This impressive record of economic growth is not limited to BRIC countries. Martin Wolf (2010) of the *Financial Times* provides data on 'emerging country shares of global output', based on information obtained from the IMF, the Federal Reserve, and Schroders. These sources forecast that among countries with emerging economies, Turkey will contribute the highest share of global output by 2015 (with more than 30 per cent) on a purchasing power parity basis, followed respectively by Indonesia, Mexico, Brazil, Russia, India, and China. China's contribution is expected to be the lowest, ranging from 0 to 5 per cent. The common ground for these countries' positioning in the global system as middle-range economic powers is formulated, most obviously, in relation to their experience of economic growth. However, their geopolitical and economic significance varies.

With the exception of Canada, the countries studied in this book are usually categorized as 'middle income countries' with high rates of economic growth. They represent a group of economically and politically significant key states emerging from the global South, although each has its own historically varied trajectory of social change. The growing economic strength and political significance of these countries has led some commentators to conclude that a multipolar world of global power dynamics is arising from the regrouping of countries in the global South (e.g. Amin 2006; Arrighi 2007; Calhoun and Derluguian 2011; Frank 1998; Glennie 2011; Therborn 2011; Wallerstein 2003). In regard to the emerging new realities of global power, China and Brazil, together with India (not examined in this volume), have been acknowledged by many as formidable challengers. According to the Centre for Economics and Business Research (CEBR), Asian countries and Brazil are rapidly 'moving up', while European countries are 'falling back' (*BBC News* 26 December 2011). In the CEBR's World Economic League Table, China is predicted to maintain an economic position second only to that of the United States, while Brazil is predicted to become the sixth largest global economy, overtaking the United Kingdom in 2011.[3] In addition to having impressive economic growth rates, both Turkey and Brazil have developed multifaceted regional and global politico-economic and strategic ties. With its important geographic location, Turkey is in many respects a country connecting North and South, East and West, while Brazil has established itself as a key country in Latin America with a growing role in the Middle East and Africa. Both Canada and Mexico have ties to the United States via the North American Free Trade Agreement (NAFTA), as well as to Latin America via various other free trade agreements. In contrast to the EU and the United States, Canada has not experienced the crisis in a profound way, yet it has undertaken measures directed towards greater market intensification, assisted by various forms of 'public–private partnerships' (Chapter 4 of this volume). Canada is included in the book because it occupies a unique position in the state system and has been a player within the continuing power dominance sphere of the global North. However, it has secondary global status in economic/geopolitical terms, and, with an emphasis on the centrality of a natural-resources based economy for export, Canada shares many problems with states in the global South. This duality in its position in the state system, which is often described as a '"rich dependency" of the American empire' (Panitch and Gindin 2012: 348 n8), enables us to further illustrate the contextually distinct but globally experienced 'variegated' processes of market-oriented restructuring in the economy and society.

The economic dynamism of key southern states, including Brazil, China, and India – with their connections to energy and resource-rich regions in Asia and Africa – has been described as signifying 'the great shift' away from the predominance of the United States and the EU in the global economy (Arrighi 2007; Frank 1998; Prestowitz 2005). However, Panitch and Gindin (2012: 19, 275–300) argue that the growing significance of these states, and especially that of China, coincides with their integration into the

'American-led global capitalist order', fostering financialization rather than marking a fundamental reorientation in global capitalism or delimitation of US capitalism (cf. Therborn 2011). Our book shifts the focus away from the interaction between economic growth and global regrouping and/or geopolitical transitions. It encourages us to think of the deepening of a market-led model of development through global multi-dimensionality and in relation to the tensions and complexities of a process expressed in ontological insecurities, new inequalities, and ecological issues.

This volume does not endeavour to include 'representative' countries from all regions of the world, nor does it aim to provide a detailed account of particular development projects pursued exclusively by economically and politically significant countries from the global South. In addition, the book does not aim to explain the differences between the causes and impact of the crisis on industrialized and poorer countries. That is the subject of a recently edited work by van Bergeijk, de Haan, and van der Hoeven (2011). Moreover, the present book has not been envisaged as presenting 'alternative projects' for the reorganization of the global economy based on the varied experiences of these countries. In fact, an attempt to do so is contrary to the very conceptual frame articulated here. The sheer range and diversity of local/national conjunctures as well as the different theoretical approaches and ontological perspectives discussed in the book present a space within which we may uncover the many aspects of the global intensification of a market-oriented model of development. However, the book's interest in these aspects of deepening market rule should not lead to an assumption that the book will uncover the dual-edged nature of developments in the countries under study: that is, improvements in socio-economic conditions, on the one hand, and increasing global dependencies which may cause growing instability and hence rising inequalities (if the crisis continues in Europe and the United States), on the other. We believe that a singular concern with the crisis' impact on and consequences for the economic-growth strategies pursued by individual countries leads to a Schumpeterian-style 'methodological individualism'.

'Methodological individualism' has no single accepted definition and frequently takes on different meanings from that given by Schumpeter (Elster 1982; Hodgson 2007; Roemer 1982; Smelser and Swedberg 1994: 5). It does, however, tend to take states as key agents in decision-making processes and agents of social change, and 'national societies' as units of analysis for comparison through standard criteria of rules and procedures. The analytical starting point of this approach is the assumption that individual societies are discrete social units and can be compared and contrasted through the lens of a variable (or set of variables) – such as the crisis' impact on development strategies – in order to establish a principle of variation in the character of the phenomenon under study. This poses a risk of turning social reality into an abstraction and neglects the highly variable geo-historical, cultural specificity of context (cf. Brown, Slater, and Spencer 2002). In avoiding 'methodological individualism', we favour an approach which views the global extension of a market model from a world historical perspective. Reinhart and Rogoff (2009: 208) argue that the 'global financial crisis of the late 2000s... [stands as] a transformative moment in global economic history whose ultimate resolution will likely reshape politics and economics for at least a generation.' This approach helps articulate the historical background of global restructuring, viewing possibilities of change not through a formal comparative analysis of individual countries juxtaposed against each other through standard criteria of comparison but in relation to a shared world historical context. Indeed, our book highlights continuities as well as divergences across cases within the general framing of the global deepening of a market-oriented path of development. This is important if we are to critically reflect on the contentious politics and new inequalities of the present restructuring process.

According to Pauly (2011), economic-crisis management strategies currently revolve around the global spread of market-driven solutions, a pattern which appears to be accelerating. Henisz, Zelner, and Guillen (2005) argue that international pressures of coercion, normative emulation, and competitive mimicry have strongly influenced the domestic adoption of a market-oriented policy model throughout the world. However, our volume shows that this does not mean there is policy convergence on the practices of the model. Rather, the contributors bring forth the space-specific variations in the content, meaning, and practices of a neoliberal market model. In addressing the question of variation and differentiation, and thus, problematizing the globally valid condition of a market-centred view, and also in its consistency with Karl Polanyi's (1944) theorizing of markets as variable social constructs, this book reveals the political content of the model as a time-specific project. Moreover, the market economy model is shown to produce serious political, social, and ecological consequences. The book illustrates the various ways in which a market-oriented model – rather than merely being transferred from one jurisdiction to the other in a 'one size fits all' manner – is instituted locally/regionally. This reflects deeper processes involved in the shifting power relations, cultural practices, historical legacies, ideological alignments, and tactical alliances that promote or challenge interpretations of existing social arrangements (e.g. Chapters 2, 3, 6, and 8 of this volume). The approach taken here, also seen in the work of Ferguson (2010), Peck and Theodore (2010), and Pieterse (2000), among others, allows us to recognize that even policies which appear to be the 'same' are frequently modified and refashioned in their interactions with locally and culturally diverse normative contexts. By focusing on politicized spatial and temporal processes, this volume traces the twists and turns of an increasingly world-wide diffusion of market reforms under conditions of crisis, thereby generating localized material and discursive outcomes that are contingent on interactions with a determinate set of social relationships. The book, then, describes the global extension and deepening of a neoliberal market-economy model by examining the relations of forces of capital, citizens, and political power as actors generating, as well as responding to, new dynamics of inequality involved in the present restructuring process. Specifically, these inequalities are traced through an examination of ecology, water use, health, childcare, technology and work, migration, and economic growth.

Concepts and issues covered: The market model of development and global ontological insecurity

A significant body of literature now exists on the economic crisis, often explaining it in terms of economic slowdown and recession. However, existing scholarly work has a narrow theoretical orientation and a limited empirical foundation, focusing almost exclusively on Europe and North America (e.g. Albo et al. 2010; Foster and Magdoff 2009; Krugman 2009; Panitch, Albo, and Chibber 2011). Some analysts with a Marxist orientation interpret the global economic crisis in terms of a general tendency within capitalism for the average rate of profit to fall. This is often seen as rooted in the systemic pressure of competitive accumulation among individual capital groups (e.g. Callinicos 2010; Harman 2007; Shaikh 1999). Foster and Magdoff (2009; 2008), who hold the same general orientation, view the crisis in terms of a deep, lasting stagnation of production and investment within the underlying 'real economy' of goods and services. But these analysts acknowledge the historical specificity of crises, undertaking a comparative interpretation of the particularity of its current form. For them, the root problem of the crisis at 'this time' is to be found in the real economy experiencing slower growth, as expressed in the growing financialization of corporate-led capitalism beginning in the 1970s, and an accompanying falling ratio of wages and salaries. Most analyses from a non-Marxist perspective believe the crisis to be caused by the lack of state regulation over banks and financial markets, and the failure of the United States and EU countries to regulate the global financial system by exerting political authority over the global economy (e.g. Krugman 2009). Those with this view argue for more state regulation in order to restructure a way out of the crisis, by constraining unfettered competition in financial markets. However, profits have actually recovered since 2007, and a number of state-led responses has been forged (Levy 2010), including virtual nationalization of two of the United Kingdom's largest banks – a move previously thought practically impossible (Callinicos 2012; Giudice, Kuenzel, and Springbett 2011; King et al. 2012). Moreover, the US government has taken measures to rescue failing banks (Albo et al. 2010); and the EU has adopted austerity measures to prevent debt defaults in Greece, Italy, Spain, and elsewhere within the Eurozone (Boyer

2012). Similarly, various monetary, fiscal and austerity measures, and stimulus plans are being implemented by governments, not only in Europe and North America but also in many other places in the world (K. Busch 2010; Torres 2010; Watt 2009). Therefore, the meaning and consequences of the current economic crisis remain unclear in terms of the lack of state economic management for the stabilization of financial markets and the restoration of profits and economic growth.

Panitch and Gindin (2011), who share a Marxist orientation and an appreciation for the historical specificity of crisis, raise the question of crisis duration in relation to the indeterminacy of its resolution. This indeterminacy is contingent upon whether and how social relations can be modified and new institutions can be developed to support the resumption of accumulation at the global level. From this perspective, the nature of the current crisis and its resolution cannot be understood in terms of state intervention in the management of the economy but only in the nature and extent of general policy cooperation and global rule-making. For Pauly (2009), policy coordination at the global level includes supranational regulation, supervision, financial burden-sharing, intense collaboration, and a shared commitment to market rule, as well as joint deployment of state power. And there has been international collaboration in the immediate context of the 2007–8 crises. However, according to Panitch and Gindin (2012; 2011), global crisis management entails the integration of large states from the global South into global capitalism under US political authority, US finance, and US transnational corporations. For these authors, the question of crisis management and resolution relates to the institution of an increasingly collaborative politics for the reconstitution of global frameworks and regulatory regimes. This argument formulates global restructuring as an 'imperial challenge' facing the US state, to maintain, manage, and secure the extension of global capitalism. The challenge involves coordination of the policies of states and the behaviour of states in restructuring the resumption of accumulation, including powerful states of the global South. This in turn results in a more interdependent global capitalism in which the American state maintains and reinforces its centrality. As elaborated in my previous book, *Hegemonic Transitions, the State and Crisis in Neoliberal Capitalism* (Atasoy 2009a: 2–7), this approach is problematic in two respects: first, its emphasis on a strong state (or states) as the historic agent of social change, and second, its conceptualization of power in generic terms as the capacity to influence international outcomes. This emphasis assumes a 'cause and effect' relationship between the exercise of power and social change, requiring a demonstration of the causal interconnections in terms of their relevance for global restructuring. From this position, the burden of proof is in establishing the change-oriented goals and efficacy of consequences sought. In our view, this burden often leads to ignoring the messiness, disjunctures, frictions, and/or complexities embodied within and across context-specific economic, political, cultural, and ideological relationships (e.g. Jessop 2004). Without undervaluing the importance of state-led rule-making, as also evidenced in Chapters 6, 8, 9, and 10 in this volume, we investigate a market-oriented restructuring of the social and material conditions of life as experienced *within* spatially and historically differentiated contexts.

The present book diverges from a singular preoccupation with financial-economic crisis management and the restoration of the accumulation process. Indeed, it emphasizes the reshaping of life itself, and the livelihoods of those who are situated in the present-day crisis context (Chapters 2, 3, 4, 5, 6, and 7 of this volume). Global policy diffusion and collaboration entails the restructuring of capital and classes, the reorganization of states and political alliances, the reconfiguration of societies, and ultimately the transformation of human life. An analysis which takes seriously the question of the uneven processes of the global proliferation of a market model of development has to uncover the increasing complexity of the political process, the meaning of diversity, and the experiential sense of restructuring in the social-political-economic-cultural arrangements of society. That is why this book places greater emphasis on deeper structural issues in the material, social, and ecological conditions of life as related to various aspects of change in social reproduction and livelihood, including ecology, water use, health, childcare, technology and work, and migration.

Many countries in the global South have been integrated into global capitalism, and in general they continue to experience economic growth. However, economic impoverishment, massive social inequalities, and various forms of 'accumulation by dispossession' (Harvey 2005) are increasingly an everyday reality for large segments of the world population. The uncertainty arising from the global deepening of a market model is giving way to 'universal ontological insecurity', which Gill (2012) has conceptualized as leading towards 'global organic crises'. 'Global organic crisis' combines multiple existentially distinct *crises* of livelihood into globally manifest intersections of expression (e.g. Chapters 2, 3, 4, 5, 6, and 7 of this volume).

Within the political-cultural context of expanding ontological insecurity, we are witness to the emergence of a new and dangerous global 'class' which has recently been described by Standing (2011) as *the Precariat*. Individuals belonging to this 'class' lack the various forms of 'labour-related securities' in Keynesian-style 'industrial citizenship', and thus, are pushed into the precarious existence of the disengaged and distrustful. With this concept, Standing aims to convey the human costs of labour market flexibility, the reduction in access to social benefits, and the decline in living standards and employment conditions under neoliberalism (also see Spencer 2012: 688). What makes this group 'dangerous', according to Standing, is the chronic uncertainty, tenuous employment patterns, absence of labour-related social solidarity systems, and growing sense of human redundancy which govern the material conditions of their existence. It is these conditions, according to Standing, which generate and sustain the politics of disengagement, and are often associated with the 'thinning' of democracy and ultimately with neo-fascism. For Gill (2012), the uncertainty of social relations melded into massive inequality within the market economy calls into question the legitimacy of current institutional frameworks of market rule and a global leadership which support ever-greater integration into global capitalism. Gill hypothesizes that the current regulatory frameworks of policy collaboration, as exemplified in the Group of 20 (G-20), will deepen the global extension of a market model, resulting in the intensification of globally intersecting organic crises. Therefore, the resolution of these crises requires a different understanding of 'global leadership', which, as illustrated by Carroll (Chapter 11 of this volume), must be seen as comprising diverse movements engaged in the various questions of livelihood and social justice.

Rodrik (2011) offers his own perspective for rethinking global frames of policy cooperation – one which requires recalibration of the relations between states and the market economy towards more democratic regulation. Rodrik calls this 'the next stage of globalization'. His argument is that variation in state actions and nationally specific institutional diversity must be balanced with the global nature of markets. This balancing act would entail a shallow form of multilateralism, as it would incorporate into the global system varied combinations of national institutional arrangements in labour markets, social welfare, finance, corporate governance, and so on. In a similar manner, Cypher (Chapter 8 of this volume) also emphasizes the importance of active state intervention and increased state capacity for achieving institutional stability. In his chapter Cypher argues in favour of increased state capacity, reflecting a critical reinterpretation of what Rodrik calls 'hyperglobalization'. Rodrik describes 'hyperglobalization' as deep integration, promoted by the technocratic elites of international regulatory frameworks including the World Trade Organization (WTO). It entails the deep penetration of global frameworks into areas of domestic policy, creating incompatibilities with democratic politics while impinging on patterns of domestic diversity. Chapter 10 by Muñoz Martínez reveals how such top-down technocratic solutions are implemented at the national level through state-bureaucratic intervention. They involve mediation of conflicting interests by the capitalist classes. Rodrik, like Cypher, prefers a policy of state intervention. He believes the post-war Bretton Woods regime provides a historical reference point for reimagining a new shallow form of multilateralism, permitting governments to respond in their own ways to the social and employment needs of citizens while enabling global trade to recover. Such an arrangement would resolve the political trilemma of the world economy which, according to Rodrik, consists of tension between hyperglobalization, democracy, and national domestic politics. However, Bagchi's (2011) analysis of the neoliberal state and its restrictions on immigration and migrant labour captures the importance of recognizing the constraints placed on the search for justice by the state itself.

These debates in the literature identify important problems associated with the structurally recurring economic crises of capitalism. All offer thoughtful criticism and direct attention to the need for more democratic alternatives and transformation-oriented social/political movements. Nonetheless, there is considerable conceptual confusion in the literature as to how the concept of economic crisis and crisis management can be utilized in historically interpreting multilayered processes of change. Salient alternative explanations are required in relation to the meaning and consequences of the politics of diversity in the global political economy, given that the idea of 'economic crisis' does not tell us much about the restructuring processes underway in the cases examined in this book. Therefore, it is important to note that a number of issues and concerns do not lie within the foci of this book. These include policy debates concerning the causes and consequences of economic crises (e.g. Callinicos 2012; 2010; Eichengreen 2003; Helleiner et al. 2009; Reinhart and Rogoff 2009), global crisis management strategies adopted by international organizations (e.g. Woods 2006), and/or the impact of crisis on states (e.g. Stiglitz 2006). The fundamental significance of this book lies in its treatment of the varied processes of restructuring in order to uncover how 'market rule' as the core epistemic assumption of global crisis management is experienced, embraced, reformulated, critiqued, and challenged, both materially and discursively across cases. Further, this book illuminates the contradictory dynamics and socio-economic consequences of an economic calculus applied across a diverse world, while also reflecting on the possibilities for and constraints on alternative forms of politics. Carroll's chapter represents the one contribution which explicitly focuses on alternative forms of politics, through an examination of transnational counter-hegemonic struggles. The question of whether or not this politics of diversity is leading to a qualitative change in the global relations of power remains an empirical question beyond the scope of the present book.

As members of the Group of 20 (G-20), all countries studied in the book participate in the global management of crisis by establishing the rules and norms of the global economy. Their grouping within the G-20 is significant for the empirical context of the book, as it allows us to expose the politics of diversity in the global centrality of a market-based policy orientation. Founded in 1999, the G-20 provides a frame within which cross-border political collaboration among countries of the global North and South takes place. It includes a core group of states from the global North (Group of 7) and a grouping of 11 states from the global South, plus the Central Bank of the EU. The Group of 7 (G-7), founded in 1976, created a policy context for a 'neoliberal' phase in the global capitalist economy by asserting private market solutions to the debt crises of the 1970s and 1980s. The G-20, on the other hand, was created in response to the financial crises of the late 1990s, which further expanded market-based solutions throughout the world. By incorporating the powerful states of the global South into a method of global governance, the G-20, according to McMichael (2008: 155), gives priority to the political management of the world economy as a *singular entity*. The perspective elaborated by Soederberg (2006) suggests that this method of global governance might be postulated as a 'shared form of leadership' among states for the joint management of crisis. For Panitch and Gindin (2012), however, the establishment of the G-20 symbolizes the continuing centrality of American-state power in the making and political management of global capitalism. I do not believe the disagreement here can be reduced to whether the G-20 represents a 'shared form of leadership' or the American state alone continues to be dominant. With the growing economic and political influence of China and India, uncertainty prevails over whose rules will govern global economic integration (Quark 2012). Still, this method of global governance hinges on, and strengthens, the role of managerial bureaucrats in setting up parameters and shaping agendas via multilateral and bilateral policy negotiations for the expansion of market solutions (Gill 2008). The bureaucratic 'governing coalitions' of crisis management, unstable and fragile as illustrated by the EU's recent handling of debt crises in Greece and Italy, diminish the significance of the societal dimension and its geo-historical variation, and undermine the politicized processes of local outcomes. As pointed out by Rodrik (2011), the de-politicized, top-down mobilization of policy and global economic regulations undermines democracy and the principle of self-determination. And, as argued by Gill (2012), top-down crisis management has generally made minimal effort to address the crises of livelihood and social reproduction that afflict a majority of the world's population. For Gill, the dominant global leadership over crisis management mobilizes disciplinary, technocratic forms of governance, both to stabilize prevailing power structures and strategies of rule and to maintain a condition of de-politicization. Italy and Greece, as well as Spain, have now instituted such forms of governance in the context of EU-imposed monetary, fiscal, and austerity measures to deal with their sovereign debt crises. Although our book engages primarily with issues of ontological crises – specifically, the problems of ecology, water, health, work, childcare, and migration (Chapters 2, 3, 4, 5, 6, and 7 of this volume), it departs significantly from the scholarly preoccupation with issues of transformed global leadership which dominate Gill's 2012 book. Our book also offers insightful examples of the specific ways in which economic restructuring is taking place. This includes the Chinese government's 'transformation and upgrading' policy as tied to efforts to rebalance regional disparity (Chapter 6 of this volume), the shift to a consumption-driven (wage-led) path of growth in China (Chapter 9 of this volume), and the Brazilian government's adoption of state-led 'redistributive growth' (Chapter 8 of this volume). Various chapters of the book clearly illustrate that the precise direction of change in the forms and activities of the state as well as the material and discursive restructuring of the social remain unclear. Given this lack of clarity, our coverage of a changing global conjuncture enables us to weigh the historical significance of a single-pointed preoccupation with the concept of economic-crisis management and leadership while emphasizing the multi-faceted character of structural changes currently underway – changes which are embedded in the 'variegated' and unevenly combined systemic processes of the global economy.

In addition to probing the politics of structural change as experienced in culturally diverse ways, this volume helps us think through possibilities for a more socially responsible reorganization of the global economy during times of economic crisis. However, it is not altogether clear how social life is being reconfigured under the current global expansion of market-based solutions, nor what the ontological–ecological consequences are. Considerable insight is gained into some of these consequences from Adaman and Madra's chapter on the economization of the ensemble of social relations, including the ecology; Harris and Işlar's chapter on privatization of watercourses and urban water delivery in Turkey; Whiteside's chapter on public–private partnership hospitals in Canada; Invernisi's chapter on the impact of technological advancements in nanotechnology on labour relations; Zhang's chapter on the relocation of labour-intensive industrial firms in China from coastal areas to inland cities and provinces; and Hu's chapter on women's labour force participation and the childcare crisis in China.

Much uncertainty arises from the massive inequalities generated by the market economy. It is evident though, that these inequalities undermine the material basis of social solidarity, signalling a particular epistemic shift in the way governments relate and regulate social relations through the logic of market rule.

The empirical cases studied here are not units of formal comparative analysis, but place-specific contexts for observing and understanding diversity in politics. Breaking away from the single-site tradition, individual chapters in the book explore different forms of comparative analysis, including relational comparison and 'the extended case method' (Burawoy 1998) as a reflexive model of connecting local contexts to general process and structuring. As mentioned earlier, the book avoids 'methodological individualism', which sees a particular location as a unit of analysis, comparing its attributes in relation to that of another location. Therefore, the place-specific differences observed in this book do not present a process of articulating a 'fixed' programme of social change that would repeat itself in one geographical region after the other. Rather, each chapter aims to uncover the complex ways in which 'general' global trends associated with neoliberal market capitalism connect with regional-national-local 'diversities'. An examination of these connections will enable us to identify how the deepening of market rule and the localized effects of market-oriented restructuring are experienced in varied geo-historical contexts with different institutions, practices, and cultures.

Organization of the book

The contributors to this volume may diverge in their coverage of subject matter, empirical starting points, theoretical perspectives, and interpretations of global trends. Nevertheless, on the whole, they share a concern with the market-oriented restructuring of life in the present-day crisis context of the global economy. They also demonstrate a shared interest in the global conditions of deepening inequality and citizen disempowerment as manifestations of market rule and economic calculus. Further, they all explore spatial and temporal variation in restructuring.

The book's coverage of diverse regions, issues, and interpretations allows us to consider the prospect of new forms of political mobilization beyond economic crisis management as expressed by governments, communities, and citizen groups. This will be examined through four themes which focus on different dimensions of human life and the natural environment. Following the introductory chapter, Part I: *Commodification and Environmental Governance* deals with a market-centred view of the ecological issues that pervade neoliberal capitalism through the economization of nature, privatization of watercourses, and urban water use. Part II: *Market Developmentalism and Livelihood Change* concerns the diverse ways that health provisioning, technology and labour relations, childcare and gender-based inequalities, the economy, and government are reconfigured. This part of the book reflects on the processes of market-oriented development projects and commodification as expressed through shifting power relations, cultural practices, historical legacies, ideological alignments, and tactical alliances. Part III: *State Restructuring and Economic Development* examines the changing conditions of states and the deepening of market-led developmentalism, the implications for competitive growth, the policies of redistribution, and resulting political tensions. Part IV: *Alternative Forms of Politics* provides an opportunity to rethink global power through an examination of the role of transnational alternative policy groups in knowledge production and mobilization. This part also reconsiders the methodological significance of diversity in local politics for global social change.

Part I includes two chapters. The first, Chapter 2, 'Understanding Neoliberalism as Economization: The Case of the Environment' by Adaman and Madra, views neoliberalism as a drive not only towards privatization and marketization, but more broadly as a drive towards the economization of the ensemble of social relations through an understanding that individuals are calculative and calculable. It traces the historical genealogy of neoliberal reason back to the establishment of the Mont Pèlerin Society in the immediate aftermath of the Second World War. Their chapter claims that if the neoliberal project is to be understood as an economization of the entire realm, then the Post-Walrasian approach, whose main aim is to provide 'incentive-compatible' mechanisms, should also be included within the neoliberal project despite its egalitarian concerns. The chapter makes two claims: first, the reduction of ecological valuation to a mere aggregate of individual subjective valuations may be inappropriate for complex and uncertain ecological services; and second, environmental policies that are based on economic incentives are likely to subject the entire ecology to the economic logic of markets, 'performatively' turning it into an object of strategic-calculative logic.

Chapter 3, 'Neoliberalism, Nature, and Changing Modalities of Environmental Governance in Contemporary Turkey', by Leila Harris and Mine Işlar, presents an overview of recent environmental governance shifts in Turkey, analysing these shifts in relation to broader trends and crises related to neoliberalism. Highlighted examples include recent debates related to privatization of the country's watercourses, decentralization of resource governance functions including water user associations (WUAs), as well as use of market mechanisms such as full cost recovery and pricing for urban water delivery. Through their examination of broader histories, discourses, and processes, especially those related to European Union accession, Ottoman history, and recent policies of the ruling AK Party, the authors detail several ways in which the market-oriented practices of environmental governance are not entirely new in Turkey, and certainly not exterior to long-held views and policies in the Turkish context.

Part II, *Market Developmentalism and Livelihood Change,* includes four chapters. Chapter 4, 'Tarnished yet Tenacious: Examining the Track Record and Future of Public–Private Partnership Hospitals in Canada', by Heather Whiteside, discusses the theoretical and empirical implications of public–private partnerships (P3s), as illustrated through Canadian hospitals. The author first examines the connection between privatization, P3s, and changes in neoliberal policy, and then speculates on what P3s might say about future neoliberal policy lock-in. Following that, the legacy of health care privatization is discussed. It is argued that privatization not only has a deleterious impact on social reproduction but that P3 hospital projects have a particularly dismal track record; they offer poor value for money, transfer a significant degree of power and authority to unaccountable market actors primarily motivated by profitability concerns, and expose public health care systems to the vagaries of global financial markets (the implications of which were made especially evident by the 2008 global financial crisis). Despite these problems (new and old), P3 promotion continues unabated in Canada, not because of a proven track record of superiority, but because of dogged political and ideological commitment to market expansion.

Chapter 5, 'The Industrial Development of Nanotechnology and Its Likely Implications for Labour', by Noela Invernizzi, traces the growing world-wide integration of nanotechnology into manufacturing processes through an examination of nanotechnology products and innovation trends. The implications for the emergence of a small but growing nanotechnology labour force are also examined. Most of the global labour force currently employed in nanotechnology is composed of highly educated scientists and engineers involved in research and development (R&D) activities. Along with the increasing manufacture and commercialization of nanotechnology-enabled products, a demand for intermediately skilled positions is also emerging, particularly for highly educated technicians and other categories of skilled workers often retained in the global North. The chapter considers the adverse effects of nanotechnology adoption on current production sectors, skill distribution, and its role in generating instability and transformation in the labour market.

Chapter 6, 'Global Economic Crisis and the "Spatial Fix" of China's World Factory: The Great "Long March" Inland', by Jun Zhang, argues that increases in the GDP and export growth rates of China are largely due to the export-oriented production of inexpensive made-in-China products for consumers in the global North during a period of tightened budget constraints. China's export performance is explored in terms of a great 'long-march' inland of labour-intensive manufacturing industries from eastern coastal regions. The relocation and expansion of manufacturers in inland China has been driven by firms seeking cost-reduction, the national government seeking to maintain the stability and viability of the economy while reducing regional gaps, and the number of local state officials seeking to aggrandize their local interests. While industrial relocation from coastal to inland regions has been underway since the early 2000s, the global economic crisis has helped China's low-cost manufacturers located in the interior gain even more market share in the world – a process largely facilitated by enormous inter- and intra-provincial disparity and the availability of both local-born surplus rural workers in the interior and the return of rural–urban migrants from coastal towns. In the end, this chapter questions whether industrial relocation may generate an over-accumulation crisis in China, which could be difficult to resolve in the short run.

Chapter 7, 'Childcare Policy Reform and Women's Labour Force Participation in China', by Xinying Hu, proceeds on the basis of the argument that childcare policy in China is the most important element for women's equal participation in the labour market, and that it was once a significant policy tool in China during the planned economic era. However, market-oriented economic reforms and restructuring in the previous 30 years have generated a childcare crisis which has created significant difficulties for the labour force participation of women with children in cities across China. The childcare crisis is even more evident since the global economic crisis of 2007–8. While more women are struggling to fulfil job opportunities, government policy has not adequately addressed the current childcare gap. Women must still endure a double burden if they wish to participate in the paid labour market.

Part III, *State Restructuring and Economic Development,* includes three chapters. Chapter 8, 'Brazil: Neoliberal Restructuring or Rejuvenation of the Developmental State?', by James Cypher, examines the structural changes that have occurred in Brazil since the beginning of the 1990s, with close attention paid to economic growth and a shift in income distribution in favour of the poor. The author argues that these changes in economic growth rates and income redistribution reflect a recent turn towards 'developmentalism' and revival of the 'developmental state' – a transformation made possible in part by the fact that neoliberalism never firmly anchored itself in Brazil during the 1990s. Cypher demonstrates this in relation to Brazilian 'redistributive growth' policy through an examination of a Brazilian national industrial strategy embedded within the general processes of financialization in the global economy.

Chapter 9, 'Can China's Growth Lead the World Out of the Global Economic Crisis?', by Paul Bowles, argues that hopes for the recovery of the global economy increasingly rest on 'emerging countries' such as China. In this regard, China's leadership has spoken for much of the past decade on the need to 'rebalance' the economy and place it on a different growth path, with domestic consumption as a leading driver of growth. This chapter analyses two questions. The first is how to best characterize China's existing growth path. China is typically considered to have an export-led economy par excellence. However, this characterization is highly questionable. Second, if China wishes to shift growth paths, then, on the basis of insights generated by post-Keynesian growth models, the author concludes that a shift to a consumption-driven (wage-led) growth path may be much more problematic than is generally assumed. If restoring the global economy's growth relies upon a rebalancing in China, the prospects do not look good.

Chapter 10, 'Crisis, Social Class, and the "Fixing" of Capitalism in Mexico', by Hepzibah Muñoz Martínez, asserts that the differentiated position of diverse fractions of the capitalist class in Mexico, in relation to both capital mobility and fixity, has resulted in inner class divisions and the loss of political consensus around neoliberal policies during the current economic crisis. In an effort to rebuild political consensus around the state neoliberal agenda, the Mexican state attempted to mediate these inner class conflicts through policies that helped capitalist fractions guarantee profits in their fixed and financial investments. These two processes – the distinct relationship of capitalist fractions in Mexico to capital mobility and fixity, and the state mediation of inner class conflict – have shaped policy responses to the 2007–10 crises in Mexico. This has helped to reproduce existing power relations in the country, characterized by increasing inequality and precarious employment.

Part IV, *Alternative Forms of Politics*, includes two chapters. Chapter 11, 'Alternative Policy Groups and Transnational Counter-Hegemonic Struggle', by William K. Carroll, presents preliminary findings from the author's investigation of an emergent component of global civil society: transnational alternative policy groups (TAPGs), which research and promote democratic alternatives to neoliberal globalization. Since the mid-1970s, and particularly since the 1990s, such organizations have generated important ideas, both visionary and strategic, for a 'globalization from below'. These groups serve as 'collective intellectuals' in contestations that transect national borders and resist the neoliberal status quo while also posing alternatives to it. This chapter provides an overview of 16 TAPGs and addresses some of the challenges they face in contending with the economic/ecological crisis of global capitalism, as transnational counter-hegemonic actors on the contested terrain of global civil society.

My own Chapter 12, 'Conclusion: Rethinking the Politics of Diversity', summarizes the 'findings' of Chapters 2–11 and critically engages with the 'universalizing' pretentions of 'market rule'. It weaves together the separate, context-specific conclusions of each chapter into a critical account of the connections between the generalities observed in the global intensification of the market economy and the time- and space-dependent specificities of our cases. This discussion exposes the *social* significance of reworking the term 'crisis' *through* the situated social relations of place, beyond a universalizing, single-pointed normative commitment to economic growth.

Notes

1. Financialization refers to the increasing autonomy of the financial sector, with banks and industrial and commercial firms acting independently of one another. It also involves a wide range of economic actors in the financial markets such as banks and other financial institutions, industrial and commercial firms, and middle- and working-class households integrated into credit markets. Other important aspects of financialization include redistributive activities carried out through speculation, predation, fraud and thievery, and the proliferation of financial derivatives as a hedge against uncertainty (Callinicos 2010: 23–34; Harvey 2005: 161).
2. The Treaty on Stability, Coordination and Governance in the Economic and Monetary Union was adopted on 31 January 2012 and expresses this effort.
3. India is forecast to overtake France as the fifth largest economy by 2020.

References

Albo, G., S. Gindin, and L. Panitch (2010) *In and Out of Crisis: The Global Financial Meltdown and Left Alternatives*, Oakland, CA: PM Press.

Altvater, E. (2009) 'Postneoliberalism or Postcapitalism? Failure of Neoliberalism in the Financial Market Crisis', *Development Dialogue: Postneoliberalism – A Beginning Debate* No. 51: 73–86. Available online: http://rosalux-europa.info/userfiles/file/DD51.pdf#page=75. (accessed: 3 August 2012).

Amin, S. (2006) *Beyond US Hegemony*, London & New York: Zed Books.

Arrighi, G. (1994) *The Long Twentieth Century*, London & New York: Verso.
Arrighi, G. (2007) *Adam Smith in Beijing: Lineages of the Twenty-First Century*, London: Verso.
Atasoy, Y. (2009a) *Hegemonic Transitions, the State and Crisis in Neoliberal Capitalism*, London & New York: Routledge.
Atasoy, Y. (2009b) *Islam's Marriage with Neoliberalism: State Transformation in Turkey*, London & New York: Palgrave Macmillan.
Bagchi, A.K. (2011) 'Global Social Reproduction and the Neoliberal Order', Paper Presented at the International Workshop on *Economic Crisis and the Reorganization of the Global Economy: Trans/regional Responses*, Simon Fraser University, 9–10 September.
BBC News (26 December 2011) 'Brazilian Economy Overtakes UK's, Says CEBR'. Available online: http://www.bbc.co.uk/news/business-16332115. (accessed: 27 December 2011).
Block, F. (2000) 'Remarx: Deconstructing Capitalism as a System', *Rethinking Marxism* 12(3): 83–98.
Boyer, R. (2012) 'The Four Fallacies of Contemporary Austerity Policies: The Lost Keynesian Legacy', *Cambridge Journal of Economics* 36(1): 283–312.
Brady, D., J. Beckfield, and M. Seeleib-Kaiser (2005) 'Economic Globalization and the Welfare State in Affluent Democracies, 1975–2001', *American Review of Sociology* 70(6): 921–48.
Brand, U. and N. Sekler (2009) 'Postneoliberalism: Catch-all Word or Valuable Analytical and Political Concept?', *Development Dialogue: Postneoliberalism – A Beginning Debate* No. 51: 5–15. Available online: http://rosalux-europa.info/userfiles/file/DD51.pdf#page=173. (accessed: 3 August 2012).
Brown, A., G. Slater, and D. Spencer (2002) 'Driven to Abstraction? Critical Realism and the Search for the "Inner Connection" of Social Phenomena', *Cambridge Journal of Economics* 26(6): 773–88.
Burawoy, M. (1998) 'The Extended Case Method', *Sociological Theory* 16(1): 4–33.
Busch, K. (2010) 'European Economic Government and Wage Policy Coordination: The Eurozone Crisis Calls for Structural Reforms', Friedrich Ebert Stiftung. Available online: http://library.fes.de/pdf-files/id/ipa/07232.pdf. (accessed: 18 October 2011).
Bush, R. (2007) *Poverty & Neoliberalism*, London & Ann Arbor, MI: Pluto Press.
Calhoun, C. and G. Derluguian (eds) (2011) *Aftermath: A New Global Economic Order?* New York: New York University Press.
Callinicos, A. (2010) *Bonfire of Illusions: The Twin Crises of the Liberal World*, Cambridge and Malden: Polity.
Callinicos, A. (2012) 'Commentary: Contradictions of Austerity', *Cambridge Journal of Economics* 36(1): 65–77.
Cambridge Journal of Economics (2009) 'Special Issue: The Global Financial Crisis' 33(4) (July).
Crotty, J. (2009) 'Structural Causes of the Global Financial Crisis: A Critical Assessment of the "New Financial Architecture" ', *Cambridge Journal of Economics* (2009), 'Special Issue: The Global Financial Crisis' 33(4): 563–80.
Crow, B. and S.K. Lodha (2011) *The Atlas of Global Inequalities*, Berkeley: University of California Press.
Cypher, J. (2010) 'Mexico's Economic Collapse', *NACLA: Report on the Americas* 43(4): 51–2.
Cypher, J. (2011) 'Mexico since NAFTA: Elite Delusions and the Reality of Decline', *New Labor Forum* 20(3): 61–9.

Eichengreen, B. (2003) *Capital Flows and Crises*, Cambridge, MA: MIT Press.
Elster, J. (1982) 'The Case for Methodological Individualism', *Theory and Society* 11(4): 453–82.
Ferguson, J. (2010) 'The Uses of Neoliberalism', *Antipode* 41(Supplement S1): 166–84.
Foster, J.B. and F. Magdoff (2008) 'Financial Implosion and Stagnation: Back to the Real Economy', *Monthly Review* 60(7): 1–29.
Foster, J.B. and F. Magdoff (2009) *The Great Financial Crisis*, New York: Monthly Review Press.
Frank, A.G. (1998) *ReOrient: Global Economy in the Asian Age*, Berkeley, CA: University of California Press.
Gill, S. (2000) 'Knowledge, Politics, and Neo-Liberal Political Economy', in R. Stubbs and G.R.D. Underhill (eds) *Political Economy and the Changing Global Order*, Oxford, New York & Toronto: Oxford University Press.
Gill, S. (2008) *Power and Resistance in the New World Order*, London & New York: Palgrave Macmillan.
Gill, S. (ed.) (2012) *Global Crises and the Crisis of Global Leadership*, Cambridge: Cambridge University Press.
Giudice, G., R. Kuenzel, and T. Springbett (eds) (2011) *UK Economy: The Crisis in Perspective*, London & New York: Routledge.
Glennie, J. (2011) 'The Rise of the "South-South" Aid Agencies', *The Guardian Weekly*, March 4: 44.
Grugel, J. and P. Riggirozzi (2012) 'Post-Neoliberalism in Latin America: Rebuilding and Reclaiming the State after Crisis', *Development and Change* 43(1): 1–21.
Harman, C. (2007) 'The Rate of Profit and the World Today', *International Socialism* (115).
Harvey, D. (1989) *The Condition of Postmodernity*, Cambridge, MA & Oxford, UK: Blackwell.
Harvey, D. (2005) *A Brief History of Neoliberalism*, Oxford: Oxford University Press.
Helleiner, E., S. Pagliari, and H. Zimmermann (eds) (2009) *Global Finance in Crisis*, London & New York: Routledge.
Henisz, J.W., B.A. Zelner, and M.F. Guillen (2005) 'The Worldwide Diffusion of Market-Oriented Infrastructure Reform, 1977–1999', *American Review of Sociology* 70(6): 871–97.
Hodgson, M.G. (2007) 'Meanings of Methodological Individualism', *Journal of Economic Methodology* 14(2): 211–26.
Jessop, B. (2004) 'Developments in Marxist Theory', in K. Nash and A. Scott (eds) *The Blackwell Companion to Political Sociology*, Malden, MA: Blackwell Publishing.
King, L., M. Kitson, S. Konzelmann, and F. Wilkinson (2012) 'Making the Same Mistake Again – Or Is It *This Time* Different?', *Cambridge Journal of Economics* 36(1): 1–15.
Krugman, P. (2009) *The Return of Depression Economics and the Crisis of 2008*, New York: W.W. Norton.
Levy, J. (2010) 'The Return of the State? French Economic Policy under Nicolas Sarkozy', Unpublished paper presented at the 106th Annual Meeting of the American Political Science Association, Washington DC, 2–5 September.
Lindblom, C. and J.P. Zuquete (2010) *The Struggle for the World: Liberation Movements for the 21st Century*, Palo Alto: Stanford University Press.
Macdonald, L. and A. Ruckert (eds) (2009) *Post-Neoliberalism in the Americas*, London & New York: Palgrave Macmillan.

McMichael, P. (2008) *Development and Social Change: A Global Perspective 4th ed.*, Los Angeles: Pine Forge Press.

McMichael, P. (2012) *Development and Social Change: A Global Perspective 5th ed.*, Los Angeles: Pine Forge Press.

McMichael, P. and K. Morarji (2010) 'Development and Its Discontents', in P. McMichael (ed.) *Contesting Development*, New York & London: Routledge.

McNally, D. (2006) *Another World Is Possible: Globalization & Anti-Capitalism*, Winnipeg: Arbeiter Ring Publishing.

McNally, D. (2012) 'Slump, Austerity and Resistance', in L. Panitch, G. Albo, and V. Chibber (eds) *Socialist Register 2012: The Crisis and the Left* Vol. 48: 36–63, London: The Merlin Press.

Messkoub, M. (2011) 'Crisis, Employment and Poverty in the Middle East and North Africa', in P.A.G. van Bergeijk, A. de Haan, and R. van der Hoeven (eds) *The Financial Crisis and Developing Countries: A Global Multidisciplinary Perspective*, Cheltenham, UK & Northampton, MA, USA: Edward Elgar.

O'Riain, S. (2012) 'The GPO's Best Friend? The European Model in Crisis', *States, Power, and Societies*, Political Sociology Section, American Sociological Association, Winter 17(1).

Panitch, L. and S. Gindin (2011) 'Capitalist Crises and the Crisis This Time', in L. Panitch, G. Albo, and V. Chibber (eds) *Socialist Register 2011: The Crisis This Time*, Vol. 47, London: the Merlin Press.

Panitch, L. and S. Gindin (2012) *The Making of Global Capitalism*, London & New York: Verso.

Panizza, F. (2009) *Contemporary Latin America: Development and Democracy Beyond the Washington Consensus*, New York: Zed Books.

Pauly, W.L. (2009) 'Managing Financial Emergencies in an Integrating World', *Globalizations* 6(3):35–64.

Pauly, W.L. (2011) 'The Political Economy of Global Financial Crises' in J. Ravenhill (ed.) *Global Political Economy 3rd ed.*, Oxford: Oxford University Press.

Peck, J. and N. Theodore (2010) 'Mobilizing Policy: Models, Methods, and Mutations', *Geoforum* 41(2): 169–74.

Peck, J., N. Theodore, and N. Brenner (2010) 'Postneoliberalism and Its Malcontents', *Antipode* 41(Supplement S1): 94–116.

Pieterse, N.J. (ed.) (2000) *Global Futures: Shaping Globalization*, London & New York: Zed Books.

Polanyi, K. (1944) *The Great Transformation*, Boston: Beacon Press.

Prestowitz, C. (2005) *Three Billion New Capitalists: The Great Shift of Wealth and Power to the East*, New York: Basic Books.

Quark, A.A. (2012) 'Transnational Governance as Contested Institution-Building: China, Merchants, and Contract Rules in the Cotton Trade', *Politics & Society* 39(1): 3–39.

Reinhart, M.C. and K.S. Rogoff (2009) *This Time is Different: Eight Centuries of Financial Folly*, Princeton & Oxford: Princeton University Press.

Rist, G. (1997) *The History of Development*, London: Zed Books.

Rodrik, D. (2011) *The Globalization Paradox: Democracy and the Future of the World Economy*, New York & London: W.W. Norton & Company.

Roemer, E.J. (1982) 'Methodological Individualism and Deductive Marxism', *Theory and Society* 11(4): 513–20.

Rostow, W.W. (1960) *The Stages of Economic Growth: A Non-Communist Manifesto*, Cambridge: Cambridge University Press.

Sader, E. (2009) 'Postneoliberalism in Latin America', *Development Dialogue: Postneoliberalism – A Beginning Debate* No. 51: 171–80. Available online: http://rosalux-europa.info/userfiles/file/DD51.pdf#page=173. (accessed: 3 August 2012).

Shaikh, A. (1999) 'Explaining the Global Economic Crisis', *Historical Materialism* 5(1): 103–44.

Short, N. (2012) 'Leadership, Neoliberal Governance and Global Economic Crisis: A Gramscian Analysis', in S. Gill (ed.) *Global Crises and the Crisis of Global Leadership*, Cambridge: Cambridge University Press.

Smelser, N. and R. Swedberg (1994) 'The Sociological Perspective on the Economy', in N. Smelser and R. Swedberg (eds) *The Handbook of Economic Sociology*, Princeton, NJ & New York, NY: Russell Sage Foundation.

Spencer, A.D. (2012) 'Book Review Symposium: Guy Standing, *The Precariat: The New Dangerous Class*, reviewed by A.D. Spencer', *Work, Employment & Society* 26(4): 688–9.

Standing, G. (2011) *The Precariat: The New Dangerous Class*, London: Bloomsbury Academic.

Stiglitz, E.J. (2006) *Making Globalization Work*, New York: W.W. Norton.

Soederberg, S. (2006) *Global Governance in Question*, London & Ann Arbor, MI: Pluto Press.

The Guardian (20 March 2013) 'Cyprus Protestors Hail Rejection of EU Bailout Terms'. Available online: http://www.guardian.co.uk/world/video/2013/mar/20/cyprus-eu-bailout-video (accessed: 20 March 2013).

Therborn, G. (2006) *Inequalities of the World*, London & New York: Verso.

Therborn, G. (2011) *The World: A Beginner's Guide*, Cambridge: Polity Press.

Tilly, C. (1998) *Durable Inequality*, Berkeley: University of California Press.

Torres, R. (2010) 'Incomplete Crisis Responses: Socio-economic Costs and Policy Implications', *International Labour Review* 149(2): 227–37.

Wallerstein, I. (2003) *The Decline of American Power*, New York: The New Press.

Watt, A. (2009) 'A Quantum of Solace? An Assessment of Fiscal Stimulus Packages by EU Member States in Response to the Economic Crisis', Working Paper 2009.05, European Trade Union Institute. Brussels: ETUI aisbl.

Wolf, M. (2010) 'Three Years and New Fault Lines', *Financial Times*, 13 July.

Woods, N. (2006) *The Globalizers*, Ithaca & London: Cornell University Press.

World Bank (2001) *World Development Report 2000/2001: Attacking Poverty*, Oxford University Press.

Part I

Commodification and Environmental Governance

2

Understanding Neoliberalism as Economization: The Case of the Environment

Fikret Adaman and Yahya M. Madra

In the aftermath of the 2008 financial crisis, governments and international finance organizations began to call for and take regulatory measures in order to prevent similar breakdowns in the future, causing some commentators to quickly pronounce neoliberalism dead. Consider, for instance, a recent example: while writing this chapter, a special report in the 21–27 January 2012 issue of *The Economist* – embellished with a red and black portrait of Lenin on the cover, triumphantly holding a cigar with a dollar sign on it – lamented that the 'emerging world's new model' would be 'the rise of state capitalism'. Yet, this line of argument is based on a rather simplified and narrow reading of neoliberalism, as a purer *laissez-faire* regime where spontaneous markets reign free with minimal role for governments. A closer look at its brief history challenges this reading of neoliberalism as a project of marketization that unfolds on both the practical and ideational levels. Practically speaking, governments have always played an active role in designing, instituting and facilitating the operation of markets, not only before but also under neoliberalism. In other words, the track record of three decades of neoliberal hegemony at a global scale demonstrates that the much-invoked dichotomy between state and private capitalism fails to do justice to the intensity and depth of technocratic–bureaucratic state involvement in implementing neoliberalism (Harvey 2005; Peck 2010). In fact, if we were to follow the directions Michel Foucault (2008: 131) proposed in the late 1970s in his prescient genealogy of the neoliberal intellectual tradition, we would have to concede that the neoliberal 'turn' in economic thinking that took place in the 1970s is quite distinct from late eighteenth-century classical liberalism, which aimed at protecting markets from arbitrary state

The authors would like to thank Yıldız Atasoy and Hasan Tekgüç for their constructive suggestions.

interventions (see also Medema 2009). This neoliberal, post-welfare era represents a particular epistemic shift in the way governments relate to and regulate the entire ensemble of social relations through a governmental matrix organized around the assumption that all social agents (be they individuals, groups, enterprises, states) are calculatively rational and calculably responsive to incentives. In other words, if neoliberalism is a drive not (only) towards marketization, but rather more broadly, towards economization of the ensemble of social relations (that is, the economic, the cultural, the political, and the ecological) through governmental dispositifs, then it would be misleading to deduce the death of neoliberalism from the increasing visibility of state involvement in the economy and society at large without asking how that involvement is epistemically organized and whether or not it successfully transforms social ontology in the direction of economization (Madra and Adaman 2010). Indeed, by understanding neoliberalism as economization rather than (only) marketization, it becomes possible to foreground the implicit normative project that informs its prescriptions, delineate how this calculative episteme may function in the reshaping of the lives and livelihoods of peoples according to reproductive necessities of the circuit of capital, and demonstrate how this calculative epistemic framework and its implied normative–ontological project harbour the risk to deepen, rather than alleviate, both the economic and the ecological crises.

If one were to subscribe to this reading of neoliberalism as a drive towards economization of the economic, political, social, and ecological spheres, one could plausibly argue in our current conjuncture that, although an economic recession is still going strong in North America and Europe, leading to political crises in Southern Europe (Greece, Spain, and Italy) and potentially to the dissolution of the Euro-zone, neoliberalism remains hegemonic. In response to this deep crisis, governments are electing not to return to Keynesian-style demand-management policies through deficit – or, better yet, progressive taxation-based – spending policies as advocated by the likes of Joseph Stiglitz (2010). Rather, they continue to advocate and actually implement austerity programmes despite widespread popular unrest and opposition. More importantly, while only a small fraction within the neoliberal field still defends the market panacea paradigm unequivocally, there is very little questioning of the economizing and calculative ideologies of the neoliberal social ontological project.

In this chapter, our aim is to shed light on how the neoliberal project reproduces itself theoretically and practically in the context of ecological governance. Given the ever-deepening dual crises of environmental pollution and natural resource overuse (including the exhaustion of non-renewable energy and material sources), unveiling the relationship between neoliberalism and ecological degradation – at both theoretical and policy levels – is crucial. As Carroll (Chapter 11 of this volume) notes, an increasingly internationalizing capital, scaled up to a system of transnational production and consumption, is bringing about an ecological overshoot, evinced by, among others, species extinction, ozone layer depletion, and global warming. Yet, paradoxically and pathetically, we currently observe a myriad of cases where privatization of natural resources (such as protected areas and forests) is being promoted and financial markets are being introduced into environmental policy and conservation (such as payments for ecosystem services, biodiversity derivatives, species banking, and carbon trade). Furthermore, policy-makers who wish to guide the behaviour of citizens towards sustainability rather hastily conclude that this can only be done by setting up proper material incentive schemes that would provide the right signal to agents in their relationship with the environment (through the monetization of pollution-generating activities). Critically engaging with such policies and their ideological sources will be possible only if one subscribes to an understanding of neoliberalism as a project of economization.[1] This constitutes the essence of this chapter.

Specifically, the chapter argues that the global spread of neoliberalism as a set of ideas, interpretative grids, governmental interfaces, and institutional dispositifs in relation to the environment is premised on the conceptualization of human behaviour from a particular perspective. Here, the capacity of agents in understanding and responding to economic incentives is presupposed, and in a related manner, every human decision is assumed to be reducible to a mere cost-benefit analysis. The chapter reads the widespread and resilient hold of the neoliberal epistemic grid within theory and policy-making by situating or 'embedding' it within the historical context of intellectual continuities between neoliberal policies towards ecological problems and the general post-war intellectual legacy of neoliberalism within the mainstream of the economics discipline. For this purpose, the chapter first traces the historical genealogy of neoliberal reason back to the establishment of the Mont-Pèlerin Society, a research network or a 'thought collective' aimed at defending the idea of a free market against the post-war hegemony of Keynesian welfare state capitalism (the Beveridge Plan in the United Kingdom, New Deal in the United States, and developmentalism in the Third World). It then discusses the links, affinities, and differences not only among the usually recognized Austrian, Chicago, and Virginia schools, but also, and perhaps more controversially, the left-leaning and egalitarian post-Walrasian – better known as 'mechanism-design' – approach. Indeed, as the mechanism design approach highlights the limits and failures of markets (arising mainly due to informational asymmetries between the regulatory body and the agents [be they production or consumption units]) and advocates for their regulation as well as for the design and institution of 'incentive-compatible' mechanisms that would replace them, it tends to be read as an alternative to the neoliberal creed. Nevertheless, what appears as an 'alternative' from the neoliberalism-qua-*marketization* perspective can only be considered as a 'variant' from the perspective of neoliberalism as a project/process of *economization*. The common thread that has held these diverse groups of intellectual networks together, the chapter argues, is their ultimate belief in getting the economic incentives 'right' for paving the way towards a prosperous and harmonious society. This chapter, therefore, first invites the reader to understand neoliberalism as a governmental epistemic grid that aims to organize the entire social field through a calculative and calculable governmental logic; and second, on the basis of this reading, focuses on the particularly vulnerable and critical sphere of ecology to investigate how neoliberal governmental grid perceives ecological problems and how its policies tend to be implemented in concrete contexts.

Neoliberalism beyond marketization

As mentioned above, the narrower and *ipso facto* partial definition of neoliberalism considers it a quest for *marketization* – that is, an assemblage of deregulation, private property, trade and financial liberalization, and labour-market flexibilization, together with a reduction in the role of the state in the economy (if only at the level of representation) and especially the gradual rolling back of its welfare functions (for a critical assessment, see Plehwe, Walpen, and Neunhöffer 2006). This reading certainly has a point. The last three decades have witnessed structurally transformative national and globalizing developments (e.g. Cerny 2008; Harvey 2005; Klein 2008). The removal of trade barriers; the shift from fixed to floating currencies; the increased international capital mobility; the expansion of multinational corporations; the financialization, securitization, and commodification of areas of life previously addressed by the now retreating welfare state (that is, retirement, health care, education); and the vast amount of privatizations have altogether brought about a decoupling of profits and investment, a decline in the share of wages, and a deterioration in income distribution together with increased poverty (e.g. Duménil and Lévy 2011; Epstein 2005; Marazzi 2011; Resnick and Wolff 2010). In addition, the drive to generate short-term profits and accumulate wealth, exacerbated during the neoliberal era, has continued to deplete the earth's resources to the point where today the global economy requires approximately 1.4 times the earth's capacity to regenerate resources per year (www.footprintnetwork.org).

Some scholars name this process the 'roll-back' (as in the rolling back of the post-war welfare state) phase of neoliberalism but carefully note that it is almost always accompanied by a 'roll-out' phase (Peck 2010; Tickell and Peck 2003). As the neoliberal project/process of economization stumbles along its path into various forms of market failures, social antagonisms, and ecological limits, these scholars argue, it may end up rolling out the state (or more generally the mechanisms of 'command and control') by taking a proactive role in devising market-complementary and technocratic regulatory institutions, expanding and deepening the dispositifs of social control, and implementing contingent crisis-management interventions (Peck 2010: 22–8). Indeed, when viewed from an historical perspective, the state apparatus has always been involved in the design and safeguarding of market structures: recall, for instance, Karl Polanyi's (1944) portrayal of the liberal era of the late nineteenth and early twentieth centuries. Furthermore, governments past and present have always actively and directly participated in the day-to-day operations of the economy. To begin with, global military spending resumed its rate of growth after a brief period of post-Cold War slow-down in the 1990s (http://www.sipri.org). Accompanying this process of military build-up is the unprecedented growth of the 'security' industry in the post-9/11 context. Increasing income inequality, combined with the 'fear' industry, has led to the disintegration of social cohesion and increasing segmentation of the social space – as evinced by the contrast between the growing numbers of gated communities and heavily isolated and policed shantytowns (Davis 2006; Klein 2008). Similarly, while capitalist states have witnessed dramatic restrictions in their welfare services, through public–private partnerships they continue to participate in regional redevelopment, urban renewal, and infrastructural (for example, energy) projects at the local, city, and regional levels (Chapters 3 and 4 of this volume). Most recently, in the aftermath of the 2008 financial meltdown, we observed how US and European governments were forced to function as a lender of last resort, as institutions that are supposed to bail out corporations that are themselves too-big-to-fail. Given the fact that their economic growth was also based on (potentially risky) combinations of varying but high levels of consumer indebtedness driven by an increasing availability of highly liquid short-term capital inflows (Brazil, India, Turkey), high rates of workforce exploitation (Turkey, China), and fierce (resource) extractionism (China, Russia, Turkey), a similar predicament may be expected in the BRIC and other emerging economies as well (cf. IMF 2012). As if all this was not enough, advanced capitalist states of the global North are presently implementing austerity regimes and further cutting social expenditure budgets – the United States in particular does so without curtailing security-related spending, a significant contributor to its budget deficit. Yet, all these involvements have gone hand-in-hand with the financialization of the economy. In addition to an increased share of finance in the economy (financial services becoming a, if not the, key industry) and its use switching from risk hedging to speculative motives, financialization has meant the reduction of all exchanged values, tangible or intangible, into either a financial instrument or a derivative of it (e.g. Duménil and Lévy 2011; Epstein 2005; Marazzi 2011; Plihon 2011). Neoliberalism, therefore, is to be seen as rooted in a philosophical tradition that essentializes the economizing, calculative, and calculable behaviour of agents, and reduces decisions regarding all aspects of life to a mere calculus of costs and benefits. Read as such, it should thus not be viewed only as a tendency towards marketization – the support and guidance of state-forms at different scales (from local to transnational) and the international finance organizations notwithstanding – but rather as a deeper process of de-politicizing economic life (a form of biopolitics) in which states and other institutions of command and control play an active role.

Neoliberal governmentality and its forms

Foucault's (2008) close reading of some of the key texts of neoliberal thought at his 1979 lectures at the Collège de France (see also Tribe 2009) moves beyond popular representations of neoliberalism that reduce it to a set of marketization policies. According to Foucault, neoliberalism is a response to the historical unfolding of a constitutive tension of liberal governmental reason: how might one extend the realm of freedom without inadvertently delimiting it with governmental interventions that are necessary for the extension of the realm of freedom? In contrast to classical liberalism that tried to limit government control over markets, neoliberalism answers this question by aiming at nothing less than modelling 'the overall exercise of political power' on the competitive logic of markets (Foucault 2008: 131). The emergence of neoliberalism, according to Foucault, heralds the birth of a new art of government, a 'biopolitical mode of governmentality', where the state ceases to relate to its subjects as citizen-subjects with social rights and begins to conduct its functions under the presumption that subjects will respond (predictably) to economic incentives in all aspects of their lives. In short, neoliberalism, as a combination of an ideological discourse and practices, entails a push towards de-politicization of the social through economization – that is, imposing a logic of cost-benefit analysis to *all* aspects of life under the assumption that everything is commodifiable (Fine and Milonakis 2009; Leys 2008).

The historical genealogy of neoliberal reason can be traced back to the immediate aftermath of the Second World War and the establishment of the Mont Pèlerin Society by Austrian economist and philosopher Friedrich von Hayek (Bockmann 2007; Mirowski and Plehwe 2005; Peck 2010). Serving as the meeting place of European ordo-liberals and constitutional political economists, North American 'Chicago' neoclassicals, and Virginia School of public choice economists, the Society was an important node of the neoliberal intellectual network in the post-war era. The state phobia of this intellectual network was fuelled in part by the bad aftertaste from the Nazi consolidation of state power in Germany and in part by the challenge from the then-ongoing Soviet experiment with economic planning as an alternative to capitalism. In addition to these factors, the success of the New Deal in the United States, the Beveridge plan in the United Kingdom, indicative planning in France, and various shades of developmentalism in the postcolonial world may have also played a part in constituting this fear of the state (Foucault 2008). German ordo-liberals wanted to reconstruct market institutions by reconstructing the German State according to the logic of competitive markets and taking 'the production unit' (that is, the enterprise) as the basic model-institution in reconfiguring the entire social world around the 'social market economy', where a compromise between social democracy and economic liberalism was forged in order to generate a balance between economic growth, inflation, employment, and social welfare (Foucault 2008: 75–158; see also Yamawaki 2001). Austrian neoliberals advocated the insulation of the state from the variable demands of the popular will so that the rule of law could be fully established (Vanberg 2009). And in North America, while the Chicago neoclassicals extended the marginalist neoclassical framework to legal theory, the analysis of household, and the critique of education, health, labour, and other areas of social policy that the New Deal had already reached (Becker 1976), members of the Virginia school of public choice developed what is essentially a neoclassical critique of the bureaucratic logics of the post-war welfare state through the rubric of rent-seeking models (Krueger 1974).

The common thread in all these approaches has been a desire to embed the economic sphere within the technocratic and purportedly neutral discourse of economics, and thereby de-politicize the functioning of the economy. Ordo-liberals know very well that markets do not come to existence on their own and thus need to be constructed and instituted by the state, but would like to accomplish this in such a way that the state's mode of intervention is modelled along the calculative logic of the enterprise (Vanberg 2001). Austrians are well aware that the rule of law should be established by the state qua extra-market power, but would like to insulate the state from the democratic demands of the popular will (Hayek 1948; Kirzner 2000). The American neoliberals of both the Chicago and the Virginia schools are also highly cognizant of the fact that it is impossible to eradicate the role and functions of the state from a democratic society (for even the contractual law, the foundation of market society, is contingent upon the monopolization of violence in the hands of the state), but would like to develop an economic critique of its welfare policies by submitting them to perpetual efficiency audits and constitutionally delimit its budgetary discretions (Brennan and Buchanan 1985; Friedman 1962).

Nevertheless, in order to fully appreciate the hegemonic power of neoliberalism, it will be useful to turn our attention to another school of thought – one that is normally not cited among the family of neoliberal approaches. Referred to as the post-Walrasian school, or the mechanism-design approach, this school of thought highlights various market failures that emanate from information failures (adverse selection and moral hazard), and argues that markets and non-market institutions are all different kinds of mechanisms that elicit a certain desired performance from rational agents (qua *homo economicus*), with varying levels of success (for a classic and foundational statement of this position, see Arrow 1974). In terms of this approach, since markets do not necessarily deliver economically efficient outcomes, any kind of institutional mechanism will do the job, as long as it is 'incentive-compatible' and gives the 'right' signals to rational agents (Hurwicz 2008; Stiglitz 1993). The idea here is that in cases where the market mechanism fails to function properly because agents have private information they do not want to reveal (as in the case where, faced with a regulator's willingness to obtain firm-specific information on the cost structure of abatement, the firm will have incentive *not* to reveal its true cost structure), a mechanism should be set up such that all agents fare best when they truthfully reveal private information. Consider, for instance, the following set-up: given the continuing importance of agricultural non-point source pollution, regulatory bodies need information on farmers' risk preferences as well as their technologies and input use in order to best assess their responses to different policy options and design effective policies. Yet, because of the asymmetric distribution of information and because farmers will have no reason (incentives) to reveal private information, regulatory bodies will have to come up with incentive-compatible policies. It is indeed possible (as presented, for example, in Peterson and Boisvert 2004) to design a mechanism that successfully solves this class of problems – that is to say, the proposed mechanism will provide the appropriate incentives to change inputs and hence environmental quality in the desired direction – but due to the very existence of asymmetric information, these policies will be more costly compared to the hypothetical situation where the regulators have all the required information. Similar applications have been proposed for environmental problems where regulatory success depends on accessing the private information that agents would normally not reveal. An important implication of this school of thought is that it offers an intellectual framework for the reform of the state-forms (local, regional, national, transnational) according to the strictures of economic logic. In other words, according to our extended definition of neoliberal reason as the process/project of de-politicization through economization, this latter school of thought also falls under the rubric of the neoliberal framework, even though it does not advocate private property and marketization *per se*.

States as agents of economization

Neoliberal reason is therefore not simply (only) about market expansion and the rolling-back of the welfare state but more broadly about reconfiguring the state and its functions so that the state governs its subjects through an interface of economic incentives rather than direct coercion. In other words, subjects of the neoliberal state are not citizen-subjects with political and social rights but rather economic subjects who are supposed to comprehend (hence, calculative) and respond predictably (hence, calculable) to economic incentives (and disincentives). There are mainly two ways in which states under the sway of neoliberal reason aim to manipulate the conduct of their subjects. The first, based on the behaviourist assumption that economic agents respond predictably to economic (but not necessarily pecuniary) incentives, is either through markets or through expert-designed incentive-compatible institutional mechanisms. The second involves a revision of the way the bureaucracy functions. Here, the neoliberal reason functions as an internal critique of the way bureaucratic dispositifs organize themselves: the typical *modus operandi* of this critique is to submit the bureaucracy to efficiency audits and subsequently advocate the subcontracting of various state functions to the private sector via either full-blown privatization or public–private partnerships.

While in the first case citizen-subjects are treated solely as economic beings, in the second the state is conceived as an enterprise (that is, a production unit) – an economic agency whose functions are persistently submitted to various forms of economic auditing, thereby suppressing all other (social, political, ecological) priorities through a permanent economic scrutiny. Subcontracting, public–private partnerships, and privatization are all different mechanisms through which contemporary governments embrace the discourses and practices of current multinational corporations. In both cases, however, economic policy decisions (whether they involve macroeconomic or microeconomic matters) are isolated from public debate and deliberation and treated as matters of technocratic design and implementation, while regulation, to the extent it is warranted, is mostly conducted by experts outside political life – so-called independent regulatory agencies. In the process, democratic participation in decision making is either confined to an already highly commodified, spectacularized, mediatized electoral politics, or to the calculus of opinion polls, where consumer discontent can be managed through public relations experts. As a result, a highly reductionist notion of economic efficiency ends up being the only criteria with which to measure the success or failure of such decisions. Meanwhile, individuals with financial means are free to provide support to those in need through charity organizations or corporations via 'social responsibility' channels.

Here, two related caveats should be noted to sharpen the central thrust of the argument proposed in this chapter. First, separation of the economic sphere from the social-ecological whole is not an ontological given, but rather a political project. By treating social subjectivity solely in economic terms and deliberately trying to insulate policy-making from popular politics and democratic participation, the neoliberal project of economization makes a political choice. Since there are no economic decisions without a multitude of complex and over-determined social consequences, the attempt to block (through economization) all available political modes of dissent, objection, and negotiation (that is, 'voice') of those who are affected from the said economic decisions is itself a political choice. In short, economization is itself a political project.

Yet, this drive towards technocratization and economization – which constitutes the second caveat – does not mean that the dirty and messy distortions of politics are actually being removed from policy-making. On the contrary, to the extent that policy-making is insulated from popular and democratic control, it becomes open to 'distortions' by the politics of rent seeking and speculation – ironically, as expected by the representatives of the Virginia School. Most public–private partnerships are hammered behind closed doors of a bureaucracy where states and multinational corporations divide the economic rent among themselves. With growing concentration of capital at a global scale, various strategic and key industries such as armaments, chemical, health care, and petroleum (Klein 2008) gain enormous leverage over governments. It is extremely important, however, to note that this tendency towards rent seeking is not a perversion of the neoliberal reason. For much of neoliberal theory (in particular, for the Austrian and the Chicago schools), private monopolies and other forms of concentration of capital are preferred to government control and ownership. Furthermore, for some (such as the Virginia and the Chicago schools), rent seeking is a natural outcome of human 'opportunism' – even though neoliberal thinkers disagree among themselves as to whether rent seeking is essentially economically efficient (as implied by the 'capture' theories of the Chicago school) or inefficient (as implied by the rent-seeking theories of the Virginia school) (Madra and Adaman 2010).

This reconfiguration of the way modern states in advanced capitalist social formations govern the social manifests itself in all domains of public and social policy-making. From education to health, and employment to insurance, there is an observable shift from a rights-based policy-making regime forged through public deliberation and participation to a policy-making regime governed solely by the criterion of economic viability. In this regard, as noted above, the treatment of subjectivity solely in behaviourist terms of economic incentives functions as the key conceptual choice that makes the further technocratization of public policy possible.

Within this general terrain, neoliberal thinking and practices certainly have a significant impact on nature. The next section will focus on the different means through which various forms of neoliberal governmentality propose and actualize the economization of the environment.

Economization of the environment: Diverse paths

In recent years, the interrelated dual crises of environmental pollution and natural resource overuse (including the exhaustion of non-renewable energy and material sources) have globally become objects of neoliberal policy-making. In the area of environmental policy, markets and market-like mechanisms are increasingly being used to provide both consumers and producers proper incentives to protect nature. These mechanisms range from marketable pollution permits (that is, cap-and-trade) to price-per-bag policies for shoppers and households, from natural resource privatization to reliance on the futures and derivatives in the energy (for example, oil) and precious metal (for example, gold) markets (Heynen McCarthy, Prudham, and Robbins 2007). Yet, and not surprisingly if one adopts the framework presented above, these developments have been contemporaneous with the mounting dominance of neoliberal governmentality within the state apparatus, which at times does not shy away from acting as an active economic player, beyond its usual neoliberally sanctioned functions as a rule-setter and regulator. In the petroleum industry, for instance, the public–private partnership model is quickly becoming the standard rather than the exception (Madra 2010). While national oil companies (NOCs) are becoming increasingly important in the extraction of petroleum, multinational oil companies (MOCs) still control the downstream industry (from refineries to distribution networks in consumer markets), and in many cases, NOCs seem to be forming partnerships with MOCs. This picture, needless to say, replicates itself in almost all extraction activities (from copper to gold) throughout the globe. The impacts of prevailing power inequalities on social and ecological life notwithstanding, the common thread in all these approaches has been a stated desire to apply a strict cost-and-benefit methodology in the use of ecosystem services: either by letting the market analyse this through the price mechanism or by assigning a monetary value to the ecosystem (contingent valuation being the most commonly used technique). This perspective is no doubt more clearly present in cases where natural resources are privatized with the motto that ownership rights will provide agents with appropriate incentives to protect nature, as will be taken up in more detail below.

From a historical perspective, in the post-war era, Keynesian macroeconomics combined with welfare economics constituted the framework of mainstream economic theory and policy, and environmental protection took the form of legal regulations concerned mainly with conserving biodiversity and establishing maximum permissible levels of toxic components. Although market instruments were also applied, as in the case of Pigovian taxes to deal with environmental externalities by forcing economic agents to internalize environmental costs through taxes (Turner, Pearce, and Bateman 1993), to a large extent, nature was considered to belong to the public and governments were obligated to protect it. Furthermore, the process was dominantly driven by experts and conservationists who typically informed policy through area-specific terminology and language. Hence, the processes of valuation and the establishment of protected areas were both significantly different from those that would be handled during the neoliberal era.

Yet, despite their mandates to protect nature, post-war governments of all stripes (capitalist, socialist, and non-aligned), thanks in part to free-flowing cheap oil, were able to sustain high rates of economic growth, where the working populace received an increasing share of the national income, paralleling sustained productivity increases (Mitchell 2011). However, with the energy crisis of the 1970s, post-war regimes began to experience intensified internal contradictions, and the neoliberal project (with significant variations) began to gain hegemonic ground worldwide through varying combinations of consent and coercion. Demand management policies aiming to maintain full employment were replaced by austerity regimes that prioritized relieving the pressure on the supply side (through tax cuts) and controlling the inflation rate. This shift of focus in macroeconomic policy, partly justifying itself through the 1970s energy crisis, was accompanied by the ascendency of an 'economic way of thinking' in all realms of social life. The 1970s also witnessed the increasing severity of accumulated ecological problems as well as a radically augmented awareness and politicization of environmental pollution and natural resource overuse – the first Earth Summit was organized in 1972 in Stockholm (del Mar 2011). Within the realm of environmental policy, this shift manifested itself in the escalating use of monetary valuation as a basis for conservation decisions and economic policy measures. With the advent of neoliberalism, and especially starting with the 1990s, the use of markets to protect environmental resources and the privatization of natural resources increased substantially, along with mechanisms designed to tackle information-related problems in the field of environmental policy.

In their aptly titled *Free Market Environmentalism*, originally published in 1991, Anderson and Leal (2001), following the Mont Pèlerin tradition and harmonizing the Chicago and the Austrian traditions, proposed forcefully that market environmentalism – the use of market institutions together with well-defined, enforced, and transferable private property rights on environmental assets and services – is the only viable solution for protecting environmental resources. Once the problem is framed in this manner, what fails is not the market mechanism *per se*, but rather the underlying vision of a paternalistic government that tries to control the environment directly by retaining ownership rights over it and imposing regulations. Reformulating the environmental problem in the individualistic terms of an exchange relationship represents it as a pure economics problem, the remedy to which is nothing but economic measures (Adler 2002). When property rights are clearly delineated, the argument goes, owners will have an incentive to avoid pollution problems and therefore gain by making sure that the threat is abated. On the flipside, liability for pollution, and possible litigation and prosecution, are seen as powerful motivators for economic actors (individuals or enterprises) to control any actions that may hamper the interests of others. Similarly, the best way to deal with natural resource use is argued to be again through allocating and creating private property rights so that beneficiaries take the necessary steps to make the best use of them. For instance, if fishing rights in a lake are given to a firm, it is argued that it will have an incentive to refrain from overfishing and degrading the environment; in contrast, allowing the general public to fish as they wish will unavoidably lead to overfishing as a result of their free-riding actions – the outcome that Hardin (1968) named as the 'tragedy of the commons'. The state, then, is seen as providing no panacea for the problem at hand; bureaucrats, in addition to the possibility of corruptive rent seeking (the Virginia point), will be incapable of generating the information necessary to deal with the problem in the first place (the Austrian point).

Here, three underlying conceptual shifts may be identified as pertaining to the treatment of citizen-subjects, the bureaucracy, and the state. First, citizen-subjects are treated solely as economic agents that behave atomistically. They are assumed to respond to economic incentives (defined in terms of property rights) and legal reprisals, free-ride when the opportunity arises, and be able to engage in a rational manner. The consolidation of the treatment of the citizen-subject as *homo economics* establishes a key conceptual condition for the economization of the environment. Within this context, it would be best to understand the creation and allocation of property rights merely as a particular form of policy implementation of this underlying drive towards economization. Second, when the proponents of the Virginia school of public choice applied this vision of economic actors to the bureaucracy and its constituent actors, they were merely driving the key neoliberal axiom ('individuals respond to incentives') to its logical conclusions (that the bureaucracy may indeed be prone to corruption and rent-seeking activities). They concluded that the negative social welfare effects of governmental failures outweigh those that emanate from market failures. (Here, it should be noted in passing that no conclusive empirical evidence supported the argument that government failures would be greater than market failures.) Finally, the Austrian school perceived the economic problem as one of the social mobilization of knowledge, which is by definition tacit (that is, fragmented and dispersed). Consequently, through the interaction of rival entrepreneurial activities, the state will inevitably perform less effectively in that mobilization process – a stance the school developed during their engagement in the so-called calculation debate that run around the 1930s and 1940s, about whether or not rational economic calculation was possible under state ownership of the means of production (Adaman and Devine 1996). Furthermore, the liberal reason of the Austrian school dictates that all hierarchical structures are to be challenged. To summarize, on the one hand, bureaucratic waste, economic rent seeking, and slackness are seen as endemic problems in the political (state) control of natural resources; on the other, competition in the marketplace is perceived as providing a powerful incentive for actors to acquire and discover information needed to enhance efficiency, and above all natural asset management.

Differences between the Chicago and the Austrian schools should also be acknowledged, however. Theoretically, for the first, the idea of using markets to allocate environmental resources originated in Ronald Coase's seminal essay from 1960 (Coase 1960; see also Medema 1994). The Coasean solution (subsequently formulated by George Stigler) is based on defining property rights for ecological resources and letting people express values through trade. Hence, it is buyers and sellers who evaluate these values in monetary terms. Disputes are therefore settled through bargaining and the exchange of property rights, with no need for governmental regulation. As a result, provided that transactions are costless, in the sense that time and other resources allocated to the bargaining process are so infinitesimal that they are treated as zero costs, externalities will be accounted for within the contractual frame of markets. This Coasean framework has provided the basis not only for the privatization of ecological assets but also for the marketable permits system, the applications of which include air and water pollution control, management of water and land use, and fisheries (US Environmental Protection Agency 2000; Stavins 2008). Yet, the system requires that a permissible level of pollution (for example, the total sulphur dioxide to be emitted in a given area) or a maximum use of an ecological asset (for example, the total catch level of a particular type of fish in a particular geography) be ascertained. In accordance with its trust in the sovereignty of citizens' preferences, the Chicago approach suggests the application of different techniques (as in the case of the contingent valuation method) to estimate individual valuations and aggregate them to form the value of the ecosystem in question in order to determine the said cap.

The Austrians, on the other hand, while embracing the Coasean theorem as a rationale for privatization, express doubts about the marketable permits system on the grounds that the system requires an *a priori* setting of a cap. Instead, they claim that, given interpersonal conflicts over natural resource use, the solution to ecological problems could be achieved through free interactions of economic agents under the rule of law and private property. The conflict between those who use the atmosphere as a carbon sink and change the climate and others who rely on an unchanged climate would be an obvious case to consider. In such a case, the Austrian argument would take the following form: if property rights were allocated and the appropriate legislative procedures existed, economic agents in such a liberal environment with a fully fledged legal system would be able to determine the best trajectory to establish harmonious reconciliation between economic activities and nature – and thus no need for any governmental intervention (Adler 2009; Cordato 2004; Dawson 2011; Pennington 2005; Rothbard 1982). When pressed, they would suggest that 'the lack of property rights today does not mean that a useful property-rights solution is forever impossible' – an argument based on the hope that '[a]dvances in technology may yet allow the establishment of enforceable rights to ... even the presence of an atmosphere that clearly does not promote damaging climate change' (Stroup 2008). Naturally, both the Chicago and the Austrian neoliberal positions object in principle to any challenge to private agents' time horizon (and therefore whether they are myopic or not) on the (normative) basis of individual sovereignty, and thus do not recognize, let alone consider, an alarmingly increasing number of cases where businesses are quick to exploit natural resources for which they were granted property rights.

Finally, the post-Walrasian neoliberal approach suggests that in formulating environmental policies (such as setting out environmental taxes) the existence of imperfect information among agents should be explicitly acknowledged and intelligently designed incentive mechanisms be devised to tackle them. Proponents see no structural differences among varying ownership regimes over the efficiency of a system; but rather they focus on the different ways in which incentive schemes in each regime are formulated. Moreover, because they view the market as just one out of a list of possible mechanisms, they are certainly not unquestioningly committed to privatization or marketization, and have faith in the capability of technocrats and experts for devising incentive schemes. More specifically, when faced with environmental pollution problems where regulators lack accurate information on the perpetrators (for example, in a given industry, pollution abatement costs may be unobservable), the optimal environmental policy would involve the development of a mechanism where it is in the perpetrator's best interest to truthfully reveal any relevant private information (abatement costs, in the example above). A significant bulk of the relevant literature, both applied and theoretical, draws upon Baron and Myerson's (1982) well-known framework on price regulation of a natural monopolist where its costs are unknown. The regulative framework is based on the 'revelation principle', first proposed by Gibbard (1973), that sets out the rules that are feasible and subject to incentive constraints in economic problems associated with adverse selection or moral hazard, or both (Gottinger 2001; Jebgerg and Lando 1997; Spulber 1988). Meanwhile, when faced with tragedy-of-the-commons class of problems that are marked by natural resource overuse and where the actions of agents are unobservable (such as regulators who experience severe difficulties in checking whether individual fishermen exceeded their quotas or not), the theory proposes that the problem of overuse can be successfully confronted if a socially optimal equilibrium is achieved and maintained through appropriately designed 'trigger strategies' (a player using a trigger strategy initially cooperates but punishes the opponent if a certain level of defection is observed) that facilitate repeated interactions (Rubinstein 1979).

As noted above, a major difference of the post-Walrasian approach from the Austrian and the Chicago approaches pertains to the status of property rights and the market mechanism. For the latter two, already discussed in length, private property and marketization are the two key institutions for a successful environmental policy. From the perspective of the mechanism-design approach, however, as long as institutions are incentive-compatible, their ownership structures in and of themselves do not matter; a well-designed institution with public or cooperative ownership could potentially be at least as efficient as an institution with private ownership (Adaman and Devine 1996; Bardhan and Roemer 1992). Furthermore, in contrast to Chicago and Austrian economists who favour current unequal patterns of ownership and income, most members of the post-Walrasian approach would be uneasy with private property on the grounds that this may very likely replicate, if not reinforce, current inequalities (Stiglitz 1994). Coming to the status of the market mechanism, as suggested above, markets are just one of many available mechanisms, and in cases where information is imperfectly available the market mechanism will be unable to provide efficient outcomes. Nevertheless, while this divergence of opinion regarding the efficiency of private property and the desirability of the market mechanism is indeed a difference that matters, and (in a related manner) while politically speaking post-Walrasians would opt for more egalitarian solutions that equalize opportunity, the mechanism-design approach to environmental regulation shares a common underlying assumption with the environmentalism of the Chicago and the Austrian schools: individuals respond to economic incentives. They differ only in the way they define the possible universe of economic incentives: for post-Walrasians, creating markets are equally valid as setting out a Pigovian tax scheme, or imposing a quota (with an accompanying penalty mechanism). Yet, since their primary concern is the existence of asymmetric information among regulatory bodies and economic agents, and since they believe that markets are likely to fail in such cases, they concentrate mainly on mechanism design.

To wrap up, this section laid out different paths that economization of the environment may take as a result of the hegemonic hold that neoliberal theory and practice have enjoyed for over three decades. In drawing this picture, we followed Foucault in conceptualizing neoliberalism as an ideology, manifested in social, material, and epistemic realms, which claims that economic subjects, perceived as calculative and calculable agents, can (and indeed should) be governed through economic incentives. This framework not only covers the so-called standard neoliberal positions of the Austrian and the Chicago schools (with the addition of the Virginia approach), which are on the right end of the political spectrum and defend current unequal patterns of ownership and income, but also the post-Walrasian school, which is situated on the left end of the political spectrum and, while taking a rather sceptical stance against private ownership and the market mechanism, argues for a more egalitarian society. Therefore, Foucault's framework does not only implicate the privatization and marketization, or in short the financialization, of the environment as a part of neoliberal theory and practice – on which there is a vast literature (e.g. Arsel and Büscher 2012) – it also implicates incentive-compatible mechanisms that are based on a similar understanding of the individual as a calculative and calculable agent – even if such mechanisms do not rely on the institution of private property or even the market device. Imagine a society (for instance, along the line of Stiglitz 1994), where the means of production are under public ownership and a group of experts (a central planning bureau, if one wishes to adopt the old terminology) design incentive-compatible mechanisms to make sure that subjects act properly; in other words, a society where information asymmetries will cause no impediments in the quest of controlling ecological degradation. We suggested that even a scenario such as this should be seen as a variant of neoliberal ideology. To sum up, to the extent that the logic of economization remains intact, it will be of a secondary importance whether or not the system is regulated; natural resources are fully or partially privatized; the state acts as an active agent or just takes the administrative role; the behaviour of subjects is regulated through markets or institutions with incentive mechanisms.

In lieu of conclusion

Most ecological issues involve irreducible uncertainty and complexity. When making decisions on such irreducibly uncertain and complex phenomena, an exclusive reliance on the aggregation of the solipsistic preference orderings of autonomous individuals might end up producing highly problematic outcomes. If indeed individual preferences are largely determined by their socio-economic and political surroundings (Jacobs 1997), an anthropocentric epistemic context incentivized through monetary gains, which promotes a myopic vision and solipsism, will be an unlikely candidate to cultivate 'pro-nature' preferences. Equally valid is the argument that the current state of scientific knowledge is subject to considerable uncertainty when it comes to ecological issues, and as such knowledge produced by scientific analysis alone cannot form an adequate basis for decision making (Ravetz 2011). Consequently, for this task it would be inappropriate to reduce environmental valuation to a mere aggregation of individual subjective valuations through a market or market-like mechanism (as the Chicago and the Austrian neoliberal positions would support) or leave it solely to the discretion of a group of scientific experts (as some of those who subscribe to the mechanism-design approach would have it). Furthermore, as most ecological issues are about inter- and intra-generational distributional conflicts, Chicago and Austrian neoliberalism would inevitably be biased in favour of those who have market power, since decisions would largely depend on the preferences of influential market agents (due to a variety of possible reasons, ranging from differential access to information to unequal distribution of assets).

In making decisions with substantial consequences pertaining to both current and future lifestyles (such as the overall growth rate, distributional trajectories, technological path, consumption habits, risk attitude [say, *vis-à-vis* nuclear energy]), the market response or aggregate individuals' valuations derived through a set of available techniques may substantially differ from what could be obtained through collective deliberation and negotiation by various stakeholders, including the scientific community (Özkaynak, Adaman, and Devine 2012). This criticism applies not only to neoliberal positions that favour the current unequal distribution of power but also the post-Walrasian approach, which although concerned with distributional issues keeps relying on the calculative and calculable agency assumption. An alternative approach would argue that in incommensurable cases, where all relevant aspects cannot be captured along a single dimension (such as those derived from monetary cost-benefit analyses), a multi-criteria methodology, which would involve not only economic but also political, moral, scientific, and cultural inputs from a variety of stakeholders, would be more appropriate (Martinez-Alier, Munda, and O'Neil 1999; Munda 2008). The key promise of participatory decision-making procedures, where deliberatory dispositifs and multi-criteria techniques are employed, is that a consensus-building process from below can be best materialized by taking into account the (potentially conflictual) positions of different stakeholders including, of course, the scientific community (Adaman 2012). In this regard, they constitute a formidable path to be explored as an alternative to the surreptitiously normative neoliberal governmental dispositifs, designed by experts from above, under the assumption that all actors are calculative and calculable.

The current indiscriminate application of neoliberal policies over the entire scope of the social field has brought about such political, economic, cultural, and ecological devastation that many of us gladly welcome suggestions for any type of reform to halt this process – even if some of these policies act as though the behaviourist manipulation of economic incentives were the only viable policy tool available. Consider the case of carbon markets, for instance, where the cap is decided either by a scientific body or through aggregate individual preferences. The fact of the matter is that, far from addressing the inefficiencies that emanate from opportunistic and manipulative activities, these mechanisms are vulnerable precisely because they end up soliciting manipulative, predatory, and rent-seeking behaviour (since they were designed to function under such behavioural assumptions in the first place). In other words, these solutions subject a commons such as global climate into the economic logic of markets and 'performatively' turn it into an object of strategic-calculative logic (Çalışkan and Callon 2010; 2009; MacKenzie 2009; MacKenzie, Muniesa, and Siu 2007; Spash 2011). Consider, furthermore, the case of price-per-bag policies. Laboratory experiments and anthropological evidence both suggest that charging a price for some activity that should in fact be treated as a duty or a commitment may well create perverse results (Bowles and Hwang 2008; Campbell 1998). Monetizing the pollution-generating activity instead of limiting (or banning) the activity itself (along with providing an awareness programme) could result in an increase of the unwanted activity. Similarly, the debate on resource extraction and energy production seems to be focusing on whether they should be nationalized, privatized, or be run as public–private partnerships. Nevertheless, the problem with the private versus public dichotomy, given our reading of the contemporary state as an agent of economization, is precisely that both forms, to the extent that they are informed by the different variants of neoliberal reason, serve to isolate these critical areas from the deliberations and political demands of various stakeholders and the general public, limiting the only channels for communication available to them to the price (or price-like) mechanisms. However, perhaps most importantly, neither can be immune towards all types of rent-seeking activities that occur behind the closed doors of technocracy, which operates in an area where the state fades into the market in the various forms of dispositifs.

Needless to say, economic activities that degrade environment are not recent phenomena that are exclusive to what is now increasingly being called the neoliberal era. If anything, post-war Keynesian developmentalism (mainly because of the availability of cheap oil) is responsible for an enormous amount of environmental pollution and ecological degradation (Mitchell 2011). In this sense, it would be wrong to present neoliberalism as being the only responsible mode of governmentality for the dual crises of climate change and natural resource depletion. Yet, this does not change the fact that the neoliberal reason (in its free-market and mechanism-design variations) is pushing its agenda in an era where both of these crises are reaching catastrophic levels, and it is highly questionable whether neoliberal methods of handling environmental pollution and extraction crises will be capable of addressing long-term concerns. Unsurprisingly, social movements against the ways of neoliberal reason are gaining momentum all over the world. At this junction, the difference between defensive movements of resistance, which can always be defeated, diffused, co-opted, or incorporated, and transformatory and progressive movements, which work towards more democratic, self-governing, and rights-based societies, should be openly acknowledged. Alternative policy groups, especially (but by no means exclusively) those working at a transnational level, will continue to play an important role in that regard, by *inter alia* advocating global justice and ecological salvation, creating and mobilizing veridical knowledge and promoting practices and relations that prefigure alternative futures (Chapter 11 of this volume). Similarly, at more regional and local levels, community and solidarity economy efforts and initiatives will also play a pivotal role in cultivating non-anthropocentric, non-exploitative, and non-extractive economies of cooperation and sharing (Gibson-Graham 2006). In this chapter, our contribution to the invaluable efforts of those who are contesting neoliberal globalization, in terms of either resisting to its destructive and irreversible social and ecological consequences or forming alternative modes of production, appropriation, distribution, and circulation of values, has been to remind the reader of the following: to be able to move beyond the horizon of neoliberal reason instead of confining ourselves only to a critique of the marketization or financialization processes, it is necessary to critically engage with the variegated, diverse, and always context-dependent processes of the economization of life and nature at a more profoundly epistemic level.

Note

1. This understanding of neoliberalism as (an ever-unfolding process of) economization resonates with the representation of neoliberalism as a 'variegated' and 'flexibly mutating regime of "market rule"' offered by Peck and his colleagues (Peck and Theodore 2010; Peck, Theodore, and Brenner 2010) and explored by the various contributors to the present volume. While we agree with the argument regarding the flexibility and diversity of neoliberalism, we further argue that this flexibility and diversity arise because neoliberalism, beyond marketization, is a process of economization of the social – a radical process of re-conceptualization of the core social issues from the interpretative grid of economic calculus. This understanding also enables us to address some of the concerns raised in relation to the concept of 'post-neoliberalism'. An increase in governments' regulative involvement in the economy, attention towards social-redistributive issues, or a decline in the role that competitive markets play in the economy may very well go hand in hand with increasing economization of social and environmental spheres in the broadest sense. Precisely because the understanding of economization steps outside the state–market dichotomy, it enables us to entertain a sceptical approach towards concepts such as 'post-neoliberalism'.

References

Adaman, F. (2012) 'Power Inequalities in Explaining the Link between Natural Hazards and Unnatural Disasters', *Development and Change* 43(1): 395–407.

Adaman, F. and P. Devine (1996) 'The Economic Calculation Debate: Lessons for Socialists', *Cambridge Journal of Economics* 20(5): 523–37.

Adler, J.H. (2002) 'Book Review of *Free Market Environmentalism* by Anderson and Leal', *The Cato Journal* 22(1): 182–8.

Adler, J.H. (2009) 'Taking Property Rights Seriously: The Case of Climate Change', *Social Philosophy and Policy* 26(2): 296–316.

Anderson, T.L. and D.R. Leal (2001) *Free Market Environmentalism*, second edition, New York, NY: Palgrave Macmillan.

Arrow, K.J. (1974) *The Limits of Organization*, New York: W.W. Norton.

Arsel, M. and B. Büscher (2012) 'Changes and Continuities in Neoliberal Conservation and Market-based Environmental Policy', *Development and Change* 43(1): 53–78.

Bardhan, P. and J. Roemer (1992) 'Market Socialism: A Case for Rejuvenation', *Journal of Economic Perspectives* 6(3): 101–16.

Baron, D.P. and R.B. Myerson (1982) 'Regulating a Monopolist with Unknown Costs', *Econometrica* 50(4): 911–30.

Becker, G.S. (1976) *The Economic Approach to Human Behavior*, Chicago: University of Chicago Press.

Bockmann, J. (2007) 'The Origins of Neoliberalism between Soviet Socialism and Western Capitalism: A Galaxy without Borders', *Theory and Society* 36(4): 343–71.

Bowles, S. and S.H. Hwang (2008) 'Social Preferences and Public Economics: Mechanism Design When Social Preferences Depend on Incentives', *Journal of Public Economics* 92(8–9): 1811–20.

Brennan, G. and J. Buchanan (1985) *The Reason of Rules: Constitutional Political Economy*, Indianapolis, IN: Liberty Fund, Inc.

Campbell, J.L. (1998) 'Institutional Analysis and the Role of Ideas in Political Economy', *Theory and Society* 27(3): 377–409.

Cerny, G.P. (2008) 'Embedding Neoliberalism: The Evolution of a Hegemonic Paradigm', *The Journal of International Trade and Democracy* 2(1): 1–46.

Coase, R.H. (1960) 'The Problem of Social Cost', *Journal of Law and Economics* 3(4): 1–44.

Cordato, R. (2004) 'Toward an Austrian Theory of Environmental Economics', *The Quarterly Journal of Austrian Economics* 7(1): 3–16.

Çalışkan, K. and M. Callon (2009) 'Economization, Part 1: Shifting Attention from the Economy towards Processes of Economization', *Economy and Society* 38(3): 369–98.

Çalışkan, K. and M. Callon (2010) 'Economization, Part 2: A Research Programme for the Study of Markets', *Economy and Society*, 39(1): 1–32.

Davis, M. (2006) *Planet of Slums*, London & New York: Verso.

Dawson, G. (2011) 'Free Markets, Property Rights and Climate Change: How to Privatize Climate Policy', *Libertarian Papers* 3(10): 1–29.

del Mar, D.P. (2011) *Environmentalism*, New York: Longman.

Duménil, G. and D. Lévy (2011) *The Crisis of Neoliberalism*, Cambridge, MA: Harvard University Press.

Epstein, G.A. (ed.) (2005) *Financialization and the World Economy*, Cheltenham, UK: Edward Elgar.

Fine, B. and D. Milonakis (2009) *From Economics Imperialism to Freakonomics: The Shifting Boundaries between Economics and Other Social Sciences*, London: Routledge.

Foucault, M. (2008) *The Birth of Biopolitics: Lectures at the Collège de France 1978/1979*, Michel Senellart (ed.) and Graham Burchell (trans.), Basingstoke: Palgrave.

Friedman, M. (1962) *Capitalism and Freedom*, Chicago: Chicago University Press.

Gibbard, A. (1973) 'Manipulation of Voting Schemes: A General Result', *Econometrica* 41(4): 587–601.

Gibson-Graham, J.K. (2006) *A Postcapitalist Politics*, Minneapolis: University of Minnesota Press.

Gottinger, H.W. (2001) 'Incentive Compatible Environmental Regulation', *Journal of Environmental Management* 63(2): 163–80.

Hardin, G. (1968) 'The Tragedy of the Commons', *Science* 162(3859): 1243–8.

Harvey, D. (2005) *A Brief History of Neoliberalism*, Oxford: Oxford University Press.

Hayek, F.A. (1948) *Individualism and Economic Order*, Chicago: University of Chicago Press.

Heynen, N., J. McCarthy, S. Prudham, and P. Robbins (2007) *Neoliberal Environments: False Promises and Unnatural Consequences*, London: Routledge.

Hurwicz, L. (2008) 'But Who Will Guard the Guardians?' *American Economic Review* 98(3): 577–85.

IMF (2012) *World Economic Outlook: Coping with High Debt and Sluggish Growth.* Available online: http://www.imf.org. (accessed: 15 December 2012).

Jacobs, M. (1997) 'Environmental Valuation, Deliberative Democracy and Public Decision-Making Institutions', in J.B. Foster (ed.) *Valuing Nature? Economics, Ethics, Environment,* London: Routledge.

Jebgerg, L. and L. Lando (1997) 'Regulating a Polluting Firm under Asymmetric Information', *Environment and Resource Economics* 10(3): 267–84.

Kirzner, I.M. (2000) *The Driving Force of the Market: Essays in Austrian Economics,* London: Routledge.

Klein, N. (2008) *The Shock Doctrine: The Rise of Disaster Capitalism,* Toronto: Vintage.

Krueger, A.O. (1974) 'The Political Economy of the Rent-Seeking Society', *American Economic Review* 64(3): 291–303.

Leys, C. (2008) *Total Capitalism: Market Politics, Market State,* London: Merlin Press.

MacKenzie, D. (2009) *Material Markets: How Economic Agents Are Constructed,* Oxford: Oxford University Press.

MacKenzie, D., F. Muniesa, and L. Siu (eds) (2007) *Do Economists Make Markets? On the Performativity of Economics,* Princeton: Princeton University Press.

Madra, Y.M. (2010) 'Political Economy of Oil', in R. Free (ed.) *21st Century Economics: A Reference Handbook,* Newberry Park, CA: Sage Publications.

Madra, Y.M. and F. Adaman (2010) 'Public Economics after Neoliberalism: A Theoretical-Historical Perspective', *European Journal of History of Economic Thought* 17(4): 1079–106.

Marazzi, C. (2011) *The Violence of Financial Capitalism,* Cambridge, MA: MIT Press.

Martinez-Alier, J., G. Munda, and J. O'Neil (1999) 'Commensurability and Compensability in Ecological Economics', in M. O'Connor and C. Spash (eds) *Valuation and the Environment: Theory, Method and Practice,* Cheltenham & Northampton: Edward Elgar.

Medema, S. (1994) *Ronald H. Coase,* London: Macmillan.

Medema, S. (2009) *The Hesitant Hand: Taming Self-Interest in the History of Economic Ideas,* Princeton: Princeton University Press.

Mirowski, P. and D. Plehwe (eds) (2005) *The Road from Mont Pèlerin: The Making of the Neoliberal Thought Collective,* Cambridge: Harvard University Press.

Mitchell, T. (2011) *Carbon Democracy: Political Power in the Age of Oil,* London & New York: Verso.

Munda, G. (2008) *Social Multi-Criteria Evaluation for a Sustainable Economy,* Heidelberg & New York: Springer.

Özkaynak, B., F. Adaman, and P. Devine (2012) 'The Identity of Ecological Economics: Retrospects and Prospects', *Cambridge Journal of Economics* 36(5): 1123–42.

Peck, J. (2010) *Constructions of Neoliberal Reason,* Oxford: Oxford University Press.

Peck, J. and N. Theodore (2010) 'Mobilizing Policy: Models, Methods, and Mutations', *Geoforum* 41(2): 169–74.

Peck, J., N. Theodore, and N. Brenner (2010) 'Postneoliberalism and Its Malcontents', *Antipode* 41(Supplement S1): 94–116.

Pennington, M. (2005) 'Liberty, Markets and Environmental Values: A Hayekian Defense of Free Market Environmentalism', *Independent Review* 10(1): 39–57.

Peterson, J.M. and R.N. Boisvert (2004) 'Incentive-Compatible Pollution Control Policies Under Asymmetric Information on Both Risk Preferences and Technology', *American Journal of Agricultural Economics* 86(2): 291–306.

Plehwe, D., B. Walpen, and G. Neunhöffer (eds) (2006) *Neoliberal Hegemony: A Global Critique,* London & New York: Routledge.

Plihon, D. (2011) 'Financialization of the Economy – A Brief Introduction', *Conference Report, European Cross Networking Meeting on the Global Crises*, 28–29 October 2011, Paris.

Polanyi, K. (1944) *The Great Transformation*, Boston: Beacon.

Ravetz, J.R. (2011) 'Postnormal Science and the Maturing of the Structural Contradictions of Modern European Science', *Futures* 43(2): 142–8.

Resnick, S.R. and R.D. Wolff (2010) 'The Economic Crisis: A Marxian Interpretation', *Rethinking Marxism* 22(2): 170–86.

Rothbard, M.N. (1982) 'Law, Property Rights, and Air Pollution', *The Cato Journal* 2(1): 55–99.

Rubinstein, A. (1979) 'Equilibrium in Supergames with the Overtaking Criterion', *Journal of Economic Theory* 21(1): 1–9.

Spash, C.L. (2011) 'Carbon Trading: A Critique', in J. Dryzek, R. Norgaard, and D. Schlossberg (eds) *Oxford Handbook on Climate Change and Society*, Oxford: Oxford University Press.

Spulber, D.F. (1988) 'Optimal Environmental Regulation with Asymmetric Information', *Journal of Public Economics* 35(2): 163–81.

Stavins, R.N. (2008) 'Environmental Economics', in S.N. Durlauf and L.E. Blume (eds) *The New Palgrave Dictionary of Economics* (Second Edition), London & New York: Palgrave Macmillan.

Stiglitz, J.E. (1993) 'Post Walrasian and Post Marxian Economics', *Journal of Economic Perspectives* 7(1): 109–14.

Stiglitz, J.E. (1994) *Whither Socialism?* Cambridge, MA: The MIT Press.

Stiglitz, J.E. (2010) *Freefall*, New York: W.W. Norton.

Stroup, R.L. (2008) 'Free-Market Environmentalism', *Library of Economics and Liberty*. Available online: www.econlib.org/library/Enc/FreeMarketEnvironmentalism.html. (accessed: 12 October 2011).

Tickell, A. and J. Peck (2003) 'Making Global Rules: Globalizaton or Neoliberalization?', in J. Peck and H. Yeung (eds) *Remaking the Global Economy*, London: Sage.

Tribe, K. (2009) 'Political Economy of Modernity: Michel Foucault's Collège de France Lectures of 1978 and 1979', *Economy and Society* 38(4): 679–98.

Turner, R.K., D. Pearce, and I. Bateman (1993) *Environmental Economics: An Elementary Introduction*, Baltimore: The Johns Hopkins University Press.

US Environmental Protection Agency (2000) *Guidelines for Preparing Economic Analyses*, Washington, DC: US EPA.

Vanberg, V. (2001) *The Constitution of Markets: Essays in Political Economy*, London: Routledge.

Vanberg, V. (2009) 'Liberal Constitutionalism, Constitutional Liberalism and Democracy', *Freiburg Discussion Papers on Constitutional Economics, 09/04*, Freiburg: Walter Eucken Institute.

Yamawaki, N. (2001) 'Walter Eucken and Wilhelm Röpke: A Reappraisal of their Economic Thought and the Policy of Ordoliberalism', in Y. Shionoya (ed.) *The German Historical School: The Historical and Ethical Approach to Economics*, London: Routledge.

3
Neoliberalism, Nature, and Changing Modalities of Environmental Governance in Contemporary Turkey

Leila M. Harris and Mine Işlar

This piece analyses some of the recent environmental governance changes in Turkey that could be described as neoliberal: privatization of watercourses, decentralization of water user associations (WUAs), and increasing use of market instruments, such as full cost recovery and privatization of urban water. In line with debates on variegation and neoliberalism (Brenner, Peck, and Theodore 2010), we argue that there are key historical traces and contextual factors that make the contemporary situation in Turkey unique and interesting with respect to broader debates on neoliberal environmental governance. Neoliberal practices and policies build on, accentuate, and articulate with these historical and contextual specificities. Historically, there are key connections to Ottoman policies and legacies, situating current policies as a disjointed continuation of some earlier and longer-term efforts (even as in other ways, contemporary policies also represent a sharp break from earlier policies and norms). The European Union accession process, recent economic crises, and the recent politics associated with the Islamic AK party all similarly bear a clear imprint on the pathways and effects of neoliberal environmental governance practices in this context. Our aim here is to untangle, and situate, contemporary environmental governance practices in Turkey in relation to some of these historical and contextual processes and pathways. To do so contributes to debates related to neoliberal natures, variegated neoliberalisms, as well as other contemporary environmental policy debates. It also contributes to one of the general aims of this volume to interrogate the specificities of economic reform (and crises) in varied contexts.

Overview of contemporary neoliberal environmental governance in Turkey

In its most general sense, the term 'neoliberalization' refers to 'a politically guided intensification of market rule and commodification' (Brenner, Peck, and Theodore 2010: 184). There has been considerable interest over the past several decades in detailing the specific effects of neoliberalization, particularly as they might unfold differently across contexts, or as they extend into resource and environmental realms (Heynen et al. 2007; Mansfield 2007). In their recent work, Brenner, Peck, and Theodore (2010) call for greater attention to *variegation*, referring to the systematically uneven, or variegated, character of these processes, including focus on the differentiated geographies, modalities, and pathways of neoliberalization processes. Among the key questions they suggest are ripe for further analysis, they identify a critical need to interrogate how neoliberalism unfolds differently in relation to different geo-institutional processes and histories, as well as the ways that neoliberalism remakes that uneven landscape – often intensifying uneven development of regulatory forms across places, territories, and scales. In brief, to what extent are regulatory and geo-institutional differences exploited, intensified, or reworked through neoliberalization processes (see also Chapter 1 of this volume)?

Turkey is one of many countries that have embarked on a path of neoliberalization, particularly from the Özal period in the 1980s onwards. This transformation has been fostered to significant extent by multilateral institutions such as the International Monetary Fund (IMF) and the World Bank. As is also true with many other contexts, with these changes, the role of the state has not necessarily diminished, but has transformed from being the provider of public utilities and services such as electricity, gas, telecommunications, and water to being the regulator of a business or investor-friendly environment to encourage private sector involvement in provision of these services (Ferguson 2009; Peck 2001).

Work by Kibaroğlu, Başkan, and Alp (2009) provides an overview of the neoliberalization of water-related sectors in Turkey with discussion of the devolution of irrigation, privatization of hydroelectricity, as well as some of the primary elements of related resistance movements. Given this, we only revisit key elements of this context and these changes here, with particular focus on some of the historical and contextual dimensions of these shifts. As a general background, economic and political instabilities such as those associated with the global oil crisis in 1973, the Cyprus war of 1974, and changing labour and remittance practices linked to the European Economic Community, all were instrumental in preparing the ground for a neoliberal policy turn in Turkey (Atasoy 2005). A leading figure of the economic liberalization, Turgut Özal was effective in what has been called the 'There Is No Alternative'-rhetoric (at times also attributed to Margaret

Thatcher), adopting the Washington consensus, and convincing many that economic difficulties could not be overcome without long-term financial adjustments (Yalman 2009). Before the military coup in September 1980, Özal (then a minister in the Demirel government) introduced an economic programme known as the January 24 Decisions. This policy package was designed to implement structural adjustment packages of the IMF and World Bank with aims to promote free trade as well as the decentralization and the deregulation of governance. After the coup, the military regime that took power provided a secure environment for the implementation of these reforms without labour and social opposition (Balkan and Sungur 2002). According to Yalman (2009), this is an important feature of 'structural adjustment' for Turkey, specifically that such reforms began at a moment when the political structure was under complete reorganization. Thus the geo-institutional landscape was open to significant alteration and reconfiguration. These structural adjustment policies went beyond efforts to stabilize the economy, as they also included broader policy shifts and development policies characterized by a strong market system of resource allocation (Yalman 2009). Özal's party, ANAP, stayed in power from 1983 until 1989 and is considered the main architect of Turkey's neoliberal reforms, laying the groundwork for changes that continue into the present day (Kibaroğlu, Başkan, and Alp 2009).

With rising industrialization and growing environmental awareness of the 1980s, 'the environment' eventually gained mention in the current Turkish constitution (adopted during the military regime in 1982). It states in Article 56: 'Everybody has the right to live in a healthy and balanced environment and that improving the environment, protecting the health of environment and preventing environmental pollution is the duty of both the state and individual.'[1] However, as Cerit-Mazlum (2006) argues, despite this constitutional language, Turkey's approach to the environment has been largely shaped by a national growth and developmental discourse (cf. Adaman and Arsel 2005), and other broader political-economic reforms consistent with neoliberalization. In brief, in many policies, economic development is implicitly situated as a precondition for environmental protection, with more weight in policy circles and political discourse being afforded to goals of economic growth and development than to environmental protection per se. Accordingly, environmental concerns that do enter into political debate are often also strongly linked to industrial needs, with major foci including energy politics, as well as economic and trade relations. Some have interpreted this 'let's not sacrifice development for the sake of environment' approach as representing a major obstacle to the maturation of environmental policies in this context (Cerit-Mazlum 2006), while others suggest that environmental legislation in Turkey is fairly well developed, yet suggest there is insufficient implementation that results in significant and on-going environmental challenges (Adaman and Arsel 2005).

How then has the neoliberal turn affected the environmental governance in Turkey? Not surprisingly, the neoliberal turn has increasingly entered the domain of resource use, access, and governance, albeit somewhat more slowly than in other sectors and policy domains. In the past two decades, significant legislative reforms have been passed leading to major changes in the governance of natural resources. These policies were both consistent with structural adjustment policies and also have been generally consistent with the neoliberalization of environmental governance as it has unfolded in diverse contexts across the globe (Heynen et al. 2007; Mansfield 2007).

For instance, *Law No. 3291* enacted in 1986, allowed significant resource sectors to be opened up to free enterprise and privatization by authorizing the Council of Ministers to privatize the State Economic Enterprises (SEEs) which controlled key sectors of Turkish industry such as manufacturing, iron and steel, as well as petrochemicals (Kibaroğlu, Başkan, and Alp 2009). Although the actual implementation process has taken a long time, 188 public companies have been completely privatized prior to 2009 (Atasoy 2009: 112). This privatization of SEEs led to a departure from statism (Yalman 2009), one of the foundational principles of Atatürk's Turkish modernization project (also known as Kemalism) that stressed the prominent role of the state in industry and more generally.[2] Yet another crucial legal reform was *Law No. 3096* enacted in 1984 in the context of the Electricity Market Act which introduced the Build-Operate and Transfer Model (BOT) to the energy and water sectors, thereby allowing the private sector to generate, transmit, and distribute electricity and to construct, operate, and manage water infrastructure such as dams, water plants, and irrigation systems (Kibaroğlu, Başkan, and Alp 2009). In essence, these are all models that serve to enable private involvement in infrastructural development, or seek to leverage private capital to enable the construction of projects, and as such alter the distribution of costs, risks, and benefits between public administration and private investors (Yılmaz 2009). Together with decentralization shifts that also were pursued in tandem with these legal reforms, private sector involvement has increased considerably in the management and operation of natural resources:

> Liberalization and deregulation of the national energy sector and its sub-sectors, including hydroelectricity production, marked a clear departure from earlier decades. Public investment had characterized the period between 1950 and 1980 and particularly the 1970s, which had seen the construction of large dams with no participation by the private sector.
> (Tutus 2006, cited in Kibaroğlu, Başkan, and Alp 2009: 291)

The most recent, and perhaps most controversial, of neoliberal shifts in natural resource sectors has been what is being referred to as the 'privatization of Turkey's rivers'. In brief, in an effort to promote electricity generation, and to promote investment by the private sector in such, the Turkish government has embarked on a large-scale effort to promote small-scale hydroelectricity facilities, known as HEP (hydroelectric power). Rights to Turkey's rivercourses are granted for a 49-year period to private companies in order to build small-scale, run-of-the-river production facilities. While the scale of each effort is relatively small, the overall scale of the effort is massive, with over 1700 HEP facilities planned for Turkey's rivers over the coming decades. Among those around 350 projects are in operation and 1418 are at various planning stages (Erdoğdu 2011), with the expectation that eventually 3 per cent of Turkey's total energy production will be provided by these run-of-river HEP facilities (Işlar 2012). Here, it is both the government's solvency and also the energy crisis that set the stage for this effort. As stated by the head of the energy section, the General Directory of the State Hydraulic Affairs (*Devlet Su İşleri*, henceforth DSİ), 'Turkey is going through an energy crisis; the energy supply cannot meet the energy demand of the growing industry so Turkey is heavily dependent on external sources. That is why the state is looking for alternative options' (Interview DSİ, 5 April 2010).

With BOT and similar methods, 'privatization' in water and other sectors is taking many forms. All told, these mechanisms enable enhanced involvement of the private sector in infrastructure development or service provision, most often without the state yielding inherent ownership of those resources. Although the state is the ultimate owner of water resources in Turkey, through concession models water rights are transformed into exclusive rights that are privately held on a temporary, albeit significant basis (49 years). There is a tension that emerges with the use rights of these rivers being held by private companies for electricity generation. Specifically, this use may conflict with the customary use rights of rural communities, which may rely on the natural ecology of the rivers for fishing and other livelihood needs (Işlar 2012). This 'privatization' exists in diverse forms, and appears to be intensifying through a range of practices.

For instance, considerable loans are now available from international or Turkish banks for renewable energy, spurring the HEP programme and associated streams of investment. Further, Turkish state agents and publications (for example, those produced by DSİ) represent Turkish hydroelectricity as relatively underdeveloped as compared to neighbouring Europe. The government actively promotes these projects, particularly in the context of attempts to align with the EU's ambition of developing 'blue energy for a green Europe' (Dalkır and Şeşen 2011: 39). Further fuelling these shifts, the hydroelectricity sector represents a significant opportunity for businesses to enter the carbon market since small-scale hydroelectricity production is considered as a renewable energy option that effectively reduces carbon emissions. Indeed, there has been rapid entry into these markets to benefit from the influx of resources now available through carbon trading

(Chapter 2 of this volume). In addition to all of these factors, small-scale hydroelectric facilities are also preferred by foreign creditors such as World Bank, and European credit agencies, due to the long history of problems with large-scale projects (Scott 1998). Given 'small is beautiful' rhetoric of many environmental campaigns, and also given the significant resistance to larger projects over the history of lending by these agencies, these funders have generally withdrawn from larger projects, favouring instead small efforts of which HEP is a primary example (for Ilısu Dam controversy, see Morvaridi 2004).

Even as the scale of the resistance to date might be smaller than that associated with the larger projects of the past, the HEP projects have nonetheless been met with significant resistance, both due to the sense that there will be ecological and livelihood losses, and also due to the decision-making and permitting processes, where there has been little community input on these 'local' 'small-scale' projects. In all of these ways, the specific pathways of neoliberalization in the water sector are moulded by a host of contextual factors across multiple scales, including the preferences of international lenders, the discourses and practices of the EU, and the continuing Turkish state efforts to fit into an evolving 'Europe'. In the section on history below, we focus on traces of other contemporary privatization and devolution shifts, particularly to connect recent privatization of urban water delivery systems (for example, İzmit, Antalya, and İstanbul) to earlier efforts during the Ottoman period.

In addition to privatization, decentralization has also been an important focus for many governance reform efforts in Turkey and around the world. This has included decentralization both to reduce state indebtedness, and also to build on more participatory forms of governance that have gained currency in policy circles of the past several decades. These reforms again need to be understood in the broader environmental and developmental context that has highlighted the importance, and favourability, of local-scale, participatory development or natural resource-management efforts (e.g. Brosius, Tsing, and Zerner 2005; Cooke and Kothari 2001; Harris, Goldin, and Sneddon 2013). However, within the context of Turkey specifically, it is also necessary to situate these reforms in the context of the institutional restructuring of the DSİ and of the Bank of Provinces.

The DSİ was established in 1953 as the entity responsible for management of drinking water in provinces and villages with populations of less than 3000 people. As a result of increasing migration to urban centres in the 1960s gradually the scope of DSİ's responsibilities has been extended to mega cities' finance and restructuring of water infrastructure and services in order to meet the demands of the growing urban population (Çınar 2006). With respect to the 1980s restructuring schemes DSİ's operational and maintenance responsibilities were gradually distributed again back to municipalities and other bodies (see *Law No. 2824* in 1983 for domestic and industrial water supply), to Water User Associations (started earlier but accelerated by the transfer programme funded by World Bank in 1993 for irrigation), and to the private sector (for irrigation, ground, and spring water) (Svendsen and Nott 1999). The General Director of DSİ stated that the World Bank chose Turkey as a model country in part because of its efficient process of decentralizing sectors such as irrigation. At the time of the significant push towards decentralization, the DSİ director described the process as follows: 'Today (in 1999) we have around 300 water user associations. New ones are on the way. 83 per cent of the land[3] is transferred to farmers. By doing so, we established Turkey's biggest hidden privatization' (Altınbilek, *Zaman Gazetesi* 12 January 1999, author's translation).

Here, what is significant is the way that norms related to democratization, or devolution, are negotiated in a way that is seen as consistent with a privatization agenda. One might think that the DSİ's role was reduced after its main responsibilities were transferred to local governments and other agencies. However, in line with many theoretical discussions related to neoliberalism (e.g. Peck 2001), the state's role in this regard was not reduced, but rather transformed, particularly to offer institutional support for market interactions and private entities. As Kibaroğlu, Başkan, and Alp (2009) argue, further legal reforms such as the *4628 Electricity Market Law*[4] in 2001 represented a critical transition by appointing DSİ as the government body in charge of implementing the initial steps for the privatization of the hydroelectricity sector. Another structural reform was enacted in 2011 when the Ministry of Forestry and Environment is separated into two ministries: the Ministry of Environment and Urbanization and the Ministry of Forestry and Water Affairs. As part of this reform, DSİ was separated from Ministry of Environment and brought under the aegis of the new Ministry of Forestry and Water Affairs. This recent change carried water affairs and thus DSİ up to a ministerial level and represents decentralization in a particular form – effectively centralizing a body that oversees an array of decentralized governance processes.

Through the decentralization of finance and the reorganization of public institutions, the Bank of Provinces has also been transformed under neoliberal restructuring. Initially operating as the Bank of Municipalities since 1933, the Bank merged with Municipal Public Works and was established as the Bank of Provinces in 1945 – representing a fundamental realignment of its functions. In brief, the Bank of Provinces functions as a state investment agency that provides financial and technical support to municipalities for investment and infrastructure, including in support of drinking water and wastewater treatment. After the 1980s restructuring reforms, its role in relation to water investment shifted away from provision of public credits and subsidies to support local infrastructure to more of a general consulting function (Çınar 2009). Municipalities have been given increasing financial autonomy and are encouraged to apply for loans and financial support from private sources. In line with these broader trends, urban water governance has also been transferred to the metropolitan municipalities' water and sewage administrations (known as the İSKİ Model) that 'operate under a commercial regime which facilitates the mobilization of financial resources via foreign loans' (Çınar 2009: 351). Accordingly, the share of foreign credits (mainly from World Bank, the European Investment Bank and the German Bank for Reconstruction) used for the sewage infrastructure has increased from 19 per cent to 48 per cent between the years 1990 and 1996 (Çınar 2006: 236). Some municipalities extended the scope of foreign financing options to privatize other dimensions of the operation and maintenance of urban water. For instance, through long-term concessions and BOT models, large multinational water companies such as France-based Suez won water-supply concessions for ten years in Antalya after the municipality was forced to privatize the system as part of a loan conditionality to accept US$ 100 million from the World Bank in 1995 (Çınar 2009: 352). However, various urban water privatization attempts failed due to resistance to increased water tariffs among other factors as can be seen in the cases of İzmir, İzmit, Antalya, and İstanbul (Hall and Lobina 2009; Çınar 2009 for discussion of three urban water privatization cases from the Turkish context). For instance, as Hall and Lobina (2009: 2) describe, for the case of Antalya, tensions heightened between the local municipality and the Suez subsidiary, particularly when the private company demanded a doubling of water tariffs and a ten-fold increase in sewerage fees. When the city refused, the concessionaire declared bankruptcy and withdrew.

While these are only several examples of what might be thought of as 'neoliberal environmental governance' in this context (admittedly, representing the research interests of both authors who primarily focus on water), they nonetheless are indicative of a broader suite of trends for Turkish policy and governance. Although we have hinted at some of the pathways and reasons for these reforms, our aim in the following sections is to better understand the impetus and effects of these trends, particularly in way that moves away from a naïve or straightforward interpretation that these changes have been simple 'impositions' from external agents such as the IFIs. Instead, we endeavour to document and trace the fertile context for the on-going neoliberalization of environmental governance in the Turkish context, both by detailing the historical lineage and pathways for some of the reforms, and also by situating these changes within the broader context important for understanding Turkish policy and governance, both with respect to geopolitics (for example, in relation to Turkey's European Union accession process), and also with respect to local political currents and trends (for example, the rise of Islamic party politics and the AK Party of the past decade). To do so, we believe, helps us to consider *variegation* as a central feature and outcome of these on-going neoliberalization processes.

Historical traces: Situating contemporary practices in relation to Ottoman–Turkish temporalities

Although we discuss governance practices of the type described in the section above as *neoliberal*, in the Turkish case, it is clear that many of these practices have historical lineage and precedent. In particular, in Ottoman times, there were several key policies that provide an indelible backdrop for the practices of contemporary environmental governance (and altered state function) that we are witnessing today. For instance, David Hall and Emanuele Lobina (2009) suggest that the first urban water privatization *ever* occurred under the Ottoman Empire. Further, many liberal ideas that characterized the early Republican period (1920s–50s) share some much common ground with these contemporary practices. Our analysis is consistent with others (e.g. Atasoy 2009) who have suggested that neoliberalism needs not be thought of as wholly new, but instead, builds on and modifies earlier liberal practices and reforms. In the Turkish case, while some contemporary practices and economic ideals may not be easily traceable to the early Republic, Kemalist ideals and practices certainly share a strong liberal political foundation, including focus on the individual, rights of women, as well as ideas such as state and nation building. In more recent times, many analysts particularly highlight the importance of the Özal period (1983–9) for Turkey's movement towards neoliberal reforms. Among the elements identified, Özal strongly focused on trade liberalization, openness to investment, and forging a strong relationship to the World Bank (Öniş 2004, also recall discussion above). This period is often described as the 'opening' for what would eventually become easily recognizable as Turkey's neoliberal phase, later evolving and extending to also include important reforms in the environmental realm of the type documented here.

Drawing on key works such as that by Salzmann (2004; 1993) or Atasoy (2009), we find several intriguing examples of the historical currents of contemporary (neo)liberal reforms, giving us some indications of how the current practices articulate with several distinct time periods throughout Turkey's history. For instance, Salzmann describes the importance of decentralization and privatization (such as privatized tax contracts, *malikane*) to Ottoman state formation. The Malikane system was introduced around 1695 as a method of internal borrowing for dealing its fiscal problems that began to appear during the seventeenth century (Genç 2004). In essence, these were contracts tendered to allow private entities working locally to collect state revenues. Somewhat ironically, these decentralized and privatized contracts were issued at the same moment when many state functions, including consolidated revenue collection, were becoming 'centralized'. As such, this centralization through decentralization mirrors some of what we describe above with the recent shifts for DSİ functions. In describing these Ottoman policies, much of Salzmann's interest is in thinking through the ways that these practices provide an interesting counterpoint to common theories of state formation, particularly those that emphasize consolidation and centralization as key features of the modern state. Her account of these practices calls to question the common idea that decentralization and privatization are new, and also challenges the fairly widespread idea (at least in Western academic debates) that decentralization, privatization, and similar practices run counter to 'modern state formation' (see also Tilly 1990 for an interest in the variety of state-making trajectories in Europe). Arguing against common social scientific accounts (particularly those influenced by the work of Weber and Tocqueville, among others), Salzmann argues that decentralization and privatization practices under the Ottoman regime constituted adaptive, alternative state formations (adaptive to particular conditions including changing warfare or agricultural practices), slightly different in character from what might be commonly recognized in discussions of other modern state forms.

As Salzmann writes with respect to both the tendency to associate policy centralization with state formation and also to link privatization and decentralization to the diminishment of state capacity, '(N)ot only does our current vantage point begin to normalize the polities of the past, but it also bids us to reconsider decentralization within longer cycles of state formation' (Salzmann 1993: 394).

While Salzmann's theoretical target is state formation, her narrative is instructive for our aim to clarify contemporary environmental neoliberalization in the Turkish context. Specifically, the fact that privatization and decentralization were important features of Ottoman state policy suggests that these practices have a long history in this context. Further, in line with Salzmann's comment above, our contemporary discussion of neoliberalism tends to normalize the idea that these policies are linked to globalization, and are Western constructs and ideals that are imported, or imposed upon, developing contexts (Öniş 2006).

While we do not deny this as a key aspect of the ways that neoliberalization is unfolding in different parts of the globe (given the influence of international financial institutions – IFIs), including in Turkey, we also take the point from Brenner, Peck, and Theodore (2010) that neoliberalization may specifically rely on, and exaggerate, geo-institutional differences with respect to institutions, cultures, or histories. Indeed, it is possible that the relationship between Ottoman historiography and decentralization, privatization, or other features commonly associated with neoliberalism represent an important starting point to more fully situate, and understand, what makes the uptake, proliferation, or effects of these policies in Turkey possible (that is, to possibly understand these as somewhat 'endemic' policy forms). Salzmann's account also begs the question of why these policies might be especially adaptive to particular shifts and broader challenges facing the contemporary Turkish state. Some of these issues are mentioned above, for instance, the particular ways that opening investment to European companies (for example, Suez) might be productive in the context of Turkey's EU bid, or ways that Turkey endeavours to fit into contemporary 'green' imaginaries of EU environmental policies (see also Erensu 2013 and Harris forthcoming).

Among other possibilities, this history might help ready the acceptance of these policies in this context, given the possibilities that contemporary policies appear to have some endemic roots. This possibility mirrors the conclusions of another study, which suggests that neoliberalization processes may find fertile ground among the imaginaries of the lay public, in that everyday environmental discourse seems to affirm a sense of civil society and individual responsibility for environmental issues, with little emphasis on state regulatory responsibility (Harris 2011). In line with these possibilities, it is also possible that decentralization or privatization may have different effects dependent on the contextual factors specific to Turkey's political, economic, and geo-institutional realities at present. Paralleling Salzmann's discussion of changing agricultural practices and changing warfare that allowed decentralization and privatization policies to be adaptive in Ottoman times, there might also be contemporary realities such as those related to rural to urban migration, or changing geopolitical considerations related to Iraq, or broader instabilities across the Middle East, that similarly make these policies particularly attractive at present. For instance, it is imaginable that with the economic and political instabilities associated with the two Gulf wars over the past several decades, Turkey has been particularly vulnerable to the need to attract foreign investment, to secure domestic energy sources, and to appease the United States or European allies given these geopolitical currents. This was especially the case with the sanctions in Iraq, as Turkey faced the loss of important trading partners and the ability to import Iraqi oil. With respect to rural to urban migration that has been a strong feature of the Turkish landscape since the 1950s, the stress on urban infrastructure also might make cost recovery and decentralization attractive, easing the burden on centralized government to extend and maintain infrastructure, particularly to *gecekondu* (informal settlements, or literally 'constructed overnight' in Turkish) and impoverished areas. Quite different connections might also be in evidence. As Turkey had previously privatized water provision during Ottoman times, and this was considered a failure (see Çınar 2009), it is possible that this history and legacy might condition an unwillingness to engage with these practices, seeing them as antithetical to Turkish cultural or contextual factors (perhaps being picked up in contemporary resistance movements). In line with this possibility, we do have some evidence of this from our work on contemporary resistance movements, for instance, with narratives that stress that 'water is from our ancestors' as part of resistance to the privatization of Turkish rivers. With all of these possibilities, we can open up new avenues of inquiry with respect to the ways that contemporary neoliberalization practices might articulate with, exaggerate, or rub up against these institutional and contextual histories in interesting ways.

To flesh out these possibilities a bit more fully with the specific example of earlier water privatization in İstanbul, a report published leading up the 2009 World Water Forum held there suggested that this cosmopolitan city represented *the first* example of failed water privatization. As they describe it, in 1882, a French Company (Générale Des Eaux) obtained a concession for İstanbul's water at a time when the city was the capital of the then faltering Ottoman Empire. This agreement was made to help repay some debts to foreign investors and was part and parcel of an entire set of concessions that were being given to foreign companies (with monopolies established for different industries, including the operation of ports, tramways, railroads, and so forth in a way which bears a resemblance to contemporary conditions, Noyan 2008). This private contract for İstanbul's water remained in place until after the establishment of the Turkish Republic and the abolishment of capitulations by the Lausanne treaty, until eventually the concession was dismantled in the 1930s with the water services of the city shifting to public ownership. Here we can see in retrospect that the privatization of water under the Ottoman Empire was linked to the empires' political, economic, and geopolitical decline, and the particular vulnerabilities that were associated with this period, including economic instabilities and crises. The situation today has some clear parallels, as again, restructuring, debt-load, and the attempt to stabilize financial markets (for example after the repeated collapses of the early 1990s) have together played a significant role in stimulating and operationalizing current privatization and decentralization efforts (consider as well the role of broader crises such as those associated with the Gulf War, as discussed above). As another example, it is a similar context of political economic crisis and vulnerability that led to the privatization of Antalya's municipal water, spurred by the World Bank in the early 1990s (Çınar 2009).

To draw out the parallels a bit more fully (even as we recognize the significant differences between these two periods), both the late Ottoman period and contemporary period are generally characterized by attempts to create investment-friendly environments, and both are motivated with expressions of desire to align more fully with world markets, and also specifically to 'catch up' to the West. As Ahmad (2000: 9) describes, the Ottoman period of capitulations, of which the earlier reforms were a part, was linked to the idea of:

> the Tanzimat statesmen (who) had believed that the open-door liberal economic policies would bring benefits to the economy from a new division of labour and from being part of a world market. They had therefore agreed to abandon all protective measures including the right to raise tariffs unilaterally.

In a somewhat parallel sense, Öniş (2011: 718) characterizes the current integrationist strategy of the AK party government as 'privatisation of public enterprises...not (as) an ideological issue. Turkey would benefit from closer integration with the global markets'. Certainly, foreign investment, privatization, and the granting of concessions are all somewhat distinct processes, and occurred in different time periods for different sets of reasons. However, issue of contextual readiness for these sorts of shifts is interesting to consider across these distinct historical moments. To consider this further, capitulations under Ottoman times can be thought of as a set of privileges given to the foreign powers – that later coalesced as more formalized rights. For instance, after a major land concession during the Ottoman period, a French ambassador interpreted this as assuring 'to foreign capital the right to develop unlimited mineral, agricultural and forestry riches of the Ottoman Empire' (Ahmad 2000: 7). By attending to this earlier period under the Ottoman Empire, we are suggesting that these specific histories, and earlier 'experiments' with privatization, or openness to public investment, might be important to understand the reception and effects of Turkey's contemporary environmental neoliberalization, including emergent and on-going resistance.

As noted above, resistance movements did invoke the earlier 'failed' histories with İstanbul's privatization in the lead up to the 2009 World Water Forum. Given the ways that the particular historiography of Ottoman decline has indelibly marked the political and cultural imagination in Turkey (cf. Pamuk 2006, as discussed in Atasoy 2009), it is also clear that there might be particular resistance to a sense that Turkey is under the thumb of Western (imperial) powers, even those represented by the large (mostly European) water multinationals. In such a narrative, the Kemalist reclaiming of public water provision in İstanbul in the 1930s might be framed as 'resistance' to the influence of French water companies, and with it the French, British, Greek, and other claims to Turkish territory that marked the decline of the Ottoman Empire leading up to the founding of the Republic. The Kemalist historiography in Turkey is the one that is largely celebrated for having reclaimed Turkish territory and its people, and taking it out of imperial hands. For all of these reasons, we expect that this longer history might also play into 'resistance' narratives and ideals, particularly regarding the 'suitability' of these practices for the Turkish context. However, the situation, particularly as it also intersects with EU debates and practices, is clearly very ambiguous, with complex support for Europeanization and modernization, and also at times resistance to the influence and force of the EU in Turkish policy and daily life (see Harris 2011 and forthcoming for discussion as this relates to environmental policies and politics).

Taking stock of other historical periods, there are other interesting trajectories that are illumined through closer consideration of the Kemalist period, as well as in relation to other features of the contemporary AK party rule.

Atasoy's (2009) account of contemporary AK party politics in Turkey helps to highlight some of these connections (see also further discussion on the contemporary period in the following section, below). As Atasoy describes, the ways that neoliberal debates play out contemporarily have a strong lineage and connection to Kemalist ideals, including those related to individual freedom, modernization, or Turkey's connection to the 'West' (as per the comments above). To make this point using an environmental example, we can draw on recent work by Atalan-Helicke and Mansfield (2012) regarding neoliberal agricultural seed governance. Analysing contemporary seed practices in Turkey they argue that these changes cannot simply be interpreted as an imposition from 'without', either by broader neoliberal actors (such as the IFIs), or through Europeanization channels. Instead, they argue that Turkish political practices and actors favour these policies based on assumed linkages to long-held desires of agricultural modernization that have been emphasized since the Kemalist period. Simply put, they argue that there is a cultural and historical predisposition to favouring policies and practices that appear congruent with discourses of modernity, progress, and developmentalism (particularly those associated with 'the West' that have long characterized Turkish political economy, see also Harris 2008).

These accounts help us to begin to sketch out the historical antecedents for particular practices we might recognize in the contemporary period as 'neoliberal', with seemingly contradictory possibilities in terms of what the effects of some of these lineages might be. The authors cited (particularly Salzmann and Atasoy) do a great deal to allow us to situate these practices in relation to other social and political processes of importance to the time periods and contexts under study (whether changing agricultural practices or warfare regimes in the Ottoman period, or changing Islamist policies contemporarily). Drawing on insights of this type, our aim is to similarly allow us to make better sense of contemporary neoliberal environmental governance in Turkey, accounting both for the longer durée by highlighting some of these historical antecedents, and also in relation to other practices, politics, and policies of the contemporary period – from rising Islamist politics to energy crises. Although this discussion of historical antecedents is quite brief, we nonetheless have sought to make the point that these particular practices (for example, decentralization or privatization) are not necessarily new to Turkey, and indeed were important characteristics of governance in this context over a hundred years ago. While the pressures and reasons for these policies looks very different during the decline of the Ottoman Empire in the context of war and state making, and the more contemporary impulse rising from AK party policies and the rapidly growing Turkish economy contemporarily, nonetheless it is important to trace these connections. To attend to variegation is both a project of tracing differences and contextual specificities, as well as highlighting the types of distinctions which matter for the specific forms and outcomes of such policies.

The contemporary turn to these policies in the environmental realm must be understood in relation to these earlier policies (just as neoliberalism is linked to, though somewhat distinct from liberalism, in all of its guises, see Peck 2001; Peck and Tickell 2002). Even as we see clear connections and lineage to earlier practices in Turkey, there are also clear distinctions that should not be underplayed. For instance, while some of the first water privatization efforts were introduced during the Ottoman period, that time period is also characterized by a strong emphasis on free water provision (for example, under the rule of Abdülhamid 1876–1918). Given that reality, the effects of the early privatization efforts were likely quite different from the strong market orientation that couples privatization with full cost recovery and similar policies at present (even as equity is also a stated aim of contemporary efforts). Similarly, there are also interesting points of tension between Salzmann's point that decentralization and privatization allowed for unique and situationally defined forms of modern state building, and other accounts that consider ways that Turkish state building was strongly linked to centralization of institutions and consolidated control of resources (cf. Harris and Alatout 2010).

These histories, and their effects for state building, institutions, and politics are interesting to connect to the contemporary moment, despite these contradictory and unclear expressions. Given the specific contextual factors that characterize the Turkish political economy at present, what are the linkages of contemporary neoliberal environmental governance policies to these longer histories of state building, shifting state–society relations, or changing citizen subjectivities? Specifically, as environmental governance increasingly emphasizes local responsibility and decentralization, what are the implications for state institutional forms, for governance possibilities, or for citizen subjectivities (cf. Agrawal 2005; Harris 2011)? Further, what are the geopolitical and other political and institutional factors of the contemporary moment that make the contemporary Turkish context ripe for on-going neoliberalization of environmental governance? Indeed, such questions are interesting to consider in the Turkish case as the idea of a strong centralized state has long resonance, beginning with one-party rule after the establishment of the Republic, and as emphasized through Kemalist reforms that aimed to consolidate a singular and unitary Turkish state and nation that effectively resisted Western imposition even as it strongly sought to connect to, and mimic, Western-style modernities (see Keyman and Öniş 2007), these ideas also connect to the Ottoman Tanzimat period (see Atasoy 2009). All of this provides interesting context and background for how decentralization, privatization, or other neoliberal environmental governance efforts might unfold in this context, and to what effect.

In the next sections, we elaborate yet other contextual factors that might be important for understanding and interpreting on-going 'neoliberal' environmental governance changes in the contemporary Turkish context.

Contemporary context: EU accession, economic crises, and AK party politics

In the previous section, we attempted to connect dimensions of on-going governance changes with historical political economic considerations in Turkey. In this section, we draw out a bit more fully several other dimensions of the contemporary period, particularly on-going political economic instabilities, the politics associated with EU accession, and rising popularity of Islamist party politics. With respect to the economic and political crises that have affected Turkey, particularly earlier financial crises in 1994, 1998, 2000–01, Turkey's political-economic instability of the past several decades led to significant 'openings' for Turkey's neoliberalization. Consider, for instance, the increasing interaction with 'external actors' (for example, the World Bank) as well as changing political and cultural concerns (Keyman and Öniş 2007). As one example of World Bank influence, consider that Kemal Derviş, following on a 22-year career at the Bank, returned to Turkey to oversee the economic recovery after the 2001 financial crisis. In terms of broader political concerns, it is also important to consider a series of crises of the state (the 1980 military coup, the 1997 coup threat, or the threats of military intervention in 2007 – the so-called e-coup), as well as the more stable period of recent years (characterized by the growth and entrenchment of the Islamic AK party, as well as continuing negotiations and reforms associated with European Union accession). All of these contemporary trends further define the contours of nature's neoliberalization in this context, and indeed, even serve to define what the very term 'neoliberalization' might mean given these specific manifestations and articulations.

To provide one example, the political destabilization and coup in 1980 shook the confidence in the idea of a strong centralized state among the Turkish polity. This is significant given the entrenched history of the strong state since the establishment of the Turkish Republic under Mustafa Kemal Atatürk in 1923. The coup had significant effect: 'the legitimacy once enjoyed has been withdrawn in the eyes of Turkish society at large, its democracy deficit has steadily increased, the national developmentalism has been seriously challenged and replaced by neoliberal economic rationality' (Keyder 1997: 14).

Here, the claim is made that reduced state legitimacy articulated with neoliberal rationalities to favour a diminished centralized state, and perhaps also an increasing role for the IFIs and other external actors. With respect to frequent economic crises as well, developing countries including Turkey have been subject to stabilization policies of the IFIs (such as that which occurred after Turkey's 2001 crisis). Some have argued that these restructurings made Turkey more vulnerable to later economic crises in that they suddenly – and prematurely – exposed the economy to vulnerabilities in the face of financial and capital account liberalization (Öniş 2006).

Others suggest, however, that modifications to the banking and other sectors through these adjustments made Turkey less vulnerable to later shocks, including those associated with the 2008 crisis (Oğuz 2011). Whatever the specific directions of this vulnerability, the economic crises and political fragilities (both so common to Turkey in the past several decades) have both served to pave the way for neoliberal rationalities and policies, including, but not limited to, the increasing influence of IFIs. The specific ways that this neoliberalization has affected resources and nature relate to these alterations to Turkish state regulatory and fiscal capacities, as well as the considerable efforts undertaken to open the Turkish economy to further investment. The result in Turkey (from these changes, but also from a number of other reforms, as well as acceptance as an accession country to the European Union) has been remarkable foreign investment, and also considerable economic growth, especially since the 2001 crisis (for instance, with average estimated foreign investment of US$ 1.4 billion per year from 1995 to 2004, and now with averages closer to US$ 20 billion per annum, see YASED 2007). Of course, this period (characterized by investments, privatization, and growth) has also come with environmental and governmental consequences. For instance, the wave of privatization began with banking, and has now extended to include privatization of water and so forth (referred to by Öniş (2011) as the 'mass privatization era', signalling foreign investment of a particular type). Or, to provide another example, the focus on debt reduction has spurred further decentralization of resource governance, such as those associated with the Water User Groups (Harris 2005; Kadirbeyoğlu 2008). In another illustration still, we can imagine the ways that considerable growth of the past two decades has consequences for resource use (cf. Tienhaara 2010), augmenting needs for resources such as energy. To the extent that energy or other resource requirements are increasingly linked to economic growth, there may also be feedbacks that spur further privatization to harness resource capacities or to develop more energy resources, such as that associated with granting rights to the rivers for hydroelectricity generation as described above.

Concerning broader EU processes, there are many ways that these have shifted the terrain of Turkish political economic conditions (Glyptis 2005; Göksel and Güneş 2005; Tocci 2005), including transformations of environmental politics in ways that contribute to the rise of new political forms, and at times a shift away from state-centric politics (Ignatow 2008). Spurring shifts of this type, the EU has made specific investments in environmental civil society, shifting the regulatory, institutional, and political dimensions of these issues more towards non-governmental organizations and away from the state regulatory apparatus (Harris 2011). Of course, the privatization of different sectors such as water provision also directly connects to

EU political processes, in that it is most often European companies that are bidding for, and getting contracts, for these efforts, just as they are for dam building based on BOT models that have also risen in favour with more recent state restructuring. For instance, through the European Investment Bank, between 1995 and 2005 the EU has provided credits for €493 million in total to be used in various sewage, wastewater, and water infrastructure projects (Topçu 2005: 295). As a World Bank adviser stated in 2009 during the World Water Forum in İstanbul, 'EU candidacy is another economic sector and (the) World Bank helps Turkey to develop projects in compliance with EU directives' (author notes from World Water Forum, İstanbul 2009).

There are yet other ways that the EU accession process, and the environmental *acquis* in particular, articulates with the broader contours of nature's neoliberalization. To provide a specific example, even as the EU Water Framework Directive (European Commission 2000) has considerable emphasis on equity concerns, one of the principles also states the following as a key objective: 'setting prices for water use taking into account the principle of cost recovery and in accordance with the polluter pays principle'. Towards this end, the EU member states must ensure, by 2010, that 'water-pricing policies provide adequate incentives to use water resources efficiently to recover the true cost of water services in an equitable manner' (European Commission 2000: 13). In general, the incredible cost that Turkey will face in meeting the *acquis* standards make it appear as though privatization is the only possible way forward. However, as Markandya (2005) concludes, privatization is not the only way of sharing the burden of upgrading environmental standards. Other options are to commercialize state-owned enterprises or to raise the financing for the investment through commercial loans. All told, there is significant pressure for reform on Turkey and other accession countries, often spurring rapid movement towards commercialization and other 'neoliberal' responses.

Other commentators and analysts have also considered the specific articulation of the EU accession process, as well as neoliberalization processes, with politics of the ruling AK party (e.g. Tuğal 2007). As Keyman and Öniş (2007: 211) suggest, the AK party has uniquely been able to 'capitalize upon (the) opportunity space provided by (this) changing domestic, regional, global context'. To provide a specific example of the ways that these politics and practices merge in complex and interesting ways, Atasoy (2009) provides a discussion of veiling to show how the Islamic agenda (to allow veiling in public buildings) melds with (neo)liberal ideas related to the rights of the individual, and also with European ideas of personal freedom (see also Gökarıksel and Mitchell 2005). Similar ideas were articulated in an interview with the *Liberal Düşünce* NGO in an interview conducted by one of the authors in 2005, whose aim is to promote liberal thought and traditions in Turkey, including a strong neoliberal impulse related to market orientation.

Indeed, apart from contemporary politics, other demographic factors also play into the contemporary discourse on privatization. For instance, the rapid rural-to-urban migration of the past several decades and rapid population growth in Turkey has resulted in an infrastructural deficit for the urban water supply (see Altınbilek 2006, for the example of İstanbul). As expressed by Environment and Forestry Minister Veysel Eroğlu, 'Our ministry supports public–private co-operation by all means', and further 'With the financial means that are controlled by the central government, it is impossible to realise the projects at hand in the short run. We will have to attract private investment' (Yücel 2008).

Thus, in ways that parallel our discussion of historical antecedents above, there are specific issues with respect to Turkey's political-economic fragility, restructuring, demographic shifts, or other issues that all articulate with, and bear an imprint upon, the why and how neoliberalization is currently taking hold in Turkey in environmental realms. We have made considerable efforts to detail some of these key historical and contextual factors, as we believe they are crucial both to situate and understand the character, function, and effects of neoliberal natures. In line with the overall interests of the volume on economic crisis, the recent and frequent economic crises in Turkey were one of many factors that serve to condition the acceptance, uptake, and proliferation of neoliberal environmental governance. Echoing Tienhaara's (2010) discussion of the relationships between economic and environmental crises, here we also see similar connections whereby the economic crises (2008 and earlier) paved the way for particular forms of intensified growth and investment. Similarly, the recovery from the 2008 crisis, and the stimulus package eventually accepted by the AK party, was very much discussed as an 'opportunity', inflected in part by the notion of green economic growth and development (that also characterized the discourse of stabilization and recovery elsewhere, such as the recent economic recovery efforts in the United States under Obama).

Another clear point to be made here, as discussed further in the conclusion, is the ways that neoliberalization doesn't stand apart from its specific articulations (Castree 2008). In this case, there are unique connections and resemblances to Ottoman policy, Kemalist modernist vision, and contemporary Islamic politics, that all fashion nature's neoliberalization. It is also worth considering that although in some senses it appears that neoliberalism is 'endemic' to the Turkish context (by articulating with earlier decentralized policies, or by playing on modernist aspirations), there are also ways that Turkey has been 'subject' to policy imposition from without. This has occurred most clearly with the reform packages following Turkey's frequent economic crises (for example, following the 2001 crisis when Turkey became the IMF's biggest lender). Similarly, Turkey's position with respect to on-going negotiations with the European Union means that Turkey is undertaking considerable reforms to meet EU expectations and to follow accession criteria. In all of these ways, we must understand neoliberal policies in the Turkish context as fashioned at the interstices of these 'internal' and 'external' forces, carrying with them all the weight of what it means to modify state institutions, regulations, and policies in ways that respond to Turkey's unique history, but also in ways that 'conform' to European or IFI expectations (with all of the postcolonial baggage that entails [see Harris 2008, or discussion in Glyptis 2005 or Atasoy 2009 on the uneasy ways that EU expectations articulate with Kemalist or Islamist politics]). In making this claim we are effectively concurring with the conclusions of Atalan-Helicke and Mansfield (2012) discussing neoliberal seed practices. As they suggest, many countries including Turkey adopt laws that favour commercialization and privatization, and with it, policies that limit non-commercial seed-saving and exchange. This results *not simply* from imposition of regulation from above (that is, from the EU or global regulatory bodies), but instead reflects that developing countries often themselves adopt dominant perspectives on the 'modern' seed and notions of agricultural 'progress'. Thus, in the case of agricultural seeds, and with respect to other aspects of nature's neoliberalization, it is imperative to think through both the 'internal' and 'external' cultural, political-economic, and institutional factors that give rise to certain policies at certain times. This is all part and parcel of documenting, and beginning to understand the constitution of, and effects of, variegated neoliberalisms.

Conclusions: Ways forward, resistance, and broader neoliberal processes

We have suggested that there is no crisp divide between what policies and practices can be thought of as 'neoliberal' in Turkish historiography. Instead, the emergent policies and practices reflect multiple influences and traditions in uneasy and dynamic ways. In making this claim, we reaffirm the point made by Peck, Theodore, and Brenner (2010) that there is no possibility of forging crisp differentiation between neoliberalism and its Others, making it difficult to capture what is 'inside' and what is 'outside' neoliberalism. Recognizing these difficulties, we nonetheless find it to be fruitful to attend to the specific ways that the contemporary environmental governance practices in Turkey mesh with broader projects and policies associated with neoliberalism, serving to identify the linkages and connections to other political economic projects and policies as they are unfolding in different times and places.

With respect to the specific articulations of seed practices, water privatization, or decentralized resource governance in contemporary Turkey, we have argued here that an appreciation for historical, contextual, or cultural factors is crucial to understand why some of these policies have been adopted, or to begin to unpack what their effects might be. To push this a bit, we have suggested that the so-called privatization of Turkey's rivers must be understood beyond a circumscribed understanding of 'neoliberal environmental governance', even as these practices clearly link to what we understand as 'neoliberalism'. Instead, it is useful to consider these contemporary governance practices in light of Turkey's imperative to 'develop' (and the energy requirements this entails), or the need to maintain a geopolitical position that is stable and favourable to Europe and the 'West'. All of these imperatives are accentuated given the broader instability that marks the region, and on-going difficulties that Turkey faces with respect to many of its neighbours for trade, foreign policy, or oil imports.[5] In this context, we might want to trace the roots of these contemporary 'privatization' efforts to the earlier examples of urban water provision in Ottoman times, or the particular global environmental governance situation that emphasizes a growing need for 'renewable' electricity sources. Renewable energy is perceived as a solution, in that it may relieve Turkey's energy dependency on neighbouring countries (since 75 per cent of its energy demand comes from imported natural gas and petrol, see Başkaya, Başkaya, and Sarı 2011; Işlar 2012). As well, there is also a geopolitical drive for renewable energy that links to Turkey's desire to take active part in market for climate change solutions such as carbon market mechanisms (Erensu 2013; Işlar 2012). Although Turkey is not obliged to reduce carbon emissions as set by Kyoto protocol and thus cannot benefit from global emissions trading, there are many projects designed for voluntary carbon markets, allowing renewable energy producers in Turkey to sell carbon credits (Dalkır and Şeşen 2011). At present, there are 151 carbon market projects in Turkey and 84 of them are HEP projects (Dalkır and Şeşen 2011: 49).

Tracing these sorts of connections and linkages, we have tried to detail several ways that neoliberal practices in Turkey are not wholly new, and certainly not exterior to long-held views and policies in the Turkish context. Instead, contemporary neoliberal agendas articulate with these longer-term practices. In contrast to Kemalist pathways, however, the contemporary moment is certainly distinct in terms of forging new state administrative forms, or state–society relations. As such, we see growing favour and incidence of so-called neoliberal environmental governance.

We also find a major gap in our understanding in terms of being able to explicate what these specific histories and imaginaries mean in terms of what 'effects' these neoliberal policies are likely to have in this context. Some hints might be gleaned from analyses such as that provided by Harris (2011) that suggests lay imaginaries in Turkey indicate a readiness and acceptance of civil society responsibility for environmental issues, deflecting attention away from state regulatory forms. Or, other work also focused on environmental politics detects some resistance to EU imposition of norms and regulations, given the perception that they might be unsuitable for the

Turkish context (see Harris forthcoming). To provide another example of how these connections might be meaningful, given the EU context and focus on 'justice' (at least as policies such as the Water Framework Directive are written) as well as the focus of the AK party on issues such as social welfare and poverty, how might these discourses and policies also serve to condition particular responses to the increased neoliberalization of environmental governance in Turkey (cf. Atasoy 2008)? For instance, might the AK party discourse on justice mean that nature's neoliberalization will unfold with safety nets for the poor, or in ways that foment particular types of resistance given contradictions in the aims of these discourses and policies?

We also see evidence for the possibility that resistance to nature's neoliberalization draws on specific understandings of the context: its history, culture, and traditions. Indeed, analysis of the resistance movement that has evolved in response to the 'privatization' of Turkey's rivers draws considerably on Turkish cultural traditions and lifeways as part of its discourse (Işlar 2012). Local communities from 81 cities of Turkey and all regions of Anatolia have expressed their concerns related to the loss of rural lifestyles, Turkish culture, and history, and worked to establish Turkey's first national water rights platform called *Türkiye Su Meclisi* (Turkish Water Assembly 2010) to contest the hydroelectricity plants built and planned in their villages. In the declaration of their 'Water Manifesto', they advocate for the acknowledgement of the non-economic value of water and nature. Similarly, TMMOB (Union of Chambers of Turkish Engineers and Architects) has been leading the charge in resistance to these policies, viewing it as in their purview as an association of Turkish engineers to show awareness to the destructive implications of power plants (interview with a former member of water commission of TMMOB, 15 January 2011). However, their role is limited since some of their members take part in the planning and the construction of these plants. From a more environmental perspective, we see evidence both for the ways that broader dimensions of environmental discourse and practice contribute to the privatization of Turkey's rivers (for example, green economies, carbon trading, or 'small is beautiful' movements). We also see counter instances, where in part the resistance to use of the rivers in this way also draws heavily on the idea of environmental harm that will occur with the significant alteration of the rivers. In addition, on-going social and legal struggles raise awareness regarding the issues of recognition of land and water rights, or the importance of local participation, changing the nature of demands during project design and implementation stages (such as the addition of customary rights reports and other requirements).

Certainly, Turkey's neoliberal environmental governance, and resistance to such, is both part of broader trends and processes. However, we have also used the opportunity of this chapter to explore some other ways that history and context matter for the form, function, and effects of these policies and practices. As Ignatow (2008) and others note, there remains a continuing need to discern the local effects of broader trends such as economic liberalization, as well as a need to specify the particular forms of neoliberalism in different contexts, including how they become indigenized (McNeill 2005). To do so is also crucial to understand *variegation* as a key feature and characteristic of neoliberalism. As Brenner, Peck, and Theodore (2010) argue, it is crucial to think through the unevenness and context specificity as key features of neoliberalism, as well as foundational to the ability of neoliberalism to morph and detour in ways that exploit these uneven geographies and differentiated features and histories. Not only does attention to variegation allow us to better understand the 'character' of neoliberalism, but this allows us to begin to make progress towards thinking through 'alternatives' to neoliberalism as they may take root in particular times in places. Thinking through this web of interconnections helps us to make sense of ways that diverse neoliberalization practices, while certainly externally aligned, may also appear as 'natural', 'endemic', or 'hostile', or 'foreign' in a context such as Turkey.

Notes

1. Given the constitutional language related to shared state and individual responsibility (or duty), it is of interest that recent research suggests that lay discourse on environmental challenges reinforce a sense of a fairly minimal role for the Turkish state and greater relative emphasis is given to individual and local responsibility (Harris 2011).
2. Mustafa Kemal Atatürk was the first president of modern Turkey after its establishment, and has been very influential in fostering a vision for a modern and secular Turkey, often referred to as Kemalism (see Bozdoğan and Kasaba 1997, or Harris 2008 for more on Kemalist modernization in Turkey).
3. Topçu (2011: 103) states that the total irrigated area in Turkey is about 5.3 million hectares of which 3.06 million hectares were developed by DSİ. Almost 2.1 million hectares have been transferred to irrigation associations and the like.
4. The 4628 Electricity Market Law became the basis for 'water rights concession contracts' that define and regulate the principles for leasing the rights of water use from rivers for 49 years by the private sector to produce electricity. After this law was enacted in 2001, there are 1700 projects in the entire country constructing Hydro Electric Power Plants (HEPP) that have already been licensed or are in the process of being licensed to private companies (DSİ Press Release 2009).
5. Even as Turkey has adopted a 'zero-problem' neighbour policy to ease relations with neighbouring countries, there are aggravated tensions with the current Syrian regime, many neighbouring countries still require a visa (for example, Greece or Bulgaria), and instabilities in Iraq and Iran continue to pose considerable problems for Turkish regional policy.

References

Adaman, F. and M. Arsel (eds) (2005) *Environmentalism in Turkey: Between Democracy and Development?* Aldershot, UK: Ashgate.

Agrawal, A. (2005) *Environmentality: Technologies of Government and the Making of Subjects*, Durham & London: Duke University Press.
Ahmad, F. (2000) 'Ottoman Perceptions of the Capitulations 1800–914', *Journal of Islamic Studies* 11(1): 1–20.
Altınbilek, D. (1999) *'DSİ'de Sessiz Sedasız Özelleştirme'*, *Zaman Gazetesi*, 12 January. Available online: http://arsiv.zaman.com.tr/1999/01/12/ekonomi/2.html. (accessed: 15 March 2013).
Altınbilek, D. (2006) 'Water Management in Istanbul', *International Journal of Water Resources Development* 22(2): 241–53.
Atalan-Helicke, N. and B. Mansfield (2012) 'Seed Governance at the Intersection of Multiple Global and Nation-State Priorities: Modernizing Seeds in Turkey', *Global Environmental Politics* 12(4): 125–46.
Atasoy, Y. (2005) *Turkey, Islamists and Democracy: Transition and Globalization in a Muslim State*, London & New York: I.B. Tauris.
Atasoy, Y. (2008) 'The Islamic Ethic and the Spirit of Turkish Capitalism Today', *Socialist Register* 44: 48–69.
Atasoy, Y. (2009) *Islam's Marriage with Neoliberalism: State Transformation in Turkey*, London & New York: Palgrave Macmillan.
Balkan, N. and S. Sungur (2002) *The Ravages of Neo-Liberalism: Economy, Society, and Gender in Turkey*, Hauppauge, NY: Nova Science.
Başkaya, S., E. Başkaya, and A. Sarı (2011) 'The Principal Negative Environmental Impacts of Small Hydropower Plants in Turkey', *African Journal of Agricultural Research* 6(14): 3284–90.
Bozdoğan, S. and R. Kasaba (eds) (1997) *Rethinking Modernity and National Identity in Turkey*, Seattle, WA: University of Washington Press.
Brenner, N., J. Peck, and N. Theodore (2010) 'Variegated Neoliberalization: Geographies, Modalities, Pathways', *Global Networks* 10(2): 1–41.
Brosius, P., A. L. Tsing, and C. Zerner (2005) *Communities and Conservation: Histories and Politics of Community-Based Natural Resources Management*, Lanham, MD: Rowman and Littlefield.
Castree, N. (2008) 'Neoliberalising Nature: The Logics of Deregulation and Reregulation', *Environment and Planning A* 40 (1) 131–52.
Cerit-Mazlum, S. (2006) 'Dış Politika Sorunu Olarak Çevre: Rio'dan Johannesburg'a Türkiye'de Çevre Dış Politikasi ve STK'lar' (From Rio to Johannesburg: Turkey's Environmental Foreign Policy and Civil Society)', in S. Cerit-Mazlum and E. Dogan (eds) *Sivil Toplum ve Dış Politika, Yeni Sorunlar, Yeni Aktörler*, İstanbul: Baglam.
Çınar, T. (2006) 'Su Hizmetlerinin Özelleştirilmesinde Model Ülkeler ve Türkiye Örnegi' (Model countries in the Privatization of Water Services. Example from Turkey), *Toplum ve Hekim*, 23(1): 41–52.
Çınar, T. (2009) 'Privatisation of Urban Water and Sewerage Services in Turkey: Some Trends', *Development in Practice* 19(3): 350–64.
Cooke, B. and U. Kothari (2001) *Participation: The New Tyranny*, London: Zed Books.
Dalkır, O. and E. Şeşen (2011). *Çevre ve Temiz Enerji*. Available online: www.dsi.gov.tr/docs/haber_dokumanlari/2011/.../cevre_temiz_enerji.pdf. (accessed: 28 March 2013).
Erdoğdu, E. (2011) 'An Analysis of Turkish Hydropower Policy', *Renewable and Sustainable Energy Reviews* 15: 689–96.
Erensu, S. (2013) 'Abundance and Scarcity amidst the Crisis of "Modern Water": The Changing Water-Energy Nexus in Turkey', in L. Harris, J. Goldin, and C. Sneddon

(eds) *Contemporary Water Governance in the Global South: Scarcity, Marketization, and Participation*, London: Routledge.
European Commission (2000) *Water Framework Directive: 2000/60/EC- of the European Parliament and of the Council of 23 October 2000 Establishing a Framework for the Community Action in the Field of Water Policy*. Available online: http://eurlex.europa.eu/LexUriServ/LexUriServ.do?uri=OJ:L:2000:327:0001:0072:EN:PDF. (accessed: 4 April 2013).
Ferguson, J. (2009) 'The Uses of Neoliberalism', *Antipode* 41(S1): 166–84.
Genç, M. (2004) 'A Study of the Feasibility of Using Eighteenth-Century Ottoman Financial Records as an Indicator of Economic Activity', in H. İslamoğlu-İnan (ed.) *The Ottoman Empire and the World Economy*, Cambridge: Cambridge University Press.
Glyptis, L.A. (2005) 'The Cost of Rapprochement: Turkey's Erratic EU Dream as a Clash of Systemic Values', *Turkish Studies* 6(3): 401–20.
Gökarıksel, B. and K. Mitchell (2005) 'Veiling, Secularism, and the Neoliberal Subject: National Narratives and Supranational Desires in Turkey and France', *Global Networks* 5(2): 147–65.
Göksel, D. N. and R. B. Güneş (2005) 'The Role of NGOs in the European Integration Process: the Turkish Experience', *South European Society and Politics* 10(1): 57–72.
Hall, D. and E. Lobina (2009) *The Private Sector in Water in 2009*. PSIRU, Business School, University of Greenwich. Available online: http://gala.gre.ac.uk/1706/1/2009-03-W-companies.pdf. (accessed: 15 March 2013).
Harris, L. M. (2005) 'Negotiating Inequalities: Democracy, Gender, and Politics of Difference in Water User Groups in Southeastern Turkey', in F. Adaman and M. Arsel (eds) *Environmentalism in Turkey: Between Democracy and Development?* Aldershot, UK: Ashgate: 185–200.
Harris, L. M. (2008) 'Modernizing the Nation: Postcolonialism, (Post)Development, and Ambivalent Spaces of Difference in Southeastern Turkey', *Geoforum* 39(5): 1698–708.
Harris, L. M. (2011) 'Neo(liberal) Citizens of Europe: Politics, Scales, and Visibilities of Environmental Citizenship in Contemporary Turkey', *Citizenship Studies* 15(6/7): 837–59.
Harris, L. M. (forthcoming) 'Imaginative Geographies of Green, Unmapping Difference, Postcoloniality and Affect in Environmental Narratives of Contemporary Turkey', *Annals of the Association of American Geographers*.
Harris, L. M. and S. Alatout (2010) 'Negotiating Hydro-scales, Forging States: Comparison of the Upper Tigris-Euphrates and Jordan River Basins', *Political Geography* 29: 148–56.
Harris, L. M., J. A. Goldin, and C. Sneddon (eds) (2013) *Contemporary Water Governance in the Global South: Scarcity, Marketization, Participation*, London: Routledge.
Heynen, N., J. McCarthy, S. Prudham, and P. Robbins (eds) (2007) *Neoliberal Environments: False Promises and Unnatural Consequences*, London & New York: Routledge.
Ignatow, G. (2008) 'Transnational Environmentalism at Europe's Boundaries: Identity Movements in Lithuania and Turkey', *Current Sociology* 56(6): 845–64.
Işlar, M. (2012) 'Privatised Hydropower Development in Turkey: A Case of Water Grabbing?' *Water Alternatives* 5(2): 376–91.
Kadirbeyoğlu, Z. (2008) *Decentralization and Democratization: The Case of Water User Associations in Turkey*. PhD Thesis. McGill University.

Keyman, E. F. and Z. Öniş (2007) 'Globalization and Social Democracy in the European Periphery: Paradoxes of the Turkish Experience', *Globalizations* 4(2): 211–28.
Keyder, Ç. (1997) 'Whither the Project of Modernity? Turkey in 1990s', in S. Bozdoğan and R. Kasaba (eds) *Rethinking Modernity and National Identity in Turkey*, Seattle: University of Washington Press.
Kibaroğlu, A., A. Başkan, and S. Alp. (2009) 'Neo-Liberal Transitions in Hydropower and Irrigation Water Management in Turkey: Main Actors and Opposition Groups', in D. Huitema and S. Meijerink (eds) *Water Policy Entrepreneurs: A Research Companion to Water Transitions around the Globe*, Cheltenham: Edward Elgar.
Mansfield, B. (2007) 'Property and the Remaking of Nature-Society Relations, Introduction to the Special Issue', *Antipode* 39(3): 393–405.
Markandya, A. (2005) 'Turkey on the Path to EU Accession: the Environmental Acquis', in B. Hoekman and S. Togan (eds) *Turkey: Economic Reform and Accession to the European Union*, Washington, DC: World Bank and Center for Economic Policy Research.
McNeill, D. (2005) 'Narrating Neoliberalism', *Geographical Research* 43(1): 113–5.
Morvaridi, B. (2004) 'Resettlement, Rights to Development and the Ilısu Dam, Turkey', *Development and Change* 35(4): 719–41.
Noyan, D. (2008) 'Reluctant Modernization: The Cultural Dynamics of Water Supply in Istanbul, 1885–950', *Technology and Culture* 49(3): 675–700.
Oğuz, S. (2011) *The Response of the Turkish State to the 2008 Crisis: A Further Step Towards Neoliberal Authoritarian Statism*. IIPPE. Available online: http://www.iippe.org/wiki/images/a/ac/Oguz_IIPPE_Ankara.pdf. (accessed: 15 March 2013).
Öniş, Z. (2004) 'Turgut Özal and His Economic Legacy: Turkish Neo-liberalism in Critical Perspective', *Middle Eastern Studies* 40(4): 113–34.
Öniş, Z. (2006) 'Varieties and Crises of Neoliberal Globalisation: Argentina, Turkey and the IMF', *Third World Quarterly* 27(2): 239–63.
Öniş, Z. (2011) 'Power, Interests and Coalitions: The Political Economy of Mass Privatisation in Turkey', *Third World Quarterly* 32(4): 707–24.
Pamuk, O. (2006) My Father's Suitcase, *Nobel Lecture*. 7 December 2006. Available online: http://nobelprize.org/nobel_prizes/literature/laureates/2006/pamuk-lecture_en.html. (accessed: 25 July 2011).
Peck, J. (2001) 'Neoliberalizing States: Thin Policies/Hard Outcomes', *Progress in Human Geography* 25(3): 445–55.
Peck, J. and A. Tickell (2002) 'Neoliberalizing Space', *Antipode* 34(3): 380–404.
Peck, J., N. Theodore, N. Brenner (2010) 'Postneoliberalism and Its Malcontents', *Antipode* 41(1): 94–116.
Salzmann, A. (1993) 'An Ancien Régime Revisited: "Privatization" and Political Economy in the 18th Century Ottoman Empire', *Politics and Society* 21(4): 393–423.
Salzmann, A. (2004) *Toqueville in the Ottoman Empire: Rival Paths to the Modern State*, Leiden: Brill Academic Publisher.
Scott, J. C. (1998) *Seeing Like a State*, New Haven, CT: Yale University Press.
Svendsen, M. and G. Nott (1999) 'Irrigation Management Transfer in Turkey: Process and Outcomes', in *EDI Participatory Irrigation Management Case Studies Series*. Available online: http://www.inpim.org/files/documents/sve_turk.pdf. (accessed: 15 March 2013).
Tienhaara, K. (2010) 'A Tale of Two Crises: What the Global Financial Crisis Means for the Global Environmental Crisis', *Environmental Policy and Governance* 20(3): 197–208.

Tilly, C. (1990) *Coercion, Capital and European States: AD 900–1992*, Cambridge & Oxford: Cambridge University Press.

Tocci, N. (2005) 'Europeanization in Turkey: Trigger or Anchor for Reform?' *South European Society & Politics* 10(1): 73–83.

Topçu, F. (2005) 'Suda Dış Kredi: İzmit Örnegi' (External Credits in Water: Example of İzmit), in T. Çınar and H. Özdinç (eds) *Su Yönetimi*, Ankara: Memleket Yayinlari.

Topçu, S. (2011) 'Water for Agriculture: A Major and Inefficient Consumer', in A. Kibaroğlu, W. Scheumann, and A. Kramer (eds) *Turkey's Water Policy: National Frameworks and International Cooperation*, Berlin: Springer.

Tuğal, C. (2007) 'Nato's Islamists: Hegemony and Americanization in Turkey', *New Left Review* 44: 5–34.

Turkish Water Assembly (2010) *Water Manifest of the Turkish Water Assembly*. Available online: http://english.turkiyesumeclisi.net/uploads/6/7/0/8/6708484/watermanifestoftheturkishwaterassembly.pdf. (accessed: 15 March 2013).

Yalman, G. (2009) *Transition to Neoliberalism: The Case of Turkey in the 1980s*, İstanbul: Bilgi University Press.

YASED (2007) *International Investors association of Turkey*. Foreign Direct Investment Report. Available online: http:/www.yased.org.tr/webportal/English/istatistikler/tudyi/yr/Documents/FDIReport-june07.pdf. (accessed: 25 July 2012).

Yılmaz, I. (2009) *Public-Private Sector Partnership Models in Turkey*. Turkish British Chamber of Commerce and Industry. Available online: http://www.tbcci.org/Newsletter/September2009/PUBLIC-PRIVATE%20SECTOR%20PARTNERSHIP%20MODELS%20IN%20TURKEY.pdf. (accessed: 15 March 2013).

Yücel, G. (2008) 'Turkey's Water Future in Europe', *Global Water Intelligence* 9(3). Available online: http:/www.globalwaterintel.com/archive/9/3/general/turkeys-water-future-in-europe.html. (accessed: 15 March 2013).

Part II

Market Developmentalism and Livelihood Change

4

Tarnished Yet Tenacious: Examining the Track Record and Future of Public–Private Partnership Hospitals in Canada

Heather Whiteside

Public–private partnerships (P3s) with the for-profit private sector first emerged in Canada in the mid-1990s and have been steadily growing in popularity ever since. More recently, proliferation since the mid-2000s has been sustained largely through infrastructure projects developed within provincial health sectors. By 2011, P3 hospitals accounted for half to three-quarters of all P3 projects in British Columbia (BC) and Ontario respectively, the Canadian provinces most enthusiastic for P3s (see Partnerships BC n.d.; Infrastructure Ontario n.d.).[1] With large hospital re/development in particular, P3s are now the principal way in which these infrastructure projects and their accompanying support services are delivered. While the rise of P3s is a global phenomenon, which is in no way unique to Canada, specificity when evaluating this policy matters. By focusing on Canadian P3 hospitals, we are able to uncover how global neoliberal processes operate at the ground level (in the form of particular P3 projects) and how this unfolds within a specific sector (health care). In so doing it becomes evident that location- and sector-specific conditions shape the implementation of larger neoliberal forces.

The growing exposure of the Canadian public health care system to the logic of capitalist profitability and commodification via P3 adoption is typically passed off as a new and innovative approach to 'alternative service delivery' (Hodge and Greve 2005: 7–8). This would seem to suggest that procuring public infrastructure and services through for-profit providers is simply one innocuous policy option among many. However, as P3s contribute to a transformation in the prevailing social relations of power,

The author would like to thank Yıldız Atasoy and the anonymous reviewer for their helpful comments on earlier draft versions of this chapter.

they will instead be examined here for their connection to what David Harvey (2003) calls 'accumulation by dispossession'. Like other forms of privatization (for example, selling state assets), P3s promote dispossession by creating new markets for private investors and allowing for an expansion of market rule. However, unlike other forms of privatization, P3s also allow for the flourishing of accumulation by dispossession within especially sensitive areas of public policy which would not otherwise be suitable candidates for more overt privatization initiatives. This is achieved at least in part through the depoliticization of health infrastructure and service decision making. Within a public health care system P3s thus offer the advantage of opening up an untapped pool of potential investment sites, but this occurs largely by stealth. This latter feature is particularly relevant in Canada given the popularity of the public health care system.

This chapter will discuss the theoretical and empirical implications of P3 policy, as illustrated through Canadian hospitals. The nature of this discussion is twofold. First, the connection between privatization, P3s and neoliberal public policy will be examined, along with speculation as to what the entrenchment of the P3 model might say about the intensification of neoliberalism in the aftermath of the global economic crisis. Second, the legacy of health care privatization will be discussed. Here it will be argued that not only does privatization have a deleterious impact on social reproduction and long-term service planning and integration, but that P3 hospital projects have a particularly dismal track record: they offer poor value for money, transfer a significant degree of power and authority to unaccountable market actors primarily motivated by profitability concerns, and expose public health care systems to the vagaries of global financial markets (the implications of which were made especially evident through the 2008 global financial crisis). Despite these problems (new and old), P3 promotion continues unabated in Canada, meaning that P3 policy tenacity is sustained not through a track record of superiority but through dogged political and ideological commitments made to market expansion and dispossession.

Neoliberalism and privatization

A key distinguishing feature of the neoliberal era (roughly 1980–present), and a theme explored in various ways throughout this volume, is an emphasis on marketization: market-led economic and social restructuring (Jessop 2002: 461). Work done by Peck and Tickell (2002) on the 'roll-back' and 'roll-out' versions of the neoliberal restructuring processes alerts us to the equally destructive and prescriptive elements of marketization. Policies associated with the former include cuts to social programmes, full-scale privatization, and deregulation; the latter includes, by contrast, social programme reform (rather than simply programme cuts), establishing partnerships with the private sector (rather than full-scale privatization), and re-regulation (rather than deregulation). A greater emphasis on technocratic decision making is similarly present with roll-out neoliberalization. Policies which encourage and support market intensification therefore take many forms across the neoliberal era.

Along with the dynamics of marketization we must also consider the norms inherent in neoliberal forms of governance. For instance, given its longevity in the face of recurrent crises, contradictions, and dislocations, Keil (2009) has proposed a third dimension of neoliberal restructuring: rolling with an unstable, but increasingly normalized market order, which he dubs 'roll-with-it' neoliberalization. This involves the normalization of 'neoliberal practices and mindsets' such as the norm of competition (Keil 2009: 232). In this same vein, Adaman and Madra (Chapter 2 of this volume) point to another important facet of neoliberal normalization – the practice of 'economization', which accounts for the depoliticization of economic logic and incentives, 'based on the understanding that individuals are calculative and calculable'. Both market expansion and the normalization of normative neoliberal discourse and practice occur with privatization policy.

First, privatization enhances the breadth and depth of capitalist markets through accumulation by dispossession. Reminiscent of 'original accumulation' as described by Marx, dispossession involves the expansion of market relations in a number of ways, namely through mechanisms to create new markets and redistribute assets (Harvey 2003). Thus dispossession denotes a particular form of market expansion, specifically when that is achieved by incorporating into the realm of private accumulation that which has come to exist 'outside' of these circuits of capital (Harvey 2003). Through this predatory mechanism, new investment and profit-making opportunities are created.[2]

In Canada, dispossession as privatization has evolved over the neoliberal period, beginning with the sale of some of the public sector's most potentially profitable assets in the 1980s,[3] and later shifting into the more obscure realm of 'privatization by stealth' via P3s beginning in the 1990s.[4] Similar to full-scale privatization, P3s are best thought of as a form of accumulation by dispossession. Whereas traditional public works projects (physical and social infrastructure) are wholly owned and controlled by the public sector, with contracts awarded to a private company for a limited and specified role (such as the construction portion), P3s establish binding long-term contracts that incorporate the logic of the private sector into the provision of public goods (Hodge and Greve 2005: 64). This is reflected in Cohn's (2004: 2) definition of P3s as 'instruments for meeting the obligations of the state that are transformed so as to involve private property ownership as a key element in the operation of that instrument'. Though public assets are not directly sold, P3 contracts nonetheless carve out avenues for potentially profitable private sector investment by contractually guaranteeing future revenue streams in areas that could otherwise prove unprofitable, or too politically sensitive to fully privatize. Hospitals, roads, highways, water treatment facilities, and schools are now among the top candidates for partnership agreements. The profit motive permeates all elements of these projects, and market social relations are expanded throughout the lifetime of the P3.

Second, the entrenchment of P3 policy occurs not only through the nature of these contracts but also through the normalization of 'a de-politicization of the social', as indicated in Chapter 2. Depoliticization occurs when authority and decision making in areas of social concern (such as health care and health services) are shifted away from government and into the private sector. With P3s this happens through the awarding of multi-decade contracts to the for-profit managers who operate P3 projects as well as through the private consultants, transaction advisors, accountants, and auditors that come to inform P3 policy. Colin Hay (2007: 80–7) also suggests that depoliticization can occur when social issues are demoted from the governmental sphere to the public sphere. P3s conform to this type of depoliticization as well given that they shift public infrastructure and service decisions out of the formal democratic arena (where decision makers are accountable and public deliberation takes place) and into the far less transparent realm of arm's length public sector managers. In Canada, as is the case elsewhere (see Jooste and Scott 2012; Rachwalski and Ross 2010), this role has become dominated as of late by the quasi-public sector agencies created to promote and evaluate P3s, sometimes referred to as 'P3 agencies' (see Farrugia et al. 2008). Structured as semi-autonomous Crown corporations, Canada's provincial P3 agencies (for example, Partnerships BC and Infrastructure Ontario) are relatively insulated from public accountability and their decision making reflects private sector rationales (such as economization).[5]

Dispossession and public–private partnerships

Dispossession via public–private partnerships operates to reshape lives and livelihoods in several ways. Most obviously it involves the decades-long privatization of work historically conducted by public sector employees. This leads to a deterioration of wages and working conditions (examined later in the chapter) and thus, as Huws (2012: 64) argues, to the expropriation of rights previously won by labour. Not only does this affect the staff working for P3 private operators, but it also erodes the bargaining position of the labour movement overall given that many of the strongest unions in Canada are in the public sector. Furthermore, this can hold negative implications for workers in general to the extent that past struggles for universal public services are undermined in the process (Huws 2012: 64–5).[6]

A less obvious implication for the reconfiguration of state and society (an issue more broadly discussed in the Introduction to this volume) is the financialization of public sector activities which constitutes a relatively unique feature of P3-related dispossession.[7] Harvey (2003: 147) explains that financialization has become an important avenue for accumulation by dispossession given its predatory and crisis-prone nature (for example, allowing for ponzi schemes, asset destruction through inflation, and pension fund raiding). Privately financed P3s add to this phenomenon in three ways.

First, under the auspices of 'risk transfer' private partners assume responsibility for hypothetical project risks such as cost overruns and delays in exchange for lucrative investment opportunities. Though each project is unique, investors often expect real rates of return in the 15–25 per cent range (Gaffney et al. 1999: 116; Hodge 2004: 162), making P3 arrangements attractive investment opportunity for capital. Second, if a P3 is refinanced once it has entered into the relatively low-risk operational phase of the project, the private partner is often able to secure cheaper forms of debt (such as through bond financing rather than bank debt, see Loxley 2010: 68), which can further increase the profitability of this arrangement. Finally, there is also a dimension of self-dispossession which occurs when the institutional investor that finances a P3 is a public sector pension fund. The Ontario Municipal Employees Retirement System and Ontario Teachers' Pension Plan, for example, have been involved in several Canadian P3s in the past (see Loxley 2010). By entwining workers' savings (pensions) with vehicles of privatization, a material reliance on P3s is created, often involving the very same public sector workers or unions whose interests are simultaneously undermined in the process. With this latter feature we see that short-run benefits can pose long-run contradictions for those working for P3 private providers.

Dispossession via P3s therefore occurs at different tempos and in different ways, and holds a range of implications (for workers, service users, taxpayers, and so on). This is of even greater concern as of late given that many important public services are now highly integrated into volatile and crisis-prone financial markets. Yet P3s not only represent dispossession, they also help to entrench this key feature of neoliberal policy – how they do so is particularly relevant in the context of crisis and its aftermath.

Public–private partnerships and neoliberal intensification

The overarching issue of neoliberal market intensification described by Atasoy (in the Introduction to this volume) persists in Canada despite, or perhaps due to, the relatively moderate impact of the 2008 crisis. The role that P3s are currently playing in this process has two key aspects: the locking-in of accumulation by dispossession and the promotion of financialization. Thus efforts to support and promote P3s, to be described in subsequent sections of this chapter, are not only expressions of neoliberal policy but also help to reinforce its practice and discourse.

First, lock-in: P3s help entrench neoliberalism through decades-long, legally binding contracts. Most project agreements last for 30 years or more which is extremely long when compared with another leading form of privatization, contracting-out, which typically lasts for only a few years at a time. Of course governments do have the option of rescinding P3 agreements, but in light of other important features of neoliberal lock-in (such as trade agreements like the North American Free Trade Agreement (NAFTA) which protect the rights of foreign investors through binding arbitration) this may be far too costly an option for most governments to consider.

A related issue is the contract bundling that is a core feature of the P3 model, meaning that no one element of the project can be severed from the agreement on the basis of poor performance or a change in government ideology. This makes it extremely difficult/costly to renegotiate P3 contracts given that all components (such as infrastructure, support services, and land agreements) are legally bound together (Shrybman 2007: 200). This feature would also make it difficult, though never impossible, for a paradigm change to sweep away any one undesirable component of an existing P3.

Second, P3s are a microcosm of the larger neoliberal accumulation strategy: P3s support and rely on neoliberal financialization (as the private finance portion typically involves large institutional investors such as pension funds, or multinational banks/financial institutions) along with being a form of accumulation by dispossession, as described above.[8] This means that P3s reproduce key neoliberal economic forms, and thus neoliberal rule is increasingly entrenched with each new partnership. Further, the use of private financial markets to fund public services and infrastructure raises the even greater concern that this practice could recreate the very same conditions that triggered the financial crisis in 2008. Examples of this include the following: P3s promote off-balance sheet accounting practices, they allow for the securitization and offshoring of funds which are then recirculated into important areas of social welfare and public policy (with risks ultimately backed by the taxpayer), the commercial confidentiality that accompanies all P3 agreements encourages low levels of corporate accountability, and they allow for profit-seeking behaviour using market refinancing and equity sales – practices which are largely beyond public control once the project agreements are in place (see Reynolds 2011; Sandborn 2008; Whitfield 2009).

Public–private partnerships and the Canadian public health care sector

Though the bulk of this section will focus on the impact that P3s have on hospital sector infrastructure and support services, it is worth also recognizing that capitalist accumulation itself presents obstacles for health and well-being regardless of whether dispossession is present. Colin Leys (2010) nicely summarizes this contradiction in the following manner: capitalism produces and relies on inequalities, yet leading research into the social determinants of health strongly indicates that there is a connection between poverty and ill health (physical, developmental, social), with health indicators varying by income group. Income and ill health are thus inversely related to one another and this means that those who are in greatest need of health care coverage are those who, if forced to fully rely on the market, are least likely to be able to secure adequate coverage. In turn this can hurt capital accumulation if the overall health of workers becomes threatened. By socializing the costs of health care through public insurance (which is the essence of Canada's medicare system), public health care not only improves health and well-being but also indirectly supports capital accumulation. The importance of this relationship is borne out historically given that one of the main factors leading to the development of medicare in Canada was the ill health experienced by factory workers and army recruits in the 1940s (Fuller 1998: 27).[9]

However, as Leys (2010: 15) also reminds us, health care 'is an ideological construct almost as much as a material reality'. While the principles of public health care in Canada, namely universality and accessibility, remain in place (for a description see Armstrong and Armstrong 2008: 30–1), within the neoliberal era this has meant that attempts to achieve these goals are now subsumed within a narrow policy discourse of efficiency, value for money, and risk transfer to the private sector, along with the material reality of fiscal austerity and the pressures of balanced budget legislation. This exacerbates tensions that already exist between capitalism, health, and health care by widening inequalities[10] and destabilizing social reproduction.

Social reproduction

Closely linked to the conflict that exists between health and capitalism, social reproduction is also threatened by the profitability imperative. Problems posed for social reproduction, a concept which 'encompasses daily life and long term reproduction, both of the means of production and the labor power to make them work' (Katz 2001: 711), were historically mediated to a certain extent by the development of a public health care system in Canada. Public health care meant not only universal access to medically necessary health services (delinking receipt of services from an ability to pay for them) but also greater job security and better pay for health care workers – the majority of whom are women (see Cohen and Cohen 2006: 124). State provision of health care insurance also translated into a reduction in the burden of unpaid work done in the home, though it is estimated that roughly 70 per cent of all care work in Canada is still provided in this fashion (Armstrong and Armstrong 2010: 163).

Accumulation by dispossession erodes this public support for social reproduction as it redistributes burdens, produces new forms of inequality, and reconfigures the dynamics of public and private authority. P3s are but one form of privatization in the Canadian health care system, other forms which affect lives and livelihoods include: service delisting (narrowing the range of services covered by public insurance), contracting-out, and the growing presence of for-profit clinics. Each type can affect social reproduction in slightly different ways, and here the focus will be on the expansion of private authority and the privatization of support services that accompany P3s. However, since P3s are a model which is expressed in different ways as individual projects, not all P3s are arranged in the same way. For instance, since 2006 P3 hospital project agreements in the province of Ontario have excluded 'soft services' (non-clinical care such as dietary, and housekeeping services), but they continue to privatize 'hard services' (such as facility maintenance and security) (Block 2008: 2). There is no such exemption in the province of British Columbia (BC) though some recent P3 hospital deals have excluded cleaning services, for example. Once the hospital is operational, soft services may still be subject to contracting-out and therefore these exclusions do not necessarily imply that services are not privatized. In other words, the scope of P3 arrangements and degree of support service privatization can oscillate over time and by project.

When discussing authority and influence in the Canadian health care system it is necessary to first recognize that private actors and decision making have always been a feature of the system, including within the public medicare system. Doctors, for example, have typically been private providers of health care services, making their own decisions as to what is medically necessary, where their private practices are located, and they face little oversight of their expenditures (Armstrong and Armstrong 2008: 36). Similarly, hospitals in Canada have historically been run privately, though on a not-for-profit basis (often by community or religious organizations). What is new, and thus constitutes a significant shift in decision making and authority, is how P3s insert the profit motive into the heart of what medicare has in large part been designed to focus on: hospital service management and provision. While this does not involve privatizing clinical care services in Canada (this practice is explicitly banned by the 1984 *Canada Health Act*), it can/does affect all non-clinical services within hospital. In terms of social reproduction, this impacts both health outcomes and labour.

Cutting corners in order to reduce costs and increase profitability through hospital support service privatization creates problems for service outcomes and quality, and as a result privatization can be directly linked to illness and death. For example, in 2009 BC's Nanaimo Regional General Hospital developed the antibacterial resistant super bug C. difficile, causing dozens to fall ill and five deaths in 2009. Though infection control is a concern in all hospitals, the BC Centre for Disease Control reports that due to understaffing and improper training by the private contractor, the privatized cleaning support staff made several crucial errors in their sanitization attempts which greatly exacerbated later attempts at infection control (Leyne 2009). This supports Cohen and Cohen's (2006: 138) contention that 'because of the special requirements and dangers inherent in a hospital setting, this type of cleaning requires a level of knowledge and skill that is acquired through years of on-the-job experience as well as special training. Such training is not typically offered by the private sector'.

A related issue with hospital support service privatization is the deleterious effect that this can have on the women and visible minorities who predominantly provide these services. This includes reduced wages, less secure employment and predictable shifts, and an introduction of neo-Taylorist labour disciplining and monitoring techniques (see Armstrong and Armstrong 2010; Cohen and Cohen 2006). Furthermore, support services provided in hospital (such as dietary, cleaning, and linen services) have been re-conceptualized under the P3 model and through contracting-out as being akin to hotel services rather than unique health care-specific services. The reduced labour costs (achieved through cuts to remuneration and training, for example) that accompanies this transformation may be of direct benefit to the multinational corporations who now employ support staff within P3 hospitals, but it proves problematic for labour as well as for patients given that these services are in fact a fundamental aspect of health care provision. Support staff 'ensure the cleanliness of rooms, furnishings, and equipment that are vital to infection control; they prepare and deliver meals; they dispose of garbage and bio-hazardous material; they do the laundry for patients and staff', and thus crucial areas of health care are affected such as hygiene, nutrition, infection control, and patient care (Stinson et al. 2005: 34).

Long-run planning and service integration concerns

On top of problems posed for labour and the quality of support services are two other major long-run concerns presented by the P3 model in health care. Both constrain and reorient public sector decision making, and thus they are particularly important considerations in light of the themes discussed in this volume as well. The first relates to the mismatch that exists between the rigid, market-based private contracts guiding the planning and development of hospital infrastructure and the long-run need for flexibility and adaptability to meet the inherently changing technological, community, and policy needs in the health sector. The second corresponds to the disintegration of global hospital service planning and the internal bifurcation of authority that occurs within P3 hospitals.

Design innovation with hospitals relates specifically to the physical adaptability of the building, as it must meet today's needs while also accommodating future economic and social requirements as well as medical advances (Barlow and Koberle-Gaiser 2008). Although this challenge is equally present with traditional public hospitals, the relatively inflexible nature of P3 contractual arrangements dampens the capacity for innovation. P3 contracts do transfer some immediate risks associated with construction (such as delays and cost overruns, as covered by the project agreement) but private partners are able to avoid long-term and uncertain risks. Ultimately these risks – such as those related to functional obsolescence, changing policies, and unidentified future health care needs – falls onto the shoulders of the public sector which bears ultimately long-run responsibility for hospital infrastructure (Pollock et al. 2002). Further, Leiringer (2006) finds that as a way of minimizing the costs associated with construction risks, P3 private partners are incentivized to use tried and true design and construction techniques, not the most forward thinking and innovative ones. Hospital design is therefore conducted by profit-oriented, risk-adverse partners with little motivating them to plan for uncertain changes which would likely occur outside of the parameters of the project agreement. Infrastructure design and planning is subsequently locked in for several decades when technological and service innovations can have much shorter life cycles, making 30 year P3 project agreements far too long to adequately meet the unique needs of the health sector.

The second long-run concern specific to P3 hospitals is found in the contradiction that exists between the privatized mode of support service delivery and the need for integrated clinical and non-clinical service planning. Sometimes referred to as an 'internal bifurcation of authority' (Mehra 2005; Shrybman 2007), this feature of P3 hospitals is produced by replacing the usual authority and oversight granted to the public sector over all services within hospitals with a P3 arrangement which awards the management of non-clinical support services to a private partner.[11] This poses a hindrance upon communication and collaboration within hospital and can lead to a disintegration of planning practices. Shrybman (2007: 198) suggests that this feature could also allow for the flourishing of two tier health care given that P3 hospitals allow private investors to 'integrate, within the public hospital setting, a parallel and privately funded health services regime'.

Examining particular P3 hospitals illustrates the track record that this form of accumulation by dispossession has in Canada's public health care sector. This exercise reveals the specific ways in which P3s have affected new hospital projects in terms of value for money and in the expansion of private for-profit decision making. This discussion will focus on two pioneering P3 hospitals in Canada: BC's Abbotsford Regional Hospital and Cancer Centre and the Academic Ambulatory Care Centre (now known as the Diamond Centre).

Canada's pioneering public–private partnership hospitals

The emergence of full-spectrum P3 hospitals in Canada – where the private partner is responsible for most of the project's design, building, financing, and operating (DBFO) – began in the province of British Columbia.[12] The province's initial P3 hospitals are the Abbotsford Regional Hospital and Cancer Centre P3 in 2003 (operational in 2008) and the Academic Ambulatory Care Centre P3 (the Vancouver General Hospital expansion and redevelopment project), later renamed the Diamond Centre in recognition of a $20 million (CAD)[13] donation by philanthropists Gordon and Leslie Diamond[14] in 2002 (operational in 2006). Both projects were sorely needed, with the new hospital in Abbotsford replacing an older, rundown and inadequate regional hospital in the area; and with the Diamond Centre allowing for the reconfiguration and consolidation of existing facilities, improving teaching and patient access to the Vancouver General Hospital's ambulatory services. These two were seen at the time to be a 'proving ground' for P3s in BC's health care sector (McInnis 2003: B5).

Creating a P3 market in this delicate sector was underpinned by the significant level of political will needed to enact this new form of accumulation by dispossession. The Abbotsford case is particularly instructive here. In the face of province-wide public opinion polls clearly indicating significant opposition to private involvement, the BC provincial government remained steadfast in its determination to have the new hospital developed as a P3 (Canada News Wire 2002: 1). Then-finance minister Gary Collins revealed why this is the case when he is quoted as saying that 'the project was not only important as an individual health facility but also for the future of the P3 model in British Columbia' (Goldsworthy 2002). From this Cohn (2008: 77) quite rightly concludes that 'some projects had to be first, and the Abbotsford Hospital was seen as a good candidate' since the Abbotsford region was a strong base of support for the ruling Liberal party and this reduced the political risks involved. Furthermore, when members of the regional health authority charged with hospital planning and management in Abbotsford, many of whom had extensive private sector finance and real estate experience, expressed scepticism with the P3 route early on in the process, the provincial government ordered the Board of Directors to accept the project as a P3 or face removal (Cohn 2008: 77).

In line with these motivations, BC's initial P3 hospitals should not be considered to be pilot projects in the sense that they were used to test *whether* P3 hospitals should be pursued, but instead they were pioneering projects used to establish *how* P3 procurement and development would proceed. This lack of considered reflection exists despite a damning report produced by the provincial Auditor General, troublesome findings by forensic accountants, and sustained public opposition. Here it is possible to only briefly summarize their track record. First, claims of P3 value for money superiority are not as straightforward as proponents suggest as there are many cost run ups and methodological problems associated with their use. Second, these projects indicate just how broad the influence of private for-profit authority is within the operation of that which remains ostensibly within the public sector, affecting all elements of the project and entrenching private sector motivations and rationale throughout the project agreement. This section concludes with a brief examination of how concerns of this sort are compounded by a reliance on global financial markets to fund important social services.

Value for money

Despite claims that these P3s could deliver better value for money than traditional public procurement (Partnerships BC 2004; 2005), both fared poor in this regard as construction began later and costs were higher than initially promised, and value for money was never clearly established with either project. The higher costs associated with P3 are particularly troublesome as not only does this undermine proponents' arguments that they help curb wasteful government spending (for instance, see Canadian Council for Public–Private Partnerships 2003), but it also means that less is available to be spent on other much-needed social concerns and infrastructure projects.

With respect to cost and construction time, in the case of the Abbotsford hospital construction costs increased by 68 per cent, from an estimated $211 million in December 2001 when the P3 was first announced to $355 million in November 2004 when construction actually began. This cost increase is partially due to changes in design, yet can also be traced back to the lengthy contract negotiations inherent with complex P3 arrangements. This pushed the initiation of the project into a booming construction market, and added $63 million in inflation costs alone (Cayo 2005: D5). It also meant a delay in the opening of the hospital. British Columbians were also told that the P3 route would mean faster delivery, yet despite promises that construction would begin in 2004 and the hospital would open in early 2007 (Harrison 2003: A40), bidding and contract negotiation delayed the project by nearly two years and the hospital only began accepting patients in late 2008. This is not reflected in Partnerships BC's (2005) official value for money report, and instead the hospital is labelled 'on time and on budget' since once the agreement was in place the project did conform to the stipulations laid out in the contract.

The Diamond Centre track record fares slightly better, although it too was late and more expensive than originally promised. In 2002 the P3 model was touted as a way of delivering the project by spring 2005, at a cost of $90 million (O'Connor 2004: A4); however, it ended up opening in fall 2006 at a reported cost of $95 million (Partnerships BC 2004). On top of this smaller cost overrun the Auditor General later found that this P3 actually had a final capitalized value of $123 million, a 29 per cent increase ($28 million) over the figure reported in the official value for money report (Auditor General 2011: 10). Furthermore, any documentation that could be used to support this lower figure of $95 million has gone missing, leading the Auditor General to say that he 'find[s] it disturbing that we couldn't find documents for the conduct of this particular audit and we couldn't find explanations of dollar values for this particular audit' (Select Standing Committee on Public Accounts 2011: 468).

To this list of problems is the methodological deception that can occur, further eroding claims of P3 superiority. A central component of value–for-money assessments (which compares the cost of a P3 to a 'public sector comparator' (PSC), a hypothetical model created to represent the traditional delivery method), is the application of a discount rate to the project costs as a way of calculating 'the cost of capital over time', which accounts for considerations like interest and inflation (Partnerships BC 2005: 19). Yet the choice of which discount rate to apply is not a neutral decision, it is highly political and extremely controversial. This is because the higher the discount rate used, the more attractive the P3 option becomes since it favours expenditure in later years (the P3) relative to that which is spent now (the PSC) (Gaffney et al. 1999: 117). There is evidence of methodological deception with both BC P3 hospitals.

In their 2004 value for money report, Partnerships BC claimed that the Diamond Centre P3 saved taxpayers $17 million when compared with the public procurement option, yet forensic accountants Parks and Terhart (2009) calculate that that the actual nominal price of the P3 was more than double what a public project would have cost taxpayers. Furthermore, as mentioned above, BC's Auditor General confirms that the P3 was much more expensive than the value for money report suggests. A sizable portion of the $28 million discrepancy is owed to problems with the discount rate applied to calculate the net present value of the project. By adjusting the discount rate from the inflated 7.12 per cent to a more accurate 5.37 per cent, the Auditor General found that $17 million should be added to the total capitalized value of the P3 project (Auditor General 2011: 10). This supports earlier findings by the deputy general of the British National Audit Office that P3 accounting procedures represent 'pseudo-scientific mumbo-jumbo' (Weaver 2003).

As for the Abbotsford hospital, Parks and Terhart (2009: 16) also conclude that the methodology used to determine value for money was 'biased in favour of the P3' given that the best practice discount rate used to calculate value for money was instead substituted with a higher rate by Partnerships BC, favouring the P3 model. Had the best practice rate been used, a publicly delivered hospital would have indicated a savings of roughly $80 million when compared to the P3 option.

Power and authority

Both P3 hospitals examined here are full-spectrum DBFO P3s. With the Abbotsford hospital, the private partner holds a 30-year lease on the facility and is responsible for design, construction, finance, maintenance, and management and operation of the hospital (involving general management, help desk, food services for patients and non-patients, housekeeping, laundry and linen services, material services, plant services including facility maintenance, protection services, patient portering, utilities management, and parking services) (Partnerships BC 2005: 17). With the Diamond Centre, the private partner also holds a 30-year lease and is similarly responsible for design, construction, finance, maintenance, and management and operation (involving housekeeping, security, grounds keeping, and leasing space not used by the public partner) (Partnerships BC 2004: 9–12). Responsibility for clinical functionality remains with the public partner in both cases, and responsibility for force majeure or relief efforts (such as in the case of earthquakes or floods) is shared between both partners.

The profit motive is therefore deeply embedded and power is shared between public and private partners throughout the lifetime of these agreements. This becomes especially relevant during bidding and negotiation phases which determine hospital design and cost, and during the operational phase of the hospital. While hospital design is integral for clinical functionality, in BC the impact that P3s have had on hospital operations is of greatest concern (though design flaws are still a serious concern, see Mehra 2005 for examples). The privatization of support services, run by multinational corporations like Johnson Controls International (infrastructure maintenance) and Sodexo (non-clinical health services operations) in the Abbotsford hospital and Brookfield LePage-Johnson Controls (maintenance and operations) in the Diamond Centre, corresponds to Shrybman's (2007) description of an 'internal bifurcation of authority' (as previously discussed) given that non-clinical services are managed and delivered on a private for-profit basis while clinical services remain under the purview of the regional health authorities and the BC Ministry of Health Services.

This is a significant departure from traditional hospitals where authority and control is fully retained by public sector health authorities, constituting a notable – albeit relatively invisible – restructuring of state and society. Even in the case of hospitals which have been subject to extensive support service contracting-out, the power sharing inherent with P3s goes far deeper. As mentioned earlier, with contracting-out agreements are only in place for several years at a time, rather than several decades with P3s, and service contracts are most often kept separate rather than bundled. Together these factors significantly reduce the autonomy of the P3 public partner once the project is operational since not only does the private partner not face the threat of contract termination every few years but if there is poor performance it is not possible to sever any one portion of a P3 hospital agreement without being forced to renegotiate the entire contract.

Social costs

P3 value for money analyses fare poorly when it comes to capturing the social concerns associated with the use of private for-profit service operators.

Social costs can vary but in the health care sector, as mentioned above, they typically relate to problems with inadequate training, poor hygiene control, and deep cuts made to wages and benefits (CBC 2009; Cohen and Cohen 2006; Leyne 2009). In January 2004 many of the support services at the Matsqui-Sumas-Abbotsford hospital (the hospital later replaced by the P3) were contracted out to Sodexo – the very same company that would soon be awarded the Abbotsford P3 contract.[15] Within four months (April 2004), the *Abbotsford Times* found evidence of declining standards in the hospital. For example, it reported on 'tales of blood smears in labour rooms that should be spotless, litter left behind beds in the emergency ward and inexperienced workers entering infectious isolation rooms' (quoted in Hospital Employees' Union [HEU] 2004). While there have yet to be any reports of this occurring at the P3 hospital, in fall 2012 Sodexo's cleanliness and infection control standards were once again in the news with the outbreak of the superbug C. difficile in Burnaby Hospital (which is within the same regional health authority as the Abbotsford hospital). The outbreak led the Hospital Employees' Union (HEU) to call for a housekeeping audit given that Sodexo passed cleaning standards despite the infectious outbreak. The union claims that 'hospital cleaning is based on visual appearances only' (HEU 2012). When housekeeping services are kept in-house rather than privatized the public sector retains full control over the types of cleaning products used and method of cleaning; as well as the number of staff employed. Private partners, on the other hand, have a vested interest in getting work done quickly and at a low cost.

Low wages and benefits are another feature of BC's privatized health care support services. In tandem with the emergence of P3s in the province in the early 2000s was the enactment of dispossession-enabling legislation. Bill 29–2002 (*the Health and Social Services Delivery Improvement Act*) allowed for the elimination or alteration of several key provisions in signed collective agreements, namely those that provided job security and protection from privatization, applicable to all 'non-clinical' employees in BC's health care sector. The effects of Bill 29–2002 were swift and disastrous for health care support staff in the province. Within a few short years, more than 9000 HEU members had lost their jobs, and wages were slashed to $9–10 per hour and benefits lost in newly privatized positions (Cohen and Cohen 2006). Between 2004 and 2007 the HEU had (re)organized most privatized support staff in the province. The first round of bargaining began in 2004 and this led to a $3–4/hour wage increase (HEU 2008). The next round of bargaining began in 2008 and produced a 15 per cent wage gain ($15 per hour by 2011). Bargaining has recommenced as of late 2012. While these improvements are significant, the effects of Bill 29–2002 continue to be felt over a decade after its implementation given that nominal hourly wages in 2002 were in many instances well above their 2012 levels. In contrast, P3 agreements like the one governing the Abbotsford and Diamond Centre hospitals provide for yearly inflation-adjusted increases in service payments made to private contractors.

Design-build-finance-operate (DBFO) P3s are now the norm for most BC hospital partnerships and this status is enforced through a new capital planning policy which helps further lock-in dispossession. BC's 2002 Capital Asset Management Framework (CAMF) dictates that all capital project proposals in excess of $50 million be first considered as P3s (BC Ministry of Finance n.d.). As such, should a regional health authority wish to pursue a large hospital infrastructure project the business case must be first forwarded to Partnerships BC, the provincial Crown corporation charged with both evaluating and promoting P3s.[16] Partnerships BC then analyses the business case to determine which procurement model would be best suited for the project (ranging from a DBFO P3 to traditional procurement where design is done in-house, financing is provided by the Treasury, and support services are kept within the public sector). Tellingly, since the implementation of the P3 screen, there has yet to be a single health care infrastructure project with a value above the $50 million threshold which has not been developed as a DBFO P3, and those in the $20–$50 million range now typically proceed as design-build P3s (for example, see Fraser Health Authority 2009; Interior Health Authority 2008). All large hospital projects in the province are now pursued as some form of partnership with the private sector, normalizing privatization within the public health care sector. Regional health authorities no longer employ the vast majority of support staff in BC's health sector, although the opposite was true in 2001.

Public–private partnership hospitals and global financial markets

Longstanding problems associated with P3s were recently compounded by the 2008 global financial crisis. Prior to 2007, private partner borrowing costs exceeded public costs by 2 per cent, amounting to a 60 per cent increase in total financing costs when measured in present value terms (Mackenzie 2009: 2). While these earlier interest rate differentials did little to halt P3 development by ideologically driven governments, the global financial crisis and subsequent credit crunch greatly added to these costs. Between 2007 and 2009 the interest rate spread increased to 3 or 4 per cent on average: meaning that DBFOs would cost roughly 70 per cent more with private financing (Mackenzie 2009: 2).

Volatile financial markets also led to project delays, renegotiations, and collapsed deals in many sectors and this affected P3 hospitals that had yet to reach financial close. For instance, with the Fort St. John Hospital project in BC, financial market instability meant that a new private partner was needed to bailout the original private equity partner that had been contracted to fund the $268 million hospital (Mackenzie 2009: 11). In Ontario, the

Niagara Health Systems P3 project, originally scheduled to begin construction in spring 2009, was also delayed when the private financing portion fell through (Mackenzie 2009:12).

By the onset of the 2008 financial crisis, BC's two pioneering P3 hospitals had already entered the relatively low-risk operational phase of the agreement, and thus neither hospital was adversely affected. However, financial uncertainty of another sort has been an issue: refinancing. Both hospitals were originally financed by the Dutch bank ABN AMRO. However, in 2005 ABN AMRO's chose to sell its share in each partnership to Australian investment bank Macquarie; and in 2007 they were sold once more to John Laing PLC. These P3 hospitals thus had three different owners in as many years (2005–7) (Canadian Union of Public Employees 2011: 11). Refinancing is a huge source of profits for private P3 partners (see Whitfield 2009) though in BC gains made through refinancing are not shared with the public partner, and deals made of this nature are largely beyond the control of public authorities.

Despite serious concerns raised by refinancing issues and the global financial crisis, several Canadian provinces continued to initiate new P3s throughout the crisis. BC and Ontario in particular remained committed, announcing new infrastructure projects in areas relating to health care, transportation, incarceration, water treatment, and other important sectors in 2008–9 (see Partnerships BC: n.d.; Infrastructure Ontario: n.d.). Support for individual projects was also accompanied by longer-term initiatives. This was achieved through the assistance of specialized government agencies like Partnerships BC, and similar initiatives in other provinces and at the federal level. This, along with screens applied to infrastructure funding and procurement rules that favour P3s (such as BC's Capital Asset Management Framework), is yet another source of lock-in for P3 policy in particular, and the neoliberal trend towards marketization and economization in general.

Concluding remarks

The 2008 global financial crisis posed significant economic and political challenges in a wide range of ways, including for P3s as a new avenue of accumulation by dispossession, especially when they are privately financed. That the attractiveness of P3s suffered only minor setbacks makes little sense from a depoliticized value for money perspective. Instead it, along with their poor pre-crisis track record, indicates that at base this form of 'alternative service delivery' has always been an ideologically driven policy choice favouring dispossession – not an inherently superior procurement model. In fact, as discussed here, the reality of P3s is such that instead of offering better value for money, their higher costs mean that less money is available in the long run for other projects and services; the authority transferred to for-profit private investors holds negative implications for social reproduction;

and the use of private financing exposes public health care to crisis-prone global financial markets. Yet despite this tarnished track record P3 promotion shows little signs of abating in Canada.

The tenacity of state support offered for P3s holds important implications for the future of neoliberalism as it embeds market-based logics of dispossession and financialization within the public sector. By entrenching these features, neoliberalism is intensified. This impacts social reproduction in an immediate sense as it makes health sector employment more precarious (in terms of wages and working conditions) and can lead to a deterioration of the quality of health services. Further, from a long-run perspective it can also hinder the overall sustainability of the public health care system given that P3 hospitals are more costly than the public option, innovation is stifled through their overly ridged multi-decade long contracts, and internal hospital service planning suffers from disintegration given an internal bifurcation of authority.

Long-term commitments made to more expensive hospital infrastructure can also create a serious debt overhang, producing cost pressures which may lead to service cuts down the line. Through a series of Freedom of Information requests in 2011, it has recently been reported that in the UK NHS Trusts are now locked into long-term P3 deals where they are 'forced to pay "hyper-inflated" charges for basic services' such as '£242 to put a padlock on a garden gate at a trust in North Staffordshire, £466 to replace a light fitting and £75 for an air freshener in Cumbria and £15,000 to "install a laundry door following feasibility study" at a trust in Salisbury' (Hope 2012). Being locked into costly, long-running P3 hospital deals led to the June 2012 bankruptcy of South London Healthcare NHS Trust; and soon after it was revealed that an additional 22 NHS Trusts faced 'unsustainable' financial conditions as a result of expensive P3 hospitals (Alleyne 2012). Thus far problems of this magnitude have yet to surface in Canada, although in light of performance agreements prohibiting local health authorities in some jurisdictions from running a deficit, it is clear that P3 payments will take priority over other health service needs in Canada as well. These long-standing drawbacks have been made all the more evident through the 2008 financial crisis. Through the support of specialized government agencies like Partnerships BC and capital planning frameworks like BC's CAMF which favour P3s, there are now so few large public infrastructure projects being initiated in the health sector that P3s are increasingly the standard model.

However, we should not underestimate the changes that have taken place in P3 markets since they first emerged in the 1990s – especially as this relates to the financial crisis and organized resistance to privatization. It is likely that the global volume of annual P3 deals may never return to the heyday of 2002–7 given that this was an era of cheap credit and euphoric financialization (Canadian Council for Public–Private Partnerships 2009: 1).

Furthermore, resistance has led to small victories in recent years. In Ontario, for example, union and community activism helped lead to the 2006 exclusion of non-clinical care such as dietary, laundry, and housekeeping services from future P3 project agreements (Canadian Union of Public Employees 2007). Concerns around debt refinancing have also led to the inclusion of clauses within Ontario's P3 hospital project agreements which stipulate that financial gains reaped through debt refinancing must now be shared with the relevant public hospital board (Loxley 2010: 110). While these small victories may one day add up to a significant change, a prohibition on the future privatization of social services would be a crucial first step towards significantly undermining neoliberal rule. This makes P3-targeted resistance a strategic and practical consideration for not only specific sectors and countries, but for much larger resistance campaigns as well.

Notes

1. However, it must be noted that the proportion of P3 hospitals to total P3s fluctuates over time and the P3 model has been expanding into new sectors.
2. For a more nuanced discussion and critique of accumulation by dispossession see, for example, Ashman and Callinicos (2006) and Whiteside (2012).
3. Federal sales have included the Canadian National Railway (1995), Air Canada (1988), and portions of Petro Canada (1991) (McBride 2005: 103). Provincially, this has included Alberta Government Telephones (1990), Nova Scotia Power Corporation (1992), and the Potash Corporation of Saskatchewan (1989) (McBride 2005: 104).
4. More than 100 P3s have been established in various Canadian jurisdictions and sectors since they first emerged in the mid-1990s (see Iacobacci 2010: 1).
5. For more on this issue, see Whiteside (2013).
6. However, a word of caution is required here. With most P3s in Canada the government becomes the purchaser of services and infrastructure, not the public, and thus the universal nature of public services may not be undermined per se. In this circumstance, as is the case with P3 hospitals, services remain universally accessible by the public but their management, organization, and some degree of future planning becomes dominated by large (often multinational) corporations driven by the profit motive, not community or public sector interests. This aspect is similar to contracting-out, though the longer time horizon and contract bundling features of P3s add a greater degree of permanence.
7. Not all P3 arrangements incorporate private financing. However, it is the essence of the United Kingdom's pioneering Private Finance Initiative and the arrangement most common to Canadian P3s ever since their emergence in the mid-1990s.
8. Financialization describes a process whereby financial markets, institutions, and actors come to gain influence over economic policy and economic outcomes at the expense of participants in the real economy of production and distribution of real products (McBride and Whiteside 2011: 83).
9. And thus insofar as P3s erode economic advantages offered by public health care systems, they will also pose a contradiction for both individual health *and* for capital. The notion that P3s can help as well as hinder capital dovetails with

the argument made by Arrighi, Ashcroft, and Scully (2010: 411) that over the long run accumulation by dispossession 'generally undermines the conditions for successful development'.

10. See McBride and Whiteside (2011) for a discussion of rising income disparity and wealth concentration in Canada during the neoliberal era.
11. Depending on the project agreement. Note that in Ontario soft support services (such as housekeeping, dietary, and laundry services) are not subject to P3 agreements though they may be contracted out by hospital boards.
12. Several years earlier, in 1998, a smaller P3 hospital opened in the province of New Brunswick (see Canadian Council for Public–Private Partnerships 2006: 31). However as this P3 had a very small capital cost (only $6.4 million) and did not include the privatization of most support services (only 'hard' services like building maintenance and upkeep of the physical plant), it does not constitute a DBFO and thus BC P3s can be considered to have been Canada's premier DBFO hospital P3s. Also, as previously mentioned, not all P3 hospitals contain this wide a range of private sector involvement. More recent agreements, particularly those in Ontario, have excluded some/all soft services.
13. All references to dollar amounts in this chapter use Canadian dollars (CAD).
14. In 2006 Gordon and Leslie Diamond donated $20 million to 'fund state-of-the-art medical equipment at the new centre, establish a new Leslie Diamond Fund for Women's Health, expand the women's and men's urological health program and help provide funding for a new CT scanner for the emergency department at Vancouver General Hospital' (Campbell 2006: 14). This portion of the hospital's redevelopment does not relate in any way to the P3 (it was established for separate purposes), yet since this is now the name of the new Centre, here the P3 will be referred to as such.
15. Sodexo is a multinational corporation specializing in food services and building maintenance in hospitals, schools, prisons, and other similar institutions. It has a record of industrial standards violations and union-busting (for example, see HEU 2004).
16. In a report for the World Bank, Dutz et al. (2006: 3) cite Partnerships BC as an example of the type of agency that may be prone to conflict of interest concerns given that it provides information and guidance, advocates in favour of the development of P3s, helps with project development, and carries out ex-post evaluations of P3s in the province. The main concern here relates to the evaluation and costing methodology used to determine value for money.

References

Alleyne, R. (2012) 'Six Other NHS Trusts at Risk of Bankruptcy', *The Telegraph* 26 June. Available online: http://www.telegraph.co.uk/health/healthnews/9356064/Six-other-NHS-trusts-at-risk-of-bankruptcy.html. (accessed: 11 March 2013).

Armstrong, P. and H. Armstrong (2008) *Health Care*, Black Point, NS: Fernwood.

Armstrong, P. and H. Armstrong (2010) 'Contradictions at Work: Struggles for Control in Canadian Health Care', *Socialist Register* 46: 145–67.

Arrighi, G., N. Aschoff, and B. Scully (2010) 'Accumulation by Dispossession and its Limits', *Studies in Comparative International Development* 45(4): 410–38.

Ashman, S. and A. Callinicos (2006) 'Capital Accumulation and the State System', *Historical Materialism* 14(4): 117–31.

Auditor General (2011) *Audit of the Academic Ambulatory Care Centre Public-Private Partnership: Vancouver Coastal Health Authority*, Victoria, British Columbia: Office of the Auditor General.

Barlow, J. and M. Koberle-Gaiser (2008) 'The Private Finance Initiative, Project Form and Design Innovation: The UK's Hospital Programme', *Research Policy* 37(8): 1392–402.

Block, S. (2008) *From P3s to AFP*, Ontario: Canadian Centre for Policy Alternatives. Available online: http://www.policyalternatives.ca/sites/default/files/uploads/publications/Ontario_Office_Pubs/2008/From_P3s_to_AFPs.pdf. (accessed: 11 March 2013).

Campbell, R. (2006) 'Doctor Executive Earns Leadership Honours', *Medical Post* 42(26): 14.

Canada News Wire (2002) 'Private Hospital in Abbotsford Opposed by 71 Per Cent of Public, Including Majority of Liberal Supporters – Poll', *Canada News Wire* 7 May, 1.

Canadian Council for Public-Private Partnerships (2003) *Hospitals: the Canadian Case for Hospital PPP Projects*, Toronto: Canadian Council for Public-Private Partnerships.

Canadian Council for Public-Private Partnerships (2006) *Canadian PPP Project Directory*, Toronto: Canadian Council for Public-Private Partnerships.

Canadian Council for Public-Private Partnerships (2009) *The Impact of Global Credit Retraction on the Canadian PPP Market*, Toronto: Canadian Council for Public-Private Partnerships.

Canadian Union of Public Employees (2007) *Activists Score P3 Hospital Win*. Available online: http://cupe.ca/health-care/a459bdee705f9a. (accessed: 11 March 2013).

Canadian Union of Public Employees (2011) *P3 Hospitals: The Wrong Direction*. Available online: http://cupe.ca/updir/CUPE_P3_Hospital_Research_Report_-_April_2011.pdf. (accessed: 11 March 2013).

Cayo, D. (2005) 'Only One Bid Received to Build, Run BC's Second Big P3 Deal', *The Vancouver Sun* 23 February: D5.

CBC (2009) 'BC Health Authorities Cut Costs to Meet Budgets', *CBC News* 15 July. Available online: http://www.cbc.ca/news/canada/british-columbia/story/2009/07/15/bc-health-authority-operational-cuts.html. (accessed: 11 March 2013).

Cohen, M.G. and M. Cohen (2006) 'Privatization a Strategy for Eliminating Pay Equity in Health Care', in K. Bezanson and M. Luxton (eds) *Rethinking Social Reproduction: Feminist Political Economy Challenges Neo-Liberalism*, Montreal & Kingston: McGill-Queen's University Press.

Cohn, D. (2004) 'The Public-Private Partnership "Fetish": Moving Beyond the Rhetoric', *Revue Gouvernance* 1(2): 2–24.

Cohn, D. (2008) 'British Columbia's Capital Asset Management Framework: Moving from Transactional to Transformative Leadership on Public-Private Partnerships, or a "Railroad Job"?', *Canadian Public Administration* 51(2): 71–97.

Dutz, M., C. Harris, I. Dhingra, and C. Shugart (2006) *Public-Private Partnership Units*, Washington: World Bank.

Farrugia, C., T. Reynolds, and R.J. Orr (2008) *Public-Private Partnership Agencies: A Global Perspective*, Collaboratory for Research on Global Projects, Stanford University, No. 39. Available online: http://crgp.stanford.edu/publications/working_papers/Farrugia_etal_PPPAgencies_WP0039.pdf. (accessed: 11 March 2013).

Fraser Health Authority (2009) *Service Plan, 2009/10–2011/12*, Victoria: Province of British Columbia. Available online: http://www.fraserhealth.ca/media/ServicePlan09.pdf. (accessed: 11 March 2013).

Fuller, C. (1998) *Caring for Profit*, Ottawa: Canadian Centre for Policy Alternatives.

Gaffney, D., A.M. Pollock, D. Price, and J. Shaoul (1999) 'The Private Finance Initiative', *British Medical Journal* 319(7202): 48–51.

Goldsworthy, R. (2002) 'Objective Based Government Remains Liberal Target in BC', *Journal of Commerce* 91(92): n.a.

Harrison, D. (2003) '2 Firms Drop Bids to Operate Services at Planned Hospital', *The Province* 28 November: A40.

Harvey, D. (2003) *The New Imperialism*, Oxford: Oxford University Press.

Hay, C. (2007) *Why We Hate Politics*, Cambridge: Polity Press.

Hodge, G. (2004) 'Risks in Public-Private Partnerships: Shifting, Sharing or Shirking?' *Asia Pacific Journal of Public Administration* 26(2): 155–79.

Hodge, G. and C. Greve (eds) (2005) *The Challenge of Public-Private Partnerships: Learning from International Experience*, UK: Edward Elgar.

Hope, C. (2012) 'PFI Contracts "Costing Departments 12 Times More Than They Raise"', *The Telegraph* 16 May. Available online:http://www.telegraph.co.uk/news/politics/9270816/PFI-contracts-costing-departments-12-times-more-than-they-raise.html. (accessed 11 March 2013).

Hospital Employees' Union (2004) 'MSA Hospital a Blood-Smeared, Filthy Mess Under Sodexho: News Report', *HEU Newsletter* 11 March.

Hospital Employees' Union (2008) 'Government Policy Paved Way For Low Wages For Hospital Cleaners and Dietary Workers', *News Release* 27 March. Available online: http://www.heu.org/news-media/news-releases/government-policy-paved-way-low-wages-hospital-cleaners-and-dietary-workers. (accessed: 11 March 2013).

Hospital Employees' Union (2012) 'HEU Calls For Overhaul of Hospital Cleaning Audits', *News Release* 1 March. Available online: http://www.heu.org/sites/default/files/uploads/news/2012/03/01/NR%2003-01-12%20BG%20Cdiff.pdf. (accessed: 11 March 2013).

Huws, U. (2012) 'Crisis as Capitalist Opportunity: The New Accumulation through Public Service Commodification', *Socialist Register* 48: 64–84.

Iacobacci, M. (2010) *Dispelling the Myths: A Pan-Canadian Assessment of Public-Private Partnerships for Infrastructure Investments*, Ottawa: The Conference Board of Canada.

Infrastructure Ontario (n.d.) *Projects*. Available online: http://www.infrastructureontario.ca/Templates/Projects.aspx?id=36. (accessed: 11 March 2013).

Interior Health Authority (2008) *Health Service Plan, 2008–2011*, Victoria: Province of British Columbia.

Jessop, B. (2002) *The Future of the Capitalist State*, Cambridge, UK: Polity.

Jooste, S.F. and W.R. Scott (2012) 'The Public-Private Partnership Enabling Field: Evidence From Three Cases', *Administration & Society* 44(2): 149–82.

Katz, C. (2001) 'Vagabond Capitalism and the Necessity of Social Reproduction', *Antipode* 33(4): 709–28.

Keil, R. (2009) 'The Urban Politics of Roll-With-It Neoliberalization', *City* 13(2): 230–45.

Leiringer, R. (2006) 'Technological Innovation in PPPs: Incentives, Opportunities and Actions', *Construction Management and Economics* 24: 301–8.

Leyne, L. (2009) 'Nanaimo Hospital Botched C. Difficile Bug Battle, Probe Finds', *Times Colonist* 20 June. Available online: http://www.timescolonist.com/les-leyne-nanaimo-hospital-botched-bug-battle-1.23225. (accessed: 11 March 2013).

Leys, C. (2010) 'Health, Health Care, and Capitalism', *Socialist Register* 46: 1–28.

Loxley, J. (2010) *Public Service, Private Profits*, Winnipeg & Halifax: Fernwood.

Mackenzie, H. (2009) *Bad Before, Worse Now*, Ontario: Hugh Mackenzie and Associates. Available online: http://www.cupe.bc.ca/sites/default/files/Bad%20Before%20Worse%20Now%20_final_%20_2_.pdf. (accessed: 11 March 2013).

McBride, S. (2005) *Paradigm Shift* 2nd edition, Winnipeg & Halifax: Fernwood.

McBride, S. and H. Whiteside (2011) *Private Affluence, Public Austerity: Economic Crisis and Democratic Malaise in Canada*, Winnipeg: Fernwood.

McInnis, C. (2003) 'Proving Ground for a New Way', *The Vancouver Sun* 18 March: B5.

Mehra, N. (2005) *Flawed, Failed, Abandoned: 100 P3s, Canadian and International Evidence*, Toronto: Ontario Health Coalition. Available online: http://cupe.ca/updir/Flawed_Failed_Abandoned_-_Final.pdf. (accessed: 11 March 2013).

Ministry of Finance (n.d.) 'Capital Asset Management', Victoria: Province of British Columbia. Available online: http://www.fin.gov.bc.ca/ocg/fmb/manuals/CPM/05_Capital_Asset_Mgmt.htm. (accessed: 11 March 2013).

O'Connor, E. (2004) 'Private Sector Admitted to VGH', *The Province* 12 April: A4.

Parks, R. and R. Terhart (2009) *Evaluation of Public-Private Partnerships: Costing and Evaluation Methodology*, Vancouver, British Columbia: Canadian Union of Public Employees.

Partnerships BC (n.d.) 'Projects'. Available online: http://www.partnershipsbc.ca/files/projects.html. (accessed: 11 March 2013).

Partnerships BC (2004) *Project Report: Achieving Value for Money Academic Ambulatory Care Centre Project*, Victoria: Partnerships BC.

Partnerships BC (2005) *Project Report: Achieving Value for Money Abbotsford Regional Hospital and Cancer Centre Project*, Victoria: Partnerships BC.

Peck, J. and A. Tickell (2002) 'Neoliberalizing Space', *Antipode* 34(3): 380–404.

Pollock, A., J. Shaoul, and N. Vickers (2002) 'Private Finance and "Value for Money" in NHS Hospitals: a Policy in Search of a Rationale?' *British Medical Journal* 324(7347): 1205–9.

Rachwalski, M.D. and T. Ross (2010) 'Running a Government's P3 Program: Special Purpose Agency or Line Departments?' *Journal of Comparative Policy Analysis* 12(3): 275–98.

Reynolds, K. (2011) 'How Flipping Equity in P3s Boosts Profits and Ends Up with the Projects Being Run from Channel Islands Tax Havens', *Policy Note*, Vancouver: Canadian Centre for Policy Alternatives. 9 March. Available online: www.policynote.ca/how-flipping-equity-in-p3s-boosts-profits-and-ends-up-with-the-projects-being-run-from-channel-islands-tax-havens/. (accessed: 11 March 2013).

Sandborn, T. (2008) 'Top Private Health Player in BC Slammed for "Windfall" Profits', *The Tyee*, 12 November. Available online: www.thetyee.ca/News/2008/11/12/JohnLaing/. (accessed: 11 March 2013).

Select Standing Committee on Public Accounts (2011) *Auditor General Report: Audit of the Academic Ambulatory Care Centre Public Private Partnership: Vancouver Coastal Health Authority*, Victoria: Province of British Columbia. 27 June. Available online: http://www.leg.bc.ca/cmt/39thparl/session-3/pac/hansard/P10627a.htm#17:1155. (accessed: 11 March 2013).

Shrybman, S. (2007) 'P3 Hospitals and the Principles of Medicare', in B. Campbell and G. Marchildon (eds) *Medicare: Facts, Myths, Problems, Promise*, Toronto: James Lorimer & Co. Ltd. Publishers/CCPA.

Stinson, J., N. Pollak, and M. Cohen (2005) *The Pains of Privatization*, Vancouver, British Columbia: Canadian Centre for Policy Alternatives.

Weaver, M. (2003) 'PFI: the Issue Explained', *The Guardian* 15 January. Available online: http://www.guardian.co.uk/society/2003/jan/15/Whitehall.schools. (accessed: 11 March 2013).

Whiteside, H. (2012) 'Crises of Capital and the Logic of Dispossession and Repossession', *Studies in Political Economy* 89: 59–78.

Whiteside, H. (2013) 'Stabilizing Privatization: Crisis, Enabling Fields, and Public-Private Partnerships in Canada', *Alternate Routes: A Journal of Critical Social Research* 24: 85–108.

Whitfield, D. (2009) 'Profiteering from Public Private Partnerships', *The Guardian* 10 December. Available online: http://www.guardianpublic.co.uk/ppp-projects-investment-funds. (accessed: 11 March 2013).

5
The Industrial Development of Nanotechnology and Its Likely Implications for Labour

Noela Invernizzi

New technologies have deep implications for labour: they transform relations between work and labour markets, including the nature and organization of work, skill requirements, job creation, and employment. Debates on the effects of new technologies on work and labour markets can be traced back to classical economists who witnessed labour substitution by machines and the abrupt disappearance of some trades during the first industrial revolution (Woirol 1996). Adam Smith (1994 [1776]) held that technology makes goods cheaper, generating more demand and then allowing the economy to reabsorb any technologically displaced labour – a perspective known as compensation theory. Karl Marx (1990 [1867]) was less optimistic. He viewed progressive unemployment as a result of the ever-increasing fixed capital-to-labour ratio that characterizes capital accumulation. Regarding changes in the labour process, Smith explored the effects of the increasing division of labour and the contraction of skills on specific activities. Marx analysed the labour-process changes arising from the progressive mechanization of production at the dawn of industrialization, showing that technology contributed to decrease production dependence on human labour through the division and deskilling of labour.

Successive technological breakthroughs, such as the emergence of science-based industry, the development of Taylorist and Fordist methods of production in the early twentieth century, and post-Second World War advances in industrial automation, led to new debates. Regarding changes in employment, scholarly opinions were often polarized between theories of

---

This chapter is based on research which I conducted as a Fellow at the Woodrow Wilson International Center for Scholars, in Washington DC, USA, through the academic year 2010–11. I also acknowledge the funding for this research given by the Brazilian National Council for Scientific and Technological Development (CNPq), award N. 303002/2010–7.

labour compensation and structural unemployment – a term coined in the 1960s. Among others, Braverman (1974) and Burawoy (1979) addressed the intensification, deskilling (or skills polarization), and alienation of labour. Blauner (1964) was more enthusiastic, considering the role of automation in overcoming the alienating effects of the production line.

Theories of labour compensation and unemployment generated by technological advances still appear in debates on the effects of microelectronics and information technologies (e.g. Freeman and Soete 1994; Soete and Dosi 1983). During the 1980s, rising unemployment levels and workforce reductions, and even the disappearance of entire categories of jobs among postal workers, bank tellers, telephone operators, and printers (Noble 1995) led scholars to explore flexibilization and reskilling of certain categories of labour (e.g. Piore and and Sabel 1984; Zuboff 1988), labour relocation along global production chains, the bifurcation of work between high-tech skilled jobs and precarious jobs, and the complex nature of technology-driven labour changes (e.g. Baldoz et al. 2001).

In spite of the different stands, this short review makes it clear that each wave of technological change entails profound transformations of labour and employment (cf. Chapter 6 of this volume). Are these effects just a neutral and inexorable outcome of technological development? In strong contrast to this perspective, following the early writings of Marx on machinery and the more contemporary work of Braverman, Noble, and Burawoy, I consider that technology implications for labour are a result – certainly not a mechanical one – of the social goals that are embedded in technological design. Conceived, developed, and used at the very heart of capital-labour contradiction, production technologies reflect, more clearly than any other, the unequal amounts of power of capital and labour while, at the same time, they are ideologically covered with the veil of neutrality of the technoscientific quest for production efficiency. New technologies do not simply seek greater technical efficiency, but rather increasing productivity vis-à-vis competitors, lowering capital and labour costs, and increasing managerial control over production and the labour process, all of them directed towards increasing corporate profits.

In this chapter, I address the likely implications of nanotechnology for labour. As an emerging multidisciplinary technoscientific field, which only recently began its entry into production processes, nanotechnology is often portrayed as the bearer of the 'next industrial revolution'. Nanotechnology refers to 'the understanding and control of matter at the scale of approximately 1 to 100 nanometers where unique phenomena enable the design and production of materials, devices and systems which have novel applications' (NTSC 2011: 1).

Nanotechnology's revolutionary promises are attributed to at least three important characteristics of nanoscale manipulation. First, very small dimensions make available and enhance new physical, chemical, and biological properties that cannot be achieved in materials with larger dimensions, opening new opportunities to explore materials and construct devices. Second, at this scale, materials have a large surface in relation to their volume, increasing their reactivity; therefore, less quantity of material can perform equally or better in terms of combustion, oxidation, and biological activity. Third, at the nanoscale, differences between living and non-living matter are blurred, and hybrid materials and devices can be designed.

While research on nanotechnology has been intensifying since the 1980s, it was only after the launching of the United States' National Nanotechnology Initiative in 2000 that it was portrayed as a revolutionary technology, able to deeply transform the economy and society at large. Both the industrialized countries of the global North and emerging economies of the global South view nanotechnology as a means to increase their competitiveness. Nevertheless, the manufacturing and commercialization of nanotechnology-enabled products continue to be concentrated in a small number of countries, transnational corporations, and nano-dedicated companies.

Nanotechnology also generates polarized debate on its social and ethical implications, as well as its potential health and environmental risks. Issues addressed by academics, civil society organizations and some international institutions include inequality (the nano divide), corporate power, privacy, unintended consequences, regulation, health risks for workers and consumers, and environmental risks (Invernizzi et al. 2008). The role of nanotechnology in labour markets and work has been scarcely researched.

This chapter is a preliminary investigation of nanotechnology adoption in industrial processes, the implications for labour that can be anticipated at this initial point of nanotechnology diffusion, and trade unions' concerns regarding nanotechnology development. The chapter is organized into three sections. The first presents some indicators that show nanotechnology is moving from research and development (R&D) laboratories to manufacturing processes, involving an incipient but growing nanotechnology labour force. The second examines some potential implications of nanotechnology for labour, based on exploratory research on product innovation based on nanotechnology. The third explores trade union perspectives by analysing position-statement documents issued by unions in different countries and interviews with union leaders and unions' technical staff. The article ends with brief final remarks.

Nanotechnology's initial steps in manufacturing[1]

Nanotechnology R&D is a very well-funded enterprise. In the United States, more than US$12 billion has been invested since the beginning of the National Nanotechnology Initiative in 2000 (Lok 2010: 18). Global funding for nanotechnology reached US$18.2 billion in 2008, almost doubling the US$9.6 billion invested three years before (PCAST 2010:17). Nanotechnology's initial development was mainly supported by public funding, but companies soon increased their investments and surpassed public funding by 2004 (Cientifica 2011: 2), encouraged by an estimated $US2.5 trillion nanotechnology market by 2015 (Hwang and Bradley 2010). This is reflected in the growing number of companies involved in nanotechnology publications and patent applications – about 17,600 companies in 87 countries between 1990 and 2008 (Roco et al. 2010a: 446) – and companies' manufacturing of the first round of nanotechnology products. Nanowerk's Nanotechnology Company Directory (Nanowerk 2010a) reports the existence of 2146 nanotechnology companies from 48 countries, half of them in the United States, 670 in Europe, 230 in Asia, and 210 in other regions of the world.

In 2009, the market of final products containing nanotechnology was worth US$224 billion, almost eight times the value achieved in 2005 (US$30 billion), while the nanotechnology intermediates market was valued at about US$29 billion (PCAST 2010: 19). The largest share (55 per cent) was in the materials and manufacturing-industry sector; the electronics and information-technology sector accounted for 32 per cent of the market; the health care and life-sciences sector represented 12 per cent, and the remaining 1 per cent of the market was in the energy and environmental sector (PCAST 2010: 19). The United States, Europe, and Asia divide the bulk of the nanotechnology market, with 36 per cent, 31 per cent, and 27 per cent respectively. The rest of the world is responsible for only 6 per cent of nanotechnology-product sales (Roco et al. 2010a: 478).

Some inventories of nanotechnology-enabled products illustrate the rapid advancement of nanotechnology in industrial production and market exchanges. The Woodrow Wilson Center Project on Emerging Nanotechnology reported 1317 consumer products in 2011, compared to 54 products in 2005 when the inventory started. More than a half of them are health and fitness products, including cosmetics, clothing, personal care, sporting goods, sunscreens and filtration devices. Following in frequency are home and garden, food and beverage, and automotive products (PEN 2011). Helmut Kaiser Consultancy (2010) estimated that there were 2500 nanotechnology-based products and applications sold on the market worldwide, a sharp increase from the 300 identified in 2001.

Another key development in the advancement of nanotechnology in manufacturing is the increasing productivity in the production of key nanomaterials as, for example, carbon nanotubes. A few years ago, carbon nanotubes were difficult to produce and traded only in low quantities. By 2004, there were 54 producers of nanotubes and nanofibres globally who manufactured 65 tons per year of these materials (Cientifica 2005). By 2007, the World Technology Evaluation Centre (WTEC 2007: 8) reported a global capacity of about 270 tons per year. Nowadays, one state-of-the-art plant alone can produce up to 500 tons a year, more than the total global production in 2007 (Nanotech Wire 2009; Plastics Today 2010). Other important nanomaterials are probably following the same trends as carbon nanotubes. Nanowerk's nanomaterials database (Nanowerk 2010b) reports 2624 different nanoparticles in use today, produced by 161 suppliers.

Even if the current value of the nanotechnology market is far from the optimistic projection of US$ 2.5 trillion for 2015, nanotechnology has unquestionably started its diffusion into industrial processes. In the area of materials and electronics, its presence is already significant. Although it is in an early stage of development, nanotechnology has begun to affect workers worldwide.

Nanotechnology implications for labour

Roco (2003: 182) estimated that about two million nanotechnology jobs would be created worldwide by 2015, of which 800,000 will be in the United States, 500,000 in Japan, 300,000 in Europe, about 200,000 in the Asia Pacific region, and 200,000 in other regions of the world.[2] This figure was updated to six million jobs worldwide by 2020 (Roco et al. 2010b: v). The consultancy firm Lux Research (2004) forecasted ten million manufacturing jobs in nanotechnology by 2014, or 11 per cent of jobs in manufacturing worldwide.

There is no statistical data regarding the actual number of workers involved in nanotechnology, not even job classifications that allow the identification of such workers. In the United States, *Small Times* estimated that 24,388 people were employed in nanotechnology companies in 2004 (NIOSH 2010). Lux Research (2007) reported 5300 nanotechnology R&D employees by the end of 2006, and expected an increase up to 30,000 by 2008. According to Roco, employment in nanotechnology has rapidly increased since 2000 and the current number of jobs in the United States, including researchers and workers, is around 160,000.[3] In Germany, nanotechnology companies provided some 50,000 direct and 114,000 indirect jobs (Luther and Malanowski 2004 in Schumann 2009: 87). A study based on 860 German nanotechnology companies registered 63,000 direct jobs in 2008 and projected that small- and medium-sized enterprises would need 43,200 new employees by 2013 (BMBF 2009: 4, 72). These data, enriched by some detailed research on nanotechnology job postings (Freeman and Shukla 2008; Stephan et al. 2007), show that the nanotechnology labour market is still small, but growing.

There are studies that provide information on personnel allocation among different nanotechnology activities within companies in Germany, the United States, and England (e.g. Aibithch 2009; Godbe Research 2006; Sing 2007; USDL 2006; Van Horn and Fichtner 2008; Van Horn et al. 2009). These studies suggest that highly educated scientists and engineers in R&D activities constitute most of the labour force currently employed in nanotechnology, consistent with the fact that this technology is in its early stages. There is also a demand for intermediately skilled positions, mainly technicians, along with the increasing manufacturing and commercialization of nanotechnology-enabled products.

It is very likely that nanotechnology development and its adoption by companies will generate adverse effects on some current jobs and skills as happened as a consequence of previous significant technological change. In this chapter, I analyse these issues based on an exploratory methodological approach developed in previous work (Invernizzi 2011; Invernizzi and Foladori 2010) to investigate potential employment changes caused by nanotechnology. I began by examining the Woodrow Wilson Center's inventory of nanotechnology consumer products (PEN 2011) in order to identify product innovations that can be associated with changes in labour. Then, based on a literature review, I contextualized those product innovations within broader nanotechnology innovation trends observed in several industrial sectors that produce nanomaterials and intermediate products used in nanotechnology-based consumer products.

I grouped products enhanced with nanotechnology into four categories of innovation that have direct implications for labour: (a) nanotechnology-based products are more efficient than their conventional competitors; (b) they are multifunctional; (c) they require fewer and/or different raw materials; and (d) they have a longer shelf-life and last longer. I examined a sample of 285 products within a total of 1317 included in the inventory of consumer products, selecting one product per company in the following industries: food and food packaging, home supplies, textile & garments, automotive, batteries, coatings, displays, and computers. Figure 5.1 shows that increased efficiency and multifunctionality are the most pervasive characteristics, present in 63 per cent and 53 per cent of the products respectively, while about 21 per cent of these products exhibit changes in materials and 16 per cent have an extended life. Although less represented, the latter are dynamic innovation trends still in the R&D phase.

Increased efficiency is a recurrent outcome of product innovation in creating a new competitive environment for the profitability of firms, and leading to the substitution of products. Some examples of nanotechnology-enhanced product qualities, functions, and performance are presented in Table 5.1.

Although the advent of new products may generate new demand, and therefore new jobs, these jobs may not be evenly distributed. With higher concentrations of nanotechnology capabilities, the more industrialized countries and a few emerging economies may create more jobs associated with these new products. However, other trends are also at play here, including the specialization of some countries in particular market niches, ongoing outsourcing, and job relocation trends. Companies have been exploiting the

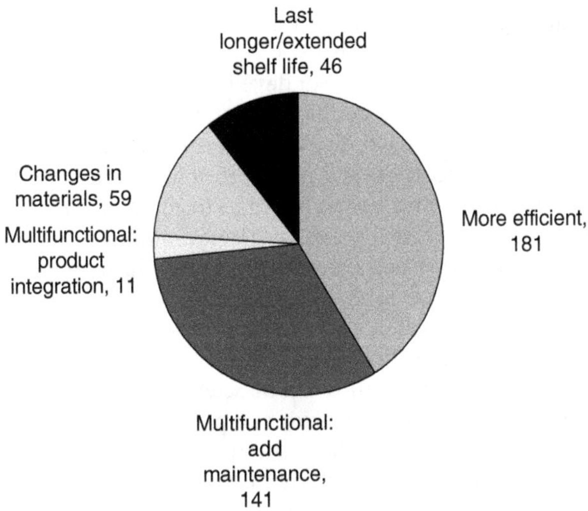

Figure 5.1 Nanotechnology product innovations
Source: Developed by the author based on the Inventory of Consumer Products (PEN 2011).

Table 5.1 More efficient products

Product	Amsoil® Ea Air Filters for cars	LifePak® Nano Anti-aging supplement	Lithium-Ion Super Charge Battery Battery for electric devices
Company	Amsoil, US	Pharmanex®, US	Toshiba Corporation, Japan
Innovation	Ea Air Filters' nanofibre media ***removes 5 times more dust*** than traditional cellulose filters.	To enhance the absorbability of nutrients, individual molecules are separated using nano encapsulation. ***Bioavailability increases by 5–10 times***	The new battery can recharge 80% of a battery's energy capacity in only one minute, ***60 times faster*** than the typical lithium-ion batteries in wide use today.

Source: Developed by the author based on PEN (2011) and companies' websites.

advantages of offshoring, including access to cheap labour, lower taxes, new markets, and proximity to raw materials.

Nanotechnology may reinforce this process and add some new features. A survey conducted by NCMS (2009: 18) in the United States indicates that 30 per cent of the 270 respondent nanotechnology companies are already involved to varying degrees in offshoring. Several nanotechnology consumer products in the PEN (2011) inventory are manufactured in other countries than the company's headquarters.[4] For developing countries, there is a major risk that imported new goods could substitute local production and jobs. A period of labour market instability is thus very likely in the coming years in the sectors that are incorporating nanotechnology more aggressively.

Nanotechnology is helping several products to add new functions, in some cases becoming more context-responsive. These *multifunctional* products can be divided into two groups. Some products add new functions to their main purpose, such as maintenance or self-preservation. Another form of multifunctionality takes place when two or more products that were produced and sold separately merge into one new product that performs multiple functions. Examples of both groups can be seen in Table 5.2.

Multifunctional products that add self-preserving functions tend to make many low-skilled and labour-intensive jobs redundant, due to falling demand for cleaning, washing, ironing, and repairing activities and decreased demand for products used in these activities. One example includes the sterilization of hospital buildings, instruments, and tools, heavily facilitated by the incorporation of bactericide coatings into paints, metals, plastics, and textiles. Other innovations may reduce more specialized maintenance activities in industrial facilities and buildings. Increasingly reactive, 'intelligent' products that respond to maintenance demands are about to reach the market. For instance, the 'self-healing' coating, used in car and home paints is able to repair scratches, bringing surfaces back to their original condition when exposed to sunlight. Intelligent packages are designed to detect food deterioration, scavenge O_2, control moisture, release preservatives, and communicate food conditions to the consumer.

The second kind of multifunctional products demonstrate a trend towards greater interaction and even the merger of branches of production. Although there are few products of this kind on the market (some examples are presented in the lower part of Table 5.2), it is an active R&D area. Some products under experimentation are construction materials with embedded solar cells, sensors, and nanomemories to be used in 'smart houses', textiles capable of releasing drugs and cosmetics, store energy, and portable electronics, that is, the incorporation of entertainment or other electronic devices into the garments. Personalized intelligent food, with special nutrients, cosmetics, and medicines that interact differently with each consumer's needs is also in store. This trend may reconfigure current industrial sectors and the distribution of the labour force among them. If there is a merger of sectors, it is likely that there will be fewer jobs available and a demand for broader, less sector-specific skills. The agglomeration of functions in one product also leads to the centralization of transport, distribution, marketing, and commercialization, which may possibly result in fewer jobs in these fields.

Table 5.2 Multifunctional products

a) Products add maintenance functions			
Product	Herbol-Symbiotec	Pilkington Activ™	Double L® Chinos
Company	Akzo Nobel/BASF, Germany	Pilkington, UK	L.L. Bean®, US
Innovation	***Dirt repellent coating for façades*** Dirt does not stick to the wall. Rain droplets disperse and dry quickly. Prevents algae and fungal growth. *It is an 'anti-aging for façades'.*	***Self Cleaning Glass*** A nano-thin layer breaks down dirt and other organic materials and prevents them from sticking to the glass.	***Wrinkle- and stain-resistant pants*** Nano-Care treatment at the molecular level of the fibre increase its density, so liquid cannot soak through and the fabric is more wrinkle resistant.
b) Convergence of different products into a single, multipurpose one			
Product	Sensatex™ SmartShirt	Nano-Sized Self-assembled Liquid Structures	Demron™ Full Body Suit
Company	Sensatex™ – US	NutraLease Ltd.– Israel	Radiation Shield Technologies
Innovation	***Textiles + electronics*** Shirt enables remote monitoring of a wearer's movement, heart rate and respiration in real-time through a nanotech conductive fibre grid knit into the fully washable shirt.	***Cosmetics + Pharma + food*** Nanoencapsulation system allows the integration of hydrophobic compounds into cosmeceutic and nutraceutic functional foods.	***Textile + defense*** Garment that shields the human body against ionizing radiation, while leaving its wearer fully mobile. Provides protection from a wide range of ballistic, chem-bio and radiological threats. One garment for all threats.

Source: Developed by the author based on PEN (2011) and companies' websites.

Nanotechnology-enabled products originate from *different materials*. In the case of natural raw materials, nanotechnology innovations can both reduce their demand by substituting them for nano-based materials and increase their demand for nanotechnology enhancement, in both cases altering current production structures. Textile fibres that almost perfectly imitate wool's superior characteristics are an example of the former, while the upgrading of cotton fibres to circumvent undesirable qualities (such as soaking

Table 5.3 Imitating wool characteristics with nanotechnology treatments for fibres

Wool characteristics	Nano treatments for fibres that imitate wool
Hydrophobic exterior (water repelling) and hydrophilic interior (water holding).	*Nano –Dry* *3XDry®* *Dry-Zone R506* *SingTex Ice Cool*
Soft touch	*Nano Touch* cover
Odorless, naturally anti-microbial	*SmartSilver*™ *E47 Nano Silver*
Flame retardant	SiO flame retardants
Water repellency gives moderate stain resistance	*Nano-Sphere, Texcote, Nanotex, Nano Care* Dirt and water run off the surface.

Source: Developed by the author based on PEN (2011) and companies' websites.

Table 5.4 Cotton enhancement with nanotechnology

Product	Effect
Performance cotton 3XDry®	3XDry® makes textiles water and stain repellent on the outside and water absorbent on the inside. The fabric is also highly breathable and dries 6–8 times faster.
Nano Protex *Nano Care*	Makes cotton stain, fade, shrink and wrinkle resistant.

Source: Developed by the author based on PEN (2011) and companies' websites.

and wrinkles) is an example of the latter. Tables 5.3 and 5.4 show some nanotechnology-based fibre treatments used to achieve both outcomes.

Previous studies suggest that nanotechnology-induced changes in raw materials entail a significant risk of labour displacement in agriculture and mining in developing countries (ETC 2008; 2005; 2003; Meridian Institute 2007; Sarma and Chaudhury 2009). Changes in demand also affect other intermediate materials that are being substituted by new nano-based materials that exhibit superior performance or other advantages, as shown in the examples in Table 5.5.

In previous research on Brazilian nanotechnology applications, I identified a group of materials that are subject to reduced demand and/or potential substitution by new materials with nanotechnology: steel and other metals, fibreglass, glass, different kinds of plastics, pharmaceutically active

Table 5.5 Substitution of intermediate materials

Product	Car exterior parts (GM Safari, Astro, Impala)	Bonderite®	Radio Frequency Shielding Paint
Company	General Motors, US	Henkel, Germany	NaturalNano®, Inc. – US
Innovation	Olefine-based nanocomposite material ***substitutes for plastics and other materials*** with better performance.	Zirconium-based nanotechnology is a ***green alternative to iron phosphate*** used in anti-corrosion coating for metals. It reduces energy consumption during application.	Paint with halloysite nanotubes for radio frequency shielding, with the ability to selectively turn on and off the impact of such shielding for authorized/unauthorized users. Substitutes for extensive use of ***conductive wiring and construction materials.***

Source: Developed by the author based on PEN (2011) and companies' websites.

materials, natural fibres, and chemical substances (Invernizzi 2011). Corporate R&D activities are focusing on several composite materials with increased performance, customized materials built from the bottom-up (for example, perfect synthetic diamonds), harvesting minerals such as gold and post-silicon electronics. These changes in materials, which are at the very centre of nanotechnology development, will alter the distribution of the workforce among different sectors. Given that the exploitation of materials is closely linked to natural resources, both at a national and international level, changes in demand may very well lead to a new regional and international division of labour.

Nanotechnology innovation is also oriented to assure long-lasting products and products with longer shelf-life spans. While the first characteristic is related to a competitive strategy of providing markets with superior-quality products, the second is related to the durability of perishable products while they are in the commercialization phase. Table 5.6 shows some examples.

Long-lasting products (which also help other products, infrastructure, and machines to last longer) reduce demand for themselves, while requiring less maintenance, therefore negatively affecting jobs at constant demand levels. Longer shelf-life reduces waste of perishable products, consequently decreasing the need for supplemental agricultural production and related activities

Table 5.6 Long lasting products, longer shelf life spam

a) Long lasting products			
Product	Behr® PREMIUM PLUS® Paint	Materia Truck Catalyst	NanoSafe™ Battery
Company	Behr® Process Corporation, US	Daihatsu, Korea	Altair Nanotechnologies Inc., US
Innovation	Harder, self-preserving exterior paint.	Self-Regenerating Catalyst. Extends the life of the catalytic converter.	Conventional lithium batteries last 2 years. New lithium battery with nano titanate has a lifetime of up to 25 years.
b) Longer shelf life spam			
Product	Aegis® OX barrier	Canola Active Oil	N-Coat
Company	Honeywell, US	Shemen Industries, Israel	Multifilm Packaging Co., US
Innovation	Clay nanocomposites prevent escape of O_2 from PET beer bottles. Beer stays fresh for 6 months (working on 18 mo.)	Shelf-life twice as long as any other edible oil.	Laminate with gas barrier properties. Keep nuts, dry foods, and snacks fresh for longer periods.

Source: Developed by the author based on PEN (2011) and companies' websites.

at constant demand levels, but it can also open new opportunities for fresh food exports. Because these products can remain in storage and on supermarket shelves for longer periods, and because packages are being upgraded with self-control devices, activities involving the transport of goods, tracking stock, and checking on the state of the products will likely be reduced.

The analysis so far suggests that nanotechnology-enhanced product innovation has a labour-saving bias. It also has the potential to disrupt job and skill distribution among sectors and countries. At this early stage of its development, there are no studies conducted at the plant level that show how the introduction of nanotechnology is changing labour processes in different industrial sectors. Based on the historical observation of technology development within industrial capitalism, it can be argued that process innovations usually have adverse effects on employment because new technologies are mainly applied to increase production efficiency and automation, which increases labour redundancy. It is therefore possible to expect that two areas in which nanotechnology innovation is strong (that is, computers and sensors) will greatly improve automation in many industries, thus altering labour markets (e.g. Pinto 2010).

Trade union perspectives on nanotechnology

This section provides a preliminary exploration of trade union views on nanotechnology and its implications for the labour force. I base my analysis on published documents and interviews. The published documents consist of 13 public declarations, signed by significant national unions in Europe, Latin America, North America, and Australia as well as large international union confederations, in which unions assess likely implications of these technologies for labour and make specific demands on the subject (see Annex A.1). I have identified these documents through an internet search using keywords in English, Spanish, and French. In addition, I conducted seven interviews with union leaders and technical advisors to unions during 2011. Most of these leaders and advisors were involved with the aforementioned declarations, and are still active in nanotechnology discussions. The unions and union confederations interviewed include: the European Union Confederation (ETUC); the International Union Confederation (ITUC), the Latin American Regional Union of Food, Farm, Hotel, Restaurant, Tobacco and Related Workers (IUF); the Australian Council of Trade Unions (ACTU), the American Federation of Labor and Congress of Industrial Organization (AFL-CIO), the ABC Chemical Workers' Union, Brazil, part of the Worker's Central Union (Químicos ABC/CUT), and the union of the Arkéma Lacq-Mourenx company, of France's General Confederation of Workers (Árkema/CGT).

Trade unions' discussion on nanotechnology implications for the labour force is incipient. There is only a small group of major international and a few national trade-unions associations that have been addressing the issue since 2004. This period coincides with a rise in nanotechnology R&D and production activities. In their position statements, these unions emphasize the potential risks of nanotechnology, workplace safety issues and the demand for regulation as the principal points in question. Concerns with other implications are still addressed in general terms as 'social and ethical issues'. Only two declarations explicitly address nanotechnology's potential effect on employment and skills. Three of these documents were also signed by NGOs and other stakeholders. Table 5.7 summarizes the main matters of concerns expressed in the declarations.

The unions' focus on health and environmental risks, workplace safety, and regulation is in response to at least three important issues. First, some NGO activities alerted unions to the potential risks of nanotechnology, starting with the call for a moratorium by the ETC Group in August 2002, at the World Summit on Sustainable Development in Johannesburg. The ETC Group based this claim on evidence of potentially severe environmental and human health risks of nanotechnology (ETC 2003). The call for a moratorium polarized the debate at the very moment that governments worldwide were launching nanotechnology programmes and funding was climbing.

Table 5.7 Trade unions' matters of concern regarding nanotechnology expressed in public declarations

Trade unions, Country or Region	**Matters of concern**					
	Insufficient knowledge	**Health and environmental risks**	**Lack of work-place safety measures**	**Need for nano-specific regulation**	**Social and ethical implications**	**Effects on jobs and skills**
Trade Unions Congress (TUC), United Kingdom	X	X	X	X		
Australian Council of Trade Unions (ACTU), Australia		X	X	X	X	
International Food Workers – IUF, Latin America and Caribbean Section	X	X	X		X	X
Civil Society – Labour coalition*, International		X		X	X	
Coalition of civil society, public interest, environmental and labour organizations**, international.	X	X	X	X	X	

European Trade Unions Confederation (ETUC), Europe	X	X	X	X	X	X
Dutch Trade Union Federation (FNV), Netherlands	X	X	X	X		
Unite the Union (UNITE), Britain and Ireland	X	X	X			
Int. Fed. of Workers in Chemical, Energy and Diverse Industries (ICEM), NGOs and government, Latin America and Caribbean		X	X		X	
Canadian Union of Public Employees (CUPE), Canada	X	X	X	X		

Note: ETUC published two declarations and ACTU published three (see Annex A.1).
Source: Developed by the author based on trade unions' declarations.
* Signatory Unions: IUF, AFL-CIO and United Steelworkers of America (USWA).
**Signatory unions: IUF, AFL-CIO, ITUC, Bakery, Confectionary, Tobacco Workers and Grain Millers International Union (BCTGM), USWA.

Scientific evidence was scarce at that time, and research on the potential risks of nanomaterials was advancing slowly, compared to the much more rapid pace of nanotechnology development. Still, scientific evidence to suggest that various nanoparticles do present risks rose over the last decade, as demonstrated by databases of published scientific articles on nanomaterials' risks elaborated by the International Council on Nanotechnology (ICON) at Rice University, and by NanoCeo (*Nanotechnology Citizen Engagement Organization*). This scientific literature on risks shows, for example, that carbon nanotubes may behave like asbestos and that other nanoparticles may present high toxicity. Since nanoparticles' size is so small, they can be easily inhaled or absorbed through the skin (Schulte and Salamanca-Buentello 2007). Given that current evidence has been obtained in *in vitro* or *in vivo* tests, there is not conclusive proof that humans will suffer the same consequences. Thus, scientists can only posit reasonable doubt that nanotechnology poses risks to human health and the environment (Kulinowski 2009; Maynard 2006). It is important to note that several union declarations cite some of these scientific studies to support their demands.

Although several social groups are expected to be exposed to the potential harm of nanoparticles, workers are the most vulnerable, since they are involved in all stages of the production cycle, from the production of nanomaterials, through their incorporation into several intermediate and final products, to the final disposal of used products. Therefore, health risks are a central concern for trade unions.

Second, discussions on the regulation of nanotechnology started with the OECD in 2007, with the appointment of the OECD Working Party on Nanotechnology (WPN) as an advisory body in devising policy for the responsible development of nanotechnology science and innovation. The European Commission has also been actively engaged in standardization and regulation of nanotechnology. Regulation has central strategic importance for governments that see nanotechnology as key to increasing their competitiveness in the future. Perspectives on how to deal with potential health and environmental risks vary greatly among countries. Trade unions are pressing for specific and mandatory regulation in their public statements. Two of our interviewees, at the European Trade Union Confederation and the Australian Council of Trade Unions, indicated that the unions had been invited to participate at some discussion tables.

Third, the open wounds remaining from past examples of disastrous workplace harms constitute ample reason for union leaders to be cautious with nanotechnology. In spite of the advances in workplace safety regulation, workers are still subject to well-known risks on a daily basis. Since nanotechnology is being introduced into the workplace and markets without prior safety assessments and regulation, workers are worried about having another asbestos tragedy:

> We have growing concerns vis-à-vis the transparency of companies to reveal information concerning health hazards. The feeling I get from many unions is 'we don't want to repeat an asbestos case,' or even with chemicals, as materials out in the market that we cannot control and, in 50 years, will become a major source of disease. We have this feeling that we might be repeating history, and it is a very frustrating feeling for many unions.
>
> (Interview #2, ITUC)

> One of the questions that workers fruquently ask when they are dealing with new substances...: 'is this another asbestos?' ...I think it is a very logical question given the long history of exposure to asbestos by workers in the US and around the world.
>
> (Interview #6, AFL-CIO)

The International Union of Food Workers (IUF) views the insufficient public information on nanotechnology's potential risks in a similar way as happened with genetically modified organisms. According to the IUF former secretary general, this is because the same companies are working on both bio and nanotechnology. He also emphasized historical learning as the source of their cautionary approach to nanotechnology:

> We have a precautionary position. Why precautionary? Because [nanotechnology] emerges within a context. In what context do nanotechnology and its possible risks emerge? ...According to ILO and WHO, there are 30 million work accidents per year in Latin America (2009 data). These accidents result in 240,000 deaths per year. This means 657 deaths per day...Workers are not suicidal! This happens because of negligence, because companies want to cut costs on workers' protection.
>
> (Interview #3, IUF)

Trade unions' mistrust of companies is based on their historical experience with workplace safety issues and because of the secrecy surrounding their nanotechnology activities. Unions demand that workers be informed and be given an active role in risk prevention and risk management. All interviewees stressed that unions do not know what companies are using nanotechnology and in which processes. Companies are not identifying nanomaterials, nor are they providing data sheets. Current regulations in most countries do not require companies to inform workers regarding a new substance unless is has been declared hazardous. One declaration produced jointly by various trade unions and NGOs in June 2007, titled *Civil Society-Labour Coalition Rejects Fundamentally Flawed DuPont-ED Proposed Framework*, demands mandatory and transparent regulation, rejecting the voluntary guidelines proposed by the Dupont company and an NGO named Environmental Defense. Soon after, a larger group of unions and NGOs signed a declaration titled *Principles for the Oversight of Nanotechnology and Nanomaterials.* It contains eight fundamental principles for an effective oversight and assessment of nanotechnology, including those nanomaterials that are already in widespread commercial use. The principles are: A Precautionary Foundation; Mandatory Nano-specific Regulations; Health and Safety of the Public and Workers; Environmental Protection; Transparency; Public Participation; Inclusion of Broader Impacts; and Manufacturer Liability. The declaration stresses that workers and their representatives must be involved in ensuring workplace safety without fear of retaliation.

Only two public declarations directly address likely changes in employment and skills caused by the introduction of nanotechnology in production. However, six declarations assert that nanotechnology will have broad economic, social, and ethical implications and will affect workers in their workplaces, as citizens, and as consumers. The interviews provided additional information on this subject.

The European Trade Union Confederation addressed employment issues in two declarations published in 2008 and 2010. The first grants job creation as one potential benefit of nanotechnology, but welcomes jobs only if they are tied to a responsible and transparent nanotechnology development. The second resolution takes a more sceptical stand and expresses concern regarding potential inequalities created by changes in employment patterns, work processes, and work conditions. According to the person I interviewed in this union confederation (Interview #1, ETUC), nanotechnology may create new jobs but will also require new skills, so unions fear that new jobs may be restricted to a very specialized group of workers with high skills, while other workers may be left behind. Thus, unions are increasingly concerned with the safety of potential new employments, both in terms of workers' health and job stability.

According to another interviewee (interview #2, ITUC), the International Trade Union Confederation, which represents workers from around the world, admits that job creation is one positive side of nanotechnology development, but also argues that the overall picture is much more complex. For example, nanotechnology may represent new job opportunities for workers in the chemical sector, who are well-organized and enjoy relatively good labour protection compared to other categories. Other workers see opportunities in nanotechnology's promise of revamping some industrial sectors in decline, such as cars and construction materials. However, according to the interviewee, what is new in the discussion on nanotechnology is that workers are not 'buying' into the employment-generation promise without considering occupational health and safety issues. ITUC has been developing what is called a *transition framework* for structural changes in the economy to be organized in a socially fair manner and to avoid workers' suffering from these changes. Thus, ITUC demands such policies as the retraining and employment of workers and unemployment benefits, in addition to workers' meaningful participation in decision making. This framework will help the union to address nanotechnology-related labour changes.

It is relevant to examine the reasons why other trade unions have not mentioned employment changes. The AFL-CIO interviewee (interview #6) said that probably none of the 55 union members are discussing potential implications of nanotechnology on employment or, if there is some discussion, it is very restricted. However, he believes that this will be a major issue at some point in the future, if nanotechnology projections are realized. He observed that the lack of discussion is due to the lack of information. Unions and workers do not have information about companies that are using nanotechnology. Moreover, nanotechnology is not perceived as a revolutionary technology by workers:

> When you read the press, or stuff coming out from the US government's NNI [National Nanotechnology Initiative], they talk about a nanotechnology revolution, but I don't think that at the shop floor level, at the workplace, people see it at all as a revolution, if they see it at all! They see new materials, we have seen new materials over the years, and this new materials happen to be new materials with something called a nanoparticle in it, whatever that means, and they don't necessarily know what that means. So, I think that there is a basic lack of knowledge on what this... technological development is all about. [Previous technological changes were about] a new machine we never had before, a new version of a machine that does a lot more. And here it is... nanomaterials into a tennis racket or golf club!
>
> (Interview #6, AFL-CIO)

In addition to lack of information on nanotechnology, another interviewee, the former secretary general of the IUF (interview #3) mentioned that workers are already overwhelmed in Latin America and the Caribbean with more tangible and urgent employment problems, such as job outsourcing and deregulation. Even though nanotechnology may entail job-loss risks in the future, this is far from workers' more immediate and pressing job problems of today. Therefore, the union is focussing first on health risks posed by nanotechnology, and then on employment risks. Nevertheless, the IUF's 2006 declaration insisted that the International Labour Organization should undertake an urgent study on nanotechnology's possible implications for work and employment conditions in agriculture and the food industry (both of which the union represents) (Foladori and Invernizzi 2008). Also the Brazilian Chemical Union, in the São Paulo metropolitan region, is beginning to formulate a position to the effect that the introduction of nanotechnology should be accompanied by retraining and productivity gains for workers. If not, this new technology may increase inequalities in the Brazilian labour market (Interview #5, Químicos ABC/CUT).

Although it sits at the forefront in discussions of nanotechnology risks and regulation, the Australian Council of Trade Unions (ACTU) does not address employment issues. The interviewed union representative (interview #4) is, however, cognizant that nanotechnology has much broader implications for workers than health and environmental risks. She is worried that only a small circle of individuals within the union understands that nanotechnology 'is going to be big and not just socks that don't smell'. In her view, since it is advancing so quickly, unions may be too late to respond to changes. The French CGT chemical union leader, who represents workers in a company that produces carbon nanotubes, is very clear in his concerns: 'Employment is for the production of products. What is the interest in getting a new job if we are going to lose our lives? For us, it has to be a safe product, or we won't produce it' (Interview #7, CGT).

Unions seek great worker participation in the process of nanotechnology development and regulation. The unions most involved in discussions with their national governments are in Spain, France, Holland, Denmark, Finland, and Ireland (Interview #1, ETUC). The European Trade Union Confederation has struggled to participate in ongoing discussions with the European Commission working groups. However, participation is not easy. Regulation and standardization cover technical matters, and trade unions have neither the necessary expertise nor an adequate number of experts.

The union's difficulties in securing qualified participation in discussions was also highlighted by the ITUC interviewee (interview #2), who stressed the difference between participation and meaningful involvement in discussions. According to the interviewee, although they were invited to participate in several forums, the level of discussion is deliberately very technical, so their capacity to intervene is limited. The union does not have enough technical resources to produce data and analyse technical documents. Their participation is often confined to demands of a general nature, asking for the implementation of the precautionary principle, consultation, and democracy. These demands are often dismissed as not belonging to the technical tables of negotiation.

Australian trade unions have actively participated in discussions with the government agency that regulates chemical substances, along with industry, NGOs, and other stakeholders. The current government is sympathetic to workers' participation, although industrial lobbies are trying to convince the government that unions are overstating risks, posing obstacles that may reduce Australia's competitiveness in nanotechnology (Interview #4, ACTU).

In the United States, the AFL-CIO Occupational Health and Safety representative has been invited to participate in several activities organized by the government. However, there are only two people from trade unions active on nanotechnology discussions in the whole country, which restricts workers' meaningful participation. Brazilian chemical workers were not invited to government discussions, but they have managed to participate at the Nanotechnology Competitiveness Forum since mid-2010 (Interview #5, Químicos ABC/CUT). In the case of the French Chemical union, individual workers have been invited to participate at the public debates organized by the government, but not through trade-union representation (Interview #7, CGT).

The lack of technical expertise has led several unions to join forces with NGOs. ETUC, ITUC, ACTU, IUF, USWA, and ICEM have worked closely with NGOs in producing some common declarations. Since they share similar concerns regarding health and safety risks posed by nanotechnology, they may strengthen those alliances in the future.

At this point, given the lack of transparency about whether or not nanotechnology is being used in industry, union negotiations with companies are not common. There are only three trade unions among the ones considered in this study that made advances. During a collective agreement negotiation in 2009, the Chemical Workers Union of the ABC region in Brazil pressed for a clause, requiring companies to provide workers with information and the inclusion of nanotechnology in the Accident Prevention Internal Commissions. This demand was rejected. Instead, it was agreed that there should be a recommendation for the incorporation of nanotechnology in the mandatory Accident Prevention Week courses in all chemical and pharmaceutical companies (Interview #5, Químicos ABC/CUT). The IUF continues to struggle for the right to information, guaranteed by the International Labour Organization. In a Latin American conference of Unilever workers in 2010, it was agreed that the unions would press for a clause in their collective agreements on the right to information regarding nanotechnology use in their workplaces. The IUF is proceeding in the same way with other major agricultural and food transnational companies (Interview #3, IUF). The Dutch Trade Union Federation, FNV, and the Confederation of Netherlands Industry and Employers negotiated some protective measures based on the Precautionary Principle, including pilot nano-reference values of exposure (SER 2009).

Final remarks

Although the optimistic nanotechnology market projections made at the beginning of the last decade have not materialized, companies researching and developing nanotechnology materials over the last ten years have multiplied, and a number of them have been marketing nanotechnology-enabled products. However, research on nanotechnology implications for labour remains scarce. My exploratory research based on the analysis of product innovation trends shows that new jobs, job losses, inter-branch redistribution of workers, and changes in the regional and international division of labour are very likely outcomes of the progressive diffusion of nanotechnology.

Workers and their unions have just begun to address the implications of this emerging technology for labour and are pressing to have their interests heard at this early stage of nanotechnology development. A number of position statements have been made public, in which unions mainly call for workplace safety measures and the strong regulation of new materials. Broader implications for employment and skills have been less-frequently addressed. Views on nanotechnology's potential for job creation, which were particularly common among unions in Europe, are now giving way to more complex thinking that includes potential adverse effects.

Theories of technology emphasize the socially constructed nature of technology. Social construction of technology reflects a process in which different interests are unequally represented. In these early phases of nanotechnology construction, contradictory views are at stake and different groups – scientists, industrialists, environmental groups, consumer associations, workers, and so on – are trying to advance their positions. Certainly, an understanding of risks posed by nanotechnology, acceptable risks, and their management is greatly influenced by the diverse and often contradictory interests of these groups. The social costs of an industrial restructuring, with its effects on employment, do not receive the same attention by different social groups. The way in which nanotechnology will unfold will very much depend on how other social forces, apart from scientists and industrialists, will articulate their understanding of the technology and influence its development.

The deepening of the economic crisis and escalating unemployment rates certainly make it difficult for unions to advance their interests on nanotechnology. However, unions have started to formulate their concerns and entered the public discussion in a moment when deliberations and political negotiations on nanotechnology regulation have just begun. In order to be capable of influencing the path of nanotechnology advancement, unions need to be better informed and be able to articulate their positions through relational activism with member unions and grassroots organizations outside the narrow circles of leadership and technical staff. A strategy that could help to strengthen their positions is to deepen the formal and informal alliances with environmental, consumer, social justice, and other civil society organizations, with whom they share some essential concerns.

Annex A.1 List of union declarations on nanotechnology

Date	Union	Country/Region	Declaration
July 2004	Trade Unions Congress (TUC)	Great Britain	Nanotechnology Fact Sheet
August 2005	Australian Council of Trade Unions – ACTU	Australia	Inquiry into workplace exposure to toxic dust

April 2006	Australian Council of Trade Unions – ACTU	Australia	Comment on DITR (Dept. of Industry, Tourism and Resources) Nanotechnology Strategy
October 2006	International Union of Food Workers – IUF	Latin America	Nanotechnology – The IUF Resolution
April 2007	Civil Society – Labor Coalition	International	Civil Society-Labor Coalition Rejects Fundamentally Flawed DuPont-ED Proposed Framework
July 2007	Coalition of civil society, public interest, environmental and labour organizations	International	Principles for the Oversight of Nanotechnology and Nanomaterials
Jun 2008	European Trade Unions Confederation – ETUC	Europe	ETUC resolution on nanotechnology and nanomaterials
October 2008	Dutch Trade Union Federation – FNV	Netherlands	Occupational health risks of nanoparticles. Letter to the Minister of Social Affairs.
(N/A) 2008	Amicus – Unite the Union (UNITE)	Britain and Ireland	Unite the union's position on nanotechnology
April 2009	Australian Council of Trade Unions – ACTU	Australia	Nanotechnology – why unions are concerned
March 2010	Int. Fed. of Chemical, Energy and Diverse Industries Union – (ICEM), GRULAC/SAICM, IPEN	Latin American and Caribbean	Resolution on nanotechnology and manufactured nanomaterials
December 2010	European Trade Unions Confederation – ETUC	Europe	ETUC 2nd resolution on nanotechnologies and nanomaterials
December 2010	Canadian Union of Public Employees – CUPE	Canada	Health and safety issues with nanotechnology

Notes

1. I have addressed the issues discussed in this section of the chapter in greater detail in Invernizzi (2011).
2. For comparison, two million is the current number of workers in the IT sector across Europe (STOA 2007: 9).

3. Personal interview, 1 December 2010.
4. Foley and Hersam (2006) argue that R&D can be outsourced to take advantage of the existing well-trained scientific personnel in several developing countries. For example, China, with its rising performance in nanotechnology research and commercialization, can become a significant player in the global nanotechnology production and labour market (Appelbaum et al. 2008).

References

Aibithch, L. (2009) 'Qualification Structure and Demand for Further Education of German Nanotechnology Companies', in *BMBF: Federal Ministry of Education and Research Nano.de-Report 2009: Status Quo of Nanotechnology in Germany*. Available online: http://www.bmbf.de/pub/nanode_report_2009_en.pdf. (accessed: 4 November 2010).

Appelbaum, R.P., R. Parker, C. Cao, and G. Gereffi (2008) 'China's (not so hidden) Developmental State: Becoming a Leading Nanotechnology Innovator in the 21st Century', Paper Presented at the Atlanta Conference on Science and Innovation Policy 2009, Atlanta, GA. Available online: http://www.cggc.duke.edu/pdfs/Nanotech_Presentations/China_not-so-hidden_developmental_state.pdf. (accessed: 12 September 2010).

Baldoz R., C. Koeber, and P. Kraft (2001) 'Making Sense of Work in the Twenty-first Century', in R. Baldoz, C. Koeber, and P. Kraft (eds) *The Critical Study of Work: Labour, Technology and Global Production*, Philadelphia: Temple University Press.

Blauner, R. (1964) *Alienation and Freedom*, Chicago & London: The University of Chicago Press.

BMBF (2009) *Nano.de-Report 2009: Status Quo of Nanotechnology in Germany*, German Federal Ministry of Education and Research. Available online: http://www.bmbf.de/pub/nanode_report_2009_en.pdf. (accessed: 4 November 2010).

Braverman, H. (1974) *Labor and Monopoly Capital*, New York: Free Press.

Burawoy, M. (1979) *Manufacturing Consent: Changes in the Labour Process Under Monopoly Capitalism*, Chicago: University of Chicago Press.

Cientifica (2005) *Market Research Report: Carbon Nanotubes Global Production*. Available online: http://www.marketresearch.com/Cientifica-Ltd-v2574/Carbon-Nanotubes-Global-Production-1692530. (accessed: 5 December 2010).

Cientifica (2011) *Global Funding of Nanotechnology and Its Impact*. Available online: http://cientifica.com/wp-content/uploads/downloads/2011/07/Global-Nanotechnology-Funding-Report-2011.pdf. (accessed: 5 December 2010).

ETC Group (2003) *The Big Down, Atomtech: Technologies Converging at the Nano-Scale*. Available online: http://www.etcgroup.org/upload/publication/171/01/thebigdown.pdf. (accessed: 20 November 2010).

ETC Group (2005) *The Potential Impacts of Nano-Scale Technologies on Commodity Markets: The Implications for Commodity Dependent Developing Countries*, A Report Prepared for the South Centre. Available online: http://www.etcgroup.org/en/node/45. (accessed: 29 September 2010).

ETC Group (2008) *Downsizing Development: An Introduction to Nanoscale Development and Implications for the Global South*, UN Non-Governmental Liaison Service Development Dossiers. Available online: http://www.un-ngls.org/IMG/pdf/0850177_UNCTAD_NGLS_FINAL3.pdf. (accessed: 29 September 2010).

Foladori, G. and N. Invernizzi (2008) 'The Worker's Push to Democratize Nanotechnology', in E. Fisher, C. Selin, and J. Wetmore (eds) *Yearbook of Nanotechnology and Society: Presenting Futures*, New York: Springer.

Foley, E. and M.C. Hersam (2006) 'Assessing the Need for Nanotechnology Education Reform in the United States', *Nanotechnology, Law & Business* 3: 467–84.

Freeman, C. and L. Soete (1994) *Work for All or Mass Unemployment? Computerised Technical Change into the Twenty-first Century*, London & New York: Pinter.

Freeman, R. and K. Shukla (2008) *Science and Engineering Workforce Project Digest: Jobs in Nanotech – Creating a Measure of Job Growth*, National Bureau of Economic Research. Available online: http://www.nber.org/~sewp/SEWPDigestJun2008.pdf. (accessed: 13 November 2009).

Godbe Research (2006) 'Nanotechnology Industry Labour Market Study', A Presentation at the Nanotechnology Forum: A Call for Action for the California Community Colleges. Available online: http://www.ccsf.edu/Services/CTE/ove/pdfs/Godbe-%20Nanotechnology%20Presentation.pdf. (accessed: 23 October 2010).

Helmut Kaiser Consultancy (2010) *Study: Nanobased Products Inventory 2009 and Commercialization*. Available online: http://www.hkc22.com/nanobasedproducts.html. (accessed: 13 October 2010).

Hwang, D. and J. Bradley (2010) 'The Recession's Ripple Effect on Nanotech', *Small Times*. Available online: http://www.electroiq.com/index/display/nanotech-article-display/5049629279/articles/small-times/nanotechmems/materials/general/2010/april/the-recession_s_ripple.html. (accessed: 11 November 2010).

Invernizzi, N. (2011) 'Nanotechnology between the Lab and the Shop Floor: What Are the Effects on Labour?' *Journal of Nanoparticle Research* 13 (6): 2249–68.

Invernizzi, N. and G. Foladori (2010) 'Nanotechnology Implications for labour', *Nanotechnology, Law & Business* 7: 68–78.

Invernizzi, N., G. Foladori, and D. Maclurcan (2008) 'Nanotechnology's Controversial Role for the South', *Science, Technology & Society* 13(1): 123–48.

Kulinowski, K. (2009) 'Temptation, Temptation, Temptation: Why Easy Answers about Nanomaterial Risk Are Probably Wrong', *AzoNanotechnology.com*. Available online: http://www.azonano.com/article.aspx?ArticleID=2448. (accessed: 2 March 2011).

Lok, C. (2010) 'Nanotechnology: Small Wonders', *Nature* 467: 18–21. Available online: http://www.nature.com/news/2010/100901/pdf/467018a.pdf. (accessed: 2 November 2010).

Lux Research (2004) 'Revenue from Nanotechnology-Enabled Products to Equal IT and Telecom by 2014, Exceed Biotech by 10 Times', *Press Release*. Available online: http://www.luxresearchinc.com/press/RELEASE_SizingReport.pdf. (accessed: 3 November 2010).

Lux Research (2007) *Nanotech Hiring Continues to Climb*. Available online: http://www.businesswire.com/news/home/20070207005791/en/Nanotech-Hiring-Continues-Climb. (accessed: 3 November 2010).

Marx, K. (1990) *Capital: A Critique of Political Economy, Vol. I*, London: Penguin Books.

Maynard, A. D. (2006) 'Nanotechnology: Assessing the Risks', *NanoToday* 1(2): 22–33.

Meridian Institute (2007) 'Nanotechnology, Commodities and Development', A Background Paper for the International Workshop on Nanotechnology, Commodities and Development', Rio de Janeiro. Available online: http://www.merid.org/nano/commoditiesworkshop/files/Comm_Dev_and_Nano_FINAL.pdf. (accessed: 28 September 2010).

Nanowerk (2010a) *Companies and Labs Directory*. Available online: http://www.nanowerk.com/nanotechnology/research/nanotechnology_links.php. (accessed: 29 October 2010).

Nanowerk (2010b) *Nanomaterial Database*. Available online: http://www.nanowerk.com/phpscripts/n_dbsearch.php. (accessed: 29 November 2010).

Nanotech Wire (2009) *Nanocyl to Expand Global Production Capacity of Carbon Nanotubes*. Available online: http://www.nanotechwire.com/news.asp?nid=9089. (accessed: 6 December 2010).

NCMS (National Center for Manufacturing Sciences) (2010) *2009 NCMS Study of Nanotechnology in the U.S. Manufacturing Industry: Final Report*. Available online: http://www.ncms.org/blog/file.axd?file=2010%2F9%2F2009_NCMS_Nano_Survey.pdf. (accessed: 17 December 2010).

NIOSH (National Institute for Occupational Safety and Health) (2010) 'Nanotechnology'. *NIOSH Safety & Health Topics*. Available online: http://www.cdc.gov/niosh/topics/nanotech/faq.html. (accessed: 8 October 2010).

Noble, D. (1995) *Progress Without People; New Technology, Unemployment, and The Message of Resistance*, Toronto: Between the Lines Press.

NTSC (2011) *The National Nanotechnology Initiative: Strategic Plan*, Washington, DC: Executive Office of the President, National Science and Technology Council, Nanoscale Science, Engineering, and Technology Subcommittee.

PCAST (President's Council of Advisors on Science and Technology) (2010) *Report to the President and Congress on the Third Assessment of the National Nanotechnology Initiative*. Available online: http://www.whitehouse.gov/sites/default/files/microsites/ostp/pcast-nano-report.pdf. (accessed: 12 October 2010).

PEN (Project on Emerging Nanotechnologies) (2011) *Analysis*. Available online: http://www.nanotechproject.org/inventories/consumer/analysis_draft. (accessed: 22 August 2011).

Pinto, J. (2010) 'The Future of Industrial Automation', *Automation.com*. Available online: http://www.automation.com/resources-tools/articles-white-papers/articles-by-jim-pinto/the-future-of-industrial-automation. (accessed: 22 December 2010).

Piore, M. and C. Sabel (1984) *The Second Industrial Divide: Possibilities for Prosperity*, New York: Basic Books.

Plastics Today (2010) 'Bayer Bets Big on Nanotube Production', *Plasticstoday.com*. Available online: http://www.plasticstoday.com/articles/carbon-nanotubes-bayer-worlds-largest-producer-now. (accessed: 6 December 2010).

Roco, M. (2003) 'Broader Societal Issues of Nanotechnology', *Journal of Nanoparticle Research* 5: 181–9.

Roco, M., B. Harthorn, D. Guston, and P. Shapira (2010a) 'Innovative and Responsible Governance of Nanotechnology for Societal Development', in M. Roco, C. Mirkin, and M. Hersam (eds) *Nanotechnology Research Directions for Societal Needs in 2020: Retrospective and Outlook*, 441–84. Available online: http://www.nano.gov/sites/default/files/pub_resource/wtec_nano2_report.pdf. (accessed: 11 October 2013).

Roco, M., C. Mirkim, and M. Hersam (2010b) 'Nanotechnology Research Directions for Societal Needs in 2020: Retrospective and Outlook Summary', *Wtec/NSF*. Available online: http://www.nano.gov/sites/default/files/pub_resource/wtec_nano2_report.pdf. (accessed: 2 October 2013).

Sarma, S.D. and S. Chaudhury (2009) 'Socioeconomic Implications of Nanotechnology Applications', *Nanotechnology, Law & Business* 6(2): 278–310.

Schulte, P.A. and F. Salamanca-Buentello (2007) 'Ethical and Scientific Issues of Nanotechnology in the Workplace', *Environmental Health Perspectives* 115(1): 5–12.

Schumann, U. (2009) 'Skill Needs in an Innovative Sector: Nanotechnology', in *Skills for Europe's Future: Anticipating Occupational Skill Needs*, CEDEFOP European Centre for the Development of Vocational Training, Luxemburg. Available online: http://www.cedefop.europa.eu/EN/Files/5194_en.pdf. (accessed: 18 October 2010).

SER (Social and Economic Council of the Netherlands) (2009) *Provisional Nano Reference Values for Engineered Nanomaterials*. Available online: http://www.ser.nl/en/publications/publications/2012/2012_01.aspx. (accessed: 7 Jun 2012).

Sing, K.A. (2007) *Nanotechnology Skills and Training Survey: Summary of Outcomes*. Institute of Nanotechnology, UK. Available online: http://www.nanoforum.org/dateien/temp/Nanotechnology%20Skills%20and%20Training%20Suvey%20Results.pdf?.15102010220616. (accessed: 15 October 2010).

Smith, A. (1994) *An Inquiry into the Nature and Causes of the Wealth of Nations*, New York: Modern Library.

Soete, L. and G. Dosi (1983) *Technology and Employment in the Electronics Industry*, London: Pinter.

Stephan, P., G.C. Black, and T. Chang (2007) 'The Small Size of the Small Scale Market: The Early-Stage Labour Market for Highly Skilled Nanotechnology Workers', *Research Policy* 36: 887–92.

STOA (Science and Technology Options Assessment–European Parliament) (2007) *Interactions between New Technologies and the Job Market, Flexecurity and Training/Vocational Training*, European Parliament, Brussels. Available online: http://www.europarl.europa.eu/stoa/publications/studies/stoa23_en.pdf. (accessed: 20 October 2010).

USDL (United States Department of Labor) (2006) *Career Voyages: Nanotechnology*. Available online: http://www.careervoyages.gov/nanotechnology-main.cfm. (accessed: 11 August 2009).

Van Horn, C. and A. Fichtner (2008) *'The Workforce Needs of Companies Engaged in Nanotechnology Research in Arizona'*, Working Paper, John J. Heldric Center for Workforce Development, Rutgers University, New Brunswick, NJ. Available online: http: //www.cspo.org/library/reports/?action=getfile&file=189&section=lib. (accessed: 13 October 2010).

Van Horn, C., J. Cleary, and A. Fichtner (2009) *'The Workforce Needs of Pharmaceutical Companies in New Jersey That Use Nanotechnology: Preliminary Findings'*, Working Paper, John J. Heldrich Center for Workforce Development, Rutgers University, New Brunswick, NJ. Available online: http://www.cspo.org/library/type/?action=getfile&file=109&section=lib. (accessed: 13 October 2010).

Woirol, G.R. (1996) *The Technological Unemployment and Structural Unemployment Debates*, Westport, CN: Greenwood Press.

WTEC (World Technology Evaluation Center) (2007) *WTEC Panel Report on International Assessment of Research and Development of Carbon Nanotube Manufacturing and Applications*. Available online: http://www.wtec.org/cnm/CNM_final_report.pdf. (accessed: 5 December 2010).

Zuboff, S. (1988) *In the Age of the Smart Machine: The Future of Work and Power*, New York: Basic Books.

6

Global Economic Crisis and the 'Spatial Fix' of China's World Factory: The Great 'Long March' Inland

Jun Zhang

China has already become the world's second largest economy and continues to post a double-digit rate of growth despite the global downturn, even though its economy has slowed significantly since 2011 (NSB 2013; Wassener 2012). More remarkable than the numeric size of China's economy *per se* is the extraordinary scale at which labour is being combined with capital to transform raw materials into commodities (Henderson and Nadvi 2011). By 2010, China's GDP was only about 40 per cent of that of the United States, but it has since overtaken the latter as the largest manufacturer on earth (Yao and Zhang 2011). China's emerging 'world factory' has been deeply integrated into global capitalism, and the China model critically depends on exports to balance its economy (Lardy 2011; Peck and Zhang 2013), although it would be inappropriate to have China classified as an export-led economy given the primacy of its domestic markets (cf. Chapter 9 of this volume). Especially after joining the WTO in December 2001, the country has witnessed a skyrocketing of growth in trade and foreign direct investment (Naughton 2007), and accordingly an increase in China's dependence on trade and global capital (Liu et al. 2009). In 2008, mainland China already accounted for nearly 9 per cent of the world's total commodity exports, and a year later, China overtook Germany to become the largest exporter in the world (NSB 2010).

China's golden age of global trade was interrupted in mid-2008 when the financial upheaval initiated by the US subprime mortgage rate crisis began to spread across the world. China has thus far survived the crisis in better shape than many developed countries (Liu et al. 2009). Part of this can be attributed to less exposure on the part of their banks to the subprime loan problems and credit default swaps that caused severe problems in North America and Europe, although the economic contractions in those regions have indeed had a negative effect on the largest emerging economy, especially due to its high level of export dependency. Trade declined sharply from mid-2008 to early 2009, from US$243.3 billion in September 2008 to US$141.9 billion in January 2009, a decrease of 41 per cent in four months (Liu et al. 2009: 500). The decline in exports has had a serious effect, especially on some manufacturing sectors, as testified by the numerous factory closings in coastal regions. However, industrial production in China increased quickly from the second quarter of 2009 after slowing down for more than one year at the nadir of the world financial crisis (Yao and Zhang 2011). International trade after the setback in 2009 also recovered strongly in 2010. Despite the drawdown in exports, China's economy has rebounded rather quickly, registering a growth rate of 9.2 per cent in 2009 and 10.3 per cent in 2010 (NSB 2010, 2011).

China's turnaround from the economic downturn is obviously tied to the enormous stimulus package of more than one-half trillion dollars launched by Beijing to galvanize domestic growth, largely through construction projects (Dunford and Yeung 2011). Relatedly, there was an effort by the state to rebalance the regional disparity of the Chinese economy towards the goal of 'transformation and upgrading' (转型升级) (Cai et al. 2009). Indeed, since the mid-2000s, China's export-oriented industrialization has undergone dramatic restructuring to cope with the changing business environment at global, national, regional, and firm levels. The crisis forced firms in China located at the bottom of the global value chain with very thin profit margins to further cut costs in order to remain competitive. Given China's vast size and enormous regional disparity, moving to inland provinces gave many labour-intensive firms a chance of survival and a location where they can obtain much cheaper land, more favourable taxes, proximity to local markets, and surplus rural labour.

The labour-intensive world factory in China has been powered by the world's largest manufacturing workforce: more than 112 million people at the end of 2006, according to one estimate (*The Economist* 2010: 59). This workforce is not only cheap, but also largely constituted of a 'floating population' of rural–urban migrants.[1] They flock from the poverty-stricken inlands to the booming coastal towns, but are hindered in their efforts to settle down permanently in cities by China's household registration system (*hukou*). Hence, they are forced to drift back to the family farm whenever hardship beckons or they are deemed unfit or undesirable by the employer (Chan 2010a; 2009; Fan 2008). The 'long march' to the western inland of many manufacturing firms previously located in eastern coastal regions has thus been associated with a reverse of the previous spatial pattern of rural–urban migration from west to east. This is due to the fact that there is a much more abundant supply of surplus rural workers in the interior, and because workers may wish to stay closer to home to avoid the suffering of separation from family members. Therefore, the 'next China' after the crisis seems to be lying 'within China's borders, but away from its coasts' (*The Economist* 2010: 59).

Due to the massive build-up in manufacturing capacity, China's world factory has actually gained more global shares from the economic crisis. The export of manufactured products shot up 20 per cent per annum between 2000 and 2009, and the share of manufactured goods in total exports increased steadily from 88 per cent to 95 per cent (NSB 2010). After the crisis, China accounted for 19.8 per cent of world manufacturing in 2010 and overtook the United States (19.4 per cent) as the world's leading manufacturing nation (World Bank 2013: 204). Although it worked as a strong engine for the deeply distressed global economy, this manufacturing spree has added to a global imbalance due to the slow pace at which China imports goods from other countries. Partly as a result, Chinese foreign exchange reserves continued to pile up to an astonishing level of 3.25 trillion US dollars in January 2012.[2]

Intrigued by the remarkable performance of the post-crisis Chinese economy, the purpose of this chapter is to demonstrate how the recovery process of the Chinese economy from the global financial crisis and its spatial ramifications have been driven by the interplays between the capital and territorial logics of power within a unique national and global politico-economic setup. While manufacturing firms seek cost-reduction, the national government seeks to maintain the stability and viability of the economy and to reduce the regional gaps, and local state leaders seek to aggrandize their local and personal interests. A modified conceptualization of David Harvey's (2001: 284–311) notion of 'spatial fix' is adopted to explain such a mechanism of post-crisis transition. I argue that China's remarkable performance so far can be largely explained by a 'spatial fix' of the 'world factory' in the form of massive investment in infrastructural projects, especially in the previously laggard inland regions, and an associated great 'long march' of labour-intensive manufacturing industries from the coast to the inland.

Other than published materials, data used in this chapter are based on my semi-structured interviews with approximately 20 local state officials in Zhengzhou, Kaifeng, Henan Province and Shenzhen, as well as managers and workers of Foxconn, the world's largest manufacturing outsourcing service provider and a major target of inward investment promotion by inland local states during China's post-crisis spatial restructuring, in both Shenzhen and Zhengzhou, in May and June of 2011.

This chapter is organized as follows. In the next section a theoretical framework centred on the notion of 'spatial fix' is laid out. China's survival strategy through the global financial crisis and subsequent recession is then elaborated and its connection to China's regional industrial restructuring detailed. It is followed by an explanation of how the spatial fix and the rise of inland regions have been tied to race-to-the-bottom 'bidding wars' to attract mobile investments. I conclude by reflecting upon the implications of China's approach of crisis management and regional rebalancing.

Theoretical background: Spatial fix, capital logic, and territorial logic

David Harvey's trademark notion of 'spatial fix' refers to different forms of spatial (re)organization, geographical expansion and temporal deferral that serve to manage, at least for some time, crisis-tendencies inherent in capitalist accumulation (Harvey 2003; 2001). In general, spatial fixes are associated with interregional volatility and the improvized redirection of capital flows from one place to another, which may or may not be a smooth process. The term 'fix' also means literally that a certain portion of the total capital is fixed to the land in some physical form for a relatively long duration. Relatedly, some social expenditures, such as transport and communications networks and education systems, also become territorialized and rendered geographically immobile through state commitments. Harvey therefore argues that temporal deferral and geographical expansion 'fix' the over-accumulation crises that arise from the chronic tendency of capital to accumulate over and above what can be reinvested profitably in the production and exchange of commodities, as a result of which surpluses of capital and labour are left unutilized or underutilized. For Harvey, attempts to resolve capital's contradictions through internal transformation reflect the inherent tension between the 'fixity' and 'mobility' of capital at any given moment and over time. The constant search to escape the contradictions and crisis-tendencies of capitalism through profitable reinvestment of surplus capital elsewhere typically spreads these contradictions and crisis tendencies and thereby subsequently intensifies them. Harvey thus argues that a spatial fix can only be temporary, because a fixed space necessary for capital's functioning at a certain time point would have to be destroyed at a later time in order to make way for fresh accumulation and a new spatial fix.

Capital mobility and fixity are two dimensions of the same processes of capital accumulation, through which the scale and scope of capitalist production is constantly restructured and reconfigured (cf. Chapter 10 of this volume). The development of new regions usually intensifies the inter-regional competition and brings pressure of devaluation to incumbent centres of capitalist development. Due to his strong commitment to the Marxian interpretation of capitalism and societal organization, however, Harvey's earlier conceptualization basically neglects the inherent incompleteness of capitalist social formations and alternative modes of societal organization that is at least partially independent of, though intertwined with, capital accumulation (Jessop 2006; 1990). Harvey (2003) defines the process of spatial fix as characterized by the mutual adjustment and reaction of two logics of power: capital and territorial. Capital logic refers to the calculative flow of capital across and through continuous space and time, because capitalist firms intentionally exploit uneven geographical conditions and asymmetries rooted in spatial exchange relations. Territorial logic, in contrast, is tied to state power and political objectives at the national and sub-national scales.

Harvey (2003: 28) maintains that unlike the process of capital accumulation, strategic decisions of the state are arrived at and implemented in 'the rough and tumble of the political process where variegated interests and opinions clash'. Harvey's account of territorial logic, however, is already overdetermined by the more privileged logic of capital rather than unfolding independently in pure geopolitical terms (Jessop 2006). Territorial logic is a unique historical construct fundamentally shaped by the organization of social classes within a state's territory and their relations to the state, rather than just a by-product of the accumulation of capital (Tilly 1990: 15; see also Arrighi 2007; 1994). Historically, the reshaping of relations between the ruler and ruled in different contexts produced variations in the historical trajectories of state formation and contrasting forms of government (Atasoy 2009: 39; Tilly 1990: 30). Capital power and territorial power are thus mingled up in geo-historically specific ways to generate a heterogeneous economic landscape. A state's strategy of territorial and crisis management influencing the outcome of 'spatial fix' is mediated by the unique class and power structures within its territory, which make China distinctive from other countries studied in this volume, especially given China's enduring status as a transitional economy moving away from its past state-socialism (e.g. Chapter 8 of this volume; Chapter 10 of this volume).

The capitalist 'spatial fix' certainly unfolds at multiple geographic scales. Both Arrighi (2007) and Harvey (2005; 2003), in their discussion of the territorial logic of historical capitalism and the case of China, entertain the concept of 'spatial fix' at the international scale and treat China as a holistic territory, as they are particularly concerned by potential global hegemonic shifts associated with the spatial fixes. In their view, China is not only the most promising site to absorb over-accumulated capital from the global capitalist core, but also on its way to become a new global hegemon. The focus of this chapter, however, is placed on the internal 'spatial fix' within China, although in connection with the transnational fixity and mobility of capital, and pertinent inter-regional industrial restructuring.

Following Jessop (2006), I view territorialization of political power as an alternative mode of societal organization to capital logic. The state is not merely an agent of capital to secure conditions for capital accumulation, but has an independent, constitutive role in capital's economic forms and the organization of the circuits of capital, including both production and financing. As an idiosyncratic historical product, China at present is characterized by an unprecedented marriage of a Leninist party-state and an escalating program of market reforms (Peck and Zhang 2013). Like many other authoritarian regimes, China struggles with the tension between the need to foster economic development by empowering local officials and the regime's imperative to control them politically (Landry 2008). The reforms, however, did not weaken the pivotal role of the Chinese Communist Party (CCP) as the key allocator of political power and the principal orchestrator of the country's development path, even at the lowest levels of China's bureaucratic system. Under China's present regionally decentralized authoritarian regime, the governance of the national economy is delegated to sub-national governments, and regional economies (provinces, municipalities and counties) are relatively autonomous and self-contained (C. Xu 2011). At the core of China's Leninist party-state is the Soviet-style *nomenklatura* cadre management system: all appointments are vetted by the organization departments of party committees with the higher levels controlling key appointments for the next two levels down (Landry 2008). This *nomenklatura* system holds the central and local together, ensuring that the heads of provincial and municipal government and party organs were appointed by national leaders. It generates a particular political logic, as it is pervaded with 'promotion tournaments', rewarding those local officials that compete to post high GDP figures and produce visible urban development monuments, whatever the costs might be (Hsing 2010; Landry 2008; Li and Zhou 2005). This Chinese version of intense sub-national competition centred on GDP growth rate has been commonly referred as GDPism.

Local entrepreneurialism driven by an ideology of GDPism and the personal career aspiration of local party leaders within China's particular institutional setup can easily degenerate into 'bidding wars' and race-to-the-bottom competition for mobile investments, with serious, deleterious consequences (Rodriguez-Pose and Arbix 2001; Thomas 2000). The Chinese party-state, however, is increasingly desperate to preserve its political power through rapid economic growth, but unwilling and unable to deal with the necessary contradictions and paradoxes generated by such a regime wholeheartedly (Pei 2006: 7). I argue that China's post-crisis 'spatial fix' has been tied to inward-investment 'bidding wars' conducted by local states, which is inbuilt within China's ongoing market-oriented, regionally decentralized, authoritarian regime, in addition to the logic of capital accumulation. Particularly, losers in the previous round of sub-national politico-economic competition – local states of the inland provinces and cities – have jumped onto the bandwagon and fiercely battled with each other for the relocation of labour-intensive manufacturing firms from the coastal regions stressed by heightening production costs and declining global demand. As a result, the seemingly successful spatial fix led by the regional bidding war is only temporary and fragile due to the idiosyncratic mix of capital logic and territorial logic. Although such a 'spatial fix' within the present framework of the political economy has stabilized the economy and rendered made-in-China products more competitive in the global market, it is probably only exacerbating, rather than reducing, the economic imbalance, nationally and globally.

Global economic crisis and the territorial logic of spatial fix

The Chinese inter-regional system is characterized by immense disparities, and throughout the history of the People's Republic of China, economic policies have been framed, correspondingly, by an implicitly or explicitly regional approach (Wei 2010; Zhou et al. 2011). Since the end of the last century, the Chinese government has launched several national development strategies to balance regional development, including Developing the West, Revitalizing Old Industrial Bases of Northeast China and Raising Central China (He and Wang 2012; Wang et al. 2010). In the name of industrial 'transformation and upgrading' (转型升级), the state launched a nation-wide relocation and rebalancing strategy since the mid-2000s (Cai et al. 2009). It has sought to reduce industries of 'high-energy consumption, high pollution and resource consumption' in the coastal regions so that space and resources can be released to develop higher value-added industry and modern services. At the same time it has encouraged industrial relocation from coastal areas to the inland to adjust its export- processing trade policy and rebalance the national economy. Since September 2006, the central government has made several rounds of policy change, including the removal and reduction of an export value-added tax (VAT) rebate and expansion of the prohibited and restricted categories of the processing trade (Yang 2012). These changes added pressure to export-oriented firms to transform, upgrade, and relocate.

Other pressures such as labour shortage, rising wages, rising prices of limited land, water, electricity and raw materials, appreciation of Chinese currency, inflation and upsurge of raw materials, have all imposed serious challenges on the export-dominated coastal economy before the global financial crisis (Liao and Chan 2011; Wang and Mei 2009; Yang 2012). Production costs increased further due to the implementation of the New Labour Contract Law which began on 1 January 2008, and more stringent requirements to provide employees with various types of social security, as well as stricter enforcement of overtime hour limits and overtime pay (HKTDC 2011; Wang et al. 2009). However, in western areas of China, especially in those provinces associated with large-scale out-migration, such as Sichuan, Henan, Jiangxi provinces and Chongqing City, vast areas of land available for industrial development, large amounts of local-born cheap labour, and favourable investment policy, all attract firms from coastal areas to relocate and cut costs.

As a result, remarkable spatial restructuring of Chinese manufacturing industries characterized by a shift from coastal to inland regions was already underway before the economic crisis (He and Wang 2010; Wang et al. 2010). According to the analysis of He and Wang (2010), the Yangtze River Delta (YRD), the Pearl River Delta (PRD) and the Capital region were still the dominant manufacturing bases in 2007, housing capital-intensive and technologically more advanced industries. But the Chengdu-Chongqing region and the Wuhan city region had risen to become two important clusters in the inland regions. Some inland provinces such as Jiangxi, Henan, and Inner Mongolia have not only become largely industrialized but also gained significant shares of manufacturing value added while Beijing, Tianjin, Shanghai, Jiangsu, Zhejiang, and Guangdong lost shares of value added in manufacturing industries (He and Wang 2010).

The inland-oriented industrial relocation and expansion accelerated along with the spread of the global financial crisis, when China's export economy began to slow down in the second half of 2007 and was devastated in late 2008 (Liu et al. 2009). In 2009 China's exports dropped on an annual basis for the first time in 30 years, by 16 per cent (Workman 2010). The global financial crisis and world-wide economic recession resulted in the decrease of orders, tight bank credit, reduced prices demanded by customers, and payment delays by customers, thus worsening the financial situation of export-oriented manufacturers in the coastal regions (Yang 2012). However, ironically, the financial crisis also helped China's low-cost manufactures gain even more market share in the world (Barboza 2009). For example, China increased its exports to the United States, thus increasing its share of all US imports from 15.6 per cent to 19.1 per cent in the 12 months from November 2008 (Harney 2010). China's export sector has recovered very quickly since mid-2009, and by mid-2010 its exports had largely regained their pre-crisis level (NSB 2012). Due to anaemic recovery in the United States and a Europe haunted by debt crisis, however, China's export growth started to dwindle in 2012 and slumped to 7.9 per cent from 20 per cent in 2011 (NSB 2013).

Record surges in monthly growth of exports between 2009 and 2011 created a huge and sudden demand for large numbers of young migrant workers, which could not be filled, at least in the short run (Chan 2010b; Hamlin 2010). Hence, unlike the prolonged unemployment crisis which followed the economic crisis in the United States and Europe, in China a 'labour shortage' quickly reoccurred soon after the massive layoff of migrant workers from the devastated coastal factories. In 2009, the number of rural–urban migrant workers reached 152 million, exceeding the number of 140 million before the economic crisis in late 2007. However, a growing proportion of these migrant workers found jobs in the inland closer to their hometowns rather than on the east coast (Wang 2010). As a result, since the early months of 2010, Chinese factories in coastal cities have been struggling to find workers to help fill export orders.

Such a temporary labour shortage has been exacerbated by the Chinese state's response to the global recession and export downfall. A massive four trillion Yuan (US$586 billion) stimulus plan was announced in November 2008 (Dunford and Yeung 2011: 37). A series of massive infrastructure-oriented projects, especially in the inland, accounted for almost one-half of this budget. While these new projects were aimed at replacing the GDP lost by falling exports, they also created millions of construction jobs for low-skilled rural workers, especially in the interior (Cai et al. 2010). Taking an opportunity from the global economic crisis, the Chinese government has escalated its effort to restructure the national economy. In April 2010, the Ministry of Commerce announced a Central China Foreign Investment Promotion Plan, including the provinces of Shanxi, Anhui, Jiangxi, Henan, Hubei, and Hunan (Ren 2010). Seven national and provincial economic and technology development zones in these regions have been targeted as primary locations for industrial relocations. These six provinces already established seven service-outsourcing model cities and 20 relocation bases for export-oriented processing trade by 2010. The Ministry of Commerce still wanted to develop industrial-relocation model parks, in order to boost the speed of industrial relocation. The State Council has approved three National Industrial Relocation Zones in Chongqing, Anhui Wanjiang, and Guangxi Guidong (X. Xu 2011). However, the real booster for the ongoing 'great long march inland' is the investment bidding war between inland cities and regions with an abundant endowment of local-born labourers.

Investment bidding wars and the rise of the inland

Labour costs certainly are a key factor driving the locational choice of labour-intensive manufacturing companies, and should explain to a good extent the ongoing 'spatial fix' of China's world factory. On the one hand, coastal regions have witnessed a remarkable rise of minimum-wage stipulation. For example, in Dongguan and Shenzhen, the average minimum wage doubled between 2002 and 2010, after stagnating at minimal increases for almost a decade. On the other hand, vast regional wage gaps continue to exist. For example, the minimum monthly wage in 2010 was around 1100 Yuan in Shenzhen, 900 Yuan in Wuhan, 800 Yuan in Zhengzhou, and 625 Yuan in Chengdu (Figure 6.1). I argue, however, that the regional bidding wars aimed at wooing mobile capital investment, especially the large ones, and the subsequent benefits received by the relocating and/or expanding companies, have also played a crucial role in stimulating the 'spatial fix', and therefore the complementary role of territorial logic must be given full recognition in addition to capital logic.

Since the outbreak of the financial crisis and economic downturn in late 2008, many businesses have accelerated their plans to move inland in order to cut their operational and labour costs. For instance, in 2009 Intel closed down an assembly line and testing factory in Shanghai and moved operations to Chengdu, making Sichuan Province the new export base for the international microchip giant. In 2010, Hewlett-Packard started operations at a new laptop manufacturing and export base in Chongqing (Huang 2011). But the most high-profile relocation and expansion project was associated

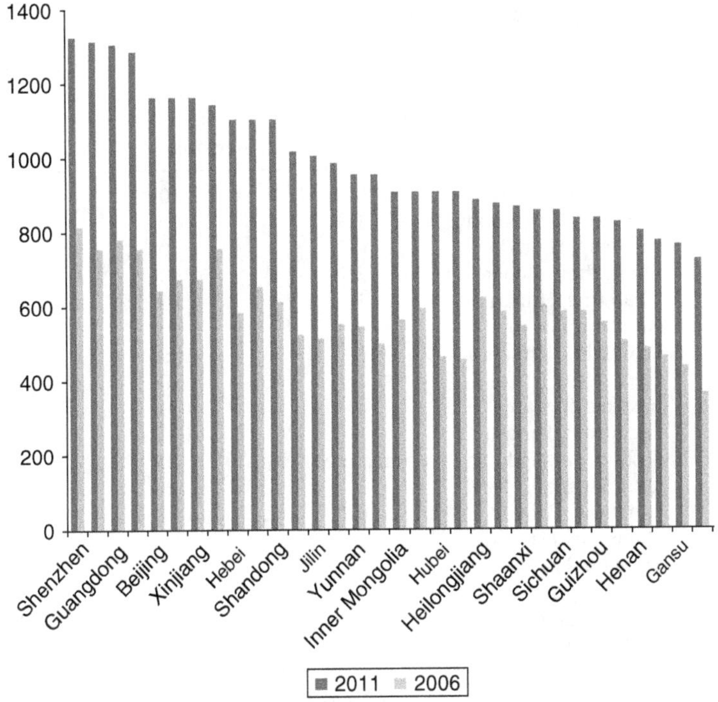

Figure 6.1 Minimum wages in provinces of China (2006 vs. 2011)
Note: Monthly wage of the highest regional category; Shenzhen is added for comparison.
Source: Ministry of Human Resources and Social Security Social Security, PRC.

with Foxconn, one of the leading labour-intensive firms in the sector of electronics on the east coast and the world's largest contract manufacturer. Foxconn, a Taiwanese company also known as Hon Hai, is now the world's largest electronics manufacturing service (EMS) provider. It was ranked 43th largest company on the Fortune 500 list in 2012.[3] Foxconn is China's largest private employer with a workforce of over 1.4 million. It is also the largest exporter in China, with a gross import and export value of US$ 244.6 billion, or 4.1 per cent of China's total volume.[4] As the premium EMS supplier to Apple, Nokia, Dell, and HP, and so on, this electronics goliath also sources supplies and designs parts, and uses its enormous size and military-style efficiency to assemble and speed a wide range of products to market. By all measurements, Foxconn is still a labour-intensive manufacturer, with direct labour in assembly, machine, warehouse, and other categories accounting for 90 per cent of its employment.[5]

Before 2007, Foxconn already had branches and subsidiaries in Beijing, Tianjin, Shanghai, Hangzhou (Zhejiang), Yantai (Shandong), Jincheng

Table 6.1 Foxconn's 'long march inland' since 2007

Starting year	Location	Planned investment size (billion USD)	Targeted employment size (1000 persons)	Planned land size (KM^2)
2011	Hengyang, Hunan	0.1	30	0.5
2010	Huizhou, Guangdong	1.3	80	0.5
2010	Jincheng, Shanxi	0.7	20	0.3
2010	Zhengzhou, Henan	3.7	300	10
2010	Changsha, Hunan	1	30	0.5
2010	Nanning, Guangxi	0.8	40	0.5
2009	Chengdu, Sichuan	10	500	10
2009	Chongqing	1	50	2
2008	Jiashan, Zhejiang	1	100	1.2
2008	Changshu, Jiangsu	1	100	1
2007	Foshan, Guangdong	(acquired)	20	0.16
2007	Qinhuangdao, Hebei	1	35	3
2007	Langfang, Hebei	0.1	150	3.5
2007	Shenyang, Liaoning	1	10	1
2007	Yingkou, Liaoning	1	10	3
2007	Nanjing, Jiangsu	1	10	1.3
2007	Huaian, Jiangsu	1.8	100	2.5
2007	Wuhan, Hubei	3	300	6.6

Source: Compiled by the author based on an interview with the Foxconn manager in charge of park construction, and supplemented by media reports.

(Shanxi), and a few other locations. However, Foxconn's most aggressive relocation and expansion have occurred since 2007 (Table 6.1). Foxconn became unfavourable to Shenzhen, especially after a serial tragedy in May 2010 when 14–6 suicide attempts by migrant workers resulting in 12 deaths took place in the first five months of the year in Foxconn's Shenzhen complex (Barboza 2010a). Although an increasingly unfavourable business in Shenzhen, Foxconn is still considered highly desirable for boosting local investment and GDP for the state leaders of inland cities and provinces. Riding on the tide of the 'long march inland', interior and neighbouring provinces, such as Hunan, Jiangxi, Guangxi, Sichuan, Anhui, Yunnan, and Hubei, have all gone to PRD and YRD areas to invite business and attract investment, frequently with their governors or mayors leading the team and ready to offer astonishing incentive packages. Foxconn is certainly on the top of their priority list.

Before signing an investment contract with Chengdu in 2009, Foxconn requested that the local government get ten square kilometres of land ready for a Foxconn Industrial Park, and finish 11 massive plant buildings hosting 30,000 workers in three months, among numerous other privileges. The local government accepted the challenge and handed over the plant buildings to Foxconn in 80 days. Neighbouring Chongqing surpassed the speed record of Chengdu: by working 24/7, it took Chongqing only 50 days from signing the contract on 4 August 2009 to the first day of operation of the production base. For Chongqing, the Foxconn project, together with HP and Cisco, was a key component of its plan to become a major manufacturing hub in southwest China, spearheaded by the IT sector, a logistics hub, and a civil aviation (Huang 2011). With a total population of 32 million – roughly equivalent to the population of Canada – Chongqing is still a predominantly rural society with 70 per cent poverty stricken rural dwellers. Chongqing's ambition is to offer urban housing and jobs for one million farmers every year over the next decade through attracting investors such as Foxconn.

But the Chongqing record was itself soon to be broken by Zhengzhou, the capital city of Henan Province. Henan has a population of over 100 million and has been one of the largest suppliers of out-migration workers: one fifth of Foxconn's current workers are from Henan. To win the bidding war for Foxconn, a special Application Office for Zhengzhou Comprehensive Tariff-free Zone was established, with the integrated function of export processing, tax-exempted logistics and port (Liu and Dong 2010). The first Foxconn plant in Henan registered on 5 July 2010 and was located in Zhengzhou Export-Processing Zone. The favourable policy treatment received by Foxconn includes: tax exemption for imported raw materials, exemption of value-added tax and consumption-tax for export products, and waiver of corporate income tax for the first two years with 50 per cent deduction for the next three years.[6] In addition, there are favourable terms for utilities such as water and electrical power supply, and most importantly, the land was offered to Foxconn almost for free, which according to local officials can be as large as 20 square kilometres. Foxconn also received various subsidies from both the provincial and municipal governments for personnel recruitment and product shipments. To facilitate Foxconn's massive hiring of shop-floor workers in a short time period, the mission was taken up as a political duty by the local government and a quota was allocated throughout the administrative hierarchy, from the provincial, municipal, and township, all the way to the village level. Due to the increased transportation costs after the relocation, Henan devoted a special fiscal subsidy for the export-processing zone where Foxconn is located: one Yuan from the provincial government and four Yuan from the municipal government for every ten dollars of export value. However, neither the local government nor the company was willing to disclose the details of the favourable tax and land package offered, largely because it has been too generous and there are concerns that once the exceptionally favourable terms are disclosed, other investors may demand something similar (Liu and Dong 2010).

Why are local state leaders willing to sacrifice so much to bid for Foxconn? The answer is the sudden, massive increase in GDP and export figures and the creation of jobs brought about by Foxconn. These are considered remarkable political achievements by provincial and local officials under the party-state's *nomenklatura* system, and crucial to their success in the 'promotion tournaments'. Foxconn-Zhengzhou Park began operation in 2011. By March 2013 it employed around 300,000 workers and produced 400,000 sets of iPhone5 daily, accounting over 50 per cent of the global supply (Luk 2013). Such explosive growth was even beyond the expectation of Henan's General Party Secretary Lu Zhangong, who proudly mentioned to the media in 2010 on several occasions that the first phase alone of the Foxconn project after its completion 'will create 180,000 jobs and double or even triple the export value of the whole province' (quoted in Chen 2010). Moreover, to a laggard inland province like Henan, Foxconn's presence also means tax revenue and an opportunity to jump-start its weak IT industry. Consequently, for local state leaders an investor with the calibre of Foxconn is definitely a magic economic and political boost that is too good to give up.

Crisis managed or delayed?

The short-term effect of such inter-regional competition for mobile investments and subsequent spatial fix has certainly been impressive. A large number of cities and regions in China's vast central and western hinterlands have clearly become the winners in this movement of an industrial 'long march inland' accelerated by the global financial crisis. The share of industrial value-added as a proportion of the national total accounted for by inland regions rose from 37.5 per cent in 2007 to 40 per cent in 2010, signifying a regional rebalancing of industrial production activities in favour of inland areas (MIIT 2011). According to materials from the Henan Department of Industry and Information Technology, in 2010, Henan received extra-provincial relocating investment of 151.4 billion Yuan, an increase of 27.8 per cent over 2009 (Table 6.2). In only one year, 1132 projects of industrial relocation were signed, 1049 projects continued from the previous year or started in the same year, and 519 projects were completed. As illustrated by the Foxconn case, these projects are usually very large: projects with a unit investment amount over 500 million Yuan accounted for 81 per cent of the total amount. Unsurprisingly, the majority of these relocating investments were from the four most developed regions in China: YRD, PRD, Bohai Rim (or the Capital Region), and Southeast Fujian, accounting for 79.8 per cent of the total. All of these projects are centred on manufacturing and 90 per cent of the investments went to various industrial parks developed by the government at provincial or local levels: 180 provincial industrial parks received 71.8 per cent, or 108.8 billion Yuan of the total relocation investment. Within the province, the capital city of Zhengzhou was the biggest winner with an investment of 47.4 billion Yuan. Luoyan ranked second with 15.2 billion Yuan.

Table 6.2 Henan province as the receiver of industrial relocations (2010)

Unit: million yuan	Realized external investment	Signed projects		Ongoing projects		Completed projects		Expected output value	Expected tax revenues	Expected jobs added
		No.	Total	No.	Total	No.	Total			
Total	151,444	1,132	277,583	1,049	90,884	519	46,959	69,973	9,842	100,212
Based on size of investment										
>0.5 billion	71,854	133	177,066	89	32,930	15	9,652	8,945	1,483	20,571
0.1–0.5 billion	50,822	382	69,920	342	35,184	157	24,890	42,760	5,147	40,511
50 million–100 million	17,886	271	20,009	248	14,331	118	7,339	11,004	2,190	20,487
below 50 million	10,882	346	10,589	370	8,439	229	5,077	7,264	1,022	18,643
Based on investor origin										
Yangtze River Delta	41,668	330	79,345	280	23,414	135	12,959	22,828	2,826	28,276
Pearl River Delta	27,411	242	58,251	222	20,614	84	6,975	9,396	1,658	22,002
Southeast Fujian	18,226	172	43,291	131	9,496	67	7,300	7,737	1,567	16,323
Bohai Rim	33,449	156	54,361	154	18,646	70	6,591	9,591	1,423	11,483
Other developed areas	30,691	232	42,335	262	18,715	163	13,135	20,421	2,367	22,128

Source: Henan Department of Industry and Information Technology, unpublished report.

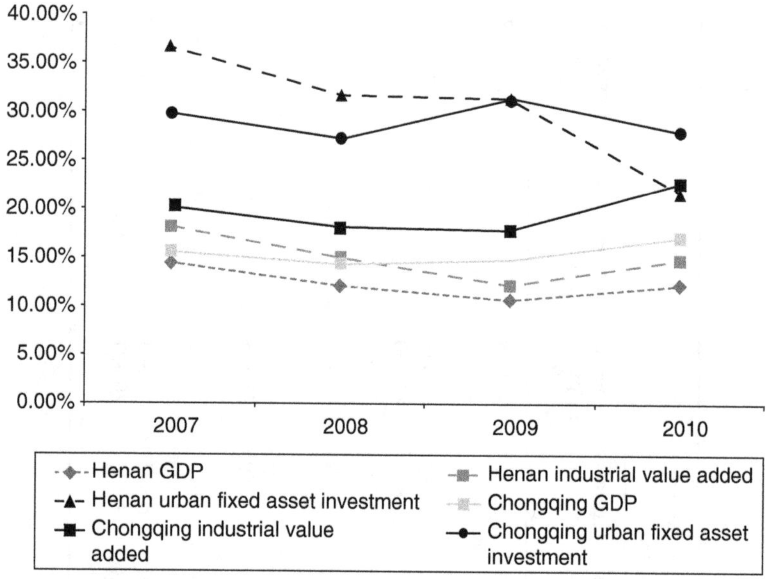

Figure 6.2 A comparison of GDP and investment growth rates between Chongqing and Henan: 2007–10
Source: HSB and CSB, 2007–10.

Largely as a result of the piling up of these new investment projects, both Chongqing and Henan, similar to other inland provinces and regions, posted remarkable double-digit GDP growth figures (Figure 6.2). Chongqing's GDP growth rate in 2010 was as high as 17.1 per cent. In both regions, the rapid GDP growth can be largely explained by even faster growth of industrial output – 23 per cent for Chongqing and 15 per cent for Henan in 2010. In turn, the skyrocketing of GDP and manufacturing growth has been enabled by massive urban fixed asset investments. Although it has shown some sign of decline from 2009 to 2010, GDP growth was still as high as 22 per cent for Henan and 28 per cent for Chongqing.

Apparently, post-crisis restructuring has demonstrated the escalation of Chinese local governments' insatiable appetite for growth and investment. Such extreme pro-business policies already generated overproduction, global imbalance, and dangerous consequences for land, labour, and environment even before the crisis (Tao et al. 2010). Most of the relocated firms have been hosted in newly constructed or expanded industrial parks or economic development zones. This has led to a new 'great leap forward', in the building of more, larger, and better industrial parks for manufacturers. For example, Henan Province alone has established more than 200 industrial parks, and in 2010, these parks had a fixed asset investment in the amount of 533.1 billion Yuan.[7] Some 'new land enclosure movements' have already been revealed behind the proliferation of new industrial parks and zones in the name of industrial transformation upgrading (cf. Hsing 2010), reminiscent of the 'zone fever' in the middle of the 1990s (Cartier 2001).

In order to ensure that enterprises settle in the industrial parks within their jurisdictions, localities must spend significant financial resources on basic infrastructure, including land, road, water, and electricity. This is clearly demonstrated by the massive size of Foxconn's proliferating industrial parks and the enormous costs shouldered by local governments to meet Foxconn's demand for land, infrastructure and facilities. The regional bidding wars for mobile investments were made possible in the first place by China's enduring 'socialist' land-tenure system, making land a perfect vehicle to achieve aggressive local developmentalism at the expense of farmers (Hsing 2010; Lin 2009; Lin and Ho 2005). This system offers local governments the vantage point from which to exploit their lucrative, simultaneous roles as land-owner, regulator, planner, and developer, capturing windfalls from land conversion and development, typically at the expense of farmers. This is further assisted by the half-reformed, state-controlled bank system. While the land tenure system offers rudimentary protection against the extremes of deprivation, it exposes farmers especially to the arbitrary power of local officials, which creates a tidal wave of land grabs, rural grievances and social unrest affecting the lives of tens of millions of households (Hsing 2010; Lin 2009; Peck and Zhang 2013).

Unsurprisingly, the 'bidding wars' have also led to the piling up of fixed asset investment in most inland regions. In Chongqing, for example, fixed asset investment had been increasing approximately 30 per cent per annum from 2007 to 2010 (CSB 2011). Although it only contains approximately 2 per cent of China's total population, Chongqing's total value of projects under construction in 2009 reached 2 trillion Yuan and was still rising. Even more impressive, Henan Province's urban fixed asset investment has been increasing at a speed exceeding 30 per cent in the past eight years and reached 1.4 trillion Yuan in 2010 (HSB 2010). Unquestionably, the massive investments have added tremendous financial burden to local governments. The debt of local governments in China at provincial, prefecture and county levels increased from less than 2 trillion Yuan in 2008 to 7 trillion Yuan in 2009, and by the end of 2010 it stood at 10.7 trillion Yuan, a figure that exceeded the year's revenue of 8.3 trillion Yuan (Wen et al. 2011: 26). A total of 46.4 per cent of the local debt, almost 5 trillion Yuan, was built up from over 10,000 local government financing platform companies, financing vehicles set up by local authorities. Since approximately 80 per cent of the debt is in the form of bank loans, it poses a potential risk to China's banking system in the form of bad debts. Entering into 2012, the Chinese economy started to languish, both exports and industrial output slowed sharply and stocks of unsold goods piled up (Wassener 2012). This time, a mountain of debt left behind by the 2008 stimulus package significantly reduced Beijing's ability to re-stimulate the economy, and the low hanging fruit of infrastructure investment was already plucked in the previous round of construction spree (Dunford and Yeung 2011). With overseas orders plummeting and costs rising, many exporters in southern China are looking to the domestic market to make up the shortfall in sales (Jacob and Zhou 2012). Significant increases in domestic, especially household, consumption, however, can hardly be forthcoming, because any serious effort to elevate domestic consumption would entail political reforms of some sort. CCP leaders have paid lip service to promoting domestic consumption for more than a decade, but overall economic policies still favour investment and exports, which have become increasingly unsustainable when the gap between overproduction and under-consumption keeps expanding (*The Economist* 2012; cf. Chapter 9 of this volume).

Certainly, this costly 'long march inland' of the world factory has offered China temporary relief from pressures generated by the global economic crisis and a rectification of the accumulated domestic imbalance due to the coast-dominated, migrant-dependent economic structure. However, it is still highly questionable whether such industrial re-territorialization will ultimately provide a payback to offset the exorbitant costs, and put China on an ideal path of industrial innovation and upgrading. The ultimate rebalancing of the Chinese economy requires a significant reduction of heavy reliance on gross investment and exports for growth by enriching ordinary Chinese workers, thereby boosting domestic private consumption (Chapter 9 of this volume). This is unlikely to happen in the near future, however, as cheap labour is still the predominant 'competitive advantage' of the 'world factory' (see Chapter 7 of this volume, for the social effects of China's cheap labour policy). Even after rebalancing, the vast majority of China's industrial workers are still employed by Foxconn-style, low-skill, low-margin, low-wage, high-volume factories; although with re-territorialization many of them may be able to stay much closer to their parents and family members. Such a change has not brought about much advancement in workers standard-of-living, skill-base, and job prospects. As Foxconn-style EMS firms and other Chinese manufacturers compete fiercely on small profit margins, their production is based on a massive build-up of modern manufacturing techniques and Taylorist work organization using assembly lines with strict segmentation and control of low-skilled operators (Duhigg and Barboza 2012). Although the final products shipped out of Foxconn are fashionable and technologically sophisticated items such as iPhone and iPad, the proportion of value-added in China is minimal. For an iPhone4 with a market price of US$600 dollars, only US$6.54 is captured by Foxconn, the assembler (Barboza 2010b). Even with the most generous state subsidies, Foxconn-style manufacturers operating at a very thin profit margin are highly dependent on their dominant clients such as Apple and highly vulnerable to market volatility and cost increases. 'We've concluded [that] Hon Hai's labour-intensive model is not sustainable', says Mr. Wang at iSuppli Research, 'Though it can keep hiring 800,000 to one million workers, the problem is [that] these workers can't keep working like screws in an inhuman system' (Barboza 2010b: B1).

Conclusion

Thus far China has survived the global economic crisis and posted remarkable figures of GDP and export growth. In this chapter I argue that the massive scale 'spatial fix' of China's labour-intensive manufacturing industries through a great long march inland has made an important contribution to lowering production costs and to making made-in-China products competitive in the present global market. This inland-oriented industrial relocation and expansion have certainly been driven by a universal capital logic, constantly searching for sites with cheaper labour and resources. It is occurring in a context where China in general has become the most promising site to absorb over-accumulated capital from the global capitalist core. But this transnational spatial fix has not taken place automatically or homogeneously in China.

I argue that China's ongoing post-crisis 'spatial fix' has been tied to inward-investment 'bidding wars' between local states, enabled by China's unique territorial logic independent of the logic of capital accumulation. China with its continental land size has always been characterized by immense regional economic disparity. As a result, the Chinese state has recurrently sought to rebalance the national economy and to reduce the gap between coastal and inland areas, especially since the late 1990s. More importantly, China's territorial logic is a unique construct rooted in its history of state socialism and planned economy, characterized by a distinctive trajectory of state formation and state-society relation. Although the economy has become increasingly market-oriented, economic restructuring is still largely coordinated and controlled by the authoritarian, hierarchical party-state. The Leninist *nomenklatura* cadre management system, supplemented by the enduring omnipresent economic influence of the Chinese Community Party, has given rise to a strong local state entrepreneurialism driven by local leaders' career concerns and an ideology of GDPism. The resultant inter-jurisdictional competition has degenerated into race-to-the-bottom 'bidding wars' for mobile investments with deleterious consequences.

When losers in the previous round of sub-national politico-economic competition have battled each other to attract mobile investments – typically labour-intensive manufacturing firms in the coastal regions stressed by heightened production costs and declining global demand – inland-oriented industrial relocation and expansion have greatly accelerated.

Undeniably, the redrawing of China's industrial map has contributed to a temporary rebalancing of its economy. This rebalancing should also benefit the distressed world economy, thanks to a stable Chinese economy making a sizable contribution to global economic growth.

However, the result of this rebalancing, through a massive dedication of public resources to attracting and retaining mobile investment and easing China's shortage of domestic demand and export dependence, is limited. The seemingly successful spatial fix led by the regional bidding war is fragile and may be short-lived. Active local entrepreneurialism and fierce regional 'bidding wars' are shallow and reactive rather than proactive responses that in the long-term may even worsen rather than ease structural contradictions such as the lack of innovation and domestic consumption and the inherent weakness of an authoritarian regime without institutionalized systems of checks and balances. The very competitiveness of made-in-China products is still built largely on China's cheap labour, but this is contradictory to the goal of raising domestic private consumption, which would require a significant wage increase for China's massive low-skilled factory workers (Chapter 9 of this volume). The predominant low skill, low value-added form of production characterized by Taylorist work segmentation and control is unlikely to be a promising solution to the upgrading of labour skills and augmenting of labour compensations (cf. Chapter 5 of this volume). The meagre rise of labour wages may be far from enough to offset output expansion, and China's approach to crisis management may be further worsening its chronic domestic problem of over-production and in turn the global imbalance (Hung 2008).

The deep and comprehensive subsidies offered to producers, enabled by the overwhelming power of the party-state, have frequently been at the cost of land-dispossessed farmers and tremendous fiscal burden by local states through a risky mechanism of debt financing. Therefore, policy competition for mobile investment also raises the delicate question of how to ensure the accountability of government officials, particularly those involved in the negotiation of discretionary incentive packages. It points out the need for governments to be able to monitor their own use of incentives, and the necessity for co-operation among governments, horizontally and vertically, to ensure that competition for mobile investments does not lead to a beggar-thy-neighbour situation or a zero-sum game. Unfortunately, these questions are unlikely to be answered in any satisfactory manner under China's present single-party authoritarian political framework.

Notes

1. In 2009 average manufacturing labour cost per person in China was US$0.81 an hour, or just 2.7 per cent of the cost of their American counterparts, even after a 17 per cent increase in cost over the year before (*The Economist* 2010: 59).

2. Foreign reserve data are available from the homepage of China's State Administration of Foreign Exchange. Available online: http://www.safe.gov.cn/wps/portal/sy/tjsj_lnwhcb. (accessed: 15 October 2012).
3. 'Profile of Hon Hai Precision Industry'. Available online: http://money.cnn.com/magazines/fortune/global500/2012/snapshots/11204.html. (accessed: 1 May 2013).
4. Data from Foxconn's homepage is available online: http://www.foxconn.com.cn/groupprofile.html. (accessed: 1 May 2013).
5. The world of EMS is invisible to consumers. But it is a huge industry with just a handful of companies like Foxconn, Flextronics, and Jabil Circuit, manufacturing and assembling for all the global electronics brands. They compete fiercely on price to earn very slim profit margins.
6. Interview with government officials of Zhengzhou Economic and Technology Development Zone in charge of the Foxconn project, 24 May 2011.
7. Interview with officials from Henan Committee of Development and Reform, Zhengzhou, 20 May 2011.

References

Arrighi, G. (1994) *The Long Twentieth Century*, London & New York: Verso.

Arrighi, G. (2007) *Adam Smith in Beijing*, London & New York: Verso.

Atasoy, Y. (2009) *Islam's Marriage with Neoliberalism,* London & New York: Palgrave Macmillan.

Barboza, D. (2009) 'People's Republic of Exports: Slump Is Making China an Even Stronger Trade Presence', *The New York Times*, 14 October, B1, B8.

Barboza, D. (2010a) 'Electronics Maker Promises Review After Suicides', *The New York Times, 26* May, B1.

Barboza, D. (2010b) 'Supply Chain for Iphone Highlights Costs In China', *The New York Times*, 5 July, B1.

Cai, F., D. Wang, and Y. Qu (2009) 'Flying Geese within Borders: How China Sustains Its Labor Intensive Industries?' [中国产业升级的大国雁阵模型分析], *Economic Studies* [经济研究究] 9: 4–14.

Cai, F., D. Wang, and H. Zhang (2010) 'Employment Effectiveness of China's Economic Stimulus Package', *China & World Economy* 18: 33–46.

Cartier, C. (2001) ' "Zone Fever", the Arable Land Debate, and Real Estate Speculation: China's Evolving Land Use Regime and Its Geographical Contradictions', *Journal of Contemporary China* 10: 445–69.

Chan, K. W. (2009) 'The Chinese *Hukou* System at 50', *Eurasian Geography and Economics* 50: 197–221.

Chan, K. W. (2010a) 'The Global Financial Crisis and Migrant Workers in China: There Is No Future as a Labourer; Returning to the Village Has No Meaning', *International Journal of Urban and Regional Research* 34: 659–77.

Chan, K. W. (2010b) 'A China Paradox: Migrant Labor Shortage Amidst Rural Labor Supply Abundance', *Eurasian Geography and Economics* 51: 513–30.

Chen, Z. (2010) 'How Did Henan Grab Foxconn [河南如何抢到富士康?]' *Southern China Weekends* [南方周末], 23 August. Available online: http://www.infzm.com/content/49066. (accessed: 25 August 2011).

Chongqing Statistical Bureau (CSB) (various years) *Chongqing National Economic and Social Development Statistical Report*. Available online: http://jtj.cq.gov.cn/html/tjsj/tjgb/.(accessed: 1 May 2013).

Duhigg, C. and D. Barboza (2012) 'In China, Human Costs Are Built into an iPad', *New York Times*, 25 January. Available online: http://www.nytimes.com/2012/01/26/business/ieconomy-apples-ipad-and-the-human-costs-for-workers-in-china.html?pagewanted=all. (accessed: 25 September 2012).

Dunford, M. and G. Yeung (2011) 'Towards Global Convergence: Asian Dynamism and the Elusive Quest for Western Growth from the Fordist to the Financial Crisis and After', *European Urban and Regional Studies* 18(1): 22–46.

The Economist (2010) 'The Next China: China's Labor Market', 31 July: 58–60.

The Economist (2012) 'Special Report: China's economy?' 26 May: 3–20.

Fan, C. (2008) *China on the Move: Migration, the State, and the Household*, London & New York: Routledge.

Hamlin, K. (2010) 'China Reaching a Lewis Turning Point as Inflation Overtakes Low-Cost Labor', *Bloomberg News*. Available online: http://www.bloomberg.com/apps/news?pid=20601068&sid=aOEXbd09bloM. (accessed: 25 September 2012).

Harney, A. (2010) 'The China Export Edge', *The Wall Street Journal*, March 30: 15.

Harvey, D. (2001) *Spaces of Capital: Towards a Critical Geography*, New York: Routledge.

Harvey, D. (2003) *The New Imperialism*, Oxford: Oxford University Press.

Harvey, D. (2005) *A Brief History of Neoliberalism*, Oxford: Oxford University Press.

He, C. and J. Wang (2012) 'Regional and Sectoral Differences in the Spatial Restructuring of Chinese Manufacturing Industries during the Post-WTO period', *GeoJournal* 77: 361–81.

Henan Statistical Bureau (HSB) (various years) *Henan Province National Economic and Social Development Statistical Report*. Available online: http://www.ha.stats.gov.cn/hntj/tjfw/tjgb/qstjgb/A06200701index_1.htm. (accessed: 1 May 2013).

Henderson, J. and K. Nadvi (2011) 'Greater China, the Challenges of Global Production Networks and the Dynamics of Transformation', *Global Networks* 11: 285–97.

Hong Kong Trade Development Council (HKTDC) (2011) *China's New, Improved World Electronics Factory: Moving Up the Value Chain in the 12th Five-year Program*. 5 May. Hong Kong: HKTDC.

Hsing, Y. (2010) *The Great Urban Transformation: Politics of Land and Property in China*, Oxford: Oxford University Press.

Huang, P. C. C. (2011) 'Chongqing: Equitable Development Driven by a "Third Hand"?' *Modern China* 37: 569–622.

Hung, H. (2008) 'Rise of China and the Global Overaccumulation Crisis', *Review of International Political Economy* 15: 149–79.

Jacob, R. and P. Zhou (2012) 'Industry Turns Attention to Domestic Market'. Available online: http://www.ftchinese.com/archiver/2012-05-24. (accessed: 25 September 2012).

Jessop, B. (1990) *State Theory: Putting the Capitalist State in Its Place*, Cambridge: Polity.

Jessop, B. (2006) 'Spatial Fixes, Temporal Fixes and Spatio-Temporal Fixes', in Noel Castree and Derek Gregory (eds) *David Harvey: A Critical Reader*, Malden, MA, USA; Oxford, UK: Wiley-Blackwell.

Li, H. and L.A. Zhou (2005) 'Political Turnover and Economic Performance: the Incentive Role of Personnel Control in China', *Journal of Public Economics* 89: 1743–62.

Landry, F. P. (2008) *Decentralized Authoritarianism in China: The Communist Party's Control of Local Elites in the Post-Mao Era*, New York: Cambridge University Press.

Lardy, N. (2011) *Sustaining China's Economic Growth after the Global Financial Crisis,* Peterson Washington, DC: Institute for International Economics.

Liao, H. F. and R. Chan (2011) 'Industrial Relocation of Hong Kong Manufacturing Firms: Towards an Expanding Industrial Space beyond the Pearl River Delta', *GeoJournal* 76: 623–39.

Lin, G. C. S. (2009) *Developing China: Land, Politics, and Social Conditions,* London: Routledge.

Lin, G. and S. Ho (2005) 'The State, Land system, and Land Development Processes in Contemporary China', *Annals of the Association of American Geographers* 95: 411–36.

Liu, H. and S. Dong (2010) 'Behind the Scene of Foxconn's Settlement in Zhengzhou' [富士康落户郑州幕后], *China Business* [中国经营报], 30 October.

Liu, W., C. W. Pannell, and H. Liu (2009) 'The Global Economic Crisis and China's Foreign Trade', *Eurasian Geography and Economics* 50: 497–512.

Luk, L. (2013) 'Foxconn Steps Up Hiring as Apple Readies Next IPhone', *Wall Street Journal,* April 16. Available online: http://online.wsj.com/article/SB10001424127887323346304578423930445976530.html. (accessed: 4 May 2013).

Ministry of Industry and Information Technology (MIIT) (2011) 'Industrial Economy Performance Report in China 2010'. Available online: http://finance.people.com.cn/GB/14004435.html. (accessed: 25 September, 2012).

National Statistical Bureau (NSB) (2010) *China National Economic and Social Development Statistical Report 2009.* Available online: http://www.stats.gov.cn/tjgb/ndtjgb/qgndtjgb/t20100225_402622945.htm. (accessed: 1 May 2013).

National Statistical Bureau (NSB) (2011) *China National Economic and Social Development Statistical Report 2010.* Available online: http://www.stats.gov.cn/tjgb/ndtjgb/qgndtjgb/t20110228_402705692.htm. (accessed: 1 May 2013).

National Statistical Bureau (NSB) (2012) *China National Economic and Social Development Statistical Report 2011.* Available online: http://www.stats.gov.cn/tjgb/ndtjgb/qgndtjgb/t20120222_402786440.htm. (accessed: 1 May 2013).

National Statistical Bureau (NSB) (2013) *China National Economic and Social Development Statistical Report 2012.* Available online: http://www.stats.gov.cn/tjgb/ndtjgb/qgndtjgb/t20130221_402874525.htm. (accessed: 1 May 2013).

Naughton, B. (2007) *The Chinese Economy: Transitions and Growth,* Cambridge, MA: MIT Press.

Peck, J. and J. Zhang, (2013)'A Variety of Capitalism . . . with Chinese Characteristics?' *Journal of Economic Geography* 13 (3): 357–96.

Pei, M. (2006) *China's Trapped Transition: The Limits of Developmental Autocracy,* Cambridge: Harvard University Press.

Ren, J. (2010) 'China's Central Region Foreign Investment Promotion Plan Promulgated' [中国中部地区外商投资促进规划出台], 30 April. Available online: http://politics.people.com.cn/GB/1026/11496087.html. (accessed: 25 September 2012).

Rodriguez-Pose, A. and G. Arbix (2001) 'Strategies of Waste: Bidding Wars in the Brazilian Automotive Sector', *International Journal of Urban and Regional Research* 25: 134–54.

Tao, R., F. Su, M. Liu, and G. Cao, (2010) 'Land Leasing and Local Public Finance in China's Regional Development: Evidence from Prefecture-Level Cities', *Urban Studies* 47: 2217–36.

Thomas, K. P. (2000) *Competing for Capital: Europe and North America in a Global Era,* Washington DC: Georgetown University Press.

Tilly, C. (1990) *Coercion, Capital, and European States, AD 990–1990,* Cambridge, Massachusetts & Oxford, UK: Basil Blackwell.

Wang, M. (2010) 'Benefiting from the Trend of Labour Shortage, Rural Migrant Workers' Employment Prospect Gets Brighter' [受益劳动力短缺趋势, 农民工就业形势前景乐观], *China Social Science* [中国社会科学报], 11 February.

Wang, H., R. P. Appelbaum, F. Degiuli, and N. Lichtenstein (2009) 'China's New Labour Contract Law: Is China Moving towards Increased Power for Workers?' *Third World Quarterly* 30(3): 485–501.

Wang, J. and L. Mei (2009) 'Dynamics of Labour-Intensive Clusters in China: Relying Exclusively on Labour Costs or Cultivating Innovation?' *International Institute for Labor Studies,* Discussion Paper 195, Geneva.

Wang, J., X. Tong, L. Mei, Y. Zhang, T. Lin, J. Wang, P. Li, W. Tan, F. Pan, P. Chen, M. Ma, Q. Chen, H. Liu, J. Song, B. Ren, P. Li, J. Jiang, and L. Zhu (2010) *Beyond Industrial Clusters: Theoretical Exploration of Industrial Clusters in China,* Beijing: Science Press (in Chinese).

Wassener, B. (2012) 'Manufacturing in China Slows Further', *New York Times,* August 23. Available online: http://www.nytimes.com/2012/08/24/business/global/manufacturing-in-china-continues-to-slow.html?ref=china. (accessed: 12 October 2012).

Wei, H. (2010) *Regional Policy in China: Review and Outlook* [中国区域政策—评价与展望], Beijing: Economic Management Press [经济管理出版社].

Wen, X., Y. Zhang, N. Yu, and L. Tian (2011) 'The Life Threatening Debts through Government Financing Platform Companies' [命悬平台贷款], *New Century* [新世纪] 26–35, 13 June.

Workman, D. (2010) 'China trade statistics', 22 February. Available online: http://import-export.suite101.com/article.cfm/china-trade-statistics-2009. (accessed: 13 July 2010).

World Bank (2013) *China 2030: Building a Modern, Harmonious, and Creative Society,* Washington DC: World Bank.

Xu, C. (2011) 'The Fundamental Institutions of China's Reforms and Development', *Journal of Economic Literature* 49: 1076–151.

Xu, X. (2011) 'Riverside Area of Chongqing as a Model Zone of Industrial Relocation Receiver Has Been Approved, National Third and Second in the West' [渝沿江承接产业转移示范区获批 全国第三西部第二], 6 February. Available online: http://www.cq.xinhuanet.com/2011-02/06/content_22008516.htm. (accessed: 16 July 2011).

Yang, C. (2012) 'Restructuring the Export-Oriented Industrialization in the Pearl River Delta, China: Institutional Evolution and Emerging Tension', *Applied Geography* 32: 143–57.

Yao, S. and J. Zhang (2011) 'Chinese Economy 2010: Post Crisis Development', Briefing Series – Issue 67. China Policy Institute, School of Contemporary Chinese Studies, The University of Nottingham. Available online: http://www.nottingham.ac.uk/cpi/documents/briefings/briefing-67-china-economic-review-2010.pdf. (accessed: 1 May 2013).

Zhou, Y., Y. Sun, Y. H. D. Wei, and G. C. S. Lin (2011) 'De-centering "Spatial Fix" – Patterns of Territorialization and Regional Technological Dynamism of ICT Hubs in China', *Journal of Economic Geography* 11: 119–50.

7
Childcare Policy Reform and Women's Labour Force Participation in China

Xinying Hu

Social policy, specifically childcare policy, was historically a critical tool in promoting women's labour market participation during the 'socialist' regime in China. Prior to economic reforms, the central government clearly specified the welfare function of childcare in relieving women's household burden, thereby enabling women to more equally participate in production work under the socialist planned economy. However, in the last 30 years, as China has restructured the centrally planned socialist economy of the 1949–79 period towards a more export-oriented industrial economy (Arrighi 2007: 351–78), the Chinese government has been more interested in national growth than relieving women from household responsibilities and promoting welfare support for working women with children. As the economy has gradually opened up to market competition, social reproduction expenditures, especially those in state-owned enterprises, have been considered as costs to market efficiency and economic growth by the government. Therefore, public funding for childcare has been restrained and even cut. And cost-cutting in the domain of social reproduction greatly affects women's employment opportunities, as women are still the primary caregivers in Chinese society.

It is my contention that changes in the public provision of social services in China, including childcare, have consequences not only for children's

Portions of this chapter were previously published in Xinying Hu, *China's New Underclass: Paid Domestic Labour*, London & New York: Routledge (2011). I acknowledge the publisher for permission to reprint. Throughout the writing of this chapter, I have received numerous comments, feedback, and revisions from Dr. Yıldız Atasoy, editor of this book. I am grateful to her for all of these, and particularly grateful for her insightful revisions in regard to the mixed system of China's social welfare regime and the Township and Village Enterprises. I am also thankful for the anonymous reviewer's comments on the role of childcare policy and data use.

development and parents' childrearing responsibilities, but also for the labour market participation of women with children and the associated relations of gender equity. This chapter provides a historical analysis of the transition in China's childcare policy over the last 30 years in order to show how a shift in state ideology in social-policy making has affected women's labour participation in the Chinese society.[1] The primary data sources used in this analysis are publicly available published government policy documents regarding childcare and early childhood education, as well as media source materials. These documents made it possible to gain a general picture of the changes in dominant policy perspective. I will attempt to demonstrate that the rising privatization of childcare in recent years has added to women's unpaid household responsibilities, increased the pressure on women in balancing paid work and family life, and caused a shift away from the 'socialist' norm of achieving a more equal gender-based family relationship where women and men can both be workers as well as caregivers. I will also briefly examine the direction of childcare policy after the 2007–8 global economic crisis, as China's economic growth trajectory took a turn away from a focus on urban coastal areas towards rural inland areas (Chapter 6 of this volume). My goal here is to assess the degree to which current government policy alternatives will undermine the 'caring state' (Daly 2001: 45) characteristics of the previous socialist regime which promised greater gender equality in labour markets.

Childcare policy and gender equality in the pre-economic reform era

In classical Marxism the primary determining factor in history is the production and reproduction of immediate life, which includes the production of the means of existence and the production of human beings themselves (Engels [1884] 2010). In general, women's involvement in both aspects of productivity is central to a Marxist understanding of the historically specific dynamics of gender equity in society. Nonetheless, classical Marxist thought often views women's participation in public production as a symbol of women's 'liberation'. Engels ([1884] 2010) argued that women's liberation can only be achieved by bringing the whole female sex back into public industry and making them independent wage earners. In order to do this, women have to be freed from private housework and domestic duties (including childcare). These tasks are then to be collectivitized (Engels [1884] 2010: 105). A Marxist perspective on women's liberation, consistent with a Marxist concept of gender equality, was widely introduced in the socialist economies of the former Soviet Union and most former socialist-bloc Eastern European countries, as well as China. In China, during the 'socialist' era (from 1949 to the late 1970s), government childcare policy was conceived in terms of encouraging women's participation in productive activity – a policy framework that linked the relation of women to both production and reproduction.

After the new China was founded in 1949 as a centrally planned 'socialist' economy, the Chinese government was explicitly committed to redefining and improving the position of women in both society and the family. The *Common Program*, China's basic law of development adopted by the People's Political Consultative Conference in 1949, stated in Article 6 that:

> The People's Republic of China shall abolish the feudal system, which holds women in bondage. Women shall enjoy equal rights with men in political, economic, cultural, educational and social life. Freedom of marriage for men and women shall be put into effect.
>
> (www.chinalawedu.com 27 April 2006)

In 1950, the government passed the *Marriage Law* to safeguard women's rights and interests in relation to family life. This law was the first to guarantee women's equal status. To facilitate and encourage women's participation in public life, the government established policies directed towards the building of a comprehensive childcare system based on state welfare spending and direct investment in childcare services. As argued by Zeng (2006: 11), early childhood education in China at that time was considered an important aspect of both childcare and children's development, with an emphasis on promoting women's employment in the productive sphere.

The governments' programme of early childhood education and care (ECEC) during the socialist era consisted of three types, all conceived within the highly complex social provisioning system (or welfare, broadly understood) of socialist China. These were work-unit childcare centres, public childcare centres run by education departments, and collectively owned childcare centres and nursery facilities. Of these three types, only collectively owned childcare centres pertained to rural farmers living in villages, and rural areas were organized into collectives known as brigades and production teams. These three types of childcare programmes were all incorporated into the overall state-welfare effort based on the work-unit system in urban areas and the collective system in rural areas. In general, work-unit based childcare programmes targeted urban working populations with non-agricultural household registration. Farming families in rural areas belonged to rural collectives and were not covered within the work-unit welfare system. Although not the norm, there were also work-unit based daycares in rural townships and counties. For example, those individuals in rural areas who worked for government organizations or in state-owned enterprises (SOEs) also held non-agricultural registration and were covered within the work-unit based childcare system. Given these historical complexities in China's social-welfare system, it is important to emphasize from the outset that this chapter's main focus is on changes in childcare-service policies as they apply to urban areas, unless stated otherwise.

In the early years after 1949, state-owned and collectively owned productive enterprises were widely established in China in an effort to build a socialist national economy (The Chinese University of Hong Kong 2009). In 1951, the government introduced *Regulations on Labour Insurance* to provide various welfare benefits based on the principle of lifetime employment in SOEs (The Chinese University of Hong Kong 2009). In the *Regulations on Labour Insurance* established in 1953, the State Council of the central government again clarified that enterprises should open collective labour insurance entities such as nurseries and childcare centres. The Regulations specified the social welfare nature of childcare centres and nurseries for working-class people (Hu 2011: 65). In addition to workers, nearly all urban residents, including government employees and those in related sectors such as education and healthcare were included in such a work-unit based welfare system. Every urban resident was allocated a work unit and thus entitled to various benefits, including public childcare service (The Chinese University of Hong Kong 2009; Zhang 2009). The childcare centres run by work units in state-run enterprises and organizations were the pillar of the Chinese ECEC system, particularly in urban industrial areas. These were also closely tied to state-welfare provisioning for working parents.

National ECEC policies and regulations in China were promoted by the Ministry of Education. Early in 1952, the Ministry of Education issued *Regulations for Kindergartens*,[2] which specified that the childcare centres' task was to

> educate pre-schoolers and make their body and mind fully developed before entering elementary schools; at the same time, lighten mothers' burdens towards children in order for them to have time to participate in political life, production labour and cultural educational activities.
>
> (China National Society of Early Childhood Education 1999: 49)

In addition to developing a national policy on early child development, the ministry and its affiliates in provincial and municipal-level governments also provided direct funding for childcare facilities. Along with the work-unit childcare centres, the kindergartens run by the educational department were the other main governmental source providing quality childcare service and early education, largely to working parents in urban areas. In China, this type of kindergarten is known as a 'public kindergarten', as it is theoretically owned by the 'people' and funded directly by government budget. The Ministry of Education also has branches in rural areas, operating kindergartens through local county-level education bureaus. However, these kindergartens run by rural county-level local governments only take children who hold a non-agricultural household registration. Farmers' children are not entitled to attend, and must instead attend collectively owned kindergartens.

Collectively owned childcare centres and nursery facilities constitute the third type of ECEC organization in China, operating in both urban and rural areas. In 1955 the Chinese government proposed a 'walk on two legs' policy, which aimed to institute a system for the development of both public and collective childcare facilities in the country (He and Jiang 2007: 4). Of the 'two legs', one referred to public facilities directly funded by the government budget, and the other referred to collectively owned facilities. In urban areas, collectively owned centres were governed by neighbourhood committees, representing the lowest level of government organization inside a city. In rural areas, the centres were run by collectives composed of village production teams and brigades. Collectively run centres were not seen as typical public facilities since they were owned by village and city neighbourhood committee collectives which autonomously managed their own expenditures. Nevertheless, these childcare centres were still considered to be public owned because they were governed collectively either by neighbourhood committees or rural collectives, not by private individuals or for-profit organizations.

In sum, all three types of childcare centres in China were publicly owned; their differences lie within the differentiated meaning of public ownership in terms of their sources of funding – that is, between the 'big public', referring to a representation of the public by the government, and the 'small public', referring to a representation of the public by collectives and SOEs. Work-unit based facilities were operated and funded by the 'small public' of the work units; public facilities were operated by the 'big public' through education departments and funded directly by the government budget. Collectively owned kindergartens were operated and funded by the 'small public' of neighbourhood committees and rural collectives.

Private childcare centres existed for only a short time after 1949. The Chinese government gradually transformed these centres formerly owned by organizations such as churches and private individuals, into one of the types of publicly owned childcare centres described above (Tang and Ju 2010: 175). The transformation process was completed in 1954 (Tang and Ju 2010: 175) and no purely private childcare centres continued to exist within the socialist ownership structure of China, a structure emphasizing collective, public provision of social welfare. This system began to change after the gradual implementation of economic reform programmes beginning in the late 1970s.

The childcare system consisting of these three types of childcare and nursery facilities greatly supported women's labour force participation, enabling women with children to balance work and family/childcare responsibilities. Although it is not possible to assess the extent to which the public-childcare system assured greater gender equity in China, government welfare policy had important gender-equity consequences. It took into account parents' concerns with the number of available childcare spaces, the operating hours of childcare centres, their geographic location and proximity to workplaces, and their financial cost. I will now provide a breakdown of these various aspects in order to explain the policy advantages.

In providing childcare spaces, many new centres were opened. From 1949 to 1978, the number of childcare facilities and children in these facilities increased dramatically. In 1949, there were only 1300 childcare facilities and 13,000 children enrolled in them. Thirty years later, by 1978, the total number of childcare facilities and children enrolled in them had risen to 164,000 and 7,878,000 respectively (China National Society of Early Childhood Education 2003: 33; Tang 2005: 39).

The centres' hours of operation were quite convenient for parents. Day care centres which took preschool children from three to seven years olds typically operated for 8–12 hours per day. There were no winter and summer breaks. All pertinent rules and regulations were clearly specified in the *Regulations for Kindergartens* outlined in 1952 (China National Society of Early Childhood Education 1999: 50). Nurseries took care of zero to three years olds. Maternity leave was for 56 days at the time. After maternity leave, working mothers could send their infants to nurseries. In order to support working parents, nurseries provided nurses to look after sick children. Consequently, when a child became sick, the mother did not have to ask for a leave (Liu, Zhang, and Li 2008: 32).

Geographically, work-unit based childcare centres were opened in workplaces and workers' residential areas. Neighbourhood childcare centres were tailored to the needs of neighbourhood residents, and, for the most part, were conveniently located within walking distance of children's homes and parents' workplaces.

Most significantly, childcare centres provided high-quality service at very low cost. For example, according to the information gathered from an interview I conducted with a parent in November 2007 (Hu 2011),[3] the key programmes run by educational departments cost no more on average than one sixth of a couple's monthly income at the end of the 1960s. Work-unit childcare facilities charged only a small fee to cover the cost of care and three meals per day (Sidel 1972: 37). Such services were seen as part of government welfare provisioning for workers. For low-income families, neighbourhood childcare centres provided services at a rate of nearly half that of public childcare centres. Other specific measures were adopted to ensure that working-class families could afford childcare. For example, if a family experienced financial difficulty in paying for nursing and teaching fees, their children's expenses could be either deducted or waived by the childcare centres (He and Jiang 2007: 4).

Children of working mothers were given priority for admission. This was specified in Article 20, Chapter 5 of the *Regulations for Kindergartens* in 1952

(China National Society of Early Childhood Education 1999: 53). However, there is no available statistical data to confirm the actual implementation of this policy. In fact, I have found an overall lack of statistical data on all of the policy issues for the entire era of the 1950s. Therefore, I rely on policy papers and government documents from my primary sources of information.

From these policy initiatives we can surmise that during the centrally planned economy period, Chinese governments viewed childcare as a tool to promote women's labour force participation and thus made tremendous efforts to improve women's status in society. Unfortunately, there is no publicly available data with which to assess the actual role of public childcare facilities in enabling women with children to enter into the agricultural and industrial productive labour force. Still, the employment rate of women was profoundly improved. For example, according to my calculations based on *China Labour and Wage Statistics Data 1949 and 1985* (National Bureau of Statistics of China 1987) in urban areas, between 1949 and 1978, the proportion of female employees in state-owned work units increased four-fold, from 7.5 per cent to 28.5 per cent. At the same time, the number of female employees in state-owned work units increased 5.5 times from 1949 to 1957, and 35 times from 1949 to 1978. In rural areas, before 1949, almost no women participated in agricultural production outside the home.[4] However, after the 1957 collectivization of agriculture, 60–70 per cent of all women between the labour-age of 16 and 60 participated in collective agricultural work. During the Great Leap Forward movement (1958–60), nearly 90 per cent of rural women participated in agricultural production teams and brigades, labouring in crop planting and harvesting. In following years, the portion of rural women participating in rural agricultural work remained high; by 1964, 95 per cent of rural women between the age of 16 and 60 were involved in agricultural production within rural collectives (Huang 1990: 62).

The work-unit based welfare system instituted during this period is based on a dual-earner/state carer model. In this model, women were encouraged to participate in public production as equals to men while the state provided various forms of public childcare through centres and nurseries. Women's needs as mothers and workers were fully acknowledged; the state aimed to provide women with employment-based income security and social services while at the same time children could receive education and professional care. This system helped women achieve greater gender equality in labour market participation by providing access to universal support from the state.

The model lasted until the end of 1970s when the government began to institute export-oriented national economic development reforms and restructure the work-unit based welfare system. Since the 1980s, and especially since the mid-1990s, childcare services have gradually shifted from an emphasis on the public/collective provisioning of welfare under a nationally planned 'socialist' economy to more individualized social protection through private savings (Peng and Wong 2010: 665). Privatized childcare financing, pricing, and delivery have tended to produce negative consequences for social equality, including gender equality (Hu 2011: 69). However, it is important to note that SOEs and government institutions continue to play a role in China's public welfare provisioning.

Economic policy change, welfare restructuring, and childcare policy

Although some have viewed China's economic growth since the 1980s as an outcome of policy adherence to a neoliberal model of economic development (Kwong 2006), the Chinese government has been highly selective in restructuring the economy, proceeding at a slow pace in privatizing public sector economic entities and key social programmes (Arrighi 2007: 356; Stiglitz 2002: 125–6; also see Chapter 9 of this volume). Although implemented gradually, China's economic reforms have had consequences for public welfare provisioning.

Work-unit based provisioning of welfare has increasingly been considered a burden, especially the viability of SOEs within the increasingly competitive relations of China's new economy. Therefore, the privatization of childcare services has been encouraged, which means that individual citizens and the private sector must play a bigger role in early childhood education and care. Women's interests in balancing work and childcare responsibilities do not play a significant role any longer in the government's consideration of ECEC policy. This is evident when one considers that greater emphasis has been placed on the early education of children rather than public childcare-service provisioning (Du and Dong, 2010). ECEC has being reformulated as early childhood education (ECE), which is currently delivered via a mixed bag of collective, state-owned and private entities. Childcare is no longer assumed to be part of public welfare provisioning and has increasingly been viewed as the responsibility of individual families/parents.

'Social Forces' and national childcare policy transformation

The running of schools by 'social forces' has been part of the national education policy in China since 1982. The Constitution of 1982 stipulated that the state encourage collective economic entities, state-owned enterprises and institutions, and other social forces, to operate various educational facilities (Tang and Ju 2010: 176). The notion of 'social forces' is used as a synonym for privatization in China. Social forces include non-government entities, private organizations, and individuals. Early childhood education as part of the general education of children also fits into this policy. In May 1984, the Ministry of Education forwarded the *Interim Procedures of Beijing Municipality on Running Schools by Social Forces*, emphasizing that various schools run by social forces are important constituents of the socialist education system in China (China National Society of Early Childhood Education 1999: 201). The ministry also confirmed that the state policy of encouraging the operation of schools by social forces would be long term (China National Society of Early Childhood Education 1999: 202). In 1988, the Ministry of Education (then named State Committee of Education) passed the *Interim Regulations on the Management of Running Schools by Social Forces* and reaffirmed the policy for developing private education (China National Society of Early Childhood Education 1999: 281). In following years, government policy strongly supported the privatization of education. In 1997, the State Council adopted the *Regulations of Running Schools by Social Forces*, which once again actively encouraged and strongly supported the privatization of education. Adopted in December 2002, the *Law of the People's Republic of China on Promotion of Privately-run Schools* formally established the legal status of private education in Chinese educational history (Tang and Ju 2010: 176).

The government also urged individual citizens and households to take responsibility for ECE. Individuals' role in ECE has been affirmed in the *Opinions on Enterprise Kindergartens* (1995), formulated by relevant national ministries and committees.[5] This document declares that 'early childhood education concerns tens of thousands of families, and the state, collectives, enterprises and public institutions, as well as individual citizens all bear responsibility and obligation to the cause of its development' (China National Society of Early Childhood Education 1999: 409). This is the first time that the government emphasized the individuals' duty to ECE. It is in stark contrast to the 1952 *Regulations for Kindergartens* which stresses the need to lighten the burden of mothers in order for them to participate in economic production.

ECE is now been viewed as a right of children and has been incorporated into the child development plan in the 1990s. In 1992 the State Council promoted the *China National Program for Child Development of 1990s*. Investing in children's education became the focus of this programme, while the care of children is not even mentioned. Rianne Mahon's (2011: 81) study on (child) care policy of the OECD and the World Bank has argued that under neoliberalism, childcare policy has been inclined to ignore women's needs and become 'less (as) a matter of equality between men and women than (as) a means for levelling the playing field between boys and girls with regard to access to education'. China's reformulation of early childhood development discourse reflects a similar tendency. In changing the direction of childcare policy to early childhood education, social policy-makers in China are not motivated by a normative commitment to greater equality but by considerations relating to the role of education in long-term economic growth. The Chinese government has also reduced its role in providing direct funding for early childhood education (Zhang 2009) and public childcare services, while encouraging 'social forces' to become increasingly involved in these areas.

Government input in ECE has been considerably limited in recent years despite China's rapid economic development (Zhang 2009). For example, from 1997 to 2004 total government appropriations for education in general more than doubled, increasing from 186.3 billion Yuan to 446.6 billion Yuan. However, only 1.2 per cent of this funding was used for early childhood education on a yearly basis (Zhang 2009: 16). In 2005, there was only a 0.1 per cent increase in government funding for ECE, amounting to 1.3 per cent of educational spending.

Along with limited state financial support, there has been an overall reduction in public childcare services. Public kindergartens run by the Department of Education have seen their funding resources privatized and the number of work-unit childcare centres and collectively owned centres has declined.

The decrease of public childcare services

The privatization of funding resources has occurred in public childcare centres operated by educational departments at all levels from the central government to local government. Budget cuts are the usual way in which these childcare centres are pressured to change, resulting in an increase in parents' share of funding for care services. Some local governments have not only stopped financing kindergartens but required parents to absorb the cost of childcare by charging them rental fees for facilities. Parents are also financially responsible for a variety of different fees, including nursing, teaching, and sometimes sponsorship fees,[6] or compulsory donations. This kind of transformed public kindergarten is gradually increasing. In Shanghai, China's largest city, the first new kindergarten of this type appeared in 1993. In less than ten years, by 2001, there were 93 transformed childcare centres, accounting for 11.70 per cent of total public-owned childcare centres (Huang 2005: 36).

With the exception of funding privatization, the number and share of kindergartens run by education departments in ECE remains almost unchanged, while there is only a slight decrease in the enrolment of children. Data from China Education Statistics for the period between 2005 and 2010 shows that the number of kindergartens run by education departments had only decreased from 4400 to 4299, with children's enrolment having dropped slightly from 29.3 per cent to 23.5 per cent (Ministry of Education of the People's Republic of China 2005–10).

Compared to the forced transformation of kindergartens operated by education departments, the number of work-unit childcare centres, especially SOE childcare centres, is rapidly dropping (Hu 2011: 71–2). On the one hand, economic reform has removed the welfare function of SOEs, and, on the other, under competitive pressures, those SOEs demonstrating poor economic efficiency have either become bankrupt, or turned into joint-venture and shareholding companies with foreign competitors and private businesses. Since 1995, with the acceleration of economic reforms, Chinese SOEs having joint venture agreements with foreign or national private companies have been encouraged to hand over their welfare facilities, such as kindergartens, schools, and hospitals created during the planned economy, to local municipal governments. The previously mentioned *Opinions on SOE Kindergartens* (1995) organized by relevant national ministries and committees, has explicitly urged enterprises, particularly those on the edge of bankruptcy, to hand over their nurseries and childcare centres to local governments. According to Du's study (2008), the transformation of ownership process is ongoing. Since no subsidies for enterprises were guaranteed from the central government, not every enterprise is willing to comply. Some childcare facilities have been shut down due to enterprise bankruptcies and restructuring; others which have survived have either been subcontracted to private organizations or individuals to reduce financial costs or handed over to local municipal governments to become publicly funded kindergartens (Du 2008: 2). The general trend in both urban and rural areas is a decline in the number of state-owned enterprise nurseries and childcare centres. From 1997 to 2010, the percentage of work-unit based childcare facilities in total numbers decreased from 11.2 per cent to 2.5 per cent, while the percentage of enrolments dropped from 11.7 per cent to 3.7 per cent (Ministry of Education of the People's Republic of China 1997–2010). In urban areas from 2001 to 2010, the number of work-unit based childcare facilities dropped from 7221 to 2912. The enrolment rate of children declined from 31.5 per cent to 11.5 per cent during the same period (Ministry of Education of the People's Republic of China 2001–10).

Collectively owned kindergartens have also been decreasing in numbers in both urban and rural areas, largely because of a decline in collective funding. In urban areas, other factors in recent years, such as city development plans related to urban reconstruction and relocation of residents have also contributed to the declining number of collectively owned kindergartens. The number of neighbourhood childcare centres in urban China has decreased every year over the last decade. There is no national statistical data available for neighbourhood kindergartens before 2005. Between 2001 and 2004, the number of public childcare centres operated by neighbourhoods and education departments was combined with national education statistics. After 2005, national statistics have separated these centres into two categories. Data show that the number of neighbourhood childcare centres has been declining year after year. From 2005 to 2010, the number of neighbourhood childcare facilities has decreased from 4571 to 2345, reduced by almost half. The children's enrolment rate has continuously dropped from 12.1 per cent to 7.1 per cent during the same five-year period (Ministry of Education of the People's Republic of China 2005–10).

Similar to the fate of neighbourhood childcare programmes in urban areas, the number of collectively owned childcare centres in the countryside have also been declining. During the 1980s, the Township and Village Enterprises (TVEs) began to become primary rural initiatives in the promotion of economic growth in China. By relaxing institutional barriers to spatial mobility, a 1984 regulation further facilitated the movement of farmers out of farming into work in nearby towns in the TVEs which were collectively owned by all inhabitants of the town or village (Arrighi 2007: 361–5). However, the TVEs had a vaguely defined and complicated ownership structure involving a variety of local arrangements. In the late 1990s attempts were made to transform TVEs into 'some form of shareholding or purely private ownership' (Arrighi 2007: 363). These enterprises do not have to provide social-welfare benefits to their workers, including childcare. Generally speaking, with the transformation of the rural collective system, the number of collectively run kindergartens and kindergarten enrolments in rural areas fell from 10,700 and 1.6 million, respectively, in 1995, to 5000 and 0.9 million, respectively, in 2003 (Du and Dong 2010: 8).

In general, the old types of kindergartens created in the centrally planned economy era which served women's interests – including employment and care responsibilities – have been shrinking in number and increasingly funded by parents. The only winners in providing childcare services after the economic reforms are the private-for-profit childcare centres. This is parallel with the government's support of privatized education.

The rise of private childcare centres

Private childcare centres have mushroomed after the economic reforms (Hu 2011: 73–5). By the end of 1991, there were 12,091 privately owned childcare centres, accounting for 7.35 per cent of total childcare centres in China (Tang and Ju 2010: 176). By 1996, the number of privately owned childcare centres reached 24,466, double the number five years previously, accounting for 13.06 per cent of total childcare centres throughout China (Tang and Ju 2010: 176). From 1997 to 2010, the number of private childcare centres and children enrolled in them has increased dramatically. In 2010, the number of private kindergartens accounted for 68 per cent of total kindergartens in China, and enrolment in private kindergartens accounted for 47 per cent of all children enrolled in kindergartens (Ministry of Education of the People's Republic of China 1997–2010).

These changes have resulted in the loss of the former welfare function of childcare centres in reconciling work and care responsibilities, with important implications for gender equity. The government's downloading of childcare responsibilities onto individual families has also caused many problems associated with accessibility and affordability of childcare services, with the attendant negative impact on women's employment (Figure 7.1).

Figure 7.1 Number of kindergartens operated by work units and the private sector in China, 1997–2010
Source: Ministry of Education of the People's Republic of China (1997–2010) *China Education Statistics*.

The influence of childcare-policy changes on women's employment and gender equality

The most significant issue arising from childcare policy changes has been the financial costs imposed on parents. Mandatory donation fees, also known as sponsorship fees, as well as teaching and nursing fees, in addition to talent-class fees, usually exceed the average family income and have now become a financial burden for many families. In 2001, the Ministry of Education conducted a survey concerning early childhood education childcare in 14 provinces and cities[7] throughout China. In total, 2352 parents, 420 childcare centres, and 588 community leaders participated in questionnaire interviews. Several childcare centres in Beijing were also investigated (Wang 2002: 4). The survey indicated that 36 per cent of childcare centres charge sponsorship fees, ranging from ¥100 to ¥10,000 per year (Wang 2002: 5). In Beijing, some childcare centres charge sponsorship fees as high as ¥30,000 per year (Liu, Zhang, and Li 2008: 71; Wang 2002: 5). As noted earlier, parents' share of funding has increased significantly following government budget cuts. Sponsorship fees have now become the main funding source for public childcare service providers. Based on a 2007 survey of 14 kindergartens and 927 families in Beijing and Shanghai by the Women's Studies Institute of China, the average monthly childcare fees charged by various childcare centres in Beijing – in addition to sponsorship fees – can be broken down as follows: public-owned kindergartens run by education departments, ¥600–1000; work-unit kindergartens, ¥600–700; neighbourhood kindergartens, ¥500–600; and private centres, ¥1300–2800 (He and Jiang 2007: 5). The minimum ¥600 monthly charge could be very burdensome given the minimum legal salary rate was only ¥730 per month in Beijing in 2007. Of the 927 families surveyed, only 14.4 per cent of parents felt that childcare fees were affordable (He and Jiang 2007: 5).

Most private childcare centres are custom-designed for high income families (Hu 2011: 73). Using 'superior' education as a selling point, private centres organize a variety of 'educational' programmes with high tuition fees. These programmes typically include talent classes in piano, dancing, and bilingual language lessons (English and Chinese) that the old traditional public kindergartens do not offer. For example, in Beijing, well-known private kindergartens charged 30–35 thousand Yuan a year in 2005, which included various programme fees and childcare expenses, almost 10,000 Yuan more than the best-known public kindergartens (Zhang 2009: 12). Increased costs have prevented average and low-income families from gaining access to affordable, quality childcare centres.

In addition to financial costs, the decreasing number of programmes and services in publicly funded kindergartens also presents a significant challenge to working mothers' needs (Hu 2011: 76). Services for children under three years old are extremely short. Under the 1989 *Regulations for Kindergartens* developed by the Ministry of Education, publicly subsidized childcare programmes would no longer cover children aged zero to two (Du and Dong 2010). Nurseries have now almost disappeared in state-owned work units and community childcare centres. Most of these centres only accept children over 2.5 years old. Without government policy support, these centres have no desire to open day nurseries for infants and toddlers. According to He and Jiang's 2007 study of 927 families surveyed in Beijing and Shanghai by the Women's Studies Institute of China, 24.8 per cent of them were unable to find a day nursery centre in Beijing for their children under the age of three. In the same survey, in Shanghai, 23.9 per cent of surveyed parents expressed the same concern of not being able to find a day nursery for their infants and toddlers (He and Jiang 2007: 5). And it is not just a problem of infant and toddler care. The situation for children three years and older is better only in large cities such as Beijing and Shanghai. For example, nearly 90 per cent of children aged three to seven are enrolled in kindergartens in these two cities (He and Jiang 2007: 5). However, according to data from China Education Statistics and Chinese Population and Employment data, the overall enrolment rate of children aged three to seven in kindergartens in the whole of China, including children in rural areas, was only 41.5 per cent in 2006 (Ministry of Education of the People's Republic of China 2007; National Bureau of Statistics of China 2008).

The hours of operation of daycare centres are also less than adequate, considering parent's work hours. Generally, daycare centres operate about ten hours a day, from 7:30–8:00 am till 16:00–17:00 pm. A typical work day in China is from 8:00 am to 17:00 pm. Taking commute-time into account, the work day is even longer. For parents' convenience, some childcare centres provide early drop-off and late pick-up service for a fee, but not every centre does so. This creates a conflict between work and childcare for parents. And it is usually the mother who has to take time off from work to drop-off and pick-up children. Many parents expect childcare centres to extend their service hours. Of 1200 surveyed parents in eight childcare centres in Beijing in 2005, 28 per cent expressed such a wish; furthermore, 41.6 per cent of them hoped childcare centres would provide boarding service for their children when a family member was sick at home. And 22.8 per cent of them still wished childcare centres would help to care for children who fell ill (Zhang 2006: 26 as cited in Liu, Zhang, and Li 2008: 71).

Due to the disappearance of work-unit and neighbourhood childcare centres, parents also often have to travel a further distance to seek childcare service. Some newly developed residential areas lack childcare facilities. According to an investigation of 73 new residential areas developed in Beijing from 1986 to 1995, only 151 childcare centres were built even though the original plans called for 179. Among the 151 built centres, about 20 per cent were not even used as childcare centres as they were either used for other purposes or set aside (Lu and Liu 2001).

Compared to the service provided to parents, especially working mothers, under the planned economy, it is obvious that current market-oriented childcare system reform has caused significant affordability, accessibility, and convenience problems. With the government's retreat from social service provisioning, the role of caregiving has fallen upon private caregivers and the market. The social policy model of dual-breadwinner/state-care under a planned economy has now become a dual-breadwinner/market or informal-care model.

As women are still considered the primary caregivers at home, less government support in social services has no doubt increased women's responsibilities. The government's expectation that families will pick up the slack has only intensified women's caregiving duties for children with minimal resources. Women's double workload has become even greater under such circumstances. Moreover, because of market competition, work pressure has increased in recent years. Even in government organizations and institutions, efficiency has become the standard by which an employee's work ethic and performance is judged. The downsizing of many organizations has only increased workload and overtime as well. *China Labour Statistical Yearbook 2011* data show that the labourers' average working time in urban areas has consistently surpassed the statutory 40 hours per week (Figure 7.2).

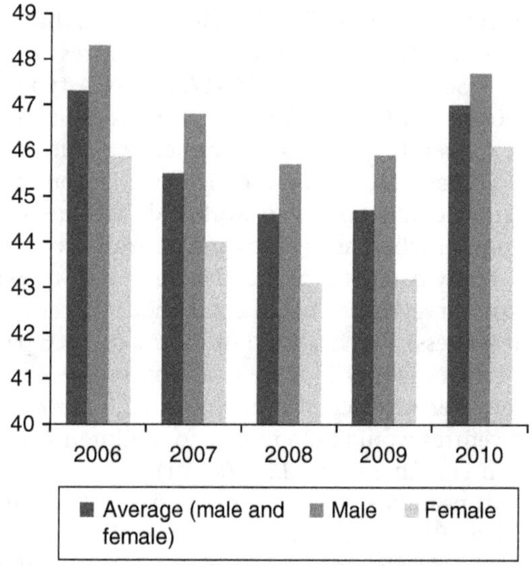

Figure 7.2 The average weekly working hours of urban employees by gender
Source: National Bureau of Statistics of China (2012) *China Labour Statistical Yearbook 2011*.

Facing double workload and intensified work pressure, the labour force participation rate of urban women with preschool-age children fell dramatically between 1990 and 2000, and more women have to reside with their parents in order to participate in the paid labour force (Maurer-Fazio et al. 2009 as cited in Du and Dong 2010: 10). Using data from the China Health and Nutrition Survey (CHNS), Du and Dong's study (2010) has established that to remain in the labour market women have become more dependent on informal care providers; and for socioeconomically disadvantaged women, this has meant increasing tension between income earning and child rearing.

Childcare policy in the aftermath of the economic crisis

The global economic crisis of 2008 has caused economic slowdown and recession in many countries in the global North and South; although China and other large emerging economies such as Brazil, India, and Turkey have not experienced significant interruptions in economic development (Introduction to this volume). Still, the economic growth rate in China has slowed considerably from a steady average of two-digit growth over the last 20 years to a single-digit increase in the last few years. The Chinese government set its GDP growth target at 7.5 per cent for 2012, compared to an 8 per cent goal in 2011 (*Global Times* 25 May 2012). The manufacturing sector has faced losses in the ongoing sluggish economic environment (*China Daily* 30 May 2012). As a result, increases in unemployment and decreases in income levels have occurred in the last few years in China, especially in relation to export-oriented industries in coastal regions. In early 2009 during the early stages of the economic crisis, 20–25 million migrant workers in China became unemployed from the coastal export-oriented industries due to numerous factory closures (Patel 2009: 34; Chapter 6 of this volume). Although China's economy rebounded very quickly between 2009 and 2010 (Chapter 6 of this volume), the slow economic growth in many developed countries and the continuing economic crisis in Europe may have negative implications for the future growth of, and employment in, China's export-manufacturing sector. For example, *The New York Times* (7 June 2012) reported that factory closures are continuing in export-dependent coastal provinces and construction sites are reducing work shifts from three a day to one in inland provinces due to economic distress.

The childcare-policy implications of recent changes in China's economy and labour-market conditions are not fully known. In the meantime, the government of China has implemented socially redistributive welfare policies to improve people's lives and extend social safety net coverage. In 2009, the central government arranged for 728.5 billion Yuan from the fiscal budget to be used for increased support of employment funding, which increased 66.7 per cent over 2008 levels. In addition, support for social housing increased by 171 per cent over 2008, along with improved support for healthcare and education (Ke 2009: 8). In the area of early childhood education (ECE), China announced the *Outline of China's National Plan for Medium and Long-term Education Reform and Development*, in July 2010. Article 6 of the plan clarifies the government's responsibilities in the provision of early child education services over the next decade for children aged three to six (Zhou 2011). While the plan identifies the government as taking the main leadership role, social-force participation is also encouraged (Zhou 2011). Social-force participation is likely to occur in both urban and rural areas, including less developed inland provinces, because local governments on each level are encouraged to incorporate early education services into city and town development plans. This means that private initiative continues to be seen as an important factor in early child education provision. Further, the central government appears to be committed to providing support through preferential terms, such as lowering the cost of land-use for building new private kindergartens and providing tax deductions for them (*People's Daily* 3 December 2010). The new plan also guarantees that private childcare centres will enjoy the same rights as public centres in terms of registration, qualification and teacher training (*People's Daily* 3 December 2010). Through these measures, the government is providing guidance and support for private kindergartens. Although there is a variety of local arrangements and practices involved in implementing the general policy of the central government, its encouragement of social-force participation in urban and rural areas will likely to play an important role in the development of ECE, particularly in rural areas.

After the release in 2010 of the *Outline of China's National Plan for Medium and Long-term Education Reform and Development*, the China State Council issued Document No. 41, entitled Issues Regarding Current Development of Early Childhood Education. This document addresses the importance of strengthening ECE in both rural and urban areas (Zhou 2011: 32). Most importantly, the central government initiated a three-year action plan which required each level of government, including provincial, municipal and national, to formulate its own three-year action plan for an ECE programme. This plan was supposed to outline the provision of support for various types of kindergarten, including state-run, collective and private programmes and services. The central government promised to increase the public funding budget for early childhood education over the next three years and improve special funding for children in the western and economically underdeveloped areas of the inland provinces, such as Gansu, Henan, and Shanxi (Zhou 2011). This special funding reflects the government's goal of improving living standards in these poor regions. Consistent with Zhang's analysis (Chapter 6 of this volume) of the movement of industrial capital into inland areas, the increasing investment in ECE also suggests a rebalancing of the Chinese government's development strategy between developed, coastal-urban regions and less developed, inland-rural areas. The central government has emphasized the promotion of ECE programmes in rural areas, and in 2010, invested 500 million Yuan in ten provinces in the western part of China to support the efforts of 61 rural counties in building ECE programmes (Zhou 2011: 34). Increased funding has also been promised for the future.

Government focus in urban areas is on providing affordable and accessible ECE programmes and services to all families, but especially to low-income families, including rural migrant workers and their children. This emphasis was conveyed in Document No. 41, which indicates that ECE programmes in urban areas should be established based on the actual population size of residents in cities, including the families of low-income and rural migrant workers. Overall in China, as Zhou's study (2011) contends, and 'for the first time in Chinese history, [Document No. 41] treats early childhood education development as an important measure for protecting and improving people's lives' (Zhou 2011: 32).

These measures indicate that the Chinese government is attempting to improve its contribution to the sphere of ECE. Increased public funding for ECE programmes in western areas, and economically less developed regions in particular suggests that the government has realized the importance of ECE for the well-being of children living in poverty. This realization is in tandem with the government's economic development objectives and the role of rural migrant labour in the promotion of economic development. As many rural workers migrate from less developed inland provinces to coastal regions to take up jobs, they tend to leave their children behind in their villages with their own older parents. Thus, the government's support for ECE may serve to facilitate children's access to early education programmes in rural areas and create equal educational opportunities for them. However, as mentioned earlier, ECE is only one aspect of the overall public provisioning of social welfare for parents with children; it appears that the growing emphasis placed on ECE is overshadowing childcare as the other component of service-provision for parents. Pre-school-like kindergarten programmes can not relieve working parents from their childcare responsibilities. Thus, many parents may have to resort to their own private means, including the unpaid work of their own family members (often non-working elderly parents) or the paid work of private caregivers. In addition to neglecting the issue of childcare, the focus on early childhood education is primarily a service provided to children aged three to six. For children under three years olds, education and care remain a family responsibility.

At the beginning of 2013, the Ministry of Education issued a notice concerning a pilot project of ECE for zero to three year olds in 14 selected areas. The project will study an ECE system that aims to provide not-for-profit service for children under three year olds, with input from public budget funding combined with funds from social forces and parents (*Beijing Youth Daily* 7 January 2013). The areas chosen for the project are in large cities only, principally Beijing and Shanghai. If successful, the project may be promoted nationwide. The pilot project is indicative of the fact that the evolution of a social policy regime in China is not unidirectional towards privatization only; it is a mixed system, which includes private ECE projects that can be expected to result in different implementation consequences for urban and rural areas. As long as early childhood education is not treated as a right or entitlement to be provided by the state free of charge, a mixed model can be expected to continue, thereby offloading the state's responsibility onto individual parents.

Regardless of the government's promise to increase the budget for early childhood education, EEC's share of total government appropriations for education remains low. In 2009, the percentage of total government appropriation for education from the GDP was 3.59 per cent, an increase of only 0.26 per cent over 2008 levels. And government appropriation for kindergartens out of total education appropriations accounted for only 1.36 per cent (Zhou 2011: 30).

Conclusion

This chapter has argued that a welfare system of social provisioning has important consequences for women's participation in the paid labour force that include the difficult challenges of balancing paid work and family relations, in addition to childcare responsibilities. The unfolding history of China's social policy regime is closely related to changes in its trajectory of economic growth. From the above analysis, we can see that the current policy emphasis on early education represents a shift from an earlier period when greater importance was given to childcare. The policy legacy of growth-oriented economic thinking which has prevailed in China for the last 30 years continues to leave its mark.

Since the economic crisis, there have been some positive changes in national ECE policy. Not-for-profit ECE programmes are expanding in urban areas, and in rural areas, with the shift of manufacturing to western inland provinces and the government's increasing support for ECE, children in the less developed provinces should benefit from ECE programmes in the near future. Nevertheless, if the programmes in both rural and urban areas do not combine childcare with education, women's labour force participation will continue to be negatively affected. Further, if the programmes are not free of charge or affordable in rural areas, parents will have to largely rely on the unpaid labour of their relatives to take care of children. Therefore, a national early childhood education and care (ECEC) policy which provides mandatory education and childcare services to all children should be widely promoted for in the pursuit of a more socially sustainable form of economic development and a social environment based on gender equality.

Notes

1. While childcare policy in both urban and rural areas will be discussed, the main focus is on urban areas. This is because the government's welfare system was concentrated in urban China due to the urban–rural divide which formed in the pre-economic reform era. In this divide, city residents enjoyed much more social welfare than rural residents.
2. In China, the term 'kindergarten' is used for a variety of different childcare institutions. Its use is different from that used in North America where the term refers specifically to the one-year education programme prior to grade one in elementary school.
3. As part of my PhD dissertation research project on domestic service and domestic workers in China, I interviewed ten parents. In this chapter I refer to information gathered from one of those interviews. For further details, see Hu, X.Y. (2011) *China's New Underclass: Paid Domestic Labour*, London & New York: Routledge.
4. Historically, the feet of women in China were bound – a tradition of female beauty which prevented them from working outside the home. Although officially banned in 1912, the tradition persisted in rural areas until the 1940s. As a result, rural women were expected to work exclusively in the home doing weaving and domestic housework rather than being involved in agricultural work in the fields.
5. These organizations include the National Education Committee, National Plan Committee, Ministry of Civil Affairs, Ministry of Housing and Urban-Rural Development, National Economy and Trade Committee, All-China Federation of Trade

Unions, and All-China Women's Federation. The National Education Committee was later renamed the Ministry of Education.

6. Sponsorship fees are similar to compulsory donations. They are a one-time fee frequently charged to parents whose children become enrolled in transformed public childcare centres. The fee is mandatory and far exceeds monthly nursing and teaching fees. The sponsorship fee is kindergarten specific. No government regulation has legalized it, but it continues to be popular in practice.
7. These 14 provinces and cities include Tianjin, Shenyang, Qingdao, Guangzhou, Sichuan Province, Guangxi Zhuang Autonomous Region, Guizhou, Gansu Province, Ningxia Hui Autonomous Region, Inner Mongolia Autonomous Region, Zhejiang Province, Anhui Province, Henan Province, and Hubei Province (Wang 2002).

References

Arrighi, G. (2007) *Adam Smith in Beijing*, London & New York: Verso.

Beijing Youth Daily (2013) 'Early Childhood Education of 0–3 Year Olds Included in Government Education Work', 7 January. A6.

China Daily (2012a) 'Sustainable Development "Facing Major Challenges"', 2 June. Available online: http://www.chinadaily.com.cn/china/2012-06/02/content_15453537.htm. (accessed: 5 June 2012).

China Daily (2012b) 'Stimulus Is Important Measure, Analysts Say', 30 May. Available online: http://www.chinadaily.com.cn/china/2012-05/28/content_15397958.htm. (accessed: 30 May 2012).

Chinalawedu.com (2006) 'The Common Program of the Chinese People's Political Consultative Conference 1949', 27 April. Available online: http://www.chinalawedu.com/news/15300/154/2006/4/xi6442364341172460029062-0.htm. (accessed: 18 February 2013).

China National Society of Early Childhood Education (1999) *Zhonghua Renmin Gongheguo Youer Jiaoyu Zhongyao Wenxian Huibian [The Collection of Important Literature on Early Child Education in the Chinese People's Republic of China]*, Beijing: Beijing Shifan Daxue Chubanshe [Beijing Normal University Press].

China National Society of Early Childhood Education (2003) *Bainian Zhongguo Youjiao [The Centenary Chinese Preschool Education]*, Beijing: Jiaoyu Kexue Chubanshe [Educational Science Publishing House].

The Chinese University of Hong Kong (2009) *A Literature Review of Family Policy in Four East Asian countries*. Available online: http://ebookbrowse.com/literature-review-of-family-policy-in-4-east-asian-societies-final-report-pdf-d86292377. (accessed: 3 May 2012).

Daly, M. (2001). 'Care Policies in Western Europe', in M. Daly (ed.) *Care Work: The Quest for Security*, Geneva 22, CHE: International Labour Office Bureau International du Travail.

Du, F.L. (2008) 'Jiating Jiegou, Ertong Kanhu yu Nuxing Laodongcanyu: Laizi Zhongguo Feinongcun de Zhengju [Family Structure, Child Care and Women's Labour Participation: The Evidence of Non-agricultural Areas in China]', in *Shijie Jingji Wenhui [World Economic Papers]* (2) (April): 1–12.

Du, F.L. and X.Y. Dong (2010) 'Women's Labour Force Participation and Childcare Choices in Urban China during the Economic Transition', Department of Economics Working Paper Number: 2010–04. Available online: http://ideas.repec.org/s/win/winwop.html. (accessed: 3 May 2012).

Engels, F. ([1884] 2010) *The Origin of the Family, Private Property and the State*, London & New York: Penguin Classics.

Global Times (2012) 'World Bank Lowered China GDP Forecast', 25 May. Available online: http://english.peopledaily.com.cn/90778/7826739.html. (accessed: 30 May 2012).

He, J.H. and Y.P. Jiang (2007) 'Cong Zhichi Funu Pingheng Jiating Gongzuo Shijiao Kan Zhongguo Tuoyou Zhengce ji Xianzhuang [On the Chinese Child-care Policy and Situation Today from the View of Supporting Women to Reconcile Work and Family Responsibilities]', *Xueqianjiaoyu Yanjiu [Studies in Preschool Education]* (8): 3–6, 29.

Hu, X.Y. (2011) *China's New Underclass: Paid Domestic Labour*, London & New York: Routledge.

Huang, J.J. (2005) 'Shanghai Zhuanzhi Youeryuan Guanlitizhi yu Banyuan Jizhi Xianzhuang Diaoyan Baogao [The Study Report of the Management System and Operation Status of Reformed Child Care Centres in Shanghai]', *Jiaoyu Fazhan Yanjiu [Exploring Education Development]* (6): 36–40.

Huang, X.Y. (1990) 'Zhongguo Dangdai Shehui Bianqian Zhong Nongcun Funu Jingji Shenfen de Zhuanhuan [Changes in the Economic Status of Rural Women in the Transformation of Modern Chinese Society]', *Shehuixue Yanjiu [Sociological Studies]* (6): 60–72.

Ke, J. (2009). 'Guoji Jinrong Weiji Fazhan Qushi ji Woguo de Yingdui zhi Ce [Development Trend of International Financial Crisis and Countermeasures of China]', *Beihua Daxue Xuebao [Journal of Beihua University (Social Sciences)]* 10(5): 4–9.

Kwong, P. (2006) 'China and the US Are Joined at the Hip: The Chinese Face of Neoliberalism', *Counterpunch*, 7–8 October.

Liu, B.H., Y.Y. Zhang, and Y.N. Li (2008) *Gongzuo he Jiating de Pingheng: Zhongguo de Wenti yu Zhengce Yanjiu Baogao [Reconciling Work and Family: Issues and Policies in China]*, Beijing: International Labour Office, ILO.

Lu, Y.J. and Z. Liu (2001) 'Beijing: Jiaoyu Cong lingsui Kaishi [Beijing: Education Starts from 0- Year-Old]', *Xinxi Ribao [Information Daily]*, 29 August, A03.

Mahon, R. (2011) 'Transnationalizing (Child) Care Policy: The OECD and the World Bank', in R. Mahon and F. Robinson (eds) *Feminist Ethics and Social Policy: Towards a New Global Political Economy of Care*, Vancouver & Toronto: UBC Press.

Maurer-Fazio, M., R. Connelly, L. Chen, and L. Tang (2009) 'Childcare, Eldercare and Labour Force Participation of Urban Women 1982–2000', paper presented at the ASSA conference, San Francisco, 3 January.

Ministry of Education of the People's Republic of China (1997–2010) 'China Education Statistics Data' (various years). Available online: http://www.moe.edu.cn/publicfiles/business/htmlfiles/moe/s6200/list.html. (accessed: 10 July 2012).

National Bureau of Statistics of China (1987) *China Labour and Wage Statistics Data 1949–1985*, Beijing: China Statistics Press.

National Bureau of Statistics of China (2008) *China Population and Employment Statistics Yearbook 2007*, Beijing: China Statistics Press.

National Bureau of Statistics of China (2012) *China Labour Statistical Yearbook 2011*, Beijing: China Statistics Press.

The New York Times (2012) 'China Cuts Lending Rates as Its Economic Growth Slows', 7 June. Available online: http://www.nytimes.com/2012/06/08/business/global/china-cuts-interest-rates.html. (accessed: 30 June 2012).

Patel, M. (2009) 'Economic Crisis and Children: An Overview for East Asia and the Pacific', Global *Social Policy*, September: 33–54.

Peng, I. and J. Wong (2010) 'East Asia', in F. G. Castles, S. Leibfried, J. Lewis, H. Obinger, and C. Pierson (eds) *The Oxford Handbook of the Welfare State*, Oxford: Oxford University Press.

People's Daily (2010) 'The Ministry of Education Interprets the 3-Year-Plan of Early Childhood Education, No More Difficulties for Entering Kindergartens', 3 December. Available online: http://www.gov.cn/jrzg/2010-12/03/content_1758599.htm. (accessed: 18 February 2013).

Sidel, R. (1972) *Women and Childcare in China: A First Hand Report*, New York: Hill & Wang.

Stiglitz, J. (2002) *Globalization and Its Discontents*, New York: Norton.

Tang, H.Y. and H.X. Ju (2010) 'Chengshi Minban Youeryuan de Fazhan Licheng yu Xianzhuang Fenxi [The Analysis of the Development and Current Situation of Private Kindergartens in Urban China]', *Liaoning Jiaoyu Xingzheng Xueyuan Xuebao [Journal of Liaoning Educational Administration Institution]* 3: 175–7.

Tang, S. (2005) 'Zhongtuo Nongcun Youerjiaoyu de Fazan yu Biange [The Development and Reform of Early Child Education in Rural China]', *Xueqianjiaoyu Yanjiu [The Study of Pre-school Education]* 6: 38–40.

Wang, H.M. (2002) 'Jiaqiang Youeryuan Shoufei Guanli Cujin Youjiao Shiye Jiankang Fazhan [Strengthen Childcare Fee Management and Improve the Healthy Development of ECE]', *Zaoqi Jiaoyu [Early Childhood Education]* 9: 4–7.

Zeng, X.D. (2006) 'Woguo Youerjiaoyu You Danwei Fuli Dao Duoyuanhua Gongji de Bianqian [The Financing Options fro Early Childhood Education: from Organization-run Welfare Model to Diversified Funding]', *Beijing Shifan Daxue Xuebao (Shehui Kexue) [Journal of Beijing Normal University (Social Sciences)]* (2): 11–6.

Zhang, Y. (2006) 'Beijing Shi Chengshi Youer Shenghuo Zhuangtai Diaocha Baogao [Investigation on Children's Life Status in Beijing]', *Xueqianjiaoyu Yanjiu [Studies in Preschool Education]* (2): 23–7.

Zhang, Y.X. (2009) 'A New Social Risk Facing the Most Disadvantaged Young Children in China: Changes in Child Care Policy and Practice and Their Impacts on Social Equality', Managing the Social Impacts of Change from a Risk Perspective Beijing Conference, April 2009. Available online: http://www.kent.ac.uk/scarr/events/beijingAb/Zhang%20yanxia.pdf. (accessed: 3 May 2012).

Zhou, X. (2011) 'Early Childhood Education Policy Development in China', *International Journal of Child Care and Education Policy*, 5(1): 29–39.

Part III

State Restructuring and Economic Development

8

Brazil: Neoliberal Restructuring or Rejuvenation of the Developmental State?

James M. Cypher

Contextualizing Brazil's contemporary political economy: How neoliberal?

The political economy of Brazil's developmental trajectory from the early 1990s to the present is the focus of this chapter. It attempts to contextualize the broad political and economic currents that have swept and spun Brazil in recent years. Brazil has become distinguished as a nation that has addressed poverty while achieving economic growth. How much of that growth is a function of redistributive policies that have had virtuous circle affects, and how much arises from an exogenous and serendipitous commodities export boom that boosted exports by 233 per cent (in US dollars) from 2002 to January 2010, and/or from other factors, remains an open question. Likewise, Brazil's recent growth has occurred in the context of extreme financial and fiscal repression. Brazil recorded the highest interest rates in the world in the early twenty-first century – ostensibly designed to thwart inflation. The fiscal budget is locked into a pattern of surplus maintenance – broken only by astute countercyclical policies during the downturn of 2008–09.

In accounting for a national trajectory it has become nearly *de rigor* in recent decades to attempt to fit an explanation of national performance into the general concepts of either *globalization* or *financialization* – or both. Regarding 'globalization', while Brazil has been impacted by rapid cross-border movements of highly liquid funds and by speculative attacks on

The author would like to thank his numerous colleagues at the Universidade Federal do Paraná, Brazil, for their assistance during prolonged periods of residence in 2010 and 2011. Particular support from João Basilio, Demian Castro, Mariano de Matos Macedo, Gabriel Porcile and Fábio Scatolin is gratefully acknowledged. Funding for this research was provided by US Fulbright Commission Research Grants in 2010 and 2011.

its currency, as well as by large-scale investments from transnational corporations (TNCs), it would be an error to interpret the dynamics of Brazil solely or largely through this neoliberal perspective. Those prioritizing such phenomena exhibit a tendency to represent the national state either as a mere receptor of international vectors – arising from greater cross-border flows of financial and productive capital – or as a state capable of pursuing only minor policies that are subordinate to the hegemonic objectives of transnational capital (Robinson 2008; Siscu, Paula, and Michel 2007). It is true that Brazil has been the largest Latin American recipient of Direct Foreign Investment (DFI) in recent years, but Brazil's noted receptivity to DFI greatly precedes the rise of the 'globalization' concept (Evans 1979). Considered in its broadest context, Eiti Sato (2011: 83) stated: 'Brazilian economic policy has been remarkably anti-globalization – [for example], against integration to global markets.' Brazil has maintained, at least since the 1930s, a low level of reliance on the external market. One conventional measure of international integration – the ratio of exports/GDP – registered a mere 9.1 per cent in 2000, rising thereafter to 14.4 per cent in 2004, but then falling to 9.6 per cent in 2010 (IPEA, various years). In contrast, Mexico's heavily integrated economy registered a 35 per cent export/GDP ratio in 2011 – 3.6 *times* Brazil's 2010 ratio.

William Tabb (2012: 37) defines *financialization* as 'the dominance of the financial industry over other economic activity [where] financial markets powerfully determine the state of the overall economy'. For complex, historically determined reasons Brazil's structure has evolved into a very particular conformation to this concept. Current *neo-developmentalist* policy (Bresser-Pereira 2012), discussed below, is setting a course that subtly challenges the entrenched national financial-rentier power bloc. Bruno et al. (2011) and Erber (2011: 39–45) have, respectively, developed the concepts of 'finance-led growth' and 'the convention of restrictive finance'. This *convention* is made up of the web of mutually supporting interests that constructed a 'sound money' hegemonic bloc consisting of the Central Bank, the Finance Ministry, the nationally owned private banks, and that slim wealthy slice of the populace regally sustained by exorbitant interest paid on the government's debt. As far as interest payments are concerned, it is important to note that from 1993 through 2005 the banks and other financial intermediaries received an equivalent of 7.2 per cent of GDP via their market transactions with the public debt and other forms of lending, while wealthy families and non-financial corporations received another 22.2 per cent of GDP (Bruno et. al. 2011: 740). For Bruno and his co-authors, finance-led growth is a structural situation wherein '*investment decisions are "subordinated", hierarchically, to the levels of real returns offered via the financial markets*' – meaning that the productive side of the economy is either subordinate to or essentially excluded by the interests of the convention of restrictive finance (Bruno et al. 2011: 736. Italics in original). These deeply entrenched interests serve to explain the resistance to the neo-developmentalist policies that have arisen since 2003, but they do not explain the creation of, or the growing momentum behind, the rival neo-developmentalist project (Erber 2011: 45–8). This chapter explains and evaluates this recently emerged project – which is not to be located in the broad realms of either globalization or financialization.

Furthermore, this chapter seeks to uncover central and relational causal factors of Brazil's political economy while eschewing universalist deductive methodologies that imply 'that [economic] laws can be applied independent of historical time and geographical place' (Hall and Ludwig 2010: 945). Neoclassical economics holds to such a method, while the analysis presented here utilizes methods of 'institutionalism' as pioneered by Thorstein Veblen and a structuralist analysis of Brazil as developed by Celso Furtado.

Veblen broke with neoclassical economics which assumed that static, market-dominated, national economies exhibited a stable tendency towards full-employment equilibrium, while the distribution of national output conformed to market-based principles that justly rewarded one-and-all in direct proportion to their efforts and productivity. Instead, he focused on the political economy of nations, emphasizing historically embedded path-dependent processes driven by forces of circular and cumulative causation (Cypher 2009; Hodgson 1996; Veblen [1915] 1954). That is, once established, a given social formation built around a project of accumulation tends to institutionalize self-sustaining processes (or 'path dependent' trajectories) – which include 'culture', ideology, and economically vested interest.

Veblen's concepts were contingent, dynamic, and evolutionary. They emerged in specifically determined, historically conditioned socio-economic contexts. Among his many concepts and theoretical formulations, several focused on the impediments to and possibilities for economic development – including the *catching-up* hypothesis (Cypher 2012). Economic change alters and undermines the extant social composition of power and wealth – which at any moment constitutes the institutionalized power structure. Hence, the privileged social strata dominating the hierarchy of power and those institutions (including ideology) that confer legitimacy on a particular institutional structure constitute a sometimes determinate, sometimes conditioning, influence on the process of social change. Change can be either regressive or progressive; it is not, according to Veblenian institutionalists, teleological (Bush 1994: 295). Although Veblen is not directly referenced in this chapter, his analytical framework and forms of dynamic analysis provide one of the methodological points of departure.

The second point of departure arises from the structuralist analysis of Celso Furtado, arguably Brazil's foremost economist. Furtado was trained in France, studying under François Perroux, who Furtado acknowledged exercised the greatest influence in the subsequent formulation of his views on Brazil's struggle to overcome underdevelopment (Vieira 2004: 31–2). Furtado shared Perroux's view that economic dynamics are derived primarily from the *sphere of production*, not exchange, and that the understanding of *power*, flowing through institutional structures, are the two fundamental building blocks of a structural socio-economic analysis (de Bernis 1994: 153–4).

Furtado broke with the universalist deductive methodology of neoclassical economics in his first international publication, arguing that orthodox economists in developing nations erroneously attempted to analyse underdevelopment while assuming that 'economic phenomena are the same everywhere' (Furtado 1958: 309). However, the situation called for a new, empirically based and historically contextualized theoretical formulation (and strategy) to overcome pervasive market failures (Furtado 1958: 315, 330, 336–7). Furtado shared Veblen's tendency to prioritize the dynamic and progressive impacts arising from the enhancement of technological capacities, while urging a national development policy that would centre on endogenous industrialization complimented by policies of income redistribution to ensure a mass-based internal market functioning as the driving force propelling balanced economic development (Bresser-Pereira 2007; da Motta e Albuquerque 2007; Furtado 1963). Furtado was of the view that underdevelopment could be overcome only through the construction of a state-led, *endogenous*, national development project, because

> the Latin American elite is socially and politically incapable of promoting the national interest. Only a strong state with broad popular support can implement the fiscal reform required to reduce the conspicuous consumption of the wealthy, redistribute income, and increase domestic savings, thus promoting a development that prioritizes social inclusion and the reduction of the historical dependence on foreign capital.
>
> (Rocha 2007: 135)

In short, Furtado anticipated most of the themes that define the recently articulated perspective of *neo-developmentalism* (Bresser-Pereira 2012; Siscu et al. 2007). The complementarities between Veblen's institutionalist political economy and the Latin American structuralist method have been well documented (Street 1967; Sunkel 1990). It is this coinciding body of analysis offered by Veblen and Furtado that underlies the methodological approach taken in this chapter.

The next section of this chapter, 'Neoliberalism's limits in Brazil', is concerned with a critical analysis of a universalist label, 'neoliberalism', commonly applied to Brazil since the 1990s. It explains why neoliberalism was never as firmly anchored in the socio-economic structure of Brazil as it was in much of Latin America. The controversial legacy of Lula's administration in terms of its growth with redistribution strategy is the subject of the following section. Here empirical material regarding wealth distribution is presented to ground a relatively abstract analysis in terms of Brazil's mode of production. Such an effort defines the given structural parameters of the Brazilian social formation and helps to highlight the underlying socio-economic structure, thereby serving to illuminate some of the causal conjunctions of the recent period. The following section is 'Structure of power and limits to redistribution', which focuses on complex questions regarding Brazil's structural bias towards income and wealth inequality. In the penultimate section 'The dynamics of state-capital relations under neoliberalism and beyond' are analysed, including the restructuring of the Federations of Brazilian capital, their think-tanks, their policy metamorphoses, and the evolution of new institutions designed to contest the hegemonic power of the *restrictive financial coalition*. The last section considered is the 'Discussion over *forms of the state* and the varieties of capitalism', which delves into a long-standing debate among those who have sought to label and encapsulate state formations in developing nations – here emphasizing the case of Brazil. All of the above sections then provide the foundation for 'Final comments' regarding the degree to which the strategy of *neo-developmentalism* has been consolidated and the scourge of neoliberalism expunged.

Neoliberalism's limits in Brazil

Since the Chicago School established a neoliberal beachhead in Chile in 1973 and quickly launched its offensive against the Southern Cone, Brazil has stood out from the rest of South America. Brazil was slow and hesitant to adopt neoliberalism in the late 1980s and early 1990s. As a consequence, neoliberalism was never as completely or firmly anchored in the socio-economic structure as in much of Latin America (Boschi 2011: 41–2). Boschi finds that the state-led institution matrix constructed in the Vargas era (1930–45 and 1951–54) successfully resisted/delayed the embedding of full neoliberalism. 'The social resistance [neoliberalism] faced served to preserve elements of [Brazil's] developmentalist past' (Boschi 2011: 41).

Brazil's 1994 *Real* Plan – engineered by then Finance Minister F.H. Cardoso – broke the forces of inertial inflation (contractual wages and other payments automatically rising, in nominal terms, as price levels rose) and subsequently allowed for Cardoso's election to two presidential terms (1994–2002). Thus, Cardoso achieved 'policy space' for change, yet he left a complex legacy both with regard to neoliberalism and inflation policy. While viewed by many as yet another neoliberal marionette, Cardoso navigated a difficult, slow, course which veered from a straight-line effort to reach one and all landing points on the Washington Consensus map (Mollo and Saad-Filho 2006: 101).

Still, as Boschi (2011: 46) noted, a 'nuclei of technical and bureaucratic excellence and [certain] development institutions' were maintained. Of note is Brazil's main development institution, the national development bank, BNDES. BNDES was created in the Vargas era in order to create and fund state-owned enterprises by vastly expanding the infrastructure.[1] Regions and some states also inaugurated important development banks. They worked in consort with BNDES and the federal government to implement a series of development plans. In the neoliberal period BNDES was charged with orchestrating the privatization (total or partial) of some state-owned firms. The privatizations were, compared to others in Latin America, relatively limited in scope and less-riddled with rent-seeking transfers of public wealth to private speculators. The fact that BNDES ably handled these privatizations – while itself escaping privatization – left largely intact a powerful state institution that would quickly become the anchor for the neo-developmentalist strategy beginning in 2003 (discussed below).

Still, as Barros de Castro (1994) has emphasized, Brazil's shallow encounter with neoliberalism undermined one of the most significant aspects of the state-led industrialization era that reigned unquestioned from the 1930s until the early 1980s. In order to contextualize this era it is important to emphasize that under state-led industrialization 'the Brazilian economy became endowed with a comparatively complete and modern industrial structure. For example, while the export of manufactured goods in 1967 accounted for only 10 per cent of total exports, it surpassed 50 per cent by 1981 and subsequently sustained this upward trajectory' (Barros de Castro 1994: 185). The slow and partial onset of neoliberalism began roughly in 1981 as Brazil's strategy of debt-led growth – total foreign debt rose 952 per cent between 1971 and 1982 – ended due the onset of global monetarism (which restricted international credits and jumped real interest rates) and the second oil shock, both occurring in 1979 (Baer 2001: 92). The price for imported oil rose by 100 per cent between 1979 and 1981, while the cost of refinancing international debt payments nearly doubled from 1979 to1981 (Baer 2001: 92–4). As a consequence, real GDP fell by 7.5 per cent from 1981 to 1983, while the crisis situation induced a realignment of policy (Baer 2001: 462). With the shift towards neoliberalism, the government ceased to recognize the long-standing entrepreneurial character of state enterprises. Under the pretext of an elusive austerity and structural adjustment, all state-owned companies (despite their markedly heterogeneous character) began to be used as instruments of macroeconomic regulation. With their autonomy drastically reduced and their financial base eroded by the state's fiscal crisis, they gradually fell prey to traditional politics (Barros de Castro 1994: 201).

By the early 1990s, as president Cardoso took power, the old growth convention, based in a rapid process of industrialization supported by and encompassing the private and public spheres, had been eclipsed. 'State enterprises, in particular, have lost their entrepreneurial drive and relative autonomy.... Gone are the sense of mission and loyalty that (mainly in the 1950s but still in the 1970s) had impelled state enterprises to spearhead economic development' (Barros de Castro 1994: 206). Thus, the fundamental and lasting change affecting Brazil's developmental capacities was the undermining of the institutionally specific, *tacit, entrepreneurial capabilities* of key state managers dispersed through the matrix of ministries, development banks and state-owned firms.

There can be no doubt that the attempt to drag Brazil into the neoliberal paradigm brought typically nefarious consequences, as Rodrik (2011; 1997) has more generally demonstrated. In the case of Brazil:

> Cardoso presented his government as the harbinger of 'modernisation' and the standard-bearer of the 'new globalised economy', and he set out to eliminate the 'distortions' arising from import substitution. However, Cardoso's policies had a severe impact on the balance of payments, local industry and employment. Imports climbed from US$27.8 billion in 1992 to US$43.1 billion in 1994 and US$75.7 billion in 1998. Over the same period, the trade balance shifted from a surplus of US$12.1 billion to a deficit of US$16.7 billion, and the current account moved from a surplus of US$6.1 billion to a deficit of US$33.4 billion. Between 1985 and 1998 consumer goods imports rose from US$376 million to US$8.2 billion, while the country's foreign travel deficit increased from US$441 million to US$4.1 billion.
>
> (Mollo and Saad-Filho 2006: 104–5)

Only eight years after the attempt to restructure Brazil's institutions a deep malaise had set in, partly due to the collateral impacts of the Mexican peso crisis of 1994–95, the Asian financial crisis of 1997, the Russian bond crisis of 1998, and Argentina's economic collapse beginning in 1999. All of these events brought speculative attacks on the *Real*, sequentially pushing Brazil into the reaches of the IFI's (international financial institutions) and their programmes of austerity/structural adjustment. But by 2002, neoliberalism was politically exhausted while the detrimental economic effects of the new policies had thrust broad sectors of the populace, and even elements of the elite, into opposition with the *status quo*. The brief time period wherein the neoliberal transition was attempted, the slowness of the process, the rising opposition to the process, and the considerable institutional inertial drag confronting the process all combined to leave Brazil with a considerable past-binding legacy of an attitudinal, conceptual, institutional, ideological, and structural nature. In no small part, this situation arose from the fact that state-led industrialization policies remained in place until the late 1980s (Vernengo 2011: 17).

The broad opening to foreign investment and trade brought trauma as well as mergers and buyouts of domestic firms. The new structural role for high interest rates – the highest in the world – induced many Brazilian family owned firms to sell out and become successful *rentiers* (Rocco 2007). Nonetheless, due to their historically established path, much of Brazilian capital fought back largely through more capital-intensive restructuring. Productivity in industry rose dramatically in the 1990s, massive layoffs ensued, but some Brazilian capital (unlike that in the Southern Cone) was able to realign itself with the brutal new reality, and wholesale deindustrialization was averted (IBRE 2010; Nassif 2008).[2] In addition, real wages rose by roughly 15 per cent in the mid-1990s, a flood of cheap consumer goods imports washed ashore and consumer credit became increasingly available (Mollo and Saad-Filho 2006: 104). In large part, these effects served to buoy domestic demand, and therefore the domestic market, since Brazil has never been an 'open' economy either in terms of exports or imports.

Most importantly, in terms of the legacy of the Cardoso administration, has been the focus on the rate of inflation. It is well known to economic historians that inflation is not a neutral, technical, concept. Some nations have a relatively high tolerance for inflation and some, such as Germany, have a zero tolerance. Brazil has had a difficult modern history with regard to inflation, with annual rates ranging between 65 and 416 per cent from 1981 to 1987, rising to well above 1000 per cent in every year but one between 1988 and 1994 (Baer 2001: 471). As a result of this cumulative experience, Brazil has undergone a structural shift from a nation with widespread indexing and an institutional predisposition towards (inertial) inflation to one where macroeconomic monetary policy, under Cardoso, Lula (2003–10) and Rousseff was unremittingly restrictive. To date, any effort to push Brazil's growth rates up to their potential has been undermined by econometric models that assume Brazil can only achieve a non-inflationary rate of growth of about 3.5 per cent (Cardim de Carvalho 2007: 31, 40). Above that limit the monetary brakes are engaged and growth is steadily undermined by state-sanctioned, but autonomous, monetary policy.

There are many objections to be made. Among the first is the widely recognized fact that economic growth can be sustained, even encouraged, when it is accompanied by relatively modest rates of inflation. In short, the idea of a trade-off between inflation and growth is false under conditions of mild or moderate inflation. Another major objection specific to Brazil is the fact that the econometric models used to predict inflation are based on parameters that are at least 15 years old. This means that the large increases in productivity achieved during the course of the 1990s in the industrial sector are not part of the potential growth capacity of the Brazilian economy. Thus, Brazil's development policy was held hostage to Central Bank projections of growth potential that are out of date. Furthermore, no econometric model can capture the nuances and complexities of the dynamics of the Brazilian socio-economic structure. Monetary policy has been guided by simplistic, reductionist concepts that fail to incorporate institutional evolution.

What is particularly of note is the fact that Brazil's distribution of income, by some measures but not by others (as discussed later), noticeably improved in the 1990s as those groups and sectors, particularly the vast and growing informal sector, excluded from the indexing schemes were no longer particular victims of institutionalized financial sector and monetary policy practices. That is, within the structure of inertial inflation, those social strata whose wages or payments were directly indexed to the inflation rate were largely protected against (dramatic) declines in their real income. Those operating in the informal sector, however, faced the full ravages of inflation – they had no market power and plenty of competitors. Thus, their humble services, however socially necessary, could not be re-priced quickly or easily, and their real incomes tended to fall dramatically.

Cardoso's legacy is more mixed and complex than some critics allege (Veltmeyer and Petras 2003). Anti-inflation policies improved the distribution of income (including for those in the informal sector) and real wages rose considerably. The neoliberal trade and tariff opening was much less dramatic and extensive than has been the case throughout Latin America. Deindustrialization, while significant in important areas, was averted. Most importantly, the attempts at broad institutional change and the dismantling of the state sector were subsequently halted or reversed in many areas. This was particularly noticeable at pivotal state institutions such as BNDES and Petrobras under Lula, and in the remarkable resurrection (in 2003) of a key development institution, the SUDENE (the Superintendency for the Development of the Northeast) originally inspired by Furtado (Cavalcante and Uderman 2009: 264). Likewise, from the outset of Lula's term and even before, and with increasing effectiveness, influential economists and state policy-makers began to make the case for the very antithesis of neoliberalism – that is, to advocate for a conscious and sustained effort by the state to construct new areas of national economic specialization, while offering a broad array of state support for strategic and priority areas. In brief, to promote for a policy that would reinvigorate Brazil's *state capacity* to conduct *Industrial Policy* (Kupfer 2003; Suzigan and Villela 1997).

Neoliberals have sought not merely profound structural changes but most especially the construction of an *irreversible* iron cage of policy rules. In Chile's case, even with a long period of consecutive rule under *Concertación* governments, not only have no reversals occurred, but the neoliberal project has been expanded in some respects while being *transformed* into an Export-Oriented (EO) project of accumulation based on the (assumed) dynamic impacts of Foreign Direct Investment (Leiva 2008: xxxv). Leiva terms this transformation 'the EO regime of accumulation', evoking the French Regulationist School 'in whose establishment and consolidation *both* neoliberal *and* neostructuralist ideas and policies play critical but different roles' (Leiva 2008: xxxv. Italics in original).[3] One of the most defining distinctions between structuralism, as pioneered especially by Furtado, and neostructuralism is the complete avoidance in the latter formulation of the conditioning themes of structural social, political and economic power. Development meant, for Furtado and his many followers, a structural change in these relations of power and they were therefore always placed at the epicentre of structuralist analysis.

With regard to neostructuralism in an Export Oriented (EO) regime of accumulation, state intervention is strictly limited to policies that support the growth of the export sector – including credits and technical assistance – while all remaining sectors are left to survive (if they can) in a neoliberal economic structure of unregulated market forces. Prioritizing the export sector means facilitating transnational corporations' unlimited access to exhaustible national mineral resources and to unregulated repatriation of profits from such activities, all based on the 'trickle-down' illusion that state policies advantageous to TNCs will be 'mutually beneficial', generating returns for the national economy. With some, minimal, cash transfers to the poorest of the poor to mitigate extreme deprivation (while encouraging their greater market participation whenever possible), the neostructural EO regime of accumulation remains, in essence, faithful to the neoliberal idea that a meritorious social order will emerge from a chaotic competitive struggle. It is this minimalist and constrained *double intervention* – to promote exports *and* to retain the smallest and most selective forms of income maintenance for the poor (forms of social coordination that will not in essence 'interfere' with a brutal, flexible, unregulated, labour market) – that defines neostructuralism: It constitutes a contradictory effort to embed the essential absence of social and economic public policies that defines neoliberalism, *but now with the trappings of a human face* (in terms of minimal 'pro-market' forms of social coordination) *within an economic structure* led by and subservient to the prerogatives of foreign capital.

Unlike other Latin American nations, Brazil's neoliberalism was more porous regarding both policy lapses and reverses, particularly in terms of its defence of national manufacturing capital. Nonetheless, the drive during the Cardoso era to open-up national manufacturing firms to international competition led many industrialists and their Federations of Industry to gradually withdraw support for Cardoso's project and to readily embrace the neo-developmentalist policies of the Lula administration (Doctor 2007). Since 2003 Brazil has introduced a variety of programmes and projects designed to delegate a crucial role to parastate firms, the state sector, and to incipient Industrial Policy. All of this has served to reinvigorate the BNDES and reintroduce planning both to stimulate national manufacturing capital and the export-oriented agribusiness sector.[4] This important aspect of the Lula-Rousseff era has been largely overlooked in the rush to condemn Lula for his indifference to MST's (Landless Rural Workers' Movement) efforts at redistributing unused agricultural lands owned by the traditional rural oligarchy and his loyalty to the most retrograde forms of monetary policy. Apparently, it has also been lost sight of in the haste to praise Lula for his support of social policies that have improved the distribution of income and lifted millions out of poverty. Brazil is now enjoying the effects of 'redistributive growth', a true novelty for Latin America, *and* the reasonable prospect of state-led policies strengthening the national industrial base while boosting the National Innovation System. Intended to embody an institutional structure designed to close a technological gap with the advance industrial nations, a National Innovation System *combines, coordinates and promotes* the research, design and innovation capabilities of the private and public sector, including national research laboratories, university science and technology facilities, and science-directed, grant-funding government agencies (Freeman 1995; Sharif 2006).

Brazil's dilemma arises from a fundamental dispute between fractions of capital. This entails the growing rivalry over national economic policy between (1) the 'neo-developmental' coalition and (2) the 'restrictive financial' coalition (Erber 2011): The former has introduced pro-labour, pro-poor policies of 'growth with redistribution' and industrial policies that involve new state-led initiatives to restructure the national industrial base (such as utilizing Petrobras as an agent to spearhead domestic industrial production in numerous 'downstream' activities including shipbuilding and many other metal-mechanic industries). The latter consists of banking corporations and other *rentier* owners of debt, (particularly the national debt, as noted in the introduction) which have adapted to and flourished under the high-interest, 'tight money' monetarist policies imposed by the Central Bank under president Cardoso (1995–2002), but continuing into 2011 under president Rousseff.

Erber (2011), Bruno et al. (2011) and Bresser-Pereira (2009) find that this restrictive financial coalition has been hegemonic, in Gramsci's use of the concept. This coalition brings together a web of interests that unites the state's macroeconomic policy-making financial entities with those of the private financial sector:

> [It] unites evermore the Central Bank with the private interests – the former seeks to maintain the stability of prices, with the later the profitability of the *status quo* that has been consolidated over the years. Both oppose structural changes that would alter the distribution of income, wealth and relative prices, increasing the risk of inflation. As a result, the coalition uses its power not only in order to promote policies that are beneficial to their interests, but also to obstruct policies that would alter the *status quo*.
>
> (Erber 2011: 44)

But, Erber emphasized that these two coalitions now *co-exist* in an unstable situation of *dual power blocs*. The subordinated but rising *neo-developmentalist coalition* is based on (1) shared growth, (2) income redistribution, (3) inclusive public health and education systems, (4) countercyclical, Keynesian-style programmes that entail credit expansion to the working class and public deficits, (5) public investments in support of technological upgrading for the private industrial sector, and (6) massive infrastructure programmes formulated and financed by BNDES, the state's development bank. Until 2011 this broad mixture of developmentalist policies tensely coexisted with the retrograde a *restrictive financial coalition* which had enabled the banks to triple their mass of profits from 2003 to 2007, as their profit rate rose from 14.8 per cent in 2003 to 22.9 per cent in 2007 (Erber 2011: 42).

It is a hypothesis of this chapter that a critical mass of state managers under President Rousseff began to challenge, in early 2011, the hegemony of the restrictive financial coalition that has drained-off a significant portion of the economic surplus. Once seen as yoked power, the Central Bank and the Finance Ministry were the institutions that restricted credit creation, pushed up (real) interest rates – to 15.8 per cent in 2003 and 14.3 per cent in 2005 – and drove up the exchange rate by 73.3 per cent from 2003 to 2010 (IPEA various years). In 2006, however, Lula appointed Guido Mantega, a Furtado-influenced developmentalist, to head the Finance Ministry. Still, Lula kept Henrique Meirelles, a strict monetarism more Freidmanian than Milton Freidman, in power. With the appointment of Andre Tombini, (a technocrat who finished his PhD in the United States, sharing the same dissertation director as Ecuador's developmentalist president Rafael Correa) interest rates have been pushed down substantially since mid-2011. Thus, the key financial policy-makers (Mantenga and Tombini) now share the deeply held developmentalist views of (1) Luciano Coutinho, the Furtado-influenced director of BNDES, (2) Antônio Raupp, Rousseff's Minister of Science Technology and Innovation appointed in 2012, (3) Fernando Pimentel, Minister of Development, Industry and Foreign Trade (MDIC), a leader in Brazil's efforts to boost national manufacturing capabilities and confront the 'currency wars' that have caused surges in imports, and (4) María das Graças Foster, Rousseff's head of Petrobras – Brazil's key state developmental institution designed to spearhead a new constellation of national firms (owned by Brazilian and foreign capital) that will constitute the state-of-the-art supply-chain for the burgeoning offshore oil industry (*The Economist* 2011b). Undermining the coalition of restrictive financial interests will not occur immediately and perhaps will not occur at all. Nonetheless, insufficient attention has been devoted to those elements that distinguish Lula's consensus approach and his deference to the power of national and international finance capital and Rousseff's 'productionist' credentials and preferences for a national development project. In short, the key state managers of Brazil exhibit high competence, deep experience and a decidedly neo-developmentalist stance – all directly in accord with that of president Rousseff.

Bresser-Pereira (2009) agrees with Erber (2011) and Bruno et al. (2011) that the ideologically dominant position regarding national policy under Lula was conceded to the *restrictive finance coalition* – preferring, however, the term 'Washington Consensus' (WC). Advocates for restrictive finance coalition argued that a strict policy of high interest rates (and an overvalued currency) would have developmental consequences. To wit, high interest rates were assumed to create an inflow of 'savings' from abroad which would supplement 'low savings' in Brazil. In the conventional neoclassical model (or in Keynesian formulations) these foreign savings are translated (automatically) into higher investment. It should be noted that such higher investment is, *by assumption*, devoted to 'capital deepening' and the 'upgrading' of the capital stock. Further, in the very process of expanding investment it is assumed that capital equipment 'embedded' in productivity-enhancing technologies will be broadly introduced. All this, it is assumed, will put Brazil on a higher growth path and reverse the stagnation and instability that has marked most of the years since 1980.

In reality, 'hot-money' funds flowing in from abroad need not find their way into capital stock expansion. Instead, speculative behaviour in financial assets or in essentially non-productive activities – such as the construction of luxury apartment buildings and boutique-dominated shopping centres catering to the opulent top 10 per cent – will absorb most foreign 'savings'.

In the WC view the interest rate policy is part and parcel of a larger totality. For one, since its effect will be to maintain an overvalued currency, it is argued that Brazil will thereby draw-in more cheaply and better made imports. This, it is assumed (by the *restrictive financial coalition*), will give domestic producers an 'incentive' to modernize and upgrade their production facilities. However, more than one outcome can be envisioned. The 'shutdown' option would be to close or sell-off the business and divert the funds acquired to the financial circuits while enjoying non-productive *rentier* returns.

Another aspect of this totality is to court Foreign Direct Investment (FDI) as a more stable means of directly raising the investment rate. Brazil's approach, consistent with the WC, has been to promote as much FDI as possible via policies that allow for the free repatriation of profits and the 'horizontal' treatment of foreign capital vis-à-vis domestic capital. According to the WC, this should bring a cornucopia of 'externalities' in terms of learning-by-doing, spin-offs, upgrading of products and processes and national innovative capacity. The issues that can be disputed in this virtuous-circle scenario have been well-researched (Cypher and Dietz 2009: 451–90). The general conclusion is that only nations that have built a *national development policy*, that is those nations that are not *passive receptors*, have been able to *selectively* accept FDI and to turn it to their own advantage.

By 2011, it appeared that Brazil's passivity regarding FDI had significantly diminished. As part of a new industrial policy – 'O Plano Brasil Maior 2011–14' – autos produced in Brazil must have local content of 65 per cent to avoid a 30 per cent tax on all imported parts and components, or imported autos (IDEA 2011). Designed for the promotion of the national auto-parts supplier chain, the new industrial-production tax also is designed to raise FDI of auto assembly plants and to damp-down auto imports. New plants will have to source 65 per cent of their inputs to national suppliers or face the 30 per cent tax. This dramatically new approach to both trade and FDI constitutes a significant challenge to the hegemony of the restrictive finance coalition which embraces the WC. More broadly, Plano Brasil Maior (under the direction of Minister Pimentel at the MDIC) is a significant furtherance of Brazil's Industrial Policy (inaugurated by Lula's administration in 2003) and another element of the challenge Rousseff's administration has presented to the *restrictive finance coalition*. Plano Brasil Maior is focused on promoting government and private sector activity in four strategic areas: (1) to increased investment in infrastructure, (2) to support manufacturing innovations, (3) to defend the internal market, and (4) to promote the foreign trade competitiveness of industry (MDIC 2011).

Looking back at the closing of the era of state-led developmentalism one finds that in the 12 year period between 1970 and 1981 investment (real gross fixed capital formation, overwhelmingly from national firms, but also including FDI) averaged 23.1 per cent of GDP (Baer 2001: 467).[5] While the WC maintained that the policies of the restrictive financial coalition would *increase* investment and *raise* its qualitative content, investment rates in Brazil averaged only 14.77 per cent in the high neoliberal period from 1984 to 2002 (Baer 2001: 467; IPEA various years). Here, an empirical-deductive methodology (that actually records and analyses empirical evidence) leads to the conclusion that these WC assumptions are based on hypothetical-deductive processes that are both institutionally bounded and demonstrably incorrect.[6] Nonetheless, according to Bresser-Pereira (2009), the tendency to maintain a failed policy arises from (1) the adoption of the thesis 'associate dependent development' which constituted the abandonment of a project to build a national industrial bourgeoisie in the 1970s; (2) the shallowness and weaknesses of the Latin American version of state-led development (commonly termed Import Substitution Industrialization); (3) the break-up of the *developmental coalition* as a result of (a) the debt crisis of the 1980s and (b) the external pressures brought to bear by the IFIs; and (4) the consent to the hegemonic formulations of the WC because local elites 'stopped thinking with their heads, took the advice of, and yielded to the pressures of, the North' (Bresser-Pereira 2009: 13).

But Bresser-Pereira was one of the three economists and sociologists (the others being F. H. Cardoso and Carlos Serra) 'who worked in the structuralist and dependency traditions and who, in the 1990s, would become the architects of the destruction of the ISI [Import Substitution Industrialization] model and of the neoliberal inspired restructuring of Brazilian capitalism' (Leiva 2008: 76). As Leiva (2008: 75–6) insists, this restructuring occurred in a piecemeal and discontinuous fashion and was never consolidated. It was not for many reasons, not the least being that Brazil's powerful business federations were staunch supporters of ISI, and they continue to find common ground with the many state policy-makers and practitioners.

As a consequence, not only was neoliberalism never fully imposed under Cardoso, but also, Brazil never took what might be regarded as the next step into the EO regime of accumulation, involving transnationalization, financialization, and flexibilization of the workforce along with a restructuring of social programmes. Over time, neostructuralists have retreated from their emphasis on equity and a project to repay the 'social debt' (such as redress for decades of low wages and insufficient public goods) towards an incomprehensible and empty advocacy of 'social covenants that promote social cohesion' (Leiva 2008: 221–2). This evolution could be noted particularly in Chile, but also in the influential policy formulations promulgated by ECLAC (or CEPAL) from the 1980s, until 2010.[7] Brazil, however, has creatively expanded on its commitment to growth with redistributive equity:

> [U]nlike Chile, structuralist economists in Brazil have not completely and fully converted into neostructuralists, renouncing a national development in which the state plays a decisive role in steering the accumulation process. Second, the discourse of 'growth with equity', though present in Brazilian debates, unfolds in a society lacking a broad-based elite consensus and whose transnational financial capital, unlike Chile's, is still struggling to impose the framework, rules, and overarching logic under which conflicts between growth and equity will always be resolved in its favor. These two elements – *the survival of unconverted structuralists and the lack of elite consensus* – have shaped economic discourse and policy formulation under two Cardoso administrations (1995–2002) as well as during the first Lula da Silva government.
>
> (Leiva 2008: 80, Italics added)

Lula's limits?

The Lula da Silva administration's eight years in power brought a variety of interpretations regarding its overall policy stance. As was the case with Cardoso, Lula was commonly condemned as a neoliberal, as emphasized by Saad-Filho (2007: 20): 'The first Lula administration showed that the PT [the Labour Party] can impose neoliberal policies more consistently and successfully than any other government, however right-wing or ideologically committed to neoliberal interests.' This view should be contrasted with that of Perry Anderson. For Lula, Anderson (2011) argues, the correct comparison is with President Kubitschek, Brazil's greatest practitioner of state-led industrialization (although Lula's focus was distinct). For his part, Leiva (2008) builds a solid case for understanding Lula as anything but a neoliberal practitioner.

Perhaps the general improvement of the lot of the poor has been the matter most strongly associated with Lula's two-term presidency (2003–10). While the PT Administration certainly did devote great attention to *Bolsa*

Família and other programmes of social uplift and inclusion, and the accolades received due to the drop in poverty rates were unquestionably merited, it is important to note that major social indicators showed improvement in the period between 1980 and 2000: life expectancy increased by 13 per cent, infant mortality fell by 56 per cent, and illiteracy fell by 48 per cent, according to official IBGE data (Bresser-Pereira 2009: 55).[8]

Due to the successful implementation of the 'growth with redistribution' policy, the distribution of income has improved, as measured by the Gini Index. However, throughout Latin America there is reason to believe that the household survey methods used to compile the data measured by the Gini Index are flawed. In Brazil's case, 76 per cent of the income measured is from wages, salaries and the self-employed (Bresser-Pereira 2009: 56). All labour income of this type constituted only 40 per cent of national income. However, the vaunted improvement in the Gini Index is actually measuring household *income compression* within a ten-fold division of the family incomes captured by the Household Survey method. The really rich and the near-rich are *not* included in the Household Survey both because such surveys are normally capped at a relatively modest level which excludes the top 10 per cent of all income receiving households. That is to say, income from bonds, stock, high-end real estate sales and related capital gains, rental incomes, and most of interest income are only very partially included in the household surveys – with as much as two-thirds of such income simply left unregistered.

The Gini measure, then, captures the improvement in incomes from the *Bolsa Família* programme and other transfer programmes, pulling the bottom one-third of the surveyed household up towards the median income. At the same time, beginning in 1999 and lasting at least through 2006 the middle class (defined as those who earn three minimum wages or above) experienced wage compression and layoffs of over two million from 2002 to 2006 (Bresser-Pereira 2009: 57). In the middle class during this period wages and salaries of new hires were 46 per cent lower than other similar workers who had been laid-off. In an unpublished study cited by Bresser-Pereira, Marcio Pochman (using a National Income Accounts approach) found that the *functional distribution of income* in the period between 1995 and 2005 showed much different result than those presumed in discussions of Brazil (Bresser-Pereira 2009: 56–7, 64). While inflation adjusted national income rose by 24.4 per cent, wage income rose by only 7.62 per cent. Other income, which primarily accounts for those items largely excluded in the Household Survey method, rose by 37.6 per cent (Bresser-Pereira 2009: 64). In short, there is every reason to believe that a complex double movement has occurred – income *compression* within the income range circumscribed by the poor, the working class and the middle class has taken place. Here then, for the overwhelming majority, we find increased income equality as the historically socially excluded strata have experienced strongly rising real income levels.

But, at the same time there has been a (largely unmeasured) soaring of non-wage income driven in large part by the enduring *rentier incomes* arising for the policy of maintaining record high interest rates. Taking the latter into account, the *overall distribution of income has not become more equal* and it is likely that it has become more unequal. (But the Gini coefficient does not record most of the high-end incomes received from *financialization.*) To the degree that these data are accurate they appear to mirror national election results in 2006 and 2010: the poor voted massively (particularly in the impoverished northeast) for the PT, the rich and near-rich tolerated the PT since they may never have done better financially, while the middle class moved away from the PT, particularly in the South where educational levels and industrial production are higher.

Structure of power and limits to redistribution

As Leiva (2008) cogently argues, the themes of a national power bloc and the retrograde nature of the industrial bourgeoisie so central to the early Cepal thinkers, particularly Furtado, have all but disappeared in Brazil and elsewhere in Latin America. This focus has been displaced by a neostructuralist discourse wherein structural socio-economic power, as exercised by landholders, industrialists and financial agents, largely disappears from analytical discussions. Yet, it is possible to uncover important remnants of the insightful structuralist methodology. In this section a brief effort is made to highlight the arguments and findings of those who follow in the structuralist tradition. In doing so, major parameters shaping the comportment of Brazil's political economy are, once again, brought to the foreground. Amann and Baer (2009) argue that Brazil remains defined by a three-fold maldistribution of assets. First to consider is the adverse path-dependent nature of Brazil's highly concentrated landholding, a legacy of the colonial and post-colonial land-grabbing processes widely practiced by the agrarian oligarchs into the twentieth century (Pereira 2003). In spite of efforts at land reform, in year 2000 farms of 1000 hectares or more constituted only 1.6 per cent of all farms but held 43.8 per cent of all arable land (Amann and Baer 2009: 38). A 2006 study shows that the largest 9.1 per cent of all landowner held a total of 78.6 per cent of Brazil's arable land (Pereira and Sauer 2011: Table I). Second, the four-firm concentration ratio (a measure of oligopoly power that sums the market shares of the top four producers in a given market and expresses the extent of concentrated economic power) in 19 industrial sectors averaged 60 per cent in 1993 and 68 per cent in 2004, with only two sectors declining, including the important and largely nationally owned auto-parts industry, which was essentially unchanged at 86 and then 85 per cent (Amann and Baer 2009: 34). Rising concentration ratios are in part attributable to the growing role of imports which has forced mergers or exit.

The compliment to these changes is reflected in the structural nature of asset concentration, which is measured only partially and indirectly through the C4 concentration ratio, but can be analysed more directly. In a sample of the Campinas region in 1996, for example, while the Gini income coefficient was 0.58, the Gini coefficient for asset ownership was 0.92 (Amann and Baer 2009: 38). At the national level 10 per cent of the population held 75.4 per cent of total wealth in 2000 (Diniz 2007: 48). A 2000 study of 459 firms in Brazil demonstrated the extremely high degree of asset concentration in terms of shareholders holdings. On average the single largest shareholder – likely reflecting the dominance of family-held firms – was 51 per cent (Leiva 2008: 136). Average ownership share of the three largest shareholders stood at 65 per cent. These concentration ratios connote vast socio-economic leverage in the policy-making sphere as well as over labour (organized or unorganized).

Landholding power and concentrated industrial power explain the highly skewed functional distribution of income of capital's share over that of labour. At the same time, the path from asset concentration to policy formulating power at the national level has been relatively direct since the 1930s – although in the case of Cardoso's administration and some of the military governments, the relation has been tense from capital's perspective. It should be noted in passing that, for reasons not explored here, the strategy of growth with redistribution, as long as it is not the *sole* strategy, has not been a focused target drawing the opposition of the peak business associations.

Education is the third factor explaining Brazil's structural bias towards income and wealth inequality. In 2000 the average number of years of schooling was only 6.4, while in Chile and Argentina it was ten. In 2001 the gap between the average number of years of schooling of the lowest to the highest income quintiles was three, while in Argentina in 2001 it was 1.8 years (Amann and Baer 2009: 39). 'Of the Brazilians making up the bottom two income quintiles of the distribution, only 5 per cent have completed secondary school, compared with 73 per cent of the richest decile' (Amann and Baer 2009: 40).

These three structural factors (oligarchic landholding, business concentration, and education inequality) of socio-economic power are unchallenged by the Lula-Rousseff approach to redistribution, a situation that leaves Brazil in a deadlocked impasse: 'given the scale of asset inequality,...it seems unlikely that the *Bolsa Família*, given its small scale proportionate to GDP, would be able to counterbalance the income effects of the enormous disparities in asset ownership' (Amann and Baer 2009: 39). An additional aspect of asset concentration has been the widespread exit of national industrialist from the sphere of production into the sphere of circulation where they now operate as rentiers. Furthermore, the massive mergers and acquisitions, particularly engineered by foreign capital (but also undertaken to a much lesser degree by national capital) have resulted in a heightened degree of asset accumulation linked to repatriation of profits and dividends. Such outflows, part of a process of denationalization that occurred in the 1990s, according to Rocco (2007: 201), resulted in a five-fold leap in annual average repatriation flows by TNCs from the 1980s to the 1995–9 period. This was the context in which national capital (minus those who had exited into the lucrative sphere of circulation as bank shareholders and/or bond clippers) commenced advocating for industrial policy in opposition to the Cardoso administration's widespread bias in favour of foreign firms.

The dynamics of state–capital relations under neoliberalism and beyond

In spite of predictions that the national bourgeoisie was largely swept away at the high point of neoliberal opening due to privatizations, mergers, and foreign buyouts, nationally owned private firms and state-owned entities retained a significant presence, as registered in Table 8.1.

Of the 40 largest firms in 1984, 19 were owned by the central government or the state governments, including the seven largest. In 1998, 11 were owned by the central government or the state government, including the two largest, while private national firms owned 11 in 1984 and 15 in 1998; foreign firms were ten in 1984 and 14 in 1998. By 1998 (registering now the top 100 firms) these figures were 27 for the nationally owned private firms, 34 for the public sector, and 39 for the transnational firms. In 1998 family firms had only 17 per cent of total revenues, government 21 per cent (down from 44 per cent in 1990) and foreign firms 40 per cent (up from 26 per cent in 1990). Shared-control firms (domestic and foreign owned) went up from 5 per cent of total revenue in 1990 to 22 per cent in 1998. These were firms where, in isolation, neither foreign-industrial capital nor foreign-financial capital controlled a majority share (Goldstein and Ross Schneider 2004: 60–1).

Continuing to take full advantage of their conglomerate structures, the *national power groups* operating family controlled firms retained a large and influential role in national policy (Mancuso, Leopoldi, and Iglecias 2010).

Table 8.1 Brazil: Largest national and transnational firms

Year	1984 (40 largest)	1998 (40 largest)	1998 (100 largest)	2010 (40 largest)	2010 (100 largest)
National private	11	15	27	14	43
National public	19	11	34	6	13
Foreign owned	10	14	39	20	44

Sources: Goldstein and Ross Schneider 2004: 60–1; Exame 2011.

This can be seen by the fact that nationally owned firms accounted for 43 of the top 100 in 2010 (Table 8.1). Foreign firms did expand their sphere in Brazil from 1998 to 2010, but their share only increased by five firms. The state sector was reduced from 34 firms to 13, and the bulk of the shift was towards nationally owned firms – their share increased by an impressive 26 firms. When focusing on the largest four, however, as can be seen from the data for 2010, the portion held by national firms is not quite as high, demonstrating that national firms lack both the capital and the technology to compete *as equals* with the largest transnationals. In terms of the largest of the large (for example, the top 40 firms), foreign firms have *doubled* their weight since 1984, primarily against the state sector, while the national bourgeoisie, contrary to the anticipations of many, has also managed to increase its role.

On a qualitative and institutional level, relations between state and capital have undergone transformations, frequently defined as 'corporatist' since their establishment in the period between 1930 and 1950. Of note is the powerful national organization, the CNI (National Confederation of Industry) established in 1938. Today the CNI orchestrates a vast network of state Federations of Industry, as well as its own Coordinator of Legislative Affairs with the objective of shaping and influencing, if not defining, national economic policy. Central focus today is upon competitiveness and the possible building of a 'knowledge-based society', and, in particular the 'Strategic Map of Industry 2007–15'. Two of the prime institutional movers of national policy under the CNI are the National Industrial Forum (est. 2004) and the Brazilian Business Coalition (CEB, est. 1996). The former brings together 50 presidents of national sectoral associations, while the latter is constituted from 170 business organizations whose prime focus is on the manner in which the Brazilian economy is integrated with the international sphere. The focus of the CEB has a great deal to do with the fact that a number of 'national champion firms', including the well-known case of Embraer, are now viable transnationals (Amann 2009; Goldstein and Ross Schneider 2004; Ross Schneider 2009a). In short, under the corporatist structure, business interests exercised little to no autonomy regarding the creation of economic policy, while the state took the lead. The neoliberal order destroyed the corporatist structure and left the national bourgeoisie vulnerable to the shifting forces of globalization and financialization.

It is important to emphasize that the Cardoso regime operated at some distance from the dominant peak business organizations for reason of 'bureaucratic insulation' and/or because Cardoso's administration embraced some version of the 'relative autonomy of the state'. In particular, starting in the 1990s, and advocated by the influential think-tank, Instituto de Estudos para o Desenvolvimento Industrial (IEDI), which holds a strong ideological affinity with the strongest business associations, the Cardoso regime was confronted by interests that sought to 'resist the anathemization of the idea of an industrial policy' for Brazil (Delgado 2010: 123). As a result, the large business associations and the *grupos* became increasingly alienated from the neoliberal model. By the beginning of 2000, 'the failure of neoliberal policies to fulfill the expectation of a return to growth was widely recognized' (Diniz 2011: 64).

This disaffection from the model promoted several institutional innovations under Lula, many of which were designed to restructure and rejuvenate Brazil's industrial base. Of note was the creation of the Economic and Social Development Council (CDES) in 2003, designed to open a dialogue between the state and civil society over the formulation and direction of policies. The CDES was dominated by national business interests and is considered to be of fundamental importance in bringing greater institutional support for the prioritization of industrial policy (Diniz 2011: 67; Doctor 2007). In 2004 the National Industrial Development Council (CNDI) was formed to facilitate consultations between the highest levels of the state (including the President and BNDES) and representatives of national industry. 'It is charged with developing public policy with regard to the development of industry, the expansion of infrastructure, the standardization of measures allowing for greater competition among firms, and the financing of entrepreneurial activity' (Diniz 2011: 67). Also in 2004 the Brazilian Industrial Development Agency (ABDI) was formed as an entity to coordinate industrial policy between the government ministries, with the sole representative of the *restrictive financial coalition* being the (outvoted) Central Bank. In 2005, according to 'the then-executive director of the IEDI... the government had restored the idea of a national business community and its role in the development of Brazilian industrial capitalism' (Diniz 2011: 68). After presenting voluminous evidence regarding the restructuring of state-capital relations that could be traced back to 1997, Diniz reached the following conclusion:

> To summarize, in terms of business-state relations, a move toward reclaiming political space occurred under Lula's first administration... The businessman-actor's logic of collective action shifted toward independence through stronger ties with centers of power. Moreover, there were clear signs that the theme of sustained growth *would assume preeminence* in the economic debate.
>
> (Diniz 2011: 73. Italics added)

It was the influence of the business associations that brought into existence *Protec* in 2003 – an institution created by parliament and designed to promote indigenous innovation in the industrial sector. Protec was part of a larger pattern wherein the industrial organizations successfully pushed for an opening for 'space for developmentalist ideas' during the 2002 election (Delgado 2010: 125). With Lula in power a new relationship was established wherein pro-growth policies have been at least partially prioritized (subject however to the continual emphasis on monetary and fiscal repression until 2011) and new channels of *direct* intermediation between capital and the state have been consolidated (Delgado 2010: 125).

Discussion over *forms of the state* and the 'varieties of capitalism'

In the face of the structural factors mentioned in the prior two sections, Kohli (2009: 387) determined that the Cardoso administration was never completely a neoliberal regime: It aimed to ensure that the state sector would continue to develop the potential of the national bourgeoisie as one viable pillar of development policy, even while using tax policies and other measures to lure TNC investments and while sanctioning denationalization mergers. Reflecting on his earlier work, President Cardoso noted that 'We were concerned with the degrees of national autonomy and therefore, with the role the state would play in development decisions' (cited in Kohli 2009: 387).

In terms of such an emphasis on state intervention, Kohli (2009: 388–99, 408) notes that Asian and Latin American nations, particularly Brazil, developed distinct path dependencies in the crucial 1950–80 period that have structurally defined (but not determined) subsequent practices and policies:

> on the whole, between 1950 and 1980, nationalist states consolidated power in most Asian countries while eliminating or mitigating the power of traditional intermediaries, minimizing the role of foreign capital, and laying the foundations for the development of indigenous technology and heavy industry. By contrast, the ruling elites in Latin America continued to rely heavily on foreign capital, failed to mitigate internal economic inequalities and the related elite–mass political gap, and constructed political economies that remained dependent on the outside world.
>
> (Kohli 2009: 407)

Ross Schneider (2009b), a careful student of socio-economic power relationships particularly in Brazil, takes the structural insights of Amann and Baer and Kohli a giant step further. He argues that the Latin American economies are *sui generis* social formations, distinct from the Anglo-Saxon model as well as that of the 'Coordinated Market Economies' of Germany and Japan, but also of the state-led Asian developing nations. Of particular note, Ross Schneider emphasizes the specificities of 'institutional continuities' in Latin America, particularly in terms of the asset concentrations highlighted above. Of particular long-standing structural importance are the importance and prevalence of national conglomerate capital (or the national 'grupos') and transnational capital. Riddled with forms of institutional retardation (such as inept financial structures, endemic political corruption, and oligarchic landholding structures) Latin American economies are described as 'Hierarchical Market Economies' – they are distinct from the other two forms mentioned above, and have not and *will not,* due to the institutionalized grip of oligarchic ownership patterns in landholding, industrial production, finance and trade, evolve into either Anglo-Saxon or Coordinated Market economies.[9] TNCs adapt to and enforce such hierarchical structures. The TNCs along with the oligarchic ownership patterns are the primary causal factors that influence other institutions, such as the state, which cannot mount a policy drive to acquire a 'national development project' or lead to the formation of the informal labour sector. Yet Brazil should be seen as *somewhat* of an outlier, the only one in Latin America, from Ross Schneider's sweeping formulation.

In a sweeping effort to engage with the concept of the 'developmental state' Amiya Bagchi has emphasized the falsity of a dichotomy between state and market as a defining feature of a developmental state. Such states are neither pro- nor anti-market, but rather dynamic social constructs, or institutions, which are able 'to combine both market and state direction in a synergistic manner' (Bagchi 2006: 233–4). For Bagchi (2006: 234) such state has three principle characteristics. A successful developmental state is (1) rid of feudal structures and institutions, while (2) its rulers must display a strong sense of inclusionary nationalism in their beliefs and actions, and (3) it must learn how to learn from other countries for promoting economic and human development. Further, a developmental state builds social capital which entails the ability 'to pursue a cohesive, long-sustained, development oriented policy' that results in the 'willingness and ability of dominant groups... to engage in the construction of enabling institutions' (Bagchi 2006: 267). Strictly interpreted, Brazil falls behind in every one of Bagchi's encapsulated measures and concepts. For example, regarding the first characteristic it should be remembered that Furtado continued to define Brazil's economy as one fundamentally structured by a colonial legacy even in the 1980s (and, presumably, today).

Peter Evans (2008) has recently argued that the requirements for a twenty-first century developmental state are even greater than ever, since the new structures of production based deeply in Communications and Information Technologies (CIT) demand an extremely large commitment to, and *capacity for,* a broad educational infrastructure. Unlike industry-driven development strategies of the twentieth century, Evans (2008: 15) argues that the currently evolved, service-driven nature, of production tends to increase the level of complexity to achieve effective state policies. Further, and particularly acute in the case of Brazil, twentieth-century success has shifted the balance between public and private power in ways that could undermine future institutional transformation. Developmental success has strengthened private capital and increased the domestic political role of transnational capital. Deeply established reliance on local private economic elites, the growing centrality of transnational capital to local accumulation and the proliferation of alliances between local and transnational capital have transformed the political landscape into something quite different than it was 40 years ago. Brazil's Achilles' heel has been its lack of commitment to a socially encompassing public education system at the primary and secondary level – a lacuna addressed only recently and partially under Lula and Rousseff. But Evans' observations run deeper than educational policy or a weak infrastructure: the contemporary challenges to the construction of a viable state apparatus intending to inaugurate and sustain policies of neo-developmentalism are far greater than those encountered in the era of state-led industrialization (1930–81).

As the most salient feature of a possible limited transition towards a developmental state structure, two factors need to be taken into consideration. First, the concept of the developmental state is relatively inclusive, complex and broad, resting on a viable vision of development and on *state capacity* (Cypher and Dietz 2009: 224–31). Attaining state capacity requires a 'developmental state formation' which is a function of three components: (1) *Power* – cohesive ability to direct and prioritize a development project and to demand performance compliance (relative autonomy); (2) *Purpose* – the mobilization of a development vision, such as neo-developmentalism; (3) *Capacity* – consisting of two interdependent elements, civil service competence (a meritocracy) and embeddedness of the state sector with the national industrial base. In the Brazilian context, redistributive growth is an inclusionary tactic, but it falls far short of a viable vision of development which would demand structural change.

Second, *state capacity* rests, in the first instance, on the professionalization of a *merit-based* cadre of state managers and their most responsible subordinates. Brazil under Rousseff is taking strides in this direction (*The Economist* 2011a: 36–7). This effort, however, has hit strong resistance – to the degree that the new administration could become deadlocked on a range of state policies due to important, but limited, steps taken to introduce a technocratic system of meritocracy. Such steps could serve to depoliticize crucial policy areas while importantly increasing the legitimacy and relative autonomy of the state. In addition, and perhaps most importantly, the new merit-based positions are not institutionally embedded. Rather, they depend on the volition of Rousseff's administration and therefore can be easily reversed under a subsequent government. The lack of a disciplined, merit-based, stratum dominating the state bureaus and departments has long been the Achilles heel of Latin America's state structures. Yet, the powerful BNDES stands out as an exception, capable of ensuring that the privatization process of the 1990s never quite degenerated into the kleptocratic scramble witnessed in most nations (Goldstein and Ross Schneider 2004: 55). Rousseff has faced a firestorm not only from opposition parties but also from the PT because she has confronted the 'business as usual' model that dominates Brazil.

Final comments

The state is the pivotal social institution, normally facilitating the reproduction of the structures of power. At certain historical conjunctures the structures of social and economic power are challenged and, occasionally altered as heretofore marginalized social strata mobilize. On one such occasion, the end of 'Republic of Coffee', Brazil never quite constructed a Developmental State (as analysed in the previous section) during the subsequent ISI era. Presently, with the recent rise of a *neo-developmentalist* strategy, it has travelled further away from the neoliberal policy matrix than any other Latin American nation. Brazil has commenced, and largely consolidated, a dual process whereby state policy has served to rejuvenate developmentalist institutions (such as BNDES) *and* create new institutions.

This has only been possible because of the crystallization of a viable social and political consensus committed to a sweeping agenda of redistribution, revitalization of the national industrial base, establishment of a national innovation system and broad policies of social inclusion. Nonetheless, deeply entrenched structural markers of inequality in landholding, wealth distribution and education have confined the scope of the current transformation, as noted in the section 'Structures of, and Limits to, Redistribution'. Even here, however, (under the sway of the neo-developmentalist agenda) such structures need not be permanent, as Brazil's 2012 Law of Social Quotas shows: the law reserves one-half of admissions at the 59 state universities providing tuition-free education for previously excluded poor and working class youth graduating from public schools (Romero 2012: A4).

Since 2007 an ongoing crisis partially arising in the financial sector in the centre nations (as highlighted in the introductory chapter of this book), partially due to massive global overproduction/excess capacity, has roiled major portions of the global economic structure. Brazil's development efforts that began in 2003 under complex and conflicted conditions moved in the direction of resolution on the national level for several years. Yet, this trajectory was disrupted by ruptures in the United States and the European economies from 2007 up to the present moment, unleashing vectors of forces that nearly derailed the forward movement of the new developmentalist project in Brazil. 'Fast policy' (entailing innovations) coupled with an adequate degree of state autonomy functioned well during 2008–09 and Brazil was able to put in place a series of Keynesian/Post-Keynesian countercyclical policies that held the downturn to a minimum and laid the basis for a strong recovery in 2010.[10]

The *restrictive financial coalition* responded to the high growth by pushing interest rates higher and restricting credit. 2011 was a mediocre year of slow growth, but (most significantly) it did allow for a new director of the Central Bank, who adopted an expansionary approach at mid-year. As emphasized in the second section this was another important step facilitating cohesion among Rousseff's neo-developmentalist state managers which suggests a fundamental turning point in state policy, now confronting/contesting financial hegemony. It is a hypothesis of this chapter that the weak growth in 2011 (2.7 per cent) is not a harbinger of a stagnationist trend – although 2012 closed with annual growth of only 0.9 per cent. With the massive, productivity enhancing infrastructure outlays spreading out over the near term, and with the impact of the versatile *Brasil Maior* plan yet to be felt, there is presently good reason to believe that Brazil will maintain momentum along a socially inclusive growth path that has emerged since 2003. 'Productionist' industrial policy centred on stimulating domestic content will lead to forward and backward industrial linkage effects – particularly from the vast investments in the strategic petroleum sector – serving to restructure the national industrial base. Finally, Brazil has moved constructively in the direction of embedding the development project in deep and broad public-private institutional structures and new forms of dialogue. Civil society has a new and important interactive role in defining and evaluating development initiatives. This is new in Latin America, but not in the cases of the successful development that have occurred in Asia.

Notes

1. > ...Some state-owned enterprises became genuine 'accumulating machines'. While GDP was growing at an annual rate of 7 per cent, investments of the largest state-owned enterprises escalated from 3.2 per cent of the total investment in 1963, to 16 per cent in 1970 and finally to 22 per cent in 1979. Moreover, investments by state-owned enterprises did not 'crowd-out' but actually encouraged private investment, which also grew at rates superior to the growth of GDP'.
   >
   > (Barros de Castro 1994: 199)
2. Deindustrialization was experienced in important sectors, and this carried important political consequences in terms of the victorious rise of the workers party (PT) by 2002 (Sader 2005: 66). In recent years the deindustrialization theme regained currency particularly as a result of the commodities boom. Booming commodities exports and a very high exchange rate value for the *Real* have caused manufacturing exports to fall as a share of total exports. Beyond this, however, the general situation is not clear. Industrial employment, for example, declined relative to total employment from 2003 through early 2012, from 17.4 to 16.5 per cent. Meanwhile the total number employed in industry *rose* from 32.5 million to 36 million (Grupo de Análise e Previsões 2012: 4).
3. The main characteristic of the neostructuralist policy framework 'is the *active promotion of new forms of social coordination beyond those offered by market forces alone*' (Leiva 2008: xxi–xxii).

4. The BNDES, in addition to establishing itself as the main long-term financing source for the manufacturing and infrastructure industries, [currently] plays a strategic role as a provider of credit lines precisely at times of cyclical variations due to international financial crises. ... In 2009 the sum of credit offered by the BNDES and by other public banks was equivalent to the total value of private banks; that is about 18 per cent of GDP

   (Boschi 2011: 48).

5. The year 2010 set a record for FDI. Still, net FDI amounted to 9.45 per cent of Brazil's total investment (ECLAC 2011: 118; IPEA 2011).
6. The WC 'solutions' were essentially static: for example (by assumption), shrinking the state to its minimal size would 'free up' resources that would then 'flow' to more productive uses, as employed by the private sector. As an important corollary, opening the country to unrestricted FDI would (again according to WC assumptions) lift the national rate of investment above levels attained prior to adoption of the WC policies. This was deemed to be the result of the fact that in the advanced industrial nations where the capital stock was large, additional growth to the national capital stock (that is, 'investment' in new capital formation) would have a relatively low rate of return. However, in 'capital short' less-developed nations the rate of return to capital was deemed to be 'high' because the national capital stock was low and insufficient. The reasoning here is based on many factors, with 'diminishing returns' to capital being foremost. Thus 'capital short' less-developed nations, operating with a surfeit of cheap labour, would 'attract' FDI from the advanced nations because in these highly industrialized nations additional capital investment would encounter lower profits due to diminishing returns caused by the depletion of high-return projects and because of higher wages paid in these nations. But, as noted, 'freeing-up' the 'capital account' to facilitate unrestricted inward flows of capital (FDI) *and* outward movements through repatriation of profits, *did not cause investment to rise* in the years cited. Of the many reasons why an increase in FDI might not increase *overall* investment one stands out: already existing companies in the host nation are frequently sold to the transnationals, resulting merely in the *swapping of asset titles*, but no new net increase in capital formation (investment).
7. ECLAC, the UN's Economic Commission for Latin America and the Caribbean, also known for its Spanish acronym CEPAL, has been the dominant source for policy-oriented research on Latin America since the late 1940s. During the era of state-led industrialization (1930–81) ECLAC's theoretical formulations were at odds with the 'modernization' theories of development, particularly advocated by the United States It was only in the beginning of 1980s that ECLAC's nationalist developmental stance was partially compromised by the tidal wave of neoliberal ideology and policy pushed by factions of the national elite throughout Latin America and by the multilateral 'development' institutions, particularly the World Bank. Since 2010 there are demonstrable indications that ECLAC has returned to its roots, now once-again advocating for structural change.
8. By 2010, there were 40 million people receiving funds from the *Bolsa* network, approximately 25 per cent of the population (World Bank 2011, cited by Kliass 2011: 20). Nevertheless, *Bolsa Família* has cost less than 1 per cent of GDP. The issue of income redistribution does not end with this programme. 'Today, Brazil

transfers more income to the elderly relative to its GDP than any other country in Latin America' (Neri 2009: 241). Between 1992 and 2006 the share of aggregate individual income of the elderly increased from 13.3 per cent to 17.6 per cent.

9. This approach offers a challenge to rival formulations as presented by Hall and Soskice (2001) and Soederberg et al. (2005) regarding the 'varieties of capitalism' operative under 'globalization' – a point made by Yıldız Atasoy on an earlier draft of this chapter.
10. Massive Keynesian-style counter-cyclical policies allowed Brazil to overcome the contagion effects of the economic downdraft set-off by the US financial implosion of 2008–09, with GDP growing at an impressive 7.5 per cent in 2010 after suffering a relatively minor downturn in 2009.

References

Amann, E. (2009) 'Technology, Public Policy, and the Emergence of Brazilian Multinationals', in L. Brainard and L. Martinez-Diaz (eds) *Brazil as an Economic Superpower? Understanding Brazil's Changing Role in the Global Economy*, Washington, DC: Brookings Institution Press.

Amann, E. and W. Baer (2009) 'The Macroeconomic Record of the Lula Administration, the Roots of Brazil's Inequality, and Attempts to Overcome Them', in J. Love and W. Baer (eds) *Brazil Under Lula*, Basingstoke, UK: Palgrave Macmillan.

Anderson, P. (2011) 'Lula's Brazil', *London Review of Books* 33(7): 3–12.

Baer, W. (2001) *The Brazilian Economy: Growth and Development*, Westport, CT: Praeger.

Bagchi, A. (2006) 'The Developmental State under Hegemony', in Jomo, K. S. (ed.) *Globalization under Hegemony*, Oxford: Oxford University Press.

Barros de Castro, A. (1994) 'Renegade Development: Rise and Demise of State-Led Development in Brazil', in W. Smith, C. Acuña, and E. Gamarra (eds) *Democracy, Markets, and Structural Reform in Latin America*, New Brunswick, NJ: Transaction Publishers.

Boschi, R. (2011) 'State Developmentalism: Continuity & Uncertainty', in M. Font and L. Randall (eds) *The Brazilian State*, Lanhan, Maryland: Lexington Books.

Bresser-Pereira, L. (2007) 'Method and Passion in Celso Furtado', in E. Pérez Caldentey and M. Vernengo (eds) *Ideas, Policies and Economic Development in the Americas*, London: Routledge.

Bresser-Pereira, L. (2009) *Developing Brazil*, London: Lynne Reinner.

Bresser-Pereira, L. (2012) 'Structuralist Macroeconomics and New Developmentalism', *Brazilian Journal of Political Economy* 32(3): 347–66.

Bruno, M., H. Diawara, E. Araújo, A. Reis, and M. Rubens (2011) 'Finance-led Growth Regime no Brasil: Estatuto Teórico, Evidências Empíricase Consequências Macroeconômicas', *Revista de Economía Política* 31(5): 730–50.

Bush, P. (1994) 'Social Change', in G. Hodgson, W. Samuels, and M. Tool (eds) *Institutional and Evolutionary Economics* (vol. 2), Aldershot: Edward Elgar Publishing.

Cardim de Carvalho, F. (2007) 'Lula's Government in Brazil: A New Left or the Old Populism', in P. Arestis and A. Saad-Filho (eds) *Political Economy of Brazil*, Hampshire, UK: Palgrave Macmillan.

Cavalcante, L. and S. Underman (2009) 'Regional Development Policies, 2003–2006', in J. Love and W. Baer (eds) *Brazil Under Lula*, Basingstoke, UK: Palgrave Macmillan.

Cypher, J. (2009) 'On the Income Gap between Nations: Was Veblen the First Development Economist?' *Journal of Economic Issues* 42(2): 361–70.

Cypher, J. (2012) 'Veblen y el origen de la hípotesis del *catching-up*', *Problemas del Desarrollo: Revista Latinoamericana de Economía* 43(169): 9–26.

Cypher, James and J. Dietz (2009) *The Process of Economic Development*, London: Routledge.

da Motta e Albuquerque, E. (2007) 'Inadequacy of Technology and Innovation Systems at the Periphery', *Cambridge Journal of Economics* 31(5): 669–90.

de Bernis, G. (1994) 'Perroux, François', in G. Hodgson, W. Samuels, and M. Tool, (eds) *Institutional and Evolutionary Economics* (vol. 2), Aldershot: Edward Elgar Publishing.

Delgado, I. (2010) 'Desenvolvimento, empresariado e política industrial do Brasil', in W. Mancuso, M. Leopoldi, and W. Iglecias (eds) *Estado, empresariado e desenvolvimento no Brasil*, São Paulo: Editora de Cultura.

Diniz, E. (2007) 'O pós-Consenso de Washington: globalização, Estado e governabilidade reexaminados', in E. Diniz (organizador) *Globalização, Estado e Desenvolvimento*, Rio de Janeiro: Editora FGV.

Diniz, E. (2011) 'Democracy, State, and Industry: Continuity and Change between the Cardoso and Lula Administrations', *Latin American Perspectives* 38(3): 59–77.

Doctor, M. (2007) 'Lula's Development Council: Neo-Corporatism and Policy Reform in Brazil', *Latin American Perspectives* 34(6): 131–48.

ECLAC (Economic Commission for Latin America and the Caribbean) (2011) *Statistical Yearbook for Latin America and the Caribbean*, Santiago: ECLAC.

The Economist (2011a) 'Dilma Tries to Drain the Swamp', 20 August: 36–7.

The Economist (2011b) 'Briefing: Brazil's Oil Boom', 5 November: 81–4.

Erber, F. (2011) 'As convenções de desenvolvimento no governo Lula: um ensaio de economia política', *Revista de Economia Política* 31(1): 31–55.

Evans, P. (1979) *Dependent Development: The Alliance of Multinational, State, and Local Capital in Brazil*, Princeton: Princeton University Press.

Evans, P. (2008) 'In Search of the 21st Century Developmental State', Center for Global Political Economy, *Working Paper no. 4* (December), University of Sussex.

EXAME (2011) 'Maiores Empresas por Vendas em 2010', *EXAME* (abril). Available online: www.exame.abril.combr/negocios/melhores-e-maiores/empresas/maiores/1/vendas. (accessed: 12 December 2011).

Freeman, C. (1995) 'The National Innovation Systems in Historical Perspective', *Cambridge Journal of Economics* 19(1): 5–24.

Furtado, C. (1958) 'Capital Formation and Economic Development', in A. N. Agarwala and S. P. Singh (eds) *The Economics of Underdevelopment*, Oxford: Oxford University Press.

Furtado, C. (1963) *The Economic Growth of Brazil*, Berkeley: University of California Press.

Goldstein, A. and B. Ross Schneider (2004) 'Big Business in Brazil: States and Markets in the Corporate Reorganization of the 1990s', in E. Amann and H.-J. Chang (eds) *Brazil and South Korea: Economic Crisis and Restructuring*, London: Institute of Latin American Studies.

Grupo de Análise e Previsôes (2012) 'Análise Tematica', *Conjuntura em Foco*, (8) año 4 (março): 1–10.

Hall, J. and U. Ludwig (2010) 'Veblen, Myrdal, and the Convergence Hypothesis: Toward and Institutionalist Critique', *Journal of Economic Issues* 44(4): 943–62.

Hall, P. and D. Soskice (2001) *Varieties of Capitalism*, Oxford: Oxford University Press.

Hodgson, G. (1996) 'An Evolutionary Theory of Long-Term Economic Growth', *International Studies Quarterly* 40(3): 391–410.

IBRE (Instituto Brasileiro de Economia) (2010) 'A desindustrialização brasileira em debate', *Conjuntura Econômica* 64(8): 8–11.

IDEA (Instituto de Estúdios para o Desenvolvimento Industrial) (2011) 'Uma Análise do Plano Brasil Maior', *Carta IEDI* (486) (23 setembro). Available online: www.iedi.org.br/cartas/carta_iedi_n_486_uma_analise_do_plano_brasil_maior.html. (accessed: 21 December 2011).

IPEA (Instituto de Pesquísa Econômica Aplicada) (various years) *Ipeadata*. Available online: www.ipeadata.gov.br. (accessed: 16 September 2011).

Kliass, P. (2011) 'Lula's Political Economy: Crisis and Continuity', *NACLA Report on the Americas* 44(2): 19–22

Kohli, A. (2009) 'Nationalist Versus Dependent Capitalist Development: Alternate Pathways of Asia and Latin America in a Globalized World', *Studies in Comparative and International Development* 44(4): 386–410.

Kupfer, D. (2003) 'Política Industrial', *Econômica* 5(2): 291–8.

Leiva, F. (2008) *Latin American Neo-Structuralism*, Minneapolis: University of Minnesota.

Mancuso, W., M. Leopoldi, and W. Iglecias (eds) (2010) *Estado, empresariado e desenvolvimento no Brasil*, São Paulo: Editora de Cultura.

MDIC (Ministry of Development, Industry and Foreign Trade) (2011) *O Plano Brasil Maior*, Brasilia: Government of Brazil: 1–22. Available online: http://www.brasilmaior.mdic.gov.br. (accessed: 18 December 2011).

Mollo, M. and A. Saad-Filho (2006) 'Neoliberal Economic Policies in Brazil (1994–2005): Cardoso, Lula and the Need for a Democratic Alternative', *New Political Economy* 11(1): 99–123.

Nassif, A. (2008) 'Ha evidencia de desindustrialização no Brasil?' *Revista de Economia Política* 28(1): 72–96.

Neri, M. (2009) 'Income Policies, Income Distribution, and the Distribution of Opportunities in Brazil', in L. Brainard and L. Martinez-Diaz (eds) *Brazil as an Economic Superpower? Understanding Brazil's Changing Role in the Global Economy*, Washington, DC: Brookings Institution Press.

Pereira, A. (2003) 'Brazil's Agrarian Reform: Democratic Innovation or Oligarchic Exclusion Redux?' *Latin American Politics and Society* 45(2): 41–65.

Pereira, S. and Sergio Sauer (2011) 'Expansión de agronegocio en Brasil', *Mundo Siglo XXI, Revista del CIECAS-IPN* (7), Table I. Available online: http://www.jornada.unam.mx/2012/02/10/opinion/032o1eco. (accessed: 2 October 2012).

Robinson, W. (2008) *Latin America and Global Capitalism*, Baltimore: Johns Hopkins University Press.

Rocco, R. (2007) 'Economic flexibilisation and denationalistation in Brazil', in A. Fernández Jilberto and B. Hogenboom (eds) *Big Business and Economic Development*, London: Routledge.

Rocha, M. (2007) 'Celso Furtado and the Resumption of Construction in Brazil: Structuralism as an Alternative to Neoliberalism', *Latin American Perspectives* 34(5): 132–59.

Rodrik, D. (1997) *Has Globalization Gone Too Far?* Washington: Institute for International Economics.

Rodrik, D. (2011) *The Globalization Paradox*, New York: W.W. Norton & Company.

Romero, S. (2012) 'Brazil enacts affirmative action law for universities', *New York Times* 31 August: A4.

Ross Schneider, B. (2009a) 'Big Business in Brazil: Leveraging Natural Endowments', in L. Brainard and L. Martinez-Diaz (eds) *Brazil as an Economic Superpower?*

Understanding Brazil's Changing Role in the Global Economy, Washington, DC: Brookings Institution Press.

Ross Schneider, B. (2009b.) 'Hierarchical Market Economies and Varieties of Capitalism in Latin America', *Journal of Latin American Studies* 41(3): 553–75.

Saad-Filho, A. (2007) 'Neoliberalism, Democracy and Economic Policy in Brazil', in P. Arestis and A. Saad-Filho (eds) *Political Economy of Brazil*, Basingstoke, UK: Palgrave Macmillan.

Sader, E. (2005) 'Taking Lula's Measure', *New Left Review* 33(May/June): 59–79.

Sato, E. (2011) 'Crisis and Beyond: Responses and Prospects', in M. Font and L. Randall (eds) *The Brazilian State*, Lanhan, MD: Lexington Books.

Sharif, N. (2006) 'Emergence and Development of the National Innovation System Concept', *Research Policy* 35(5): 745–66.

Siscu, J. L. de Paula, and R. Michel. (2007) 'Por que novo-desenvolvimentismo?' *Revista de Economia Política* 27(4): 507–24.

Soederberg, S., G. Menz, and P. Cerny (eds) (2005). *Internalizing Globalization*, Basingstoke, UK: Palgrave Macmillan.

Street, J. (1967) 'The Latin American Structuralists and the Institutionalists', *Journal of Economic Issues* 1(2): 44–62.

Sunkel, O. (1990) 'Structuralism, Dependency, and Institutionalism', in J. Dietz and D. James (eds) *Progress Toward Development in Latin America*, Boulder, CO: Lynne Reinner Publishers.

Suzigan, W. and A. Villela (1997) *Industrial Policy in Brazil*, Campinas, Brazil: Instituto de Economia, Universidade Estadual de Campinas.

Tabb, W. (2012) *The Restructuring of Capitalism in our Time*, New York: Columbia University Press.

Veblen, T. ([1915] 1954) *Imperial Germany and the Industrial Revolution*, New York: Viking.

Veltmeyer, H. and J. Petras (2003) *Cardoso's Brazil*, Lanham, MD: Rowman & Littlefield.

Vernengo, M. (2011) 'The Brazilian Economy after Lula: What to Expect?' *CESifo Forum* 1: 17–22. Available online:www.cesifo-group.de/portal/page/portal/ifoHome/b-publ/b2journal/30publforum/_PUBLFORUM11. (accessed: 3 April 2011).

Vieira, R. (2004) 'Entrevista com Celso Furtado', *História Oral* (7): 21–40.

9

Can China's Growth Lead the World Out of the Global Economic Crisis?

Paul Bowles

The current economic malaise in the Eurozone, the fragility of the recovery in the United States, and the two-decade long slump in Japan has concentrated the global economic crisis in the advanced countries. Many now pin their hopes of a global economic recovery on so-called emerging economies, especially China and India, as the new juggernauts capable of kick-starting the global economy. A 'multispeed' world, as Spence (2011) calls it, now characterizes the global economy with the engine located firmly in large developing countries. This change has led to increased interest in what Kaplinsky (2005) has termed the 'Asian drivers'.

As evidence of the role played by one of these Asian Drivers, the OECD documents how China's rise to the world's second-largest economy has dramatically increased its contributions to global growth over the past 30 years. It states (OECD 2011a: 6) that

> China's contribution to global growth has been increasing exponentially, from 5% in 1980 to 12% in 2000 and 30% in 2010. Almost 1.5 percentage points of the projected growth of 4–4.5 per cent of the world economy in 2011–12 is accounted for by China. China's economic cycle is increasingly influenced by and induces fluctuations in the rest of the world, and in OECD economies in particular.

China's future growth path therefore holds great interest for the rest of the world, the OECD countries in particular, and will be an important factor in determining whether and how fast the global economic crisis is exited.

This is a revised, abridged and updated version of Bowles (2012). I am grateful to the *Canadian Journal of Development Studies* for permission to reprint. I am grateful to Mark Setterfield for clarifying several points about Post-Keynesian growth theory and to Baotai Wang for his comments on the Chinese data. I acknowledge SSHRC for funding.

Certainly, many countries' leaders, in both the North and South, are betting on China and other large developing countries growing fast enough to pull them out of recession; this provides one reason for the increased interest in neoliberal trade policy in the post-global financial crisis period despite its evident previous failings (see the Introduction to this volume for more on the deepening of neoliberalism). An examination of the dynamics of China's growth is therefore important.

In part, the potential for China to lead the world out of the global economic crisis depends on the rate of China's growth. After decades of around double-digit annual growth, this has now begun to be questioned. Official pronouncements have lowered China's targeted growth rate to 7.5 per cent for 2012 while the annual average target for 2011–15, the period of the 12th Five Year Plan, is 7 per cent (see *China Daily* 2012). The IMF has recently lowered its growth forecasts for China to 8.0 per cent for 2012 and 8.5 per cent for 2013 (see IMF 2012). While lower than previous planned and actual growth rates, this is still a robust growth rate which would contribute significantly to global growth. However, while official Chinese pronouncements and forecasts by international agencies continue to point to high growth for China, concerns are rising. The IMF (2012) notes that 'in the medium term, there are tail risks of a hard landing in China, where investment spending could slow more sharply given overcapacity in a number of sectors'. For some the prospects of a hard landing are very high. For example, Michael Pettis (2012), an economist based at Peking University, has forecast that because of the fragile state of China's banking system, China's average annual growth rate over the next decade will barely exceed 3 per cent.

While this has focused on the level of China's growth, another set of issues concern the type of growth that China is pursuing. In particular, much attention has been paid to whether China's growth can be 'rebalanced' (see, for example, Lardy 2007). The term 'rebalancing' has usually been interpreted as meaning whether growth in China can rely less on exports and more on domestic demand as a driver of growth. This rebalancing is seen as both a way for China to sustain its growth over the longer term and to do so in a way which provides more benefits to its trading partners by increasing China's imports but without relying on the continued rapid growth of Chinese exports; indeed, as I will explain further below, it is China's pursuit of export-led growth, leading to global imbalances, that some have identified as the cause of the global financial crisis. According to this argument, to remove this cause and to permit a resumption of global economic growth requires a change in structure of the Chinese economy.

Structural and spatial changes are already occurring in the Chinese economy. In Chapter 6 of this volume Zhang offers an analysis of the 'spatial fix' underway in which Chinese manufacturing capacity is moving inland to take advantage of lower labour costs and local government incentive packages. However, as he points out, this reinforces China's export competitiveness and does nothing to move away from an over-reliance. In this sense, there is little rebalancing occurring. This chapter complements his analysis by looking more closely at what rebalancing entails and whether it is easy for China to achieve this. Using insights generated by post-Keynesian economics I argue that the task of rebalancing growth in China is formidable.

In the next section, I outline the background to the rebalancing issue and show how it has been an official policy for well over a decade but that the results to date have been very modest. In the subsequent section, I utilize post-Keynesian growth theory to explain why this might be the case and assess whether China can move to a different growth model.

China's growth path: Forces for change

China's leadership has talked for most of the past decade about the need to 'rebalance' China's economy, change its structure, and put it onto a different growth path. The intentions of China's leadership in this regard can be readily seen by the objectives set in the most recent Five Year Plans. In the 10th Five Year Plan, for example (2001–06), there was considerable talk of the need to make 'readjustments' to the growth path. These readjustments included a greater role for the service sector, addressing regional issues with increased importance given to Western development and addressing rural–urban inequalities. Together, these readjustments would serve to increase domestic demand as a source of growth. This was made clear as being both the means to, and purpose of, economic growth by Premier Zhu Rongji when announcing the plan:

> Raising the people's living standards in both urban and rural areas is the basic goal of our economic development and a crucial factor for expanding domestic demand and stimulating sustained economic growth. We must give priority to raising the people's living standards. To accomplish this we must create more jobs, increase personal income, distribute income more equitably, improve the social security system, and ensure a more comfortable life for the people.
>
> (Zhu Rongji 2001)

This shift towards a greater concern for the domestic market was a result not only of the desire to make the benefits of growth available to citizens but also to reduce the reliance on international markets. As reported in the *China Daily* (2001),

> the new five-year plan makes the expansion of domestic demands a 'long-term' principle of strategic importance. The intrinsic logic is that expanding domestic demand would provide greater leeway for maneuver

> and enhance the resistance against international economic risks in the complicated and capricious international environment.

The vulnerability of an over-reliance on exports had been illustrated in the Asian financial crisis and responding to this, as well as a concern for regional and rural–urban inequalities, the leadership signalled a change in growth direction. This change in direction became much more explicit, and the concern with rising inequalities more pronounced, with the transition to the Hu-Wen leadership in 2003.

Ma Kai, the Minister of the National Development and Reform Commission, made the new growth path clear when announcing the 11th Five Year Plan in 2006. In enumerating the objectives of the new Plan he stated:

> First, we will promote development by relying on the expansion of domestic demand, take the expansion of domestic demand, especially consumption, as a major driving force, and transform economic growth from being driven by investment and export to being driven by consumption, investment, domestic and foreign demand combined in a balanced manner.
>
> (Ma Kai 2006)

Noting that the share of domestic consumption had fallen during the previous Plan from 61.5 per cent to 50.7 per cent, he revealed that the aim would be to reverse this trend – 'adjust the relationship between investment and consumption' – with the aim of 'strengthen[ing] the driving force of consumption in economic growth'. This was to be achieved by increasing consumption through income growth 'particularly of rural residents and low-income population in urban areas' and more generally engaging in income redistribution policies (Ma Kai 2006).

In the 12th Five Year Plan (2011–15) this shift is reconfirmed with a policy priority described as being to

> establish [the] long term mechanism of expanding domestic demand. Create [a] positive consumption environment by actively yet steadily accelerating urbanization, implementing the strategy of employment as priority, deepening the distribution reform and improving social security system, gradually make the overall size of our domestic market ranks among the largest internationally.
>
> (China's Twelfth Five Year Plan 2011)

The role of income redistribution and the provision of social security as mechanisms to reduce the savings rates and boost consumption as set out in the 12th Five Year Plan reflect a continuation of the themes set out in the 11th Five Year Plan. The continued stress on the importance of the service sector and on Western regional development found in the latest plan echoes these same calls in the 10th Year Plan. There has been a consistent policy thrust over the past ten years and extending into the next five to move to a more balanced growth path in which consumption plays a greater role and investment and exports a lesser role.

Some of the measures and targets set out in the plans to achieve these objectives are indicated in Table 9.1. To these medium-term policies, we can add the boost to domestic demand given by the short-term stimulus package introduced in response to the 2008 global financial crisis (GFC). The GFC reinforced the vulnerabilities China faces from excessive reliance on export growth. These vulnerabilities, also evident in the Asian financial crisis in 1997, take the form of a sudden slowdown in export growth rates and the consequences of this for tens of millions of migrant workers who are forced to return to their rural homes as employment in the export sector falls. Thus, over-reliance on exports not only causes economic shocks, in terms of rapid changes in demand and hence income caused by international linkages, it also threatens social stability. These events have reinforced the importance to the leadership of giving a greater role to domestic consumption as a growth driver.

Table 9.1 China's five-year plans: Selected measures and targets

Plan	Selected Measures and Targets
10th Five Year Plan (2001–6)	• Increase medical and health services • Create 40 million urban jobs • Increase net per capita income of urban and rural residents by 5 per cent p.a.
11th Five Year Plan (2006–11)	• Increase urban basic pension scheme to cover 223 million urban residents (up from 174 million) • Increase coverage of rural cooperative medical care scheme from 23.5 per cent to over 80 per cent of the rural population • Create 45 million urban jobs • Increase net per capita income of urban and rural residents by 5 per cent p.a.
12th Five Year Plan (2011–15)	• Build 36 million low-income housing units • Increase basic pension coverage to 375 million urban residents and all rural resident • Create 45 million urban jobs • Increase the minimum wage rate by at least 13 per cent p.a.

The measures set out in the Five Year Plans, supplemented by the stimulus package and supported by a raft of other policy measures such as the 'Go West' strategy and the abolition of agricultural taxes, have formed part of a consistent set of domestically driven policies aimed at reducing income inequality and external vulnerability by pushing China onto a consumption-driven growth path.[1]

It should be noted that China's goal of reducing income inequality (whether realized or not) is common to many other developing countries. It is noteworthy that while the dominant neoliberal ideology in the North has meant that scant attention has been paid to decades of increasing income inequality in many countries, and took the Occupy Movement to put it back on the agenda, this has not been the case in the South. Here, there have been many examples of major policy interventions designed to reduce inequality. The National Rural Employment Guarantee Scheme in India provides one example (see Government of India 2013 for details). Cypher (Chapter 8 of this volume) documents how neo-developmentalism has gained ideological and policy traction in Brazil with redistribution being a central part of its rationale, in what Cypher terms Brazil's 'growth with redistribution' policy. Policy discourse in China resonates with that occurring elsewhere in the South but it is perhaps here that 'growth *through* redistribution' has taken its most prominent form. In the Chinese context, redistributive measures, such as those outlined in Table 9.1, are seen not as simply as tools to ensure that the benefits of growth are more widely shared; rather redistribution is seen as a way of stimulating a new type of growth based on domestic demand.

To these domestic sources, we can also add international pressures as pushing China in the same direction. The emergence of 'global imbalances' – meaning large balance of trade imbalances between countries – first attracted the attention of the IMF in 2002 and these have dominated discussion of international policy coordination since. China's export surpluses and high domestic saving rates have been seen as obstacles to sustainable global growth and, indeed, as causes of the GFC itself. With respect to solving the global imbalances, US Federal Reserve Chair Ben Bernanke (2007) argued that 'as the global perspective makes clear, the reduction of the US current account deficit also requires efforts on the part of the surplus countries to reduce the excess of their desired saving over desired investment'. Needless to say, China figured heavily in this account. Bernanke (2007) continued, with specific reference to China that

> Chinese saving rates rose rapidly (by more even than investment rates); that rise in saving was, perhaps, a result of the strong growth in incomes in the midst of an underdeveloped financial sector and a weak social safety net that increases the motivation for precautionary saving.

The international community has, therefore, also been vocal in encouraging China to address its export surplus and high saving rates and to boost domestic consumption.

Parenthetically, this analysis also resonates with heterodox/radical critiques. For example, Blackburn (2009: 129) pronounced starkly in what he admits is 'crude thinking', that 'the root cause of the [global financial] crisis was, quite simply, poverty. If Chinese direct producers had been better paid they would have furnished a larger and growing market, in ways that would have benefitted the PRC's trading partners'. Others have called for more emphasis on 'domestic demand'-led growth in developing countries including (or especially) in China (see, for example, Palley 2011 and Wade 2009).

Despite the desire of China's leaders to stimulate domestic demand and change growth paths, a change also supported and encouraged by China's trading partners, it is remarkable that private consumption in China has continued to fall as a percentage of GDP. Moreover, the composition of China's GDP in international comparative perspective stands out for the low level of private consumption. At approximately 35 per cent, it is the only country in Asia (with the exception of Singapore) where this value is less than 50 per cent (Prasad 2009: Table 1).[2]

The desired direction of policy change is therefore clear but the outcomes, as shown by the composition of GDP, still shows how far China is from achieving its goal. In order to better understand why this might be the case, and to analyse the difficulty that China faces in shifting growth paths, in the next section I examine post-Keynesian growth theory and draw inferences from that about the nature of the Chinese economy and its prospects for rebalancing.

Post-Keynesian growth theory

Growth theory in the post-Keynesian tradition is primarily concerned with the implications of income distribution for economic growth. In particular, it classifies countries' growth paths according to whether an increase in the share of wages or profits will lead to sustainable growth.[3] Of course, other causes of growth are acknowledged but the focus is on income distribution.

This framework is useful for consideration here since any attempt to change China's growth path to a consumption-led growth path will require a redistribution of income from profits to wages. As Lee (2011: 2) writes, 'demand in actual economies could be either wage led or profit led, because consumption is usually thought of as being wage led while investment and net exports are expected to be profit led'. The growth accounting approach discussed above uses the distinction between (domestic) demand-led growth (in which consumption and investment are the main drivers) and export-led growth (in which net exports play the most important role). Post-Keynesian models make a different distinction between wage-led growth (in which consumption plays the most important role) and profit-led growth (in which investment and/or net exports play the key roles).[4]

For our purposes, the analytical question becomes whether China is a wage-led economic regime, in which consumption plays the major role in enabling sustainable growth and, if it is not, whether wage-led policies can move it in that direction.

Whether an economy is a wage-led or a profit-led regime is 'not a choice variable for economic policy in any straightforward sense' (Lavoie and Stockhammer 2011: 7). A wage-led regime is one in which a change in the distribution of income towards wages will lead to continued growth; a profit-led regime is one in which it will not.

Establishing whether an economy is a wage-led or a profit-led regime depends on the structure of the economy. In particular, it depends

> in part on the existing income distribution in the country, but also on various behavioural components, such as the propensity to consume of various income recipients, on the sensitivity of entrepreneurs to changes in sales or in profit margins, and on the sensitivity of exporters and importers to changes in costs, foreign exchange values, and changes in foreign demand, as well as the size of the various components of aggregate demand – consumption, investment, government expenditures and net exports.
>
> (Lavoie and Stockhammer 2011: 7)

These 'behavioural components', while technical economic measures, can also be related to class relations and the wider political economy. For example, the propensity to consume out of wages will depend in part on the extent to which the working class has been able to achieve economic security through claims on the state through various welfare measures and on companies through employment-related benefits. The propensity to consume out of profits partly depends on social *mores* related to the display of wealth. Furthermore, the sensitivity of entrepreneurs to changes in sales or profit margins may well depend upon patterns of firm ownership and upon market structures.

In a wage-led regime, an increase in the share of national income going to wages would boost aggregate demand and growth through the following mechanisms. Firstly, consumption will increase as wage earners' propensity to consume is greater than the propensity to consume out of profits and thus aggregate consumption increases with income redistribution towards wage earners. Secondly, through the accelerator principle, the increase in consumer spending will increase investment. (This effect may be reduced if investment also depends on the profit share.) In this case, with both consumption and investment responding positively to an increase in the wage share, the economy is said to be a wage-led demand regime and a wage-led investment regime. This is the strongest case and, since investment increases, extends into increasing long-term growth. This has so far considered domestic demand-led regimes. We can now introduce an open economy by adding the impact of net exports on growth. If an increase in the wage share (and real wage) have only a small negative effect on exports then the economy is likely to be wage-led overall. Of course, if the opposite holds for the relationships described above then the economy is profit-led; attempts to shift the distribution of income in favour of labour and consumption will not increase long-run growth.

The structural differences between wage-led and profit-led demand regimes are summarized by Lavoie and Stockhammer (2011: 17) in Table 9.2. Whether an economy is a wage-led or a profit-led regime therefore relies upon the size of key behavioural variables. However, as well as these *regimes*, there are also wage-led and profit-led *policies*. These are, as their names imply, policy variables and may operate to shift the income distribution in favour of capital (through labour market deregulation and the weakening of trade unions, for example) or in favour of labour (through increased social protection and increases in worker's rights, for example). The distinction between regimes and policies is important because only if both are in alignment will the outcome be increased growth; that is, if wage-led policies are introduced in wage-led demand regimes then the outcome will be better economic growth outcomes. If wage-led policies are introduced in profit-led regimes, however, the result will be economic stagnation. The analogous result holds for profit-led policies.

How does China fit in this schema? Here Lavoie and Stockhammer make the following general argument and incorporate China within it. They argue that many countries have experienced low growth over the past three decades as a result of introducing the pro-capital profit-led policies associated with neoliberalism into wage-led demand regimes. The stagnation of

Table 9.2 Economic structure: Wage-led and profit-led demand regimes

Profit-led	Wage-led
Small differences in propensity to consume	Propensity to consume out of wages is much higher than propensity out of profits
Investment is highly sensitive to profitability and accelerator parameter is low	Investment is not sensitive to profitability and accelerator parameter is high
Very open economy with high net export price elasticity	Relatively closed economy with low net export price elasticity

the world economy, relative to the post-war 'golden age' in which pro-labour wage-led policies were dominant, is thereby explained. How was growth possible at all in these circumstances? Here they argue that neoliberalism in practice has had to rely on other external factors to compensate for the lack of domestic demand. In some countries these factors have been finance-led growth while in others it has been export-led growth. This leads them to present a 'stylized classification' (2011: 25) of important countries' growth models under neoliberalism in practice; China appears as the (sole) representative of an export-led economy located in the periphery. China then, along with Germany and Japan from the core, is identified as an economy in which 'increasing trade surpluses have been the growth engine' (2011: 27). Elsewhere (2011: 4), they define export led-growth as occurring 'where the main engine of growth has been net exports' (examples are Germany, Japan, and China).

Does China fit the 'stylized classification' as presented by Lavioe and Stockhammer? There are some reasons for doubt. Firstly, China's growth has not been driven mainly by net exports as the results from growth accounting approaches show; net exports have been contributors to growth in the most recent period but they have not been the 'main engine of growth' (see Bowles 2012 for more details; see also Dew et al. 2011). Domestic investment holds that particular title. Secondly, the temporal account used to analyse OECD growth records does not straightforwardly, if at all, carry over to China's case. To recap, their argument is that in the golden age, the growth in OECD countries as a whole was higher because demand was wage-led and pro-labour policies were followed; growth has fallen in the subsequent period of neoliberalism as pro-capital policies were introduced. Growth only occurred during this latter period due to the adoption of finance-led and export-led policies. In China, the pre-1978 period was unlikely to have been wage led given the general low levels of per capita income but heavily reliant on domestic investment as the source of growth. In the post-1978 period this has continued to be the same main source of demand, but growth has increased substantially in the reform period with net exports contributing to that since around 2000. This trajectory is quite different from the OECD history.

Nevertheless, given the dominance of domestic investment in China's growth history, does this still make China analytically a profit-led demand regime? Here, recall that this regime is characterized by an economic structure in which the propensity to consume out of profits and wages are not too different, investment is highly sensitive to profitability, and the economy is very open with a high net export price elasticity.[5]

Considering each of these variables in turn, China's propensity to consume out of profits and wages can be approximated by the savings behaviour of the corporate and household sectors. Both sectors exhibit high savings rates. Knight and Wang (2011: 12) estimate that the enterprise saving rate out of profits between 1996 and 2008 was 'consistently high, but varying between 60 and 80 per cent'.[6] In the household sector, as already noted, Prasad (2009: 18) reports that household savings, as a percentage of disposable income, 'has been on a gradual upward trend since 1990, rising to about 27 per cent in 2008'. The comparable data for 2008 for the EU27, Japan, and the United States were 5.4, 2.3, and 4.2 per cent respectively (OECD 2011b: 63).

In terms of the sensitivity of investment to profitability, this is likely to vary substantially between industrial ownership categories. As a general rule, the private (non-state) sector is much more likely to be sensitive to profitability than the state-owned sector. The state sector still continues to operate with varying degrees of a soft budget constraint, is prone to excess capacity and unsold goods, and growth (rather than profitability) continues to be a strong managerial objective. The non-state sector, consisting of domestic private- and foreign-funded enterprises, is characterized by competitive markets where the profit motive dominates and where investment might be expected to be highly sensitive to profitability.

To move beyond this generalization is complicated, however, because the ownership structure of Chinese industry now includes shareholding and limited liability companies which may be in the state and/or private sectors. The industrial ownership structure, using some broad categories, is presented in Table 9.3. Since we are interested in the sensitivity of investment to profitability, the table weights firms in each category by their share of the value of total industrial assets (which is likely to be a more accurate proxy for their investment share than their share of either total output or of total enterprises).

Table 9.3 illustrates the complex ownership structure of industry in China today. The 'pure' state-owned sector accounts for nearly 14 per cent of total assets while the 'pure' private sector, domestic and foreign, accounts for about 30 per cent.[7] In between are various hybrids involving joint ventures between foreign firms and domestic (predominantly state owned) enterprises as well as limited liability and shareholding enterprises formed by various state entities. As a rough guide, we can say that about 55 per cent of China's industrial assets are controlled by state or quasi-state enterprises (the first seven rows of figures in column two of Table 9.3 below) while 45 per cent are in the private sector (the remaining nine rows). This is only a first approximation but sufficient for our general purpose here.

China's trade/GDP ratio, a common measure of trade openness, at 55.4 per cent is relatively high for a large country and comparable to that of the United Kingdom (58.8 per cent) and France (53.0 per cent) and considerably higher than that of India (47.7 per cent), Japan (30.8 per cent), and the United States (27.7 per cent) although still lower than that of Germany (85.3 per cent). (All figures are averages for 2008–10. See World Trade Organization 2011.) Estimates of China's export price elasticity vary but recent

Table 9.3 Shares of total assets of industrial enterprises by ownership type, 2009

Type of Enterprise	Share of Total Industrial Assets (per cent)
Domestic funded	
State owned enterprises	13.9
Collectives	1.0
Cooperatives	0.5
Joint ownership	0.3
Limited liability corporations	
State sole funded corporations	7.9
Other limited liability corporations	20.5
Shareholding corporations	11.8
Private Enterprises	
Private funded	2.5
Private partnerships	0.4
Private limited liability	14.3
Private shareholding	1.3
Enterprises with funds from Hong Kong, Macau and Taiwan	9.0
Foreign funded enterprises	
Joint ventures	7.5
Cooperation enterprises	0.4
Enterprises with sole funds	7.4
Shareholding	0.8

Source: Calculated from *Statistical Yearbook of China* (2010: Table 14–1).

work indicates a significant price elasticity. For example, Ahmed (2009) reports that

> movements in the exchange rate substantially affect export growth in the direction predicted by theory; that is a greater exchange rate appreciation dampens export growth, and our estimated price elasticity is generally greater than unity, and towards the high end of price elasticities found in previous work.

My assessment of these three variables, again in the form of 'stylized facts' but drawing on empirical estimates, is summarized below in Table 9.4. I divide the variables into those exhibiting values consistent with a wage-led demand regime and those consistent with a profit-led demand regime.

Two of the three key economic variables are more consistent with the characterization of the economy as being a profit-led regime and one more ambiguous. Of course, the effect on the whole economy depends on the balance of all three but, as a first approximation, it may be reasonable

Table 9.4 The stylized facts of China's economic structure

Variable	Profit-led regime	Wage-led regime
Propensity to consume out of profits and wages	Propensity to consume out of wages and profits both relatively low	
Sensitivity of investment to profitability	High sensitivity to profitability in the private sector accounting for around 45 per cent of industrial assets	Low sensitivity to profitability in the state and quasi-state sector accounting for around 55 per cent of industrial assets
Openness of economy and export price elasticity	Trade/GDP ratio of 55 per cent is relatively high for a large country. Exports face high price elasticity	

to characterize the Chinese economy as being a profit-led regime or, less strongly, not clearly demand led. The implications of this are analysed in our concluding section.

Implications and conclusions

China's policy objective for the past decade has been to change its growth path. The analysis of post-Keynesian growth theory illustrated that, within the demand-led model the structural characteristics of the Chinese economy make it more likely to be a profit-led than a wage-led regime. This has implications for the prospects of introducing policies capable of shifting the growth path.

The measures contained in China's Five Year Plans outlined in Table 9.1 include pro-labour redistribution policies aimed at increasing wages. To these we can also add other initiatives such as the central government announcement (on 30 June 2011) that the income tax threshold would rise from 2000 RMB to 3500 RMB per month effective 1 September. Also relevant are changes to the bargaining power of labour (through the implementation of the new labour contract law in 2008, for example; see Wang et al. 2010) which is important in name although relatively modest in effect. Rising wages, which are occurring anyway as a result of labour market dynamics, are also noteworthy for their potential redistributive effects; according to official figures real wages have increased by over 10 per cent each year during 1998–2009 (National Bureau of Statistics of China 2010b: Tables 1–26 and 1–27). All of these policies are highly desirable on equity grounds. However, these pro-labour policies and market-led wage increases are not necessarily consistent with the leadership's growth objective. Post-Keynesian approaches highlight the problems in introducing wage-led policies into profit-led regimes. The result is likely to be lower growth and incoherence rather than a smooth transition to a new sustainable growth path.

The central leadership has prioritized growth and explicitly argued that China must achieve at least 7.5–8 per cent annual growth rate to absorb new labour market entrants and labour transferred into the industrial sector and thereby maintain social stability. But, as noted, introducing pro-labour policies in a profit-led regime may reduce growth and put growth and redistribution on a collision course.

What is needed, therefore, are policies to address the structural characteristics of the Chinese economy as summarized in Table 9.4. Social protection policies which lower insecurity, and thereby increase the propensity to consume out of wages, constitute one obvious area and one in which some policies (such as health and pension provisions) have indeed been introduced. Similarly, technological upgrading to decrease the price sensitivity of exports is also beneficial and has been a policy objective. If China is to succeed in redistributing income and maintaining its high economic growth rates then these structural changes will be needed if China is going to be able to successfully change growth paths. In this chapter, operating at the level of 'stylized facts', it has been argued that China is more likely to be a profit-led regime at present although this is clearly an area where more empirical work is needed. The analysis has shown, however, that the task of switching growth paths in China will be a long and difficult process.

There are also implications for the global economy and for the prospects of avoiding the economic problems – slow growth and crises – which have plagued the neoliberal era. If the rest of the world is waiting for China to pull it out of the global economic crisis by transitioning to a new high growth path then it is likely to wait in vain. Even if China did manage to shift to a wage-led growth model, this would not necessarily solve the global economic crisis in the longer term if other countries, especially those in the North, did not adapt as well. As the analysis by Lavoie and Stockhammer (2011) argues, the global growth slowdown arose because the wage-led policies adopted in the wage-led demand regimes of the North during the 'golden age' were replaced by profit-led policies in the subsequent neoliberal period. Some countries escaped the growth slowdown consequences of this by increasing demand either through export-oriented policies (for example, Germany) or through financialization (for example, the United States up until the global financial crisis). If China's shift to a wage-led regime were to be realized, if this simply encouraged Northern economies to continue with neoliberal pro-capital profit-led policies and to seek export-oriented salvation via the China market, the contradictions in the global economy would remain. The prospects for longer-term global economic recovery depend on all countries adjusting their policies and regimes, adjustments which cannot be expected to be achieved quickly.

Notes

1. The measures discussed above are all central-level policies. There are also complementary policies being adopted at the provincial level. For example, the Jiangsu provincial government has recently stated its objective as being to double the average wage level in the province by 2017. I am grateful to Hu Guoliang for bringing my attention to this point.
2. For comparative purposes, in Japan the share of consumption in GDP is 55 per cent and it is 71 per cent in the United States (Prasad 2009: Table 1).
3. Post-Keynesian models consider both demand- and supply-side effects. We restrict our attention here to the demand-side factors (for a review of these models see, for example, Setterfield 2002).
4. Strictly speaking this distinction is true for the Kaleckian version of Post-Keynesian growth theory. Kaldorian models are based on internal and external demand distinctions. The subsequent analysis is based on the Kaleckian version (Setterfield 2002).
5. Kaldorian models would also add the size of GDP components to this list.
6. One reason for this is that investment has increasingly been financed by enterprise savings. For example, the percentage of fixed asset investment financed by retained earnings increased from 55.4 per cent in 1981 to 77.4 per cent in 2009. See National Bureau of Statistics of China (2010a: Table 5–4).
7. This is calculated by adding the domestic private sector to the solely foreign- and Hong Kong-, Macau-, and Taiwan-funded enterprises. (This latter disaggregation is not given in Table 9.3).

References

Ahmed, S. (2009) 'Are Chinese Exports Sensitive to Changes in the Exchange Rate?' Board of Governors of the Federal Reserve System, *International Finance Discussion Papers*, No: 987, December. Available online: http://www.federalreserve.gov/pubs/ifdp/2009/987/ifdp987.htm. (accessed: 23 March 2013).

Bernanke, B. (2007) 'Global Imbalance: Recent Developments and Prospects', Lecture at the Bundesbank, Berlin, Germany, 11 September. Available online: http://www.federalreserve.gov/newsevents/speech/bernanke20070911a.htm. (accessed: 24 March 2013).

Blackburn, R. (2009) 'Value Theory and the Chinese Worker', *New Left Review* 56 (March–April): 128–35.

Bowles, P. (2012) 'Rebalancing China's Growth: Some Unsettled Questions', *Canadian Journal of Development Studies* 33(1): 1–13.

China Daily (2012) 'China Sets 2012 GDP Growth Target at 7.5%', 5 March. Available online: http://www.chinadaily.com.cn/china/2012-03/05/content_14755389.htm. (accessed: 24 March 2013).

China Daily (2001) 'CPPCC Members Hail New Strategic Restructuring Plan', 7 March, English Internet Edition. Available online: http://english.peopledaily.com.cn/200103/07/eng20010307_64346.html. (accessed: 27 July 2011).

China's Twelfth Five Year Plan, 2011–2015 (2011 – the Full English Version). Translation by Delegation of the European Union in China, posted 11 May 2011. Available online: http://cbi.typepad.com/china_direct/2011/05/chinas-twelfth-five-new-plan-the-full-english-version.html. (accessed: 27 July 2011).

Dew, E., J. Martin, J. Giese, and G. Zinna (2011) 'China's Changing Growth Pattern', *Bank of England Quarterly Bulletin* 51(1): 49–56.

Government of India, Ministry of Rural Development (2013) 'The Mahatma Gandhi National Rural Employment Guarantee Act 2005'. Available online: http://nrega.nic.in/netnrega/home.aspx. (accessed: 23 March 2013).

IMF (2012) *World Economic Outlook Update: New Setbacks, Further Policy Needed*, 16 July. Available online: http://www.imf.org/external/pubs/ft/weo/2012/update/02/index.htm. (accessed: 23 March 2013).

Kaplinsky, R. (ed.) (2005) 'Asian Drivers: Opportunities and Threats', *IDS Bulletin* 37(1).

Knight, J. and W. Wang (2011) 'China's Macroeconomic Imbalances: Causes and Consequences', *BOFIT Discussion Paper* (15).

Lardy, N. (2007) 'China: Rebalancing Economic Growth', in N. Lardy (ed.) *The China Balance Sheet in 2007 and Beyond*, Washington DC: Centre for Strategic and International Studies and the Peterson Institute for International Economics.

Lavoie, M. and E. Stockhammer (2011) 'Wage-Led Growth: Concept, Theories and Policies', Paper Presented at the ILO Conference on Regulating for Decent Work, Geneva, 6–8 July.

Lee, S. (2011) 'Wages and Economic Development: Towards an Alternative Model', Paper Presented at the ILO Conference on Key Lessons from the Crisis and Way Forward, Geneva, 16–17 February.

Ma Kai (2006) 'The 11th Five-Year Plan: Targets, Paths and Policy Orientation', *NDRC Minister on 11th Five-Year Plan*, 23 March. Available online: http://www.gov.cn/english/2006-03/23/content_234832.htm. (accessed: 27 July 2011).

National Bureau of Statistics of China (2010a) *China Statistical Yearbook 2010*, Beijing: China Statistical Press.

National Bureau of Statistics of China (2010b) *China Labour Statistical Yearbook 2010*, Beijing: China Statistical Press.

OECD (2011a) 'China's Emergence as a Market Economy: Achievements and Challenges', OECD contribution to the China Development Forum, 20–21 March, Beijing.

OECD (2011b) *OECD Factbook 2011–12: Economic, Environmental and Social Statistics*, Paris: OECD Publishing.

Palley, T. (2011) 'The Rise and Fall of Export-Led Growth', *Levy Economics Institute of Bard College Working Paper* (675).

Pettis, M. (2012) 'Tough Medicine and a Hard Landing for China'. Available online: http://www.creditwritedowns.com/2012/03/tough-medicine-and-a-hard-landing-for-china.html. (accessed 23 March 2013).

Prasad, E. (2009) 'Rebalancing Growth in Asia', *NBER Working Paper* (July) (15169).

Setterfield, M. (2002) *The Economics of Demand-led Growth*, Cheltenham: Edward Elgar.

Spence, M. (2011) *The Next Convergence: The Future of Economic Growth in a Multispeed World*, New York: Farrar, Straus and Giroux.

Wade, R. (2009) 'The Economic Crisis and the Developing World: What Next?' Interview with Kevin Gallagher, *Challenge*, January–February (1): 27–39.

Wang, H., R. Appelbaum, F. Degiuli, and N. Lichtenstein (2010) 'China's New Labour Contract Law: Is China Moving Towards Increased Powers for Workers?' in P. Bowles and J. Harriss (eds) *Globalization and Labour in China and India: Impacts and Responses*, New York: Palgrave Macmillan.

World Trade Organization (2011) *Trade Profiles 2011*, Geneva: WTO.

Zhu Rongji (2001) 'Report on the Outline of the Tenth Five-Year Plan for National Economic and Social Development', 5 March 2001. Available online: http://www.gov.cn/english/official/2005-07/29/content_18334.htm. (accessed 27 July 2011).

10

Crisis, Social Class, and the 'Fixing' of Capitalism in Mexico

Hepzibah Muñoz Martinez

In 2007 the American economy experienced a severe crisis which spread through credit and financial markets, leading to declining rates of investment, lower consumption and growing unemployment in the United States. In an interview at the end of 2008, Agustin Carstens, former Minister of Finance (2006–9) in Mexico and head of the Mexican Central Bank between 2010 and 2016, stated that economic stagnation in the United States would have a limited effect on the Mexican economy. When the interviewer noted that Mexico usually catches 'pneumonia' when the United States has an economic 'cold', the minister responded that this time the Mexican economy would only 'catch the sniffles' (Notimex 2008). He believed that Mexico's sound policies of fiscal austerity, public debt management and reserve accumulation would protect its economy from external shocks (Gil Diaz 2009: 29–31). However, this did not occur, and Mexico's GDP declined 6 per cent in 2009 (INEGI 2011a). According to Mexico's National Council on the Evaluation of Social Development Policy (CONEVAL), the number of people living in poverty increased by 3.2 million between 2008 and 2010 (CONEVAL 2011). The transmission mechanisms linking the American financial crisis to the Mexican economy were diminishing exports to, and workers' remittances from, the United States, Mexico's main trading and investment partner. The trade balance deficit in goods increased from 6.1 billion dollars in 2006 to 17 billion in 2008, while remittances decreased 18.75 per cent between 2007 and 2009 (OECD 2013; World Bank 2011: 175). In addition, the decrease of international capital inflows and the settlement of debt obligations in US dollars by international investors and American firms with operations in Mexico placed downward pressure on the Mexican peso

I would like to thank Yıldız Atasoy, Ruth Felder, Laura Macdonald, Susanne Soederberg, and the anonymous reviewer for their insightful comments on previous drafts of this chapter.

(Ocampo 2009: 707). Foreign direct investment decreased 13.39 per cent between 2007 and 2008 and 41.20 per cent between 2008 and 2009 (ECLAC 2010: 31). Thus, Mexico was clearly negatively affected by the impact of the US financial crisis between 2007 and 2009.

In an effort to maintain the value of the peso, the Mexican government's response to the crisis was to continue a monetary policy based on public debt management and accumulation of foreign reserves. Fiscal spending on infrastructure, production subsidies and social programmes held a secondary role in state policy. Critics pointed out that the government's monetary policy appreciated the peso, but also reduced the competitiveness of Mexican exports (e.g. Cordera et al. 2010; Tello 2009). Critics further argued that foreign ownership of banks and trade liberalization, implemented since the 1980s but accelerated after the 1994 North America Free Trade Agreement (NAFTA), intensified the negative effects of the US financial crisis on the Mexican economy. This was largely due to Mexico's continuing reliance on American markets for its exports, and the inflow of workers' remittances, in addition to portfolio and direct investments. The continuation of monetary policies during the crisis as well as the long-established economic relations between the United States and Mexico led to a diversion of funds away from production and job creation in Mexico (see: Correa et al. 2011; Vidal 2009). High unemployment and growing poverty rates during 2009 would seem to confirm this assessment of Mexican state policy.

While critics often focus on policy errors or mismanagement, this chapter argues that it is important to raise questions concerning the social and political processes that led the Mexican government to respond to the 2007 economic crisis in a particular way. Far from offering an evaluation of 'economic mismanagement', the International Monetary Fund (IMF) has actually praised Mexico's policies of high interest rates, public debt management and reserve accumulation, combined with 'competitive' low wages since the 1980s, as an effective strategy for dealing with the crisis. Unfortunately, these economic policies have been implemented without favourable results for the majority of the Mexican population. Poverty levels increased from 42.7 per cent in 2006 to 51.3 per cent in 2010 and real minimum wages have decreased by 5 per cent since 2000 (World Bank 2013; ECLAC 2012). More than half of the country's total income is held by the wealthiest 20 per cent of the population (ECLAC 2011: 67). Despite these results, the Mexican government has continued to follow the policies noted above, while other states in emerging economies such as Brazil (Chapter 8 of this volume) have undertaken a mixture of mainstream monetary policies and an expansionary role in the economy to increase domestic aggregate demand following the global financial crisis. The continuation of monetarist policies in Mexico poses an interesting question regarding the unequal power relations among domestic social forces and their role in influencing state policy choices.

Global neoliberal policy frameworks have informed the national implementation of a particular version of neoliberalism in Mexico since the 1980s, as embedded in its domestic class structure. Although there are multiple meanings associated with the concept, neoliberalism is often defined as a pathway of market-led regulatory restructuring which politically intensifies market discipline and commodification while disseminating market values throughout all aspects of life (Chapter 2 of this volume; Introduction to this volume). Thus, neoliberalism becomes a 'national regime type' (Brenner et al. 2010: 185, 202–3) and, as a policy framework, its patterns and targets are refashioned by powerful actors according to the existing institutional landscape at the national level. In an attempt to spur economic recovery, the Mexican government has adopted various market intensifying policies such as fiscal austerity, low wages, reserve accumulation and public debt management. These polices, which also constitute an overall backdrop for neoliberal global policy frameworks, have been tailored by the Mexican government to fit into the existing economic and political power structures in the country, as will be discussed later in this chapter.

The Mexican economy has recovered from a 6 per cent GDP decline in 2009 and even managed to achieve 5.3 per cent GDP growth in 2010 (IMF 2013: 154), an achievement which the IMF, as one of the global promoters of neoliberalism, has praised. On her 2011 visit to Mexico as the IMF's managing director, Christine Lagarde noted that '[T]he rapid economic recovery [of Mexico] after the global crisis is a testament to its strong fundamentals and the authorities' skilful policy management' (IMF 2011a). From this point of view, according to the IMF, the Mexican economic crisis ended in 2010, with no long-lasting consequences foreseen for Mexico's economy and society. And, Mexico, now signalled as a successful manager of the crisis, is expected to continue its neoliberal economic growth programme.

Still, the co-existence of growth recovery with increasing poverty, stagnant wages and income inequality after 2009 shows that economic recovery in Mexico is not a result of 'sound', *socially sustainable* economic policies adopted by the government, but rather, is a consequence of the intensification of market discipline which reproduces unequal power relations in the Mexican economic and political hierarchy, creating growing insecurity for many. An important question arises here: what are the forces driving the continuation of an economic model embedded in a generalized politics of market discipline and 'austerity?' This chapter aims to shed light on the persistence of the neoliberal policy reforms of monetarism (re)mobilized in response to the 2007 economic crisis by offering an analysis of the uneven power relationships *within* the capitalist class in Mexico. Further, an examination of interest differentiation within the Mexican capitalist class will provide an opportunity for assessing the policy outcomes of crisis politics.

Large Mexican companies, global manufacturing firms, foreign- and Mexican-owned banks and financial investors in both public debt and private bonds and stocks have employed different pathways to profitability which generate varied and conflicting policy demands. The resolution of these demands and the resulting political tension has characterized policy evaluation in Mexico since the 1980s. While the role of state policy-making in response to the conflicting interests of various social classes and class fractions in society is an unwieldy subject in social theory, it is an important one. This chapter endeavours to make the topic manageable by focusing on the state's policy role in mediating conflicting interests *within* the capitalist class. Far from being a technical economic-policy issue, the shaping of a policy response to the crisis in Mexico has been a matter of power balancing within the capitalist class, as figured in the political mediation of the interest diversification between profitability of productive enterprises and financial investments.

The government has adopted policies of public debt management and reserve accumulation to guarantee profits in both financial and direct productive investments. The weakening of democratic labour organizations in the country since the 1980s has created conditions which have enabled the government to pass the costs of the crisis onto working and middle classes in the form of low wages and tax increases. This chapter argues that the government's economic-growth recovery policies have been ushered in amidst the political tension and balance of power politics of the capitalist class. To demonstrate the argument, the chapter utilizes the 'fixity' and 'mobility' of capital concepts. It focuses on the role of corporations operating in Mexico, with particular attention paid to large Mexican companies which have investments abroad and also control a great share of Mexican domestic markets, including financial markets.

An analysis of the Mexican government's crisis management policies based on the concepts of fixity and mobility of capital is important for two reasons. First, the capitalist class in Mexico has enjoyed a greater influence on economic policy-making during the period under examination (2007–10). This is due to a political context of repression for progressive union activism and the insulation of state policy-making from popular pressures – a context which has been in the making since at least the 1980s (e.g. Morton 2011). However, this is not to suggest that other social forces have not had an influence on state policy in Mexico. Second, state economic policy not only mediates the struggles between capital and labour but also the political tension among various fractions of capital within the capitalist class. Capitalist demands on state policy differ according to the way firms and investors internalize the tensions between capital fixity and mobility. As a result, policy consequences do not necessarily benefit the capitalist class as a whole but depend on an intricate political process of negotiating interests.

Various social classes, including labour, relate to capital fixity and mobility in distinct ways, and this relationship is historically contingent. Given that the focus of this chapter is the policy implications of interest differentiation within the capitalist class for the resumption of economic growth in Mexico, I will not analyse the relationship of other social classes to capital's mobility.

Following this introduction, the chapter draws on the concepts of class, capital fixity, and mobility to show how the intra-class relations of capitalists influence state policy and *vice versa*. The third section provides a historical overview of policies that have departed from the import-substituting industrialization of an earlier era, thereby transforming the class structure in Mexico during the 1980s and the 1990s. This process generated an interest diversification within the capitalist class that played an important role in the shaping of the Mexican government's responses to the 2007 economic crisis. The fourth section of the chapter describes the main policies promoted by the Mexican state after the 2007 crisis and depicts the way in which the state has mediated conflicts among firms and investors by passing the costs of the crisis onto middle and working classes. This section also shows that the state's mediation of conflicting interests is both a negotiated and an antagonistic process. The final section offers a summary of the arguments developed in the chapter.

The national fixity of global capital mobility: Theoretical considerations

The chapter draws on geographical political economy to analyse the mobility and fixity of capital, and to highlight the way these dynamics shape the financial and direct investment interests of investors and firms, thus influencing class alliances and divisions over state policy in Mexico (e.g. Sheppard 2011). This approach differs from other accounts in international political economy which tend to emphasize the coercive role of international capital mobility over states in developing countries (e.g. Foster and Magdoff 2009; Thomas-Slayter 2003). Global capital mobility refers to the world-wide circulation of money as capital and credit. According to Karl Marx, capital is a social relation in which value is preserved and multiplied through the appropriation of surplus labour (Marx 1978: 40). Global capital mobility involves a momentary fixity of grounding money somewhere in order to realize profits by appropriating and using labour and nature. Firms and investors also rely on the fixity of capital in a place where capital can circulate in a coordinated way through the geographical concentration of infrastructure, transport relations, housing, labour, consumer markets, and factories. Such a space ensures the availability of labour and the necessary conditions to accelerate the exchange of goods and their transformation into money (Harvey 2001: 243–8). However, money does not have to be reinvested in the locations where it was originally appropriated. Money is therefore set in motion because firms and investors are constantly seeking to increase profits and avoid asset devaluation. As such, money is reallocated internationally to become once again territorially embedded in the form of production or investment in nationally defined currencies and interest rates for the purpose of generating profits (Harvey 2001: 312). It is in the process of spatial re-embedding of money that political tensions between capital mobility and fixity are constantly reproduced within the capitalist class, expressing varied spatial patterns of accumulation.

As Richard Bryan (1987: 261) notes, an analysis of the space where distinct fractions of capital turn their commodities into money and maintain or increase their profits *via* exploitation of nature and labour as well as through speculative financial activities is central to understanding the effects of the politically differentiated processes of accumulation on state policy. Bryan (1987: 264–7) defines four capitalist fractions in relation to the circuit of capital: national, global, investment-constrained and market-constrained. In the case of national capital, production, realization (the sale of the output of production), and reproduction (reinvestment to start a new circuit of capital) take place within the nation. In contrast, realization and reproduction occur on a world scale for global capital, while a portion of production is fixed within the nation. For investment-constrained capital, production and reproduction are fixed within the nation and realization takes place globally, whereas production and the sale of commodities occur nationally. Reinvestment in production is located at the global level for market-constrained capital.

This chapter draws on Bryan's spatial considerations of global capitalism and the state in relation to capitalist fractions. Unlike Bryan's analysis, this chapter does not define ideal-types of capitalist fractions in relation to production and the circulation of commodities. Rather, it examines the historical formation of capital fractions in the Mexican case in relation to mobility and fixity under financialization. Financialization entails an increasing role for companies in raising money in open markets, while banks seek new sources of wealth through the sale of financial products and the extraction of financial profits from the middle classes and the poor in the form of consumer debt (Marois 2012a: 143).

Financialization has transformed the composition of the capitalist class, while also both differentiating and blurring the difference of interests *within it* in relation to capital mobility and fixity. For instance, the securitization of real estate and production can create liquidity out of fixity (Fox Gotham 2009: 355–71). The existence and expansion of capital fixity also relies on the ability of landed interests and real estate developers to link their activities to financial assets. Likewise, financial investors can channel their surplus liquidity in fixed privatized assets to solve their 'surplus absorption problem' (Harvey 2010: 50). Global production firms with a financial orientation might favour the fixity of their investment in low cost locations

(Harvey 1999: 286). As such, productive and financial activities become part of the same process of international capital accumulation, which entails the internalization of the tensions between international capital mobility and national fixity within capitalist classes (Harvey 1999: 316). This process of the internalization of tensions also blurs the differences between the interests of domestic and foreign capital as national capitalists become increasingly informed by international criteria of profitability, such as investment strategies, productivity rates, and levels of economic return at home and abroad.

While social-class relationships are often defined by the fixity of relations of production within national jurisdictions (Bieler and Morton 2006: 169), financial mobility takes place within the regulatory frameworks of the international monetary system and national monetary policies (Block 1977). A complex web of complementary regulations is always required in making decisions about a multiplicity of issues, including exchange-rate adjustments, balance of payments discipline and debt management, reserve accumulation, price controls, interest rates and the problem of inflation, labour fragmentation, profit maximization, and various aspects of economic liberalization. Thus, the specific ways in which the economy is organized are never 'technical', and never 'above politics', but always historical (Block 1977). Even when national economic-policy debates are framed by a singular reference to a global policy framework of neoliberalism, policy-making is contingent upon long-lasting, historically inherited forms of national regulatory mechanisms, which in turn express a multiplicity of meanings and interests embodied in a variety of social actors and place-specific power structures (e.g. Chapter 3 of this volume; Peck 2011). This is the theoretical premise on which the present chapter is based. While acknowledging the crucial role played by global power relations and governance structures (Gill 2012) in the joint management of the mobility and fixity of capital, this chapter focuses on the administrative measures, controls, and policy regulations adopted by the nation-state of Mexico for the territorialization of capital and mediation of conflicts within the capitalist class.

The state is neither a passive entity nor an autonomous institution. Rather, it is a site of struggle where class power is institutionally materialized and mediated (Poulantzas 1974). State-policy mediation temporarily resolves conflict generated through the tension between capital mobility and fixity within the capitalist class (Bryan 1987). Once again, state policies, far from being technical or predetermined, are always historical. Class-related conflicts shape state policy and state mediation of these conflicts affects the ways in which different social agents and economic activities relate to the fixity and mobility of capital (Hirsch and Kannankulam 2011: 23). In bringing forth capital's political tensions, we can illustrate how neoliberal ideas of market discipline are transferred into policy. The conceptual utilization of capital's fixity and mobility allows us to decipher interest diversification within the capitalist class as it relates to state policy-making.

Zhang (Chapter 6 of this volume) also provides an insightful analysis of capital fixity and mobility by examining the interplay between the logic of capital in cost-reduction and profit, and the territorial logic of state power in the spatial reorganization of capitalism in China. This inclusion of territorial logic helps us avoid the subordination of all social processes to the logic of capital. Consequently, this chapter serves to further problematize the logic of capital. Greater insight into interest diversification within the capitalist class through capital's mobility and fixity demonstrates that state economic policy-making does not automatically benefit the capitalist class as a whole, and the logic of capital does not exert uniform pressure on state policy. Rather, state policy is an outcome of mediated tension from various fractions of capital which express their ability to reproduce or change the social and political conditions of policy-making.

Social class, fixity, and mobility in Mexico: An historical overview

In this section, I examine the way in which the capitalist class in Mexico articulated itself with capital mobility and fixity during the import-substitution industrialization period (1940–82) and the neoliberal period (1980 onwards). Whereas protectionist policies helped firms to partially externalize the tension between capital fixity and mobility during the import-substitution industrialization period, neoliberal policies implemented after the 1980s fully internalized this tension within firms and financial investors' interests. An additional contributing factor here was the general transformation in Mexico's social-class structure, particularly the weakening of the middle and working classes through austerity policies and the repression and co-optation of the labour movement.

Import-substitution industrialization (ISI) and the fragmentation of capitalist interests

During the ISI period, domestic markets in Mexico were protected with restrictions on imports, and foreign-direct and portfolio investment. ISI policies led to the emergence of large domestic firms in Mexico with strong links to capital fixity within the country. These firms received the benefit of state subsidies and market protection from internal and external competition, and were linked to international capital mobility through their active involvement in domestic financial groups (White 1992: 59). Some of these groups were part of international bank syndicates, which provided loans to developing countries during the 1960s and 1970s. Still, the mobility of these financial groups' assets was constrained by capital controls (Solís 1997: 19). The profits of financial groups also remained closely tied to the fixity of their capital within Mexico in the form of government protection, subsidies, domestic investment, and market expansion.

During the early period of the ISI, foreign firms were only permitted to own 49 per cent of a firm's share and had to guarantee a high level of local content in production. Their capital mobility through finance in the form of stocks and bonds was limited. There were also restrictions on foreign investment in Mexican banks and public debt. Later, with the 1965 Border Industrialization Program, the location of fully foreign-owned investment was confined to the *maquiladoras* assembly plants on Mexico's border with the United States. *Maquiladoras* were foreign-owned global corporations that imported machinery, raw materials and components on a duty-free basis while using low-wage Mexican labour. These assembly plants had to guarantee that the totality of *maquiladora* imports and produced goods was re-exported (Carrillo and Gomis 2005: 30). Their relation to capital mobility reflects their need to relocate operations internationally to cheaper production sites with minimum trade restrictions. Still, their capital mobility in the form of bonds and stocks was constrained by some capital controls (Albo et al. 2010: 48–9).

In sum, global corporations operating in Mexico through *maquiladoras* and large national firms operating either through joint-venture agreements with foreign firms or as wholly Mexican-owned companies were linked to capital mobility and fixity. However, tension between both processes was not fully internalized within firms during the ISI period because of various forms of protectionist controls pursued by the state. Market protection and subsidies allowed domestic firms to realize profits in domestic markets, while Mexican banks had rather limited links to international finance. The capital mobility of the *maquiladoras* was also confined to the northern border of Mexico, and capital flight from *maquiladoras* did not affect the entire economy. State policy during the ISI period, therefore, attenuated interest diversification between capital mobility and fixity in the country.

Neoliberalism and the internalization of capital fixity and mobility

The 1982 debt crisis marked the beginning of neoliberalism in Mexico and the 1994 peso crisis expressed the intensification of financialization. Both crises changed the balance of class forces in the country. The 1982 debt crisis began when an increase in American interest rates and a decline in oil prices forced the Mexican government to default on its foreign debt. The Mexican economy bore the costs of debt repayment by mobilizing state bureaucratic power in shifting policy through the monetary criteria of low inflation, low wages, and economic austerity. Since the 1980s, increases in taxes and the price of public services were imposed on peasants, workers and middle classes in order to pay for foreign and public debt (Correa 2006: 158–9), while government cuts further affected social programmes and the provision of food subsidies. The peso crisis of 1994 served to exacerbate the social impact of austerity measures as the government devaluated the Mexican currency, resulting in a 40 per cent decrease in the purchasing power of workers (Cowie 1999: 175). Austerity policies also led to the privatization of public companies and the reduction of public services, and hence, increased unemployment levels in the public sector.

The privatization of land and the removal of agricultural subsidies were among the main strategies adopted in the implementation of a debt regime during the 1990s. Prior to the privatization of land in 1992, land owned by peasants was organized through collective ownership *or ejidos*. The *ejido* conferred on each peasant the right to land, whose ownership was collectively organized. In this context, land owned by *ejidatarios* could not be sold or purchased in the market. With changes to the Mexican constitution in 1992, land was privatized. By allowing peasants to hold land titles, the constitution effectively transformed communal lands into private property. Austerity policies in the early 1990s also removed subsidies to agricultural inputs. As most farm subsidies were replaced by anti-poverty programmes, and tariffs and import permits for many agricultural goods were removed, peasants could no longer compete with domestic and American agribusinesses and were forced to sell their land (Gordillo et al. 1998). The privatization of *ejidos*, the removal of agricultural subsidies, and high unemployment resulted in increasing competition among a large pool of workers for low-paid jobs in cities. This change shifted the balance of class power in favour of the capitalist class as their production costs diminished with the increased supply of cheap labour in the 1980s and the 1990s.

Low labour costs were accompanied by the defeat of democratic union activism through tripartite agreements and labour arbitration councils. Since the late 1980s, federal and state governments used tripartite agreements between unions and employers to negotiate with union leaders on abandoning the right to strike. Through these agreements, which were implemented by the Institutionalized Revolutionary Party's (PRI) single-party regime to weaken local labour activism (Caulfield 2010: 149), unions relinquished their right to strike and accepted low wages while employers agreed to prevent drastic price increases. The Mexican state also undermined rank-and-file unionism through its conciliation and arbitration boards by approving a company's petition to modify a collective agreement contract, cut wages and reduce personnel (Middlebrook and Quintero 1998).

Working conditions in Mexico also deteriorated for middle classes during the 1980s and the 1990s with the dismantling of important white-collar unions, such as the bank workers union. While other white-collar unions remained in place, such as Pemex's Oil Workers Union and the

National Teachers' Union, their leaderships, in close collaboration with the presidential administrations in power, suppressed alternative voices on union matters (Aguayo Quezada 2010: 241–5). Labour legislation also allowed employers to label workers in administrative positions as *trabajadores de confianza* or 'trusted workers'. Under Mexican labour legislation, these workers were excluded from collective bargaining and the right to strike (de Buen 2000). Thus, dispossession strategies and the weakening of organized labour through state institutions shifted class power to the detriment of Mexico's peasants, and working and middle classes.

A change in the state economic-policy framework, which effectively transformed the social class structure of Mexico, also reflects the shifting relations of power within the state apparatus. Prior to the 1990s, financial groups were represented on the administration board of the Central Bank. The Finance Ministry in many cases consulted with the Mexican Association of Bankers on the laws and mechanisms which they proposed (Tello 1984: 54). Labour and the peasantry (or at least their leaders), on the other hand, were part of the PRI's corporatist structure mobilized for the stabilization of class conflicts. Mexico's financial policy, fashioned on the basis of its reliance on oil revenues, heavy state borrowing, and currency stability, mediated conflicts between these forces. In other words, throughout the 1980 and the 1990s, anti-inflationary measures were heavily reliant on *ad hoc* political mechanisms within the PRI, and social disagreements often played a role in influencing economic policy within a corporatist state-bureaucratic structure. But, through the mid-1990s, state policy based on monetary debt-management processes of low inflation, a strong currency and reserve accumulation was further centralized within the Central Bank and the Finance Ministry to limit government spending and preserve low inflation. In this way, the Central Bank and the Finance Ministry were able to externalize the imposition of financial discipline on wages, work processes, and social spending through a stronger set of rules and the policy objectives of 'sound money' and low inflation. As a result of the increasingly autonomous power of the state bureaucracy within the Mexican Central Bank and Finance Ministry, policy-making, especially in times of crisis, has become disassociated from the 'uncertainties' of democratic processes (Epstein 1992: 2).

A change in the balance of societal forces and power in the state apparatus of Mexico after the 1982 debt crisis and the 1994 peso crisis was also reflected in the changing relations of the articulation of Mexico's capitalist class to fixity and mobility. After both crises, large Mexican firms concentrated more wealth and increased their involvement in financial activities. For example, the share of total sales from the 49 largest companies in Mexico was 45 per cent in 1993. This share rose to 70 per cent in 1995 (Garrido 2005: 100). This, in addition to government privatization policies, led to the creation of large Mexican-owned companies such as Cemex and Grupo

Carso (Heredia 1995: 136). These companies were now able to control a large market-share of the Mexican economy, and have continuing importance in the Mexican economy (see Table 10.1). Several companies also diversified their investments across many industries, including telecommunications, media broadcasting, construction, banking, manufacturing, and resource extraction. This is the case for Grupo Alfa, Grupo Bal, and Grupo Carso (see Table 10.1). Economic concentration in a handful of companies not only strengthened large Mexican firms but also allowed some of these companies to expand their operations abroad, to the rest of Latin America, for example, through acquisitions (UNCTAD 2008) (see Table 10.1).

During the 1990s the financial orientation of Mexican companies increased as state policies promoted the Mexican Stock Exchange and opened capital and money markets to international investors, thereby providing a way for private firms to obtain funds outside the conventional banks. The financialization of firms, in combination with economic concentration, resulted in the dominance of a few large companies in the Mexican stock market. The issuing of Mexican stocks as a percentage of global issuance increased from 5.4 per cent in 1990 to 18 per cent in 1993 (Morera 1998: 54). By 1999, more than 50 per cent of total stock-market operations in the country were concentrated in only ten companies (BMV 2000: 28). Large Mexican firms were also allowed to issue debt in international stock markets and participate in financial operations with international investment banks (Garrido 2005: 124). While these large Mexican companies increased their financial orientation in international markets, they still sought to decrease production costs in their Mexican operations through low wages. At the same time, a strong peso, which had become a policy target since the 1990s, was beneficial to these companies because they were able to hold liabilities in foreign currency, lowering the cost of their international operations. Thus, the legacy of the economic transformations of the 1980s and 1990s in Mexico's class structure was a concentration of wealth and an increasing financial orientation among the country's largest firms. This can be seen in the concentration of 55.7 per cent of stock-market operations in Mexico by ten companies in 2010. In many cases these are the same companies which dominated financial operations in the Mexican stock market in 1999 (see Table 10.2 for an overview of companies with the largest stock market operations in Mexico in 1999 and 2010). They are all Mexican-owned, Walmart de Mexico being the only exception.

As seen in Tables 10.1 and 10.2, some of these large Mexican companies invest abroad, while also having the largest stock-market operations and maintaining a great share of domestic consumer and financial markets at the same time. América Móvil, Cemex, Femsa, and Televisa are examples of large Mexican firms that are simultaneously active in the production of goods and services for domestic markets, investment abroad and financial operations in the Mexican stock market. This shows that there

Table 10.1 The 20 most profitable Mexican private companies according to sales, return on equity (ROE) and assets in 2010; and Mexican firms with direct investment abroad in 2011

Most profitable firms by sales, ROE and Assets in 2010	**Mexican firms with the largest foreign direct investment in 2011**	**Sales abroad by percentage**	**Investment abroad by percentage**	**Workers abroad (percentage)**	**Sector**
América Móvil (It is connected to Carso Global Telecomm, Telcel and Telmex)	América Móvil	36	33.6	70	Telecommunications
Carso Global Telecom (a spinoff of Grupo Carso)	N/A	N/A	N/A	N/A	Telecommunications
Telcel (It is connected to America Movil)	N/A	N/A	N/A	N/A	Telecommunications
Telmex (It is connected to America Movil)	Telmex	94.9	50.2	92.2	Telecommunications
Cemex	Cemex	75.6	67.7	65.8	Cement
FEMSA	FEMSA	44.4	18	33.4	Beverages and beer
Grupo Bimbo	Bimbo	55	60	52.7	Food
Grupo Alfa	Grupo Alfa	54	71	51.5	Financial holding of petrochemical, food and telecommunication companies
Organización Soriana	N/A	N/A	N/A	N/A	Retail

Grupo Bal	N/A	N/A	N/A	N/A	Financial holding of mining, smelting and chemical industries (formerly known as Grupo Peñoles)
Grupo Modelo	Grupo Modelo	15.6	15.6	2.9	Beer
Grupo Carso	N/A	N/A	N/A	N/A	Financial holding of manufacturing, construction and retail companies
Grupo Mexico	N/A	N/A	N/A	N/A	Mining
Grupo Salinas	Grupo Salinas	15	28.8	16.8	Financial holding of media broadcasting, banking and retail firms
Grupo Financiero Banorte	N/A	N/A	N/A	N/A	Financial services
Grupo Industrial Lala	N/A	N/A	N/A	N/A	Food
Comercial Mexicana	N/A	N/A	N/A	N/A	Retail
Alpek	N/A	N/A	N/A	N/A	Petrochemical sector
Grupo Televisa	Grupo Televisa	16.8	22.4	10.5	Media broadcasting
Grupo Maseca (controlled by Gruma)	Gruma	65.7	18.7	63.3	Food

Note: Other large Mexican multinationals include ICA, Grupo Posadas, and Grupo Vitro. *Source*: ECLAC 2010: 52–3. *Revista Expansion* 2010: 206–7 and *America Economia* 2011.

Table 10.2 Companies with the largest stock market operations in the Mexican stock market in 1999 and 2010

Companies 1999	Market share	Companies 2010	Market share
Telmex (d)	18.92	América Móvil (d) (This company bought Carso Global Telecomm. The latter no longer quotes in the Mexican stock market)	17.77
Walmart de Mexico (f)	6.24	Walmart de Mexico (f)	11.29
Banamex (d)	6.19	Grupo México (d)	7.03
Carso Global Telecom (connected to Telmex) (d)	5.82	Inbursa (It is connected to Grupo Carso, Telmex and America Móvil) (d)	3.23
Cemex (d)	4.10	Grupo Carso (d)	3.22
Televisa (d)	4.04	Peñoles (d)	3.19
Bancomer (d)	3.56	Televisa (d)	2.74
Inbursa (connected to Grupo Carso and Telmex) (d)	3.14	FEMSA (d)	2.67
Grupo Carso (d)	1.77	Cemex (d)	2.29
Savia (d)	1.70	Elektra (Part of Grupo Salinas) (d)	2.27

*Foreign (f) Domestic (d).
Note: Bancomer and Banamex were Mexican banks with some foreign investment. In 2000, foreign banks purchased most of the shares and stocks of Bancomer and Banamex.
Source: BMV 2000: 24; BMV 2010: 36.

is interest diversification within these companies themselves. More specifically, these firms have internalized the processes of capital mobility and fixity. While domestic production and sales have reflected these firms fixity to the Mexican economy, their ties to capital mobility take the form of financial assets and investment abroad.

The structure of foreign investment in the Mexican economy also changed in the 1980s and the 1990s, after the removal of restrictions on investment in Mexican private and public debt and changes in the ownership structure of the financial sector (Kessler 2000: 50). This has had implications for the dynamics of capital fixity and mobility in Mexico and its resulting expression in intra-class struggle. In the case of the ownership structure of Mexico's financial industry, private banks were nationalized in the early 1980s and then sold to national private investors in the late 1980s. After the 1994 peso crisis, foreign banks purchased the majority of shares of Mexican financial institutions due to regulatory changes allowing more than 50 per cent foreign ownership (Marois 2010: 180; Montamen-Samadian 2000: 42). In addition, the 1994 North American Free Trade Agreement (NAFTA) made Mexico an attractive production site for international companies in the manufacturing sector. *Maquiladoras* in particular expanded beyond the northern region and became central to investment and employment in Mexico (Middlebrook and Zepeda 2003: 538). Global firms linked to *maquiladoras* were simultaneously implicated in the processes of international mobility and national fixity in the Mexican economy. While they could shift their direct and portfolio investment elsewhere, the profitability of their financial assets depended on actual activities fixed in Mexico. In the same way, international investors in Mexico's public debt relied on the state's oil sales and the state's ability to increase taxes on middle and working classes. In the case of investors with shares and bonds in companies having extensive operations in Mexico, their profits were increasingly dependent on surges in the productivity of Mexican labour, as well as domestic sales in, and exports from, Mexico.

The transition to democracy, neoliberal continuity, and the 2007–10 global crisis

The trend of economic concentration and the financial orientation of firms intensified after Vicente Fox, candidate for the centre-right Action National Party (PAN), won the 2000 presidential election after more than 70 years of the one-party regime of the Institutionalized Revolutionary Party (PRI) (Zepeda 2011: 9). By 2007, the financial liabilities of the ten largest Mexican firms were 167 per cent of their total net worth. These companies included América Móvil, Cemex, Femsa, Grupo Alfa, Grupo Modelo, Gruma, Banorte, Grupo Bimbo, Grupo Bal, and Grupo Salinas Elecktra. The capitalization of these companies through the stock market represented 169 per cent of their total assets (Alarco and del Hierro 2010: 187). Also, the Fox Administration (2000–06) gave large companies tax refunds equivalent to 98.9 per cent of the taxes originally paid by these firms (Aguayo Quezada 2010: 253). The persistence of monetarism in economic policy since the 1980s, with the outcomes of economic concentration and financialization, set the conditions from which distinct fractions of capital responded to the global financial crisis.

The impact of the 2007 economic crisis on Mexico generated different stakes for various firms and investors depending on their connections to capital's national fixity and international mobility. The capital mobility of one segment of the capitalist class often affected other segments' profits negatively. For example, several firms and investors with operations in Mexico moved their investments internationally to increase profits and avoid losses during the 2007 financial crisis. Financial investors shifted their investments to assets abroad in order to settle financial obligations in foreign currency. For example, Banamex, Citigroup's Mexican subsidiary, paid 1.4 billion dollars to its American headquarters to capitalize this bank's American operations (Redacción 2010). As a result, Mexican stocks declined 39.8 per cent and the Mexican peso depreciated 4.2 per cent in 2008, as financial investors and banks transferred money from the Mexican economy into currencies such as the US dollar (Regalado 2009: R4).

The ability of financial institutions and investors to move money internationally affected large Mexican domestic companies and Mexican-based multinationals, mainly because it put downward pressure on the Mexican stock-market index and the value of the peso. The devaluation of the peso also increased these firms' debt exposure to foreign currencies (see Table 10.3). Those Mexican firms which invested heavily in financial derivatives that bet against the devaluation of the peso were the most affected. These firms used derivatives to obtain US dollars at low interest rates, pay these loans with yields from their investment in Mexican pesos, and profit from the difference between lending rates in the United States and investment rates in the Mexican peso. Cemex, the third largest cement company in the world, reported losses of US $500 million in its derivatives operations. In fact, between 2008 and 2009, a number of Mexican firms reported losses in derivatives operations that totalled 8 billion US dollars (Reyes 2009) (see Table 10.4).

The negative effects of capital mobility from financial institutions and foreign investors did not prevent large Mexican companies from moving their money abroad. While the value of greenfield investment[1] by large Mexican

Table 10.3 Debt increase of companies in 2008 due to the American financial crisis and the devaluation of the peso

Company (sector)	**The amount of debt in relation to earnings before interest, taxes, depreciation and amortization (EBITDA)**
Ideal	7.7 times the EBITDA
Grupo Lamosa	5.5 times the EBITDA
Iusacell	4.4 times the EBITDA
Vitro	3.9 times the EBITDA
Cemex (Cement)	3.6 times the EBITDA
Alfa	1.9 times the EBITDA
Soriana	1.9 times the EBITDA
AHMSA	1.3 times the EBITDA
Telmex	1.2 times the EBITDA
FEMSA	1.1 times the EBITDA
Grupo Carso	.9 times the EBITDA
América Móvil	.06 times the EBITDA

Source: Ramírez et al. 2008.

Table 10.4 Losses in derivatives operations by October 2009 (millions of US dollars)

Company	Losses	Losses as percentage of assets
Comercial Mexicana (Retail)	1,080	25
Gruma (Corn processing)	684	18.2
Vitro	227	7.5
Alfa	191	2
Grupo Industrial Saltillo	49	4.5
Autlán	40	9.2
Grupo Posadas	38	3

Source: Ramírez et al. (2008).

firms was 842 million dollars in 2008, this increased to 1.91 billion dollars in 2009 and 2.57 billion dollars in 2010. Similar increases took place in the value of mergers and acquisitions undertaken by Mexican multinationals. These mergers and acquisitions amounted to 463 million dollars in 2008, then reached 3.24 and 3.3 billion dollars in 2009 and 2010 respectively (UNCTAD 2011: 196, 207). Firms such as Grupo Televisa, Grupo Alfa, and Grupo Carso purchased firms in the media, food, and service sector in the United States (UNCTAD 2011: 60).

Capital mobility also manifested itself in *maquiladoras* when the shares and bonds of United States-based global firms declined during the 2007 American financial crisis. This was particularly evident in the auto sector, the largest investor in Mexican *maquiladoras*, when their financial assets declined because of international overcapacity and investors' aversion to auto shares and bonds (Muñoz Martinez 2011). Global companies with *maquiladora* investments slowed production in Mexico because of financial difficulties. These firms did not invest the returns from their sales and cost-reduction measures in Mexico but channelled them into financial markets in order to fulfil financial obligations and boost the price of their bonds and stocks (Morales 2010). Still, the initial devaluation of the peso during the global crisis lowered the costs of production in Mexico, which once again made Mexico an attractive site for foreign direct investment, mostly by American companies, particularly in *maquiladoras* in the electronics and auto sectors. Examples of these American firms include General Motors, Ford, Chrysler, Sanmina, Lear Corporation, American Axle Manufacturing and Superior Industries (*Revista Expansion* 2010: 206–14). For these American companies, Mexico became more attractive than China as a site for investment in manufacturing due to rising wage levels in the latter and cheaper transportation costs from Mexico to American markets (Luhnow and Davis 2012: A12). From 2002 to 2008, Chinese manufacturing wages increased more than 200 per cent while Mexican wages rose only 7.5 per cent, in dollars, from 2002 to 2009. Average Chinese wages were only 14 per cent lower than Mexican wages by 2010 (Black and Rodriguez 2010a). However, low transportation costs from Mexico to American markets compensated for this wage gap (Black and Rodriguez 2010a). In 2010 Mexico became the second largest Latin American foreign direct investment recipient after Brazil. Foreign direct investment increased 17 per cent in 2010, and was mostly concentrated in the manufacturing and services sector, which includes food, beverages and the tobacco industry as well as metal products, machinery, and equipment industries (ECLAC 2010: 36).

Large Mexican companies had more vested interests in capital fixity in Mexico through investments in public debt, private bonds, and stocks than foreign banks and international financial investors. The former relied more on their Mexican operations, domestic markets, and peso assets to realize an important share of profits even though international capital mobility also offered them the possibility of escaping capital devaluation and finding cheap production sites outside of Mexico. Large Mexican companies required a strong peso in order to reduce exchange rate risk in their foreign direct investment and financial operations in international markets. In contrast, *maquiladoras'* main interest was not only tax exemptions but also a relatively low exchange rate. A strong peso threatened the competitiveness of their exports and diminished their gains from using cheap Mexican labour. Consequently, the interests of *maquiladoras* on peso devaluation diverged from the interests of financial investors, banks, and large Mexican companies which required a strong peso. These firms and investors were therefore not exclusively committed to either national fixity or capital mobility. Rather, they had distinct linkages to international finance and fixed processes of national production, circulation, and realization, which shaped intra-capitalist struggle and policy responses to the 2007 financial crisis.

State policy and the 'fixing of capitalism' in Mexico: The aftermath of the 2007 financial crisis

As mentioned in previous sections, the process of market restructuring initiated in the 1980s and 1990s and its resulting effects on the transformation in balance of power relations in society and within the state bureaucracy influenced state policy in 'fixing' capitalism in Mexico during the 2007 financial crisis. On the one hand, state policy aimed to secure investment within Mexico through a strong peso *via* public debt and the use of international reserves. This was a continuation of previous policies implemented in the 1990s and early 2000s (Marois 2012b: 147–50). On the other hand, policies of public debt management, reserve accumulation, low wages, and a strong currency tried to solve the problems of capitalist profitability and reconcile distinct interests of the capitalist class in relation to capital's mobility and fixity. Overall, state policy in Mexico in the immediate aftermath of the 2007 financial crisis reflected larger structural issues concerning class power in Mexico. They include the concentration of economic power in a handful of companies, the defeat of rank-and-file activism within organized labour and the imposition of dispossession strategies for the past three decades, as well as the centralization of economic-decision making within the Central Bank and Finance Ministry bureaucracy. The insulation of economic policy from popular pressures also explains why workers and the middle classes bore the costs of policy responses through regressive taxation and low wages in Mexico.

After 2007, Mexican state policy centred mostly on public debt management, and to a lesser extent, on infrastructural spending, production subsidies for exporting companies, and anti-poverty programmes. In terms of public debt management, the Ministry of Finance issued and swapped short-term instruments in pesos for long-term government debt. For example, the Ministry of Finance issued a syndicated 30-year global bond with a fixed rate, as well as a century bond due in 2110. In 2011, yield increases in public debt ranged from 0.4 per cent to 1 per cent, depending on the maturity date of the bonds (Hacienda 2011: 21, 68). Increases in the yield of government bonds and their conversion to long-term debt guaranteed high demand for the peso without causing liquidity problems for the Ministry of Finance and the Central Bank. Despite reductions in interest rates, yields in Mexican government debt have remained higher than US Treasury bonds. This has helped to ensure the worthiness of Mexico's currency, avoiding losses in peso investment due to devaluation. By December 2010, investment in Mexican assets by non-residents had an annual growth rate of 83.9 per cent, in comparison to a 10.7 per cent increase in 2009 (Banxico 2010a: 40). By 2011, non-residents held 24.70 per cent of the total public debt in Mexico (Hacienda 2011: 72).

Reserve accumulation has also guaranteed the value of the peso. International reserves increased 25 per cent in 2010 (Banxico 2010b: 58). Most of these foreign reserves came from bonds sold by the Ministry of Finance and oil sales from the state-owned oil company PEMEX. Another way of accumulating reserves was through the sale of dollar put options[2] by the Mexican Central Bank. Put options gave buyers the right to sell dollars to the Central Bank at a preferential peso rate when the Mexican peso appreciated against the dollar (Banxico 2009: 62, 64). The accumulation of reserves helped the Mexican Central Bank intervene in exchange markets to avoid peso depreciation.

These policies led to contrasting results. On the one hand, bank profits increased 7.4 per cent in 2009 (Banxico 2010a: 34) and the Mexican Stock Exchange Index rose 12.4 per cent during 2010. The accumulation of international reserves reached historical records, from 78 billion US dollars in 2007 to 113 billion in 2010 (IMF 2011b: 35). Export manufacturing expanded 30 per cent in 2010 (BBVA 2011: 7) and inflation remained close to the 3 per cent target. Current account deficits decreased from 1.5 per cent of the GDP in 2008 to 0.5 per cent in 2010. By 2009, the growth rate was – 6.2 per cent. Later, GDP growth recovered in 2010, reaching 5.3 per cent. On the other hand, direct investment declined from 10 billion US dollars in 2007 to 4.3 billion dollars in 2010 (IMF 2011b: 31, 33). The real minimum wage (based on the 2000 Mexican Consumer Price Index) fell 3.4 per cent between 2006 and 2010 (ECLAC 2012). Between 2008 and 2010, 3.2 million people became poor. By 2010, 46 per cent of the population, approximately 52 million people, did not have enough income to meet their basic need for food, health, education, clothing, footwear, housing, and public transportation (CONEVAL 2011).

The focus on reserve accumulation and public debt management was not effective in fostering investment and employment, and improving wages. So why did the Mexican government continue to implement these policies? The class structure that sustained reserve accumulation and public debt explains the centrality of these policies to the government's crisis-management strategy. The increasing financial orientation of Mexican firms, the concentration of diverse economic sectors into a few domestic and international firms, and the weakening of rank-and-file union activism shaped the way in which the politics of money management prevailed over industrial, trade, and full employment policies in the aftermath of 2007. More specifically, the internalization of fixity and mobility within firms and investors' goals influenced the predominance of debt management and reserve accumulation in formulating policy responses to the crisis.

The relationship of large Mexican firms, financial investors, and global corporations linked to *maquiladoras* in Mexico, to capital mobility and fixity was not uniform. It diverged according to their relative positions in the Mexican economy. The strength of the peso through the Central Bank's use of international reserves was particularly important for large Mexican companies because of their debt exposure in foreign currencies, particularly through derivatives. These companies bet against the devaluation of the peso in financial derivatives. When the value of the peso declined in 2007, the losses for large Mexican firms increased dramatically (Banxico 2009: 81). The Ministry of Finance and the Central Bank gave large Mexican firms access to cheap dollars from international reserves to pay their companies' liabilities in derivatives.

The supply of cheap dollars by the Mexican Central Bank allowed Mexican-based companies to pay their liabilities in US dollars. Once these companies liquidated their liabilities in foreign currency, they were able to resume their exposure to currency exchange fluctuations in 2010. Between 2009 and the first three months of 2010, Mexican private firms issued Eurobonds worth 16.6 billions of dollars. This contrasts with the 834 million of debt issued by Mexican firms in dollars the previous year (Banxico

2010a: 21). Large Mexican companies also received the benefit from the strength of the peso because they were able to maintain the value of their Mexican assets and reduce their exposure to foreign liabilities. The interests of large Mexican corporations in regard to a strong peso were compatible with those of international financial investors and banks, which also required a stable peso and profitable yields for their investments in public debt.

The emphasis on monetary and debt management was not without conflict. *Maquiladora* representatives expressed their concern over a strong peso, and the resulting loss of competitiveness for their Mexican exports (Becerril 2011). This was a recurring complaint from the *maquiladora* sector despite persisting low wages. The *maquiladora* sector's attempt to prevent the appreciation of the peso through political pressure was aimed at further lowering their export prices. Agreements and disagreements over state policy were therefore influenced by the way large firms and investors internalized the contradictions between their financial goals and nationally fixed economic activities.

State policy in mediating demands for a strong peso and competitive exports was based on maintaining stagnant wages. For example, the price of the national basic-food basket increased 8 per cent while the nominal minimum wage rose only 4.02 per cent in 2011 (CEFP 2012: 7). The low cost of labour in Mexico increased the attractiveness of the Mexican economy as a production location for both domestic and foreign firms, ensuring low export prices (Black and Rodríguez 2010b). Targeting wages temporarily solved the *maquiladoras'* concerns over export competitiveness and left the strong peso policy intact. This strategy also became compatible with the interests of large Mexican companies interested in lowering the production costs of their national operations. Both low wages and a strong peso became central to mediating the internalized contradictions of capital fixity and mobility within firms', and investors' profit goals.

Profitable yields in public debt, which sustained reserve accumulation and a strong peso, required debt repayment, and, therefore, an increase in non-oil revenues. Mexico was one of the few countries in Latin America where taxes increased after the 2007 financial crisis. One of the main sources of non-oil revenues in the country is the value-added tax (VAT), and food and medicines are exempt from this tax. In 2010, the VAT rose 1 per cent, increasing non-oil revenues between 2010 and 2011(Banxico 2011: 35). Through increases in the VAT, state policy imposed the burden of taxation on workers and the middle classes because large companies operating in Mexico can claim tax credits on the VAT. In fact, there was a 45.4 per cent increase in corporate VAT returns during 2011 in comparison to the previous year (Hacienda 2011: 27). This explains why large firms operating in Mexico did not oppose a VAT increase in income and capital gains in 2010 (Banxico 2011: 35). Thus, debt management and reserve accumulation strategies, central to mediating the internalized tensions of capital fixity and mobility, allowed the state to accumulate new resources through a regressive taxation system which imposed the financial costs of the crisis on middle and working classes.

The centrality of debt management and reserve accumulation in state policy did not prevent the implementation of two major stimulus packages. In 2008, the Felipe Calderon Administration (2006–10) announced the Program to Promote Growth and Employment (*Programa para el Impulso al Crecimiento y el Empleo* or PICE), which included public spending in infrastructure and the promotion of government procurement from small and medium enterprises. In 2009, the government also launched the National Agreement for the Household Economy and Employment to Live Better (*Acuerdo Nacional en Favor de la Economía Familiar y Empleo para Vivir Mejor* or ANEFE). This programme offered subsidies for exporting companies producing vehicles, auto parts, electronics, and machinery. The Ministry of the Economy allowed companies to engage in production stoppages and absorbed some of the labour costs. In exchange, planned job cuts had to be limited to a third of the decline of sales (Galhardi 2009). In addition, ANEFE implemented a temporary freeze on gas and electricity prices, a temporary employment programme and a scrap programme for appliances and automobiles. The 2009 agreement also expanded workers capacity to withdraw cash from their retirement fund, and increased social-security coverage of the recently unemployed. ANEFE also promoted infrastructural investment and credit access for businesses (ECLAC 2009: 20–4). Overall, government expenditure increased from 22.8 per cent of the GDP in 2007 to 26.3 per cent in 2010 (IMF 2011b: 31–2).

These stimulus packages did not improve living conditions for the majority of the population because of the state's emphasis on ensuring profitability through low wages and regressive taxation. Large firms were the main beneficiaries of government spending even though they did not pay the costs of increased taxation. The six largest construction companies in Mexico increased their profits 219 per cent in 2011, over 2010 levels (González 2011). In contrast, workers' wages in this sector increased less than 3 per cent during the same period (INEGI 2010; 2011b). Overall job and wage recovery in the manufacturing sector remained slow and social benefits were reduced 1.1 per cent (Hacienda 2011: 12). Social assistance in the form of targeted-cash transfers did not compensate for the lack of decent wages and social benefits. The concentration of the economy in a few dominant companies, and their financial orientation, regressive taxation and low wages, explains the failure of government spending to improve wages and decrease poverty.

The top 100 largest firms in Mexico provided only 3.5 per cent of the total employment in the economy in 2007 (Alarco and Del Hierro 2010: 186). Thus, the policy responses that support the interests of the capitalist class cannot be justified as crucial for creating employment via state-induced private investment in the economy. State policy responses to the crisis benefited foreign and national investors with a large stake in both international finance and productive operations and market sales in Mexico. This did not mean that the Mexican state was able to resolve intra-capitalist conflicts in its attempt to assist in the profitability problems of the capitalist class as a 'whole' (cf. Bryan 1987). Throughout 2011, for example, *maquiladoras* and other exporting sectors continued to be concerned with the appreciation of the peso (Notimex 2011), while two large Mexican companies, Televisa and Telmex, continued to fight over access to each other's sphere of activity in the telecommunications and broadcasting sector (Sigler 2012).

In sum, state policy responses remain time-specific, shaped by the balance of power dynamics within the economy. While the Mexican state tries to resolve the internalized tensions of capital between fixity and mobility, other studies (e.g. Schwegler 2008) show that the shifting relations of power within the Mexican state bureaucracy itself, as well as among political parties and other political factions, further problematize the temporary nature of that resolution. It should be reiterated, therefore, that state policy formation does not correspond directly to the general interests of the capitalist class. Rather, it involves a complicated process of 'negotiation' over policy compromise among a variety of actors including social classes, members of the state bureaucracy, and various modes of political factions (cf. Atasoy 2009). However, an unpacking of the multiple ways in which state policy responses are entangled with bureaucratic processes, power dynamics, and political hierarchies remains beyond the scope of this chapter.

Conclusion

In this chapter, I have argued that the distinct articulation of various capital groups in Mexico with global capital mobility and national fixity, and the internalization of these dynamics within firms and investors' goals, has shaped intra-class conflict, with concrete consequences for state policy-making. State policies have responded to the demands of financial investors and large Mexican companies for a strong peso, which makes possible profitable rates in government debt and lowers exchange risk exposure in foreign liabilities. These policies were not introduced without conflict. Firms and investors do not automatically accept all state policies that enforce market discipline. This is because of the varied ways in which these firms and investors have articulated with capital mobility and fixity. In order to mediate internalized tensions not only within firms but also within the capitalist class operating in Mexico, the state has imposed the burden of these policies on the working poor and middle classes through stagnant wages and regressive taxation. In this manner, the state has been able to obtain revenues to sustain the value of the peso through public debt management and international reserves accumulation while guaranteeing low production costs to firms and investors. The legacy of austerity measures, dispossession, and co-optation of organized labour since the 1980s and the 1990s has been the imposition by the state of the social costs of state crisis-management policy onto the middle and working classes of Mexican society.

Notes

1. Greenfield investment occurs when a company starts a new venture in a foreign country by constructing new operational facilities such as new factories, offices, or stores.
2. Put options are financial derivatives that involve a contract between two parties, a buyer and a seller, in which they agree to exchange an asset at a predetermined price (strike price) at a future date. This contract gives the buyer of the put option the right, but not an obligation, to resell the asset (US dollars, for example) at the strike price by the future date. In contrast, the seller of the put has the obligation to repurchase the asset at the strike price if the buyer exercises the option.

References

Alarco, G. and P. del Hierro (2010) 'Crecimiento y Concentración de los Principales Grupos Empresariales en México', *Revista CEPAL* 101: 179–97.

Albo, G., S. Gindin, and L. Panitch (2010) *In and Out of Crisis: The Global Financial Meltdown and Left Alternatives*, Oakland: PM Press.

Aguayo Quezada, S. (2010) *Vuelta en U: Guia para Entender y Reactivar la Democracia Estancada*, Mexico City: Taurus.

America Economia (2011) 'Las Empresas de la Region Más Globales'. Available online: http://rankings.americaeconomia.com/2012/multilatinas/ranking.php. (accessed: 25 April 2013).

Atasoy, Y. (2009) *Islam's Marriage with Neoliberalism*, London & New York: Palgrave Macmillan.

Banxico (2009) *Informe Anual 2009*, Mexico City: Banco de Mexico.

Banxico (2010a) *Reporte Sobre el Sistema Financiero 2010*, Mexico City: Banco de Mexico.

Banxico (2010b) *Informe Anual 2010*, Mexico City: Banco de Mexico.

Banxico (2011) *Agregados Monetarios y Flujo de Fondos, Fuentes y Usos de Recursos Financieros-saldos Como Porcentaje del PIB, 1994–2010*, Mexico City: Banco de Mexico.

BBVA (2011) *Situación Regional Sectorial, Análisis Económico*, Mexico City: BBVA.

Becerril, I. (2011) 'Preocupa a la IP Apreciación del Peso', *El Financiero*, 24 January. Available online: http://impreso.elfinanciero.com.mx/digital/reproductor.aspx?tipo=DI&diario=2011-04-27&pagActual=9. (accessed: 9 April 2013).

Bieler, A. and A. Morton (2006) 'Globalization, the State and Class Struggle: A Critical Economy Engagement with Open Marxism', in A. Bieler, W. Bonefeld, P. Burnham, and A.D. Morton (eds) *Global Restructuring, State, Capital and Labour*, New York: Palgrave Macmillan.

Black, T. and C. M. Rodríguez (2010a) 'Mexico Beats China as Cessna Shows Wages Converge With Shipping', *Bloomberg*, 8 September. Available online: http://www.bloomberg.com/news/2010-09-08/mexico-beats-china-for-u-s-companies-undaunted-by-drug-wars.html. (accessed: 25 April 2013).

Black, T. and C. M. Rodríguez (2010b) 'Mexico más Atractivo que China', *Revista Expansion*, 13 July. Available online: http://www.cnnexpansion.com/economia/2012/09/20/mexico-el-nuevo-rival-de-china. (accessed: 9 April 2013).

Block, F. (1977) *The Origins of International Economic Disorder*, Berkeley: University of California Press.

BMV (2000) *Informe Anual 1999*, Mexico City: Bolsa Mexicana de Valores.

BMV (2010) *Informe Anual 2010*, Mexico City: Bolsa Mexicana de Valores.

Brenner N., J. Peck, and N. Theodore (2010) 'Variegated Neoliberalization: Geographies, Modalities, Pathways', *Global Networks* 10(2): 182–222.

Bryan, D. (1987) 'The State and the Internationalisation of Capital: An Approach to Analysis', *Journal of Contemporary Asia* 17(3): 253–75.

Carrillo J. and R. Gomis (2005) 'Generaciones de Maquiladora: Un Primer Acercamiento a su Medición', *Frontera Norte* 27(33): 25–51.

Caulfield, N. (2010) *NAFTA and Labour in North America*, Chicago: University of Illinois Press.

CEFP (2012) *Análisis Mensual de Productos Básicos Enero 2012*, Mexico City: Centro de Estudios de las Finanzas Públicas de la Cámara de Diputados.

CONEVAL (2011) *Medición de Pobreza 2010*, Mexico City: CONEVAL.

Cordera, R., C. Zubieta, and J. Navarrete (2010) 'México Frente a la Crisis: Hacia un Nuevo Curso De Desarrollo', *Economía Informa* 6 (18): 7–60.

Correa, E. (2006) 'Changing Constraints on Monetary Policy', in L. Randall (ed.) *Changing Structure of Mexico: Political, Social and Economic Prospects*, New York: M.E. Sharpe.

Correa, E., G. Vidal, and W. Marshall (2011) 'Mexico's Economic Catastrophe: An Innocent Victim of the Global Crisis or a Homegrown Affair?' *International Economic Policy Institute Working Paper 1*. Available online: http://142.51.14.12/NR/rdonlyres/72DB2ADE-0E2F-4409-B8B9-108B54A32CD4/0/MexicoEconomicCatastrophe.pdf. (accessed: 9 April 2013).

Cowie, J. (1999) *Capital Moves: RCA's 70'Year Quest for Cheap Labor*, Ithaca: Cornell University Press.

de Buen, N. (2000) *Derechos del Trabajador de Confianza*, Mexico City: UNAM.

ECLAC (2009) *The Reactions of Latin American and Caribbean Governments to the International Crisis: An Overview of Policy Measures up to 30 January 2009*, Santiago: ECLAC.

ECLAC (2010) *Foreign Direct Investment in Latin America and the Caribbean*, Santiago: ECLAC.

ECLAC (2011) *Statistical Yearbook 2011 for Latin America and the Caribbean*, Santiago: ECLAC.

ECLAC (2012) *CEPALStat. Economic Indicators and Statistics. Labour Costs: Mexico 2000–12*. Available online: http://websie.eclac.cl/sisgen/ConsultaIntegrada.asp. (accessed: 3 October 2012).

Epstein G. (1992) 'Political Economy and Comparative Central Banking', *Review of Radical Political Economics* 24(1): 1–30.

Foster J. B. and F. Magdoff (2009) *The Great Financial Crisis: Causes and Consequence*, New York: Monthly Review Press.

Fox Gotham, K. (2009) 'Creating Liquidity out of Spatial Fixity: The Secondary Circuit of Capital and the Subprime Mortgage Crisis', *International Journal of Urban and Regional Research* 33(2): 355–71.

Galhardi, R. (2009) 'Mexico. Programa para la Preservación del Empleo', *Organización Internacional del Trabajo Notas Sobre la Crisis*, Mexico City: ILO.

Garrido, C. (2005) *Desarrollo Económico y Procesos de Financiamiento en México*, Mexico City: Siglo XXI.

Gill, S. (ed.) (2012) *Global Crises and the Crisis of Global Leadership*, Cambridge: Cambridge University Press.

Gil Diaz, F. (2009) 'Fortalezas y Debilidades de la Economía Mexicana', *Este País* 215: 29–31.

González, S. (2011) 'La Española OHL, a la Cabeza en Ganancias en 6 Meses de 2011', *La Jornada*, 1 August. Available online: http://www.jornada.unam.mx/2011/08/01/economia/022n1eco. (accessed: 8 April 2013).

Gordillo, G., A. Janvry, and E. Sadoulet (1998) 'Between Political Control and Efficiency Gains: The Evolution of Agrarian Property Rights in Mexico', *CEPAL Review* 99: 151–69.

Harvey, D. (1999) *Limits to Capital*, London: Verso.

Harvey, D. (2001) *Spaces of Capital: Towards a Critical Geography*, New York: Routledge.

Harvey, D. (2010) *The Enigma of Capital and the Crisis of Capitalism*, Oxford: Oxford University Press.

Hacienda (2011) *Primer Informe Trimestral 2011*, Mexico City: Secretaria de Hacienda.

Heredia, B. (1995) 'State-business Relations in Contemporary Mexico', in M. Serrano and V. Bulmer-Thomas (eds) *Rebuilding the State: Mexico after Salinas*, London: Institute of Latin American Studies.

Hirsch, J. and J. Kannankulam (2011) 'The Spaces of Capital: The Political Form of Capitalism and the Internationalization of the State', *Antipode* 43(1): 12–37.

IMF (2011a) 'Statement by IMF Managing Director Christine Lagarde at the Conclusion of her visit to Mexico', *Press Release 11/435*, 30 November. Available online: http://www.imf.org/external/np/sec/pr/2011/pr11435.htm. (accessed: 3 October 2012).

IMF (2011b) *Mexico, IMF Country Report*, Washington D.C., 11/250. Available online: http://www.imf.org/external/pubs/ft/scr/2011/cr11250.pdf. (accessed: 9 April 2013).

IMF (2013) *World Economic Outlook 2013: Hopes, Realities and Risks*, Washington DC: IMF.

INEGI (2010) 'Encuesta Nacional de Empresas Constructoras Octubre 2010', *Press Release 423/10*, 17 December.

INEGI (2011a) *Sistema de Cuentas Nacionales de México 2008–2011*. Available online: http://www.inegi.org.mx/sistemas/bie/?idserPadre=10200070#D10200070. (accessed: 7 January 2012).

INEGI (2011b) 'Encuesta Nacional de Empresas Constructoras Octubre 2011', *Press Release 481/11*, 19 December.

Kessler, T. (2000) 'The Mexican Peso Crash: Causes, Consequences and Comeback', in C. Wise and R. Roett (eds) *Exchange Rate Politics in Latin America*, Washington: Brookings Institution.

Luhnow, D. and B. Davis (2012) 'For Mexico, an Edge on China', *Wall Street Journal* 259(65), 17 September.

Marois, T. (2010) 'Emerging Market Bank Rescues in an Era of Finance-led Neoliberalism: A Comparison of Mexico and Turkey', *Review of International Political Economy* 18(2): 168–96.

Marois, T. (2012a) 'Finance, Finance Capital and Financialization', in B. Fine, A. Saad-Filho, and M. Boffo (eds) *The Elgar Companion to Marxist Economics*, Camberly: Edward Elgar.

Marois, T. (2012b) *States, Banks and Crisis: Emerging Finance Capitalism in Mexico and Turkey*, Chelteham: Edward Elgar.

Marx, K. (1978) *Wage Labour and Capital*, Moscow: Progress Publishers.

Middlebrook, K. and C. Quintero (1998) 'Protecting Workers' Rights in Mexico: Local Conciliation and Arbitration Boards, Union Registration, and Conflict Resolution in the 1990s', *Labour Studies Journal* 23(1): 21–49.

Middlebrook, K. and E. Zepeda (2003) *Confronting Development: Assessing Mexico's Economic and Social Policy Challenges*, Stanford: Stanford University Press.

Montamen-Samadian, S. (2000) 'Economic Integration, Capital Flows and Financial Instability', in C. Paraskevopoulos, A. Kintis, and T. Georgakopoulos (eds) *Global Financial Markets and Economic Development*, Toronto: APF Press.

Morales, R. (2010) 'Lejos de la Tormenta', *Expansion*, 4 July. Available online: http://www.cnnexpansion.com/las-500-de-expansion/2010/06/09/lejos-de-la-tormenta. (accessed: 9 April 2013).

Morera, C. (1998) *El Capital Financiero en México y la Globalización*, Mexico City: Ediciones Era.

Morton, A.D. (2011) *Revolution and State in Modern Mexico*, Boulder: Rowman and Littlefield Publishers, Inc.

Muñoz Martinez, H. (2011) 'Finanzas Globales y Producción Local: Delphi en Wall Street y Matamoros', in B. Vasquez, M. Jurado, and J. Castro (eds) *Procesos Económicos, Urbanos y Laborales en la Frontera Norte*, Tijuana: El Colegio de la Frontera Norte.

Notimex (2008) 'México, Más Fuerte que en el Pasado: Carstens', *El Universal*, 3 June. Available online: http://www.eluniversal.com.mx/notas/511647.html. (accessed: 9 April 2013).

Notimex (2011) 'Concamin, en Contra de una Intervención del Peso', *El Universal*, 2 Octubre. Available online: http://www.eluniversal.com.mx/notas/797951.html. (accessed: 9 April 2013).

Ocampo, J.A. (2009) 'Latin America and the Global Financial Crisis', *Cambridge Journal of Economics* 33(4): 703–24.

OECD (2013) *Factbook Statistics*. Available online: http://www.oecd-ilibrary.org/economics/oecd-factbook_18147364. (accessed: 22 March 2013).

Peck, J. (2011) 'Geographies of Policy: From Transfer-Diffusion to Mobility-Mutation', *Progress in Human Geography* 35(6): 773–97.

Poulantzas, N. (1974) *Classes in Contemporary Capitalism*, London: New Left Books.

Ramírez, Z., G. Velázquez, and A. Bello (2008). 'El Casino de los Derivados', *Revista Expansión*, 12 November. Available online: http://www.cnnexpansion.com/expansion/2008/11/12/doble-o-nada. (accessed: 28 March 2013).

Redacción (2010) 'Banamex Hace Ganar a Citigroup Mil 400 mdd en 2010', *Excelsior*, 23 December. Available online: http://www.excelsior.com.mx:8080/2010/12/23/dinero/698795. (accessed: 20 March 2013).

Regalado, A. (2009) 'Year-end Review of Markets and Finance 2008', *Wall Street Journal*, 2 January. Available online: http://search.proquest.com/docview/399115096?accountid=14611. (accessed: 20 August 2012).

Revista Expansión (2010) 'Las 500 Empresas Más Importantes de México', *Revista Expansión* 1043: 67–285.

Reyes, S. (2009) 'Encaminan Cambios para Regular Derivados', *El Norte*, 16 September. Available online: http://www.elnorte.com/negocios/articulo/515/1028872/default.asp?PlazaConsulta=elnorte&DirCobertura=&TipoCob=0. (accessed: 21 August 2011).

Schwegler, A.T. (2008) 'Take It from the Top (Down)?' *American Ethnologist* 35(4): 682–700.

Sheppard, E. (2011) 'Geographical Political Economy', *Journal of Economic Geography*, 11(2): 319–31.

Sigler, E. (2012) 'Slim acecha a Televisa y TV Azteca', *Revista Expansión*, 13 March. Available online: http://www.cnnexpansion.com/negocios/2012/03/12/slim-anade-otro-canal-a-su-tv. (accessed: 4 September 2012).

Solís, L. (1997) *Evolución del Sistema Mexicano Financiero*, Mexico City: Siglo XXI.

Tello, C. (1984) *La Nacionalización de la Banca en Mexico*, Mexico: Siglo XXI.

Tello, C. (2009) 'Sobre la Crisis Económica', *Este País*, 214: 8–13.

Thomas-Slayter, B. (2003) *Southern Exposure International Development and the Global South in the Twenty-First Century*, Bloomfield, CT: Kumarian Press.

UNCTAD (2008) *The Top 100 Non-financial TNCs from Developing and Transition Economies, Ranked by Foreign Assets*, Geneva: UNCTAD.

UNCTAD (2011) *World Investment Report 2011*, Geneva: UNCTAD.

Vidal, G. (2009) 'Los Oligarcas Rentistas Siguen Ganando', *Memoria*, 250: 12–17.

White, R. (1992) *State, Class and the Nationalization of the Mexican Banks*, New York: Taylor and Francis.

World Bank (2011) *Migration and Remittances Factbook*, Washington DC.: World Bank.

World Bank (2013) *Mexico. Data. World Development Indicators*. Available online: http://data.worldbank.org/country/mexico. (accessed: 23 April 2013).

Zepeda, J. (2011) 'Introducción', in J. Zepeda (ed.) *Los Amos de México*, Mexico City: Editorial Planeta.

Part IV

Alternative Forms of Politics

11

Alternative Policy Groups and Transnational Counter-Hegemonic Struggle

William K. Carroll

In *Global Slump: The Economics and Politics of Crisis and Resistance*, David McNally observes:

> Periods of enduring crisis and sporadic resistance are complex and dangerous. Desperation, anxiety, and hopelessness preside. The dominant class seems no longer to believe in itself. Rarely does it bother to espouse lofty ideals like freedom and betterment of the human condition... Rather than trying to inspire belief in their system, society's rulers seem to have no higher purpose than maintaining the status quo, squeezing profit and privilege out of a decrepit but well protected machinery of power.... Naked money-grubbing, mercenary politics, and the unconcealed use of force in the service of power are the order of the day. Governments seem content to attack the population; the rich live merely to get richer. In all these ways, the decade of austerity becomes one of social and cultural regression.
>
> (2011: 187–8)

McNally is describing the organic crisis of our time. Such a crisis, as Antonio Gramsci (1971: 276) famously wrote, 'consists precisely in the fact that the old is dying and the new cannot be born; in this interregnum a great variety of morbid symptoms appear' (cf. Gill 2012c: 234[1]). Organic crisis not only problematizes ruling-class visions and strategies while deepening the sense of despair. As old ways become unviable and as conditions of life deteriorate, popular discontent fuels outbreaks of protest which, however, stall for lack of organizational infrastructure and radical vision. Neoliberalism, as McNally (2011: 189) holds, may well be incapable of summoning up a compelling vision of the future, but much the same can be said of the Left, at least in its social-democratic guise. In an era when space opens for a radical imaginary that might posit a clear alternative to neoliberal globalization, where are the sites for such collective imagining, and how might their activities be integrated with the agency of movements?

This chapter focuses on an emergent component of global civil society: *transnational alternative policy groups* (TAPGs) that research and promote democratic alternatives to neoliberal globalization. Since the 1970s, an increasingly crisis-ridden economic globalization has fuelled concerns in the global North that democracy is being hollowed out as governments lose capacity to pursue policies that stray from what has been called the corporate agenda, even as democratic forces and practices within a number of Southern states have recently strengthened due to pressure from below – as in Latin America's 'pink tide' and the Middle East's 'Arab Spring'. Indeed, as neoliberal globalization have reshaped the political-economic terrain, North and South, transnational movements have developed as advocates of a 'democratic globalization' that endeavours to enrich human relations across space by empowering communities and citizens to participate in the full range of decisions that govern their lives (Chase-Dunn 2002; Munck 2010; Smith 2008; Smith and Wiest 2012). Alongside and in symbiosis with these movements, TAPGs have emerged – 'think tanks' that research and promote democratic alternatives to the corporate agenda of top-down globalization.

As collective intellectuals of alter-globalization, these are think tanks of a different sort from the conventional ones that advise political and corporate elites. Groups such as the Third World Institute (ITeM, Montevideo), the Centre de recherche et d'information pour le développement (Paris), the Transnational Institute (Amsterdam), and Focus on the Global South (Bangkok) create knowledge that challenges existing corporate priorities and state policies, and that advocates alternative ways of organizing economic, political, and cultural life. They disseminate this knowledge not only via mainstream media venues but through activist networks and alternative media, and they often work collaboratively with social movements in implementing these alternative ideas. This chapter provides a preliminary analysis, and addresses some of the challenges they face as transnational counter-hegemonic actors on the contested terrain of global civil society.

Global civil society has been defined as 'the realm of non-coercive collective action around shared interests and values that operates beyond the boundaries of nation states' (Glasius, Kaldor, and Anheier 2006: v). Often idealized as a coherent collection of world citizens moving forward towards social justice, global civil society is more accurately viewed as a field of conflict and struggle, distinct from the global economy and the inter-state system yet internally related to both. Although transnational networks underwriting imagined international communities reach back to the late seventeenth-century networks of Freemasons (Van der Pijl 1998), only recently has global civil society been recognized as a 'terrain for legitimizing and challenging global governance', a 'discursive space'

(Ford 2003: 129) that helps reproduce global hegemony while offering a foothold to counter-hegemonic politics (cf. Fraser 2005; Keane 2003; Munck 2006).

This terrain has long been dominated by a cosmopolitan bourgeoisie, reflecting the superior material and cultural resources of a dominant class (Van der Pijl 1998). In the twentieth century a network of business-oriented think tanks and policy groups entered the field, including the Mont Pèlerin Society and Trilateral Commission. Such hegemonic policy groups have been the object of extensive research (Gill 1990; Carroll and Carson 2003; Mirowski and Plehwe 2009; Carroll and Sapinski 2010) that has underscored their importance as sites of conventional knowledge production and mobilization (KPM), sometimes known as 'policy-planning' (Domhoff 2006). By the century's closing decades a new breed of 'advocacy think tanks' (Abelson 1995) were actively shaping the neoliberal project of market-centred society (Macartney 2008; Stone 2000). Widely implemented in the 1980s and 1990s as the political complement to economic globalization, neoliberalism tended to increase economic disparities and to degrade public goods while thinning the social basis for political consent and expanding the range of disaffected social interests (Cox 1987; Gill 1995b; Teeple 2000). By the mid-1990s neoliberal policies had provoked a variegated grassroots politics of 'alter-globalization' – resisting the 'corporate agenda' but also putting forward democratic alternatives (Coburn 2010; Smith 2008).

Some have seen in these developments a nascent counter-hegemonic bloc (Carroll 2006; Chase-Dunn 2002; Gill 2000), but this view is hardly unanimous (Day 2005; Stephen 2009). Indeed, in the decade since George W. Bush declared a war on terror much of the impetus for alter-globalization was first redirected into a massive anti-war movement in 2002–03 and then seemed to dissipate into a continuing series of anti-G8/G20 protests. The pattern, as noted in our opening quotation, has been one of sporadic resistance – campaigns that tend to stall for lack of organization and shared vision. The series of breath-taking popular struggles of 2011, focused around the militant occupation of urban space – which took on global proportions as it cascaded from Tahrir Square through Madrid to New York and scores of other cities – offers a vivid example, which is not to say that the Occupy movement was without impact, whether political or cultural. Among the problems faced by alter-globalization movements is that of *counter-hegemonic* KPM – the production and promulgation of alternative strategies and visions that, as taken up in practice, might foster a cathartic shift from the fragmented resistances typical of subalternity to a shared ethico-political project that can become 'a source of new initiatives' (Gramsci 1971: 367). The groups investigated in this research aspire to such counter-hegemonic KPM. They have furnished intellectual leadership for transnational movements and have taken up a unique yet problematic niche within the organizational ecology (Hunt and Aldrich 1998) of global justice politics.

My focus here is on specifically *transnational* alternative policy groups that *pose their politics globally*. These groups are the counter-hegemonic response to such transnational hegemonic initiatives as the International Chamber of Commerce, Trilateral Commission and World Business Council for Sustainable Development.

The changing terrain of contention

Counter-hegemony arises on a terrain shaped not only by the contradictions of class society but by the hegemonic practices and visions of the dominant historical bloc. To understand the counter-hegemonic projects that TAPGs pursue, we must first consider how hegemony is secured and maintained within late capitalism. As Fred Block (1977) observed some years ago, within capitalism a key aspect of hegemony is that the ruling class does not rule. Instead, its core interests, always in alliance with other social groups and institutions, are articulated through the agency of organic intellectuals, whose ranks include business leaders and many other organizers of practical life. Such intellectuals are 'organic' in a double sense: they are 'organizers' of an advanced capitalist way of life and their intellectual work is functionally – organically – predicated on the dominance of capital in human affairs (Vacca 1982: 62–3). The history of conventional think tanks forms part of this story of class formation from above. Linked into the circuitry of policy networks, mainstream media and corporate elites, think tanks of the right and centre have become important sites of knowledge production and mobilization in the construction of a neoliberal discursive field (Carroll and Shaw 2001; Mirowski and Plehwe 2009). Moreover, these collective intellectuals continue to proliferate. The hard right Atlas Network fosters and supports more than 400 market-oriented think tanks around the world, most of them nationally focused; the Ottawa-based Think Tank Initiative, hosted by the International Development Research Centre (IDRC), has since its establishment in 2008 funded 52 think tanks in 23 Southern countries.[2]

Set against the many high-profile purveyors of hegemonic policy, sites of cognitive praxis[3] 'from below' have been slower to form, much more modestly resourced, and until recently, have tended to focus on national theatres of political contention. All this reflects the difficulties in moving from subalternity to counter-hegemony. Think tanks of the right and centre have deep roots in the development of twentieth- century capitalism, with its rationalization of management, administration, planning and policy. In contrast, TAPGs are a recent invention. For instance, Canada's main nationally oriented left think tank, the Canadian Centre for Policy Alternatives, was founded (as an informal network) in 1980, and it was not until 1997 that the more transnationally oriented Polaris Institute, also based in Ottawa, emerged.

In a formal sense, TAPGs resemble such advocacy think tanks as the Fraser Institute: they provide intellectual leadership through research, analysis and knowledge mobilization. Yet they differ qualitatively from their conservative counterparts in three respects (see Table 11.1).

Substantively, hard-right policy groups advocate what Hayek (1976) called a market-driven politics of 'plain justice' (Carroll 2007); even mainstream policy groups advocate no more than a new regulatory regime within a neoliberal framework (Carroll and Carson 2003). TAPGs, on the other hand, are proponents of what Nancy Fraser (2005; 2010) has termed 'global justice', that combining claims for redistribution, recognition, representation, and indeed ecological salvation (Carroll and Ratner 2010).

Procedurally, hegemonic think tanks conduct policy research and engage primarily with elite political and business circles and corporate media sustaining a network of alliances or historical bloc supporting neoliberal capitalism (Stone 2000). For TAPGs, advocacy takes the form not of conventional liberal politics but of participatory democratic praxis – in

Table 11.1 Neoliberal and transnational alternative policy groups as sites of KPM

Elements in KPM	Conventional neoliberal think tanks	Transnational alternative policy groups	Challenges for TAPGs
Substantive practice	Advocate, through KPM, 'plain justice' of the market	Advocate, through KPM, global justice and ecological salvation	Global justice contradicts 'common sense;' namely, plain justice and the regnant inter-state system.
Procedural aspects	Conduct policy research and engage with elite political and business circles and corporate media	Create and mobilize veridical knowledge through participatory democratic praxis; cultivate counter-publics	Dialogical, polycentric communication and participatory KPM are less efficient than instrumental, state-centred KPM, yet TAPGs have shallow pockets.
Orientation towards future	Design and promote policies to replicate parameters of the existing way of life while solving immediate problems	Prefiguration: identify and advocate practices and relations that prefigure alternative futures	Replicating the status quo trades easily on reified assumptions of permanence; prefiguration requires strong powers of imagination and persuasion.

dialogue with movements with the intent of strengthening the capacity of counter-hegemonic publics to challenge the common sense of the day.

Finally, compared to their conventional counterparts, TAPGs are involved in *prefigurative* politics – attempting to bring new, participatory democratic practices into existence or to fruition. This implies a critical epistemology and ontology: an approach to inquiry and knowledge production that explores the alternative futures that already inhabit the present, and that considers how these elements of socio-political reality can be nurtured (Ollman 2003). The emphasis on prefiguration also distinguishes TAPGs from protest groups that in directing their limited resources to resistance and opposition often lack capacity to be proactive. In this sense, TAPGs can be seen as *catalysts* in the shift from a reactive politics of protest (as in the 1999 'Battle in Seattle' Gill 2000; Glassman 2002) to what Michelle Williams (2008) calls a 'generative politics of counter-hegemony' that seeks to transform state and economy by developing new institutions, organizations, and political actors rooted in an empowered civil society.

Each of these tasks raises challenges which are amplified by the perennial dearth of funds that is the predicament of most anti-capitalist groups. *Substantively*, the call for global justice challenges well-entrenched identifications of politics with sovereign states and goes against the grain of 'plain justice' and market civilization (Gill 1995a), which as neoliberalism has penetrated everyday life have taken on a veneer of common sense. The Westphalian 'partitioning of political space along territorial lines insulates extra and non-territorial powers from the reach of justice' (Fraser 2005: 81) while containing political identities within national borders. Within this political-economic configuration, the call for global justice may appear both unrealistic and irrelevant, and may thus fail to resonate with many people. In comparison with conventional think tanks, which trade effortlessly upon established verities of markets and states, TAPGs face a continuing uphill struggle to establish the credibility of their basic ethico-political claims.

Procedurally, dialogical communicative practices that nurture a network for democratic globalization are difficult to build and maintain. Participatory approaches are less efficient than positivist methods (St. Denis 2004) and yield knowledge whose qualitative richness is difficult to communicate in the sound bites of mainstream media. Alternative media may be more accommodating, but reach far smaller publics. Finally, the address of social movements is polycentric, and far more complicated than state-centred lobbying and interest group politics.

The commitment to *prefiguration* also brings special challenges. Conventional policy groups rely on existing structures of transnational capitalism, and consider how those structures can be replicated and extended more efficiently or with less harmful human and ecological consequences, typically through market mechanisms – free trade agreements, carbon trading, poverty reduction strategies, 3P arrangements and the like. Even when the market fails, backstopping the project is the widespread belief that, as

Margaret Thatcher put it, 'there is no alternative'. TAPGs advocate and nurture alternatives that break from hegemonic forms. This requires powers of creativity, imagination and persuasion, combined with sober appraisal of the possibilities for living otherwise that are opening up in this era of organic crisis.

Very schematically, we can conceptualize think tanks of the left and right as embedded in opposing historical blocs or as Smith (2008) puts it, global networks. Each organization develops and deploys knowledge with the strategic intent to make its bloc more coherent and effective; that is, it exercises a kind of leadership. Concretely, this entails quite different practices. Neoliberal leadership operates 'from the "top down" [and] seeks to stabilize power structures and strategies of rule, albeit with some marginal modifications under crisis conditions in ways that do not fundamentally challenge the dominant modes of accumulation and power' (Gill 2012a: 3). Neoliberal think tanks, firmly committed to capitalism and hierarchy as principles of economic and political organization, fit easily into existing elite structures: their messages, strategically focused on well-formed policy networks, are routinely conveyed by like-minded corporate media (Hackett and Zhao 1999). TAPGs, on the other hand, as collective intellectuals of an incipient global left, face the challenge of reaching a massive, diverse potential constituency and creating new political methodologies that go against the grain in giving shape to emergent oppositional practices (Carroll 2007).

Below, I do some of the spade work for researching the role of transnational alternative policy groups within alter-globalization politics. The objective is to explore, in the practices and discourses of these groups, some of the paradoxes of counter-hegemonic knowledge production and mobilization, particularly in the context of the contemporary economic and ecological crisis.

A preliminary judgement sample

This research programme is in its early days. My focus here is on a judgement sample of 16 major TAPGs, each of which satisfies these criteria:

- independence from states (each group is constituted as an NGO or network of NGOs, although it may accept funding from state or intergovernmental organizations[4]);
- a core function of knowledge production and mobilization (KPM) that challenges existing political-economic hegemonies and that presents alternatives, creates new paradigms, and so forth;
- a significant part of that KPM takes up transnational issues and speaks to transnational publics;
- the group engages a wide range of issues (it is not specialized in one domain such as water, trade or capital-labour relations).

A number of important groups come close to satisfying these criteria, and as this research programme develops we will widen the net to include them.

Table 11.2 offers a temporally sequenced description of the 16 TAPGs. Four groups formed in the mid-1970s, at the culmination of the 1960s protest

Table 11.2 Judgement sample of 16 TAPGs

Est'd	Name	Acronym	On WSF IC
1974	Transnational Institute (Amsterdam) http://www.tni.org/	TNI	YES
1975	Third World Forum (Dakar) http://www.forumtiersmonde.net/fren	TWF	*
1976	Tricontinental Centre (Lauvain-la-Neuve, Belgium) http://www.cetri.be/	CETRI	YES
1976	Centre de Recherche et d'Information pour le Developpement http://www.crid.asso.fr	CRID	YES
1984	Third World Network (Penang) http://www.twnside.org.sg/twnintro.htm	TWN	YES
1984	Development Alternatives with Women for a New Era (Manila) http://www.dawnnet.org/	DAWN	YES
1989	Instituto del Tercer Mundo (Third World Institute) (Montevideo) http://www.item.org.uy/	ITeM	YES
1990	Rosa Luxemburg Foundation (Berlin) http://www.rosalux.de/english/foundation	RLF	
1994	International Forum on Globalization (San Francisco) http://www.ifg.org/	IFG	YES
1995	Focus on the Global South (Bangkok) http://www.focusweb.org/	FGS	YES
1995	ZCom (Woods Hole, Mass, USA) http://www.zcommunications.org/	ZCOM	YES
1997	Network Institute for Global Democratization (Helsinki) http://www.nigd.org/	NIGD	YES
1998	People's Plan Study Group (Tokyo) http://www.ppjaponesia.org/index.php	PPSG	
2001	Centre for Civil Society (Durban) http://ccs.ukzn.ac.za	CCS	
2005	Alternatives International (Montreal) http://www.alterinter.org/	ALTINT	YES
2005	India Institute for Critical Action: Centre in Movement (New Delhi) http://cacim.net	CACIM	

*Participates on World Social Forum International Council (WSF IC) through World Forum for Alternatives, a joint venture with CETRI.

wave, and as the crisis of the post-war era set in. The Transnational Institute (TNI), initially the international branch of the Institute for Policy Studies (based in Washington DC), was created in 1974 as 'an international network of scholar-activists committed to social change',[5] but also as a defensive response to Chile's 9/11 – the Pinochet coup of 1973. The Dakar-based Third World Forum emerged in 1975. It has pursued a proactive political agenda, informed by Samir Amin's Marxist reformulation of dependency theory and emphasizing the strategy of 'de-linking' from global capitalism. Belgian-based Tricontinental Centre (CETRI) and Paris-based *Centre Recherche et d'information pour le developpement* (CRID) also were established with Third World foci, expressing the strong anti-imperialist thrust of the 1960s protest wave.

In the 1980s, three groups based in the global South formed. The Third World Network (TWN) and DAWN – Development Alternatives with Women for a New Era – were established in 1984, the former in Malaysia, the latter initially in Bangalore, India (currently based in Manila). The TWN grew out of a national consumers association; DAWN was established as a global network of feminist activist intellectuals of the South. The 1980s was prime time for consolidation, in much of the global North, of neoliberalism and the so-called Washington Consensus (Beder 2006), which subjected Southern countries to IMF-led austerity programmes, which in turn spurred the formation of TWN, DAWN and other progressive initiatives. DAWN in particular drew upon women's entry into the public sphere of paid work, which in the South was hastened by the Structural Adjustment Programs of the late 1970s and 1980s. Later in the decade, the end of military dictatorship in Uruguay created an opportunity to establish the Third World Institute (ITeM) in Montevideo, with ties to Third World Network. For movements in the North, however, the 1980s was a time of defensive, nationally bound campaigns, whether by British miners resisting Thatcherism (1984) or by popular groups in Canada opposing a free trade deal with the United States (1987–8) These largely unsuccessful efforts resisted the neoliberal tide without advancing forward-looking alternatives to it. Yet in 1990, Berlin-based and socialist-oriented Rosa Luxemburg Foundation was formed, initially as a small political group called the 'Social Analysis and Political Education Association'. It has since acquired a large organizational presence in Germany and globally, with offices worldwide.

In the mid-1990s TAPGs proliferated, as an intellectual aspect of the gathering global democracy movement, but also as critical responses to the crises and contradictions of neoliberal globalization. The world of TAPGs gained its first major North America-based group in 1994. An intellectual outgrowth of the struggle against NAFTA and the Uruguay Round that begat the WTO, San Francisco's International Forum on Globalization (IFG) continues to describe itself as a North-South research and educational institution critiquing the impacts of economic globalization. A year later, Massachusetts-based ZCom emerged, initially as the interactive website ZNet. Inspired by the anti-imperialist film, Z, this TAPG has made extraordinary use of the full panoply of new communications technologies in KPM.[6] Also in 1995, Focus on the Global South (FGS) formed in Bangkok and began to develop its 'deglobalization paradigm', discussed below.

In the nine years after 1996, five more TAPGs were founded. These late risers have framed their projects around the critique of capitalist globalization and the call for global alternatives, often emphasizing the need for an empowered global civil society, as do the Network Institute for Global Democratization (NIGD, based in Helsinki, established in 1997) and the Centre for Civil Society (CCS, based in Durban, founded in 2001). People's Plan Study Group, established in Tokyo in 1998 as a network of social movement activists and action-committed intellectuals, searches for democratic alternatives to global capitalism and maintains permanent research groups on transborder alliances and globalization, social movements, and other themes. Finally, two TAPGs were founded in 2005. Montreal's Alternatives International, with close ties to the Parisian complex of NGOs, emerged as a network of 'global justice' organizations dedicated to fostering solidarity and mutual understanding. The India Institute for Critical Action – Centre in Movement (CACIM), based in New Delhi, came directly out of the WSF process and has emphasized 'building and maintaining real and virtual spaces for fundamental research and critical reflection, exploration, action, and creation in the field of movement, from books, seminars and workshops to websites, listserves, and action alerts'.[7]

As social movement theorists have emphasized, activism has a cyclical character that is expressed in 'cycles of collective action' (Tarrow 1994) or 'waves of democracy' (Markoff 1996). In terms of TAPGs founded per year, Table 11.2 suggests two waves of intense TAPG formation, one from 1974–6 (1.33 TAPGs founded per year), and other from 1994–8 (one TAPG founded per year). These eight years account for nine of the 16 groups that formed over the 32-year period. The two waves appear to be articulated with the major cycles of activism over the past half-century. From the perspective of movement formation, we can see the invention and proliferation of TAPGs as an intellectual aspect of these waves. The first (which actually continued through the first half of the 1970s) is identified in the collective imaginary with Paris 1968 (Wallerstein 1989); the second (which began to build in the 1990s) identified with Seattle 1999, and took a far more international character (McNally 2006).[8] As transnational actors, TAPGs that formed in the first wave (mid-1970s) responded to the injustices and social crises engendered by the 'development of underdevelopment', including in the case of TNI the Pinochet coup of 1973 – Chile's own September 11. TAPGs emerging in the second wave responded to the injustices and crises of neoliberal globalization, a recurrent motif in the political frames through which IFG, FGS and other groups understand their projects. However, it is important to note the formation, during the 1980s, of three key Southern centres of alternative knowledge production and mobilization, as neoliberal austerity and democratization of the state (in the case of Uruguay) presented different combinations of threat and opportunity to activist intellectuals of the global South.

The relationship between global accumulation and waves of TAPG formation is even more complex. The first wave of TAPG formation coincides with the end of the post-war era of fordism in the North and developmentalism in the South, and the first generalized international recession since the 1930s (1974–5). The second coincides roughly with the accumulation of disparities issuing from neoliberal austerity, and a growing consciousness of ecological maladies that stem from endless accumulation on a world scale. It is in this wave of activism that we see the emergence of transnationally organized resistance to neoliberalism's 'new constitutionalism' (Gill 2012a: 5) – as in the 1994 Zapatista uprising against NAFTA and other inequities, the international campaign against the Multilateral Agreement on Investment (1998) and the 'Battle in Seattle' which disrupted the WTO Ministerial of 1999.

It is not surprising to find that cycles of transnational protest and capital accumulation are in some respects 'in phase' with waves of TAPG formation. On the one hand, capitalism's crises and contradictions have provided impetus for the cognitive praxis that TAPGs undertake: much of their intellectual work endeavours to explain and critique those crises and contradictions, and to advocate globally just alternatives. On the other hand, the establishment of vibrant movement communities in the 1960s/70s and 1990s created a strong demand by activists, both North and South, for alternative political knowledge and a strong supply of movement intellectuals who could, through TAPGs, produce and mobilize such knowledge.

The undulating pattern of TAPG formation recalls Polanyi's (1944) thesis that the disintegrating tendencies of capitalism provoke a 'second movement' in defence of community and society (Ashman 2004; Birchfield 1999; Gill 1995b). In a globalizing world, however, protective responses take a form different from the social democratic, state socialist and fascist projects that Polanyi analysed in depth. In the contemporary context, 'the self-defense is of a transnational character, linking together nongovernmental organizations (NGOs), environmental movements, women's movements, labor networks – a veritable transnational public designed to protect constituencies against market devastation' (Burawoy 2003: 240).

Transnational alternative policy groups strive to facilitate the formation of that public. In producing and mobilizing alternative knowledge they struggle against the market logic of capitalist disembedding while also striving to dislodge neoliberalism from its hegemonic location in popular consciousness and political policy. Somers and Block (2005) point out that the hegemony of neoliberalism *embeds the market*, ideologically, within structures of common sense – particularly in the domain of political policy but also in wider cultural fields. TAPGs are to a considerable degree engaged in discursive struggles to challenge this hegemony, but their intellectual production extends beyond critique to the advancement of alternative visions, strategies and policies. To have effect, however, this praxis must produce not simply knowledge of post capitalist alternatives; it must produce – in collaboration with the agency of allied groups – transnational counter-publics, cultures of solidarity and communities of practice that instantiate that knowledge, embedding it and beyond their own life-worlds. This sort of embedding is not centred upon national states (as in Polanyi's formulation from the 1940s); the emphasis is on constructing critical knowledge and solidarities, across borders, within global civil society – understood as a terrain of contention (Conway and Singh 2009). TAPGs direct their efforts not to one or another nationally defined citizenry, but to humanity as a whole in an ethical universalism that 'reflects the voices and practices of self-determining, self-defining individuals and communities' (Atasoy 2009: 10). In this sense their global justice politics takes up the standpoint not of nationally bound civil societies but of what Marx (1845) called 'human society, or social humanity'.

Indeed, the great challenge for TAPGs is to take KPM beyond a defensive critique of neoliberal globalization (whether centred upon national states or writ larger as in Tobin Tax schemes), into a prefigurative mode. A key site for such a shift has been the World Social Forum (WSF), and it is instructive to note that effectively three-quarters of our TAPGs participate on the WSF's International Council – its planning committee – pulling them into an 'open space' that serves as an intellectual commons for transnational movements and NGOs (see Table 11.2). However, a politics of global justice must ultimately reach beyond open-space dialogue to engage directly with capitalist and state power – whether in the form of protest politics or, as Evans (2008) notes, through allying with progressive state actors, in 'virtuous circles' of political practice that strengthen, at the global level, both movements and alternative state initiatives. Some TAPGs show evidence of such alliances.[9]

We can also see in Table 11.2 that continental Western Europe has held the largest clutch of groups (five of 16). North America – heavily over-represented as a favoured site for hegemonic think tanks[10] – is comparatively under-represented in the world of alternative think tanks. Perhaps this reflects among other things the relatively disorganized state of left politics in North America. Left think tanks of the South, (comprising seven of the 16) are of course *vastly* under-represented relative to the distribution of world population – a legacy of the material and cognitive injustices of colonialism and imperialism (Santos 2006).

The *regionalized* character of counter-hegemonic KPM is expressed not only in the location of TAPGs, but in the scope of their work. Some groups aspire to a fully global purview – TNI, IFG, NIGD, RLF and ZCom are exemplary. That all these TAPGs are based in Europe and North America suggests a continuing strain, within the world system's North Atlantic heartland, of cosmopolitan universalism in the framing of counter-hegemony. On the other hand, a number of mostly Southern-based TAPGs focus their efforts on issues and publics that are transnational yet also regional. For instance, CCS trains its efforts to a considerable degree on southern Africa; FGS has an Asian focus, as does PPSG; DAWN, TWN, ITeM and TWF all take the global South as the target for their KPM.

Importantly, these TAPGs are not all of one piece in their political projects. FGS places the 'paradigm of deglobalization' at the centre of its social vision; other groups such as NIGD (also IFG), hew more closely to a vision of democratic globalization, explicitly contrasted with neoliberal globalization; TWN trumpets Third World resurgence – reminiscent of the 1970s movement for a 'new international economic order' that was choked by the rise of transnational neoliberalism (Bair 2009). Despite this diversity, some overarching points of convergence can be discerned:

- The critique of neoliberalism – of the class power and disparities it reinforces and the problematic implications of endless, unregulated accumulation by dispossession;
- The importance of social justice and ecological sustainability as paramount values – a nascent social vision of global justice and sustainable human development (Magdoff and Foster 2010);
- The belief that such an alternative future can be achieved only through grassroots democratic movements;
- The ethical and strategic importance of North-South solidarity;
- The value of critical analysis that can inform effective and appropriate strategies for creating change.

TAPGs and the dual crisis

Earlier, I noted that alternative policy groups have formed on political terrain already occupied by hegemonic sites of KPM. But that terrain has also been reshaped by the uneven crisis of capitalist globalization. This crisis has a dual character, both economic and ecological (Harvey 2011; Magdoff and Foster 2010). Like other crises, it has not played out smoothly and uniformly, but is itself an expression, spatially and temporally, of uneven accumulation. Notwithstanding this unevenness, rising from the Volcker recession of the early 1980s, the neoliberal growth model underwrote an economic boom, punctuated by extremely unequal development, which lasted for a quarter of a century, even as it bred the conditions for chronic instability. The boom enhanced capital's structural power, sharpened inequalities and unleashed, via financialization, a massive volume of stateless fictitious capital (McNally 2011). However, the logic of accumulation by dispossession has been a highly contradictory one (Harvey 2003), and already in the 1997 Asian financial crisis the implications of declining industrial profitability, over-accumulation and anarchic capital markets could be discerned. The crisis of 1997 devastated lives and livelihoods in east Asia and ramified to Russia and then Argentina in 1998, yet its impact in the global North barely registered, as core states, mobilized within the G-7 and IMF, were able to displace the crisis into debt obligations and conditionalities that drove countries like South Korea, Indonesia and Argentina to the wall.

In Europe and North America the ensuing decade inflated a bubble economy that deferred the reckoning until 2008. When the bubble burst, neoliberalism's deregulatory logic was momentarily put into question as were the premises of endlessly expanding, credit-driven consumption. However, just as the 1997 crisis was extremely uneven in its spatial scope, the crisis of 2008ff has appeared to a great extent as a regional disruption, focussed in this case upon Europe and the United States. In much of the global South, and particularly in the BRIC countries, recent rates of accumulation have been stellar, even as global capitalism's core state have languished under the burdens of unemployment, fiscal imbalances and unredeemable sovereign debt. Still, it is doubtful that the recent pattern of rapid accumulation on the semi-periphery and slow-to-no growth at the centre can be sustained through time. Moreover, even where rates of accumulation remain robust, the global deepening of a market model combines ontologically distinct *crises* of livelihood into globally manifest intersections of expression (see Chapter 1 page 13 of this volume). Hence the language of a global crisis has real purchase, despite the crisis' unevenness of expression, whether in 1997–8 or 2008 onwards.

What is clear is that this accumulation crisis has been accompanied by a worsening ecological crisis (see Chapter 2 of this volume). In the twentieth century, as an already internationalized capitalism 'scaled up' to a system of transnational production and consumption in which most of the world's burgeoning population is ensnared, its ecological externalities also began to reach global scale. Species extinction, the thinning ozone layer and global warming are expressions of capitalism in ecological overshoot. The economic and ecological moments of crisis are interconnected, but do not follow a unitary logic. Economic crises are of their nature cyclical. Short of an exit from capitalism, they eventually resolve themselves, on the backs of workers and other subordinates, as conditions for robust accumulation are re-established – as in neoliberalism's own success in disassembling many of the impediments to accumulation that Fordism and Keynesian welfare states eventually presented. The deepening ecological crisis, on the other hand, has no bottom (Foster 2010). Without timely and radical intervention, ecological overshoot portends only a downward spiral, giving new meaning to the choice Rosa Luxemburg posed between socialism and barbarism (Angus 2010).

How have TAPGs responded to this dual crisis? Close readings of their websites offer some preliminary indications. Certainly, TAPGs take up economic and ecological issues, but to different degrees. Some provide quite extensive critical analyses of both dimensions of organic crisis, others much less so. The Transnational Institute, for instance, explicitly refers to the impending climate catastrophe and the economic crisis as a 'convergence of crises', and has led in responding to both aspects. In 1998 TNI published *Privatising Nature*, a prescient critique of market mechanisms as solutions to ecological maladies; in 2008 it spearheaded the Beijing Declaration (of 15 October), endorsed by 27 NGOs and incorporating a radical analysis of the financial crisis and a set of proposals for democratizing economic institutions.[11] In all, seven TAPGs feature in-depth analyses of the ecological crisis on their websites.[12] Eight[13] voice concern over the ecological crisis, and criticize the environmental impact of neoliberal globalization, but do not offer detailed ecological analysis.[14] In this relative sense, the ecological question differentiates our TAPGs as sites of counter-hegemonic KPM.

TAPGs also vary in how they have engaged with the crisis. Groups like the Transnational Institute and ZCom mobilize extensive networks of analysts for concise analyses of the events that comprise each immediate conjuncture of crisis. Their websites become, in effect, alternative media – nodal points for transnational counter-publics. Well-grounded, timely interventions in KPM focused on pressing concerns are indubitably of value in counter-hegemonic politics. They provide counter-publics with analyses that can be set against mainstream news narratives that tend either to reify what is a contingent reality under the rubric of 'the economy', or to vilify specific 'bad apple' personas – the Bernie Madoffs and Jérôme Kerviels.[15]

As important as it is to engage day-to-day, transnational counter-hegemonic struggle requires more. KPM singularly attuned to resistance in the immediate moment recalls Eduard Bernstein's (1899) fin-de-siècle adage, 'the ultimate aim of socialism is nothing, but the movement is everything', which has defined the politics of social democracy for more than a century. Counter-hegemonic politics requires the production and mobilization of knowledge that goes beyond the immediacy of the moment, and the immediate needs of movements in that moment. To remain on the terrain of the immediate is to cede the capacity to think and do otherwise. It is to confine one's practice to 'problem-solving', as distinct from critique (Cox 1995). 'Alternatives' become framed as more humane or environmentally sound ways of dealing with the same pragmatic problems that have already been defined within dominant discourse, and that are also taken up by organic intellectuals of capitalism's dominant class.

TAPGs and prefigurative KPM

Thus we arrive at the importance, within the organic crisis, of *prefigurative KPM*, as a companion to the day-to-day engagement with concrete issues that forms an indispensable ground for counter-hegemonic struggle. All 6 TAPGs engage in prefigurative KPM, but six devote considerable attention to this form of cognitive praxis. As intimated earlier, the visions they advance are not of all one piece, although they intersect in important ways.

The prefigurative KPM of the Third World Forum is closely associated with its founder, Samir Amin, whose *Accumulation on a World Scale* (1974) helped launch international political economy around the same time TWF was established. A global network of intellectuals, the TWF takes a critical stance on the major issues at stake in the world system and strives to identify concrete alternatives grounded in a dialectic of theory and practice 'between the scientific analysis of the problems and challenges on the one hand [and] strategies and targets of actual social movements on the other'. In what it describes as an ongoing 'search for convergence in diversity', the TWF seeks to 'identify, through the interpretation of the meaning of the movements, the more distant perspectives in which they are placed, the fundamental values and principles of the visions of society that they inspire', in order to raise 'each and everyone's awareness of the diversity vital to the construction of the future'. For TWF, the questions of democratization and development and of the *democratization of development* are key.[16]

As mentioned earlier, Focus on the Global South has placed the project of *deglobalization* at the core of its prefigurative KPM, which is undertaken by staff who facilitate transnational initiatives as well as country-based programmes from offices in Thailand, India and the Philippines. A paradigm intended to signify both the dismantling of the old and the construction of the new, deglobalization 'describes the transformation of the global economy from one centred around the needs of transnational corporations to one that focuses on the needs of people, communities and nations and in which the capacities of local and national economies are strengthened'. Focus's analytic work across five designated thematic areas – from 'defending and reclaiming the commons' to 'peace and people's security' – is informed by this prefigurative conception.[17]

The Rosa Luxemburg Foundation centres its prefigurative KPM around an educational programme rather than a research agenda in any conventional sense. Through participatory approaches such as discussion groups, its Academy for Political Education helps people gain 'the knowledge that can empower them and enable them to act'. RLF's Institute for Critical Social Analysis, founded in 2008, focuses on researching and 'strategizing left politics and *democratic-socialist transformation* of the current capitalist society'.[18] Beyond its German base, RLF is active through regional offices and partnerships with NGOs and movement groups in more than 25 countries, where its prefigurative KPM is adapted to local settings. Among its activities in south Asia, for instance, RLF supports 'new theoretical approaches to and hands-on activities for creating alternative societal and economical forms', including joint work with alter-globalization movements and local and regional socialist forums.[19]

The Transnational Institute's prefigurative KPM dates from 1999, when it undertook the *New Politics* project to document, publicize and evaluate actual experiences with direct, participatory democracy as well as the formation of new sorts of political parties emerging from movements in Latin America, Europe and Asia. The project generated hundreds of articles reflecting on the practices of social forums, movements and parties, citizen's struggles and democratization.[20] Recently, TNI reorganized its work areas, folding New Politics into an Economic Justice, Corporate Power and Alternatives programme which includes an Alternative Regionalisms initiative to build capacity for policy autonomy in the South.[21]

Two United States-based TAPGs are particularly active in prefigurative KPM. In the midst of the financial crisis of 2008 the International Forum on Globalization convened a global meeting of economists and leaders of key NGOs, to raise basic questions about the continued viability of capitalism, and then leveraged this initiative into its *Post-Capitalism* programme, which articulates 'steps to new economies of sustainability, equity and peace'. More recently, IFG launched its *Opening Silos* programme, aimed at stimulating a new 'global, intergenerational, multi-disciplinary leadership movement' – that is, the creation of organic intellectuals for global justice. Established in autumn 2011, Opening Silos exemplifies the catalytic role that TAPGs can play, vis-à-vis social movements, as centres of counter-hegemonic knowledge production and mobilization. Through a series of two-day meetings on every continent, Opening Silos encouraged new intersectional movement integration, 'crossing geographies, constituencies, program targets, even ages, toward a far more eclectic and wider ranging movement'.[22]

Lastly, ZCom's prefigurative KPM is written into its mission statement, which notes two implications that stem from its commitment to 'fundamental transformation': (1) 'successful action in the present depends very much not only on understanding current conditions but also on broad clarity about future goals and building the links between the two'; (2) 'a movement able to transform society requires massive, highly informed, participatory, unwavering allegiance which will only grow and persist if the seeds of a better future are embodied in the actions of current activists'.[23] Two major initiatives that embody these ideas are participatory economics (*PARECON*), a detailed vision for decentralized council socialism emphasizing workplace democracy, which informs the practice of various workplaces in and beyond North America, and the IOPS Project, launched in January 2012. IOPS (*International Organization for a Participatory Society*) is taking shape as

> a revolutionary organization that aims to win a better world through flexibly exploring and advocating long term vision, building the seeds of the future in the present, empowering the lives of its members, organizing in an internally classless and self-managing way, and winning changes in society that better the situations of suffering constituencies while also laying the ground work for more changes, and construction, to come.[24]

These brief accounts of prefigurative KPM illustrate how, as the production and mobilization of knowledge becomes attuned to the possibilities for a transformed future, the gap between cognition and action closes. In each instance, the point is not simply to critique mainstream policy, nor to offer policy alternatives designed to be implemented within existing institutional arrangements. Rather, prefigurative KPM consciously cultivates and promulgates radical alternatives that set in motion processes of transformation, not replication. To accomplish this, alternative policy groups need to be in close dialogue with the social movements whose collective agency can drive transformative change; indeed, much of the work of counter-hegemonic KPM involves just such a dialogue – well exemplified by the extensive movement partnerships of groups like DAWN, TNI and CCS.[25] In much the same way that participatory action research, as a methodology, subverts the distinction between knowledge production and political change, in prefigurative KPM the line between research and political action blurs, as functions of the think tank merge with those of the social movement organization.

Conclusions

The centres of alternative knowledge introduced in this chapter share a common *modus operandi* as transnationally oriented think tanks on the left. Yet they are differentiated in terms of political frames, organizational forms, and spatial locations within the global system. This diversity points to a larger reality. Taken as a whole, the 16 TAPGs comprise a spatialized organizational ecology that takes in 'open spaces' for dialogical engagement (for instance, CACIM) as well as more formally organized groups (for instance, RLF), which may have greater capacity to articulate and advocate prefigurative alternatives (Carroll 2010; Evans 2008). In much the same way that, for the right, a diverse organizational ecology of policy groups creates a rich discursive field that 'offers possibilities for nuanced debate and diverse action repertoires, all within the perimeters of permissible neoliberal discourse' (Carroll and Shaw 2001: 211), the set of TAPGs seems to offer a diversity of sites, North and South, for constructing counter-hegemonic alternatives, a creative process that requires both open spaces and more strategically oriented organizations engaged in prefigurative KPM and collective will formation. But that very diversity also points to the difficulty in combining both aspects of counter-hegemonic politics – open space and the political organization – in a single place – a classic conundrum that has beset many left parties, as well as, more recently, the World Social Forum, with its perennial debates over its identity as 'open space' or 'movement of movements'.

As the uneven, dual crisis of neoliberal globalization continues to unfold, TAPGs and other sites of transnational counter-hegemony will continue to face the challenge of engaging within changing conjunctures in ways that speak to concrete needs and ontological insecurities while helping to build intellectual and material capacity for a radically transformed world. This challenge can be expected to express itself in different modalities, according to how agencies of counter-hegemonic KPM are organized and positioned politically, culturally, and geographically.

Crises always pose a conjunction of threats and opportunities to the social actors caught up in them. On the basis of these preliminary findings, we can begin to profile the opportunities and risks that different alternative policy groups face. Groups strongly grounded within nation-states face the risk of *capture* within the perimeters of those states, yet they are positioned to help inform national-level processes of socio-political transformation. Caracas-based Centro Internacional Miranda (CIM) arguably exemplifies both sides of this paradox. Since 2005 it has functioned as a state-supported agency of the Bolivarian Revolution. It has promoted research, reflection and training on strategic issues in the process of political change, linking with economic, social and cultural initiatives within the Bolivarian Revolution (Molina 2006). Originally given a strong international mandate with a major role for foreign collaborators (effectively a state-sponsored TAPG), insiders to CIM report that more recently its brief has been narrowed to domestic popular education with a nationalist thrust, as the Venezuelan government grapples with political reaction from the domestic ruling class and its international allies, and the slow pace of socialist transformation. The risk here is one of replicating the practice of the 'old internationalism' in which 'the international dimension of struggle was subordinated to the strategic objectives of the national dimension ... the immediate objective of the struggle was primarily national and the related internationalism was instrumental to it' (Nilsen and Cox 2005, unpaginated).

On the other hand, groups that operate in transnational spaces face the challenge of *establishing the relevancies* of their analyses and initiatives to local, on-the-ground movement actors, through tangible, dialogical collaborations. Theory, including the critical discourses TAPGs produce and circulate, 'becomes a material force', as Marx (1844) put it, 'as soon as it has gripped the masses'. The corollary, however, is that ideas that remain disembedded, as abstract formulations, construct what Gramsci called 'castles in the air' (quoted in Germino 1990: 19). Efforts by groups like IFG, TNI and ZCom to embed prefigurative KPM in local contexts, reviewed earlier, indicate an awareness of the magnitude of this challenge, but closer investigation will be required to assess their effectiveness.

By the same token, Northern-based groups need to avoid tendencies towards *abstract universalism* (as in most human rights discourse), which in substance shores up Eurocentric hegemonies. Conversely, Southern-based groups need to bring the energy of anti-imperialist and Indigenous perspectives, often exemplary of 'militant particularism', into a global vision. In both North and South, what is needed is a dialectical approach to the universal and the particular. As David Harvey has argued,

> universality always exists *in relation to* particularity: neither can be separated from the other even though they are distinctive moments within our conceptual operations and practical engagements. The notion of social justice, for example, acquires universality through a process of abstraction from particular instances and circumstances, but, once established as a generally accepted principal or norm, becomes particular again as it is actualised through particular actions in particular circumstances.
> (Harvey 2001: 194, emphasis in original; cf. Ashman 2004)

For all groups, regardless of how they are positioned in the world system, what Santos (2006) calls the 'work of translation' – of bridging across languages, identities, and visions – looms large. Within WSF discussions it has become clear that 'the global left is intercultural' (Santos 2008: 261). Transnational alternative policy groups, most of them active participants at the WSF, need to elaborate practices of intercultural translation that preserve autonomy while creating common ground (cf. Carroll 2010: 185; Conway 2011). At stake in this is the reconstruction of knowledge 'in ways that permit us to be non-Orientalist' (Wallerstein 2006: 48), without simply inverting the colonial epistemic hierarchy – as in the valorization of non-Western ways of knowing over post-Enlightenment thought. In grappling with the continuing tension between emergent universals (such as, 'human rights' and 'global citizenship') and the concrete, particular contexts of life in a highly differentiated world, 'we are required to universalize our particulars and particularize our universals simultaneously in a kind of constant dialectical exchange, which allows us to find new syntheses that are then of course instantly called into question' (Wallerstein 2006: 49). The promise of transnational alternative policy groups lies in the 'inter-culturality' that can issue from their cognitive praxis as it instantiates 'a dialogical strategy of knowledge production, premised on a post-colonial sensibility' (McMichael 2009: 28). As collective intellectuals of alter-globalization, TAPGs can facilitate the formation of a 'world knowledge', conscious of its historicity and 'rooted in a politics of "strategic diversity", which situates alternative visions/knowledges in the context of shared, but differentiated, experience of the discourse and impact of global integration' (McMichael 2009: 29).

Of course, intellectual leadership in the form of alternative knowledge production and mobilization is simply one aspect of a 'process of rebuilding movements, infrastructures of dissent and oppositional capacities' (McNally 2011: 189). It would be a mistake to suppose that the various sites of counter-hegemonic knowledge production and mobilization that have grown out of global capitalism's crises and contestations are the decisive or primal forces in alter-globalization politics. Still, intellectual leadership does matter, and in the absence of a 'fifth international' pulling the diversity of left parties and progressive movements towards a creative convergence, the intellectual work of TAPGs takes on heightened importance. In this sense, the future of the global left, and the prospects for meaningful responses to the global organic crisis, depend in part on the effectiveness of TAPGs in learning from, working with, informing and inspiring critical movements, publics and progressive governments in a great variety of locations and across a wide range of issues, in a multiform politics of resistance and reconstruction.

Notes

1. Gill (2012b: 26) also observes, correctly, that organic crisis does not necessarily imply a complete breakdown of political legitimacy. 'The problem of political legitimacy for disciplinary neoliberalism has been met by strategies of depoliticization... as yet we have not seen any of the regimes governing North American or European polities being toppled.' Nevertheless, he continues, 'many problems once associated with the global South seem now to be migrating to the capitalist core of the world order' – a development that forms an important element in the global organic crisis.
2. See, respectively http://atlasnetwork.org; http://www.idrc.ca/EN/Programs/Social_and_Economic_Policy/Think_Tank_Initiative/Pages/About.aspx. (accessed: 25 March 2013).
3. On the concept of cognitive praxis, see Eyerman and Jamison (1991:55) who hold that 'it is precisely in the creation, articulation, formulation of new thoughts and ideas – new knowledge – that a social movement defines itself in society'. In this sense, the work of TAPGs forms part of the practice of social movement activism.
4. In the case of the Rosa Luxembourg Foundation, affiliated with the Party of Democratic Socialism (now Die Linke) since 1996, the electoral success of the party, particularly since the 2005 federal election, has brought extensive funds from the German state, for which parties represented in the Bundestag qualify.
5. http://www.tni.org/page/history. (accessed: 3 October 2011).
6. The year 1995 marks the beginning of ZNet, the Internet initiative that eventuated in Z Communications. This group had its origins in Z Magazine, established in 1987 as a national hard-copy serial of the US left. It evolved into an ICT-rich TAPG that fosters an interactive network of KPM through ZNet, ZSpace, ZSpeakers, and other initiatives. See http://www.zcommunications.org/. (accessed: 3 October 2011).
7. http://cacim.net. (accessed: 28 July 2011).
8. The periodization of protest waves is contingent on one's theoretical framework. Wallerstein and McNally develop their analyses on the basis of historical materialism, which is the guiding framework for this study. In contrast, Markoff grounds his account of 'waves of democracy' in a liberal-pluralist understanding of nominally democratic regimes. He views the 1960s and 1970s as an era of democratic

recession and the later 1970s into the 1990s as a period in which 'in many different countries, regimes believed to be less democratic were replaced by others believed to be more so' (1996: 11).

9. For instance, on the strength of its policy work on democratizing public services, the Transnational Institute, at the request of the Chavez government of Venezuela critically evaluated Venezuela's re-nationalization programme in the telecommunications sector. Relations between progressive (Southern) governments and TAPGs are also reflected in exchange of personnel. In 2012 Focus on the Global South appointed, as its new executive director, former Bolivian UN Ambassador Pablo Solon (well known for his having organized the Cochabamba conference on the rights of Mother Earth in 2010), replacing Walden Bello, who is now a member of the Philippines Parliament.
10. Of the 400-odd 'free market' think tanks that make up the global network supported by the Atlas Economic Research Foundation, 177 are based in the United States and Canada and 85 are based in Europe. http://atlasnetwork.org/global-network-directory/. (accessed: 25 July 2011).
11. http://www.tni.org/archives/beijingstatementoncrisis. (accessed: 26 July 2011).
12. Namely, CCS, DAWN, FGS, IFG, TWN, TNI, ZCom.
13. Namely RLF, TWF, PPSG, CETRI, NIGD, CRID, ALTINT, and ITeM.
14. CACIM, with its ardent commitment to open-space discussion, does not present any substantive content, whether ecological or economic, on its website.
15. For instance, articles posted on ZCom's Znet site on 2 August 2011 included three critical analyses of the US 'debt ceiling deal' (reached on that day) by George Monbiot, Dean Baker, and Paul Krugman, a discussion by David Case of Italy's sovereign debt crisis and its implications for the Euro, and a report by Jerome Roos on the 150,000+ who protested in Israel against 'three decades of extreme economic neoliberalism'.
16. The quoted text is from the document, 'A short presentation of the organisation', available at http://www.forumtiersmonde.net/fren/index.php?option=com_content&view=article&id=74:the-third-world-forum&catid=39:forum-du-tiers-monde&Itemid=28. (accessed: 25 March 2013).
17. http://www.focusweb.org/content/who-we-are. (accessed: 26 July 2011).
18. Founding resolution from 6 December 2008; emphasis added. http://www.rosalux.de/english/foundation/research-projects.html. (accessed: 26 July 2011).
19. http://www.rosalux.de/english/worldwide/asia.html. (accessed: 26 July 2011).
20. http://www.tni.org/node/597/by-issue. (accessed: 26 July 2011).
21. http://www.tni.org/page/about-alternative-regionalisms-project. (accessed: 24 September 2012).
22. http://ifg.org/programs/silos.html. (accessed: 11 July 2012).
23. http://www.zcommunications.org/mission.htm. (accessed: 26 July 2011).
24. http://www.iopsociety.org/mission. (accessed: 25 March 2013).
25. For RLF, the dialogue of prefiguration includes interlocutors in movements as well as activists within Germany's Left Party, for which it serves as an intellectual centre. Other TAPGs operate at a distance from formal political parties.

References

Abelson, D. E. (1995) 'From Policy Research to Political Advocacy – the Changing Role of Think Tanks in American Politics', *Canadian Review of American Studies* 25: 93–126.

Amin, S. (1974) *Accumulation on a World Scale*, New York: Monthly Review Press.

Angus, I. (ed.) (2010) *The Global Fight for Climate Justice: Anticapitalist Responses to Global Warming and Environmental Destruction*, Halifax: Fernwood Publishing.

Ashman, S. (2004) 'Resistance to Neoliberal Globalisation: A Case of "Militant Particularism"?' *Politics* 24(2): 143–53.

Atasoy, Y. (2009) 'Introduction', in Y. Atasoy (ed.) *Hegemonic Transitions, the State and Crisis in Neoliberal Capitalism*, New York: Routledge.

Bair, J. (2009) 'Taking aim at the New International Economic Order', in P. Mirowski and D. Plehwe (eds) *The Road from Mont Pèlerin: The Making of the Neoliberal Thought Collective*, Cambridge: Harvard University Press.

Beder, S. (2006) *Suiting Themselves: How Corporations Drive the Global Agenda*, London: Earthscan.

Bernstein, E. (1899) *Evolutionary Socialism*. Available online: http://www.marxists.org/reference/archive/bernstein/works/1899/evsoc/index.htm (accessed: 18 July 2011).

Birchfield, V. (1999) 'Contesting the Hegemony of Market Ideology: Gramsci's "Good Sense" and Polanyi's "Double Movement" ', *Review of International Political Economy* 6: 27–54.

Block, F. (1977) 'The Ruling Class Does Not Rule: Notes on the Marxist Theory of the State', *Socialist Revolution* 7(3): 6–28.

Burawoy, M. (2003) 'For a Sociological Marxism: The Complementary Convergence of Antonio Gramsci and Karl Polanyi', *Politics and Society* 31: 193–261.

Carroll, W. K. (2006) 'Hegemony, Counter-Hegemony, Anti-Hegemony', *Socialist Studies* 2: 9–43.

Carroll, W. K. (2007) 'Hegemony and Counter-Hegemony in a Global Field', *Studies in Social Justice* 1: 36–66.

Carroll, W. K. (2010) 'Crisis, Movements, Counter-Hegemony: In Search of the New', *Interface: A Journal for and about Social Movements* 2(2): 168–98.

Carroll, W.K. and R.S. Ratner (2010) 'Social Movements and Counter-Hegemony: Lessons from the Field', *New Proposals: Journal of Marxism and Interdisciplinary Inquiry* 4(1): 7–22.

Carroll, W.K. and C. Carson (2003) 'The Network of Global Corporations and Elite Policy Groups: A Structure for Transnational Capitalist Class Formation?' *Global Networks* 3: 29–57.

Carroll, W. K. and J. P. Sapinski (2010) 'The Global Corporate Elite and Transnational Policy Planning Network, 1996–2006: A Structural Analysis', *International Sociology* 25: 501–38.

Carroll, W. K. and M. Shaw (2001) 'Consolidating a Neoliberal Policy Bloc in Canada, 1976 to 1996', *Canadian Public Policy* 27: 195–216.

Chase-Dunn, C. (2002) 'Globalization from Below: Toward a Collectively Rational and Democratic Global Commonwealth', *Annals of the American Academy of Political and Social Science* 581: 48–61.

Coburn, E. (2010) 'Resisting Neoliberal Capitalism: Insights from Marxist Political Economy', in G. Teeple and S. Mcbride (eds) *Relations of Global Power: Neoliberal Order and Disorder*, Toronto: University of Toronto Press.

Conway, J. (2011) 'Cosmopolitan or Colonial? The World Social Forum as "Contact Zone" ', *Third World Quarterly* 32: 217–36.

Conway, J. and J. Singh (2009) 'Is the World Social Forum a Transnational Public Sphere? Nancy Fraser, Critical Theory and the Containment of Radical Possibility', *Theory, Culture & Society* 26: 61–84.

Cox, R. W. (1987) *Production, Power and World Order*, New York: Columbia University Press.

Cox, R. W. (1995) 'Critical political economy', in B. Hettne (ed.) *International Political Economy: Understanding Global Disorder*, Halifax: Fernwood Books.

Day, R. (2005) *Gramsci is Dead: Anarchist Currents in the Newest Social Movements*, Toronto: Between the Lines.

Domhoff, G. W. (2006) *Who Rules America?*, New York: McGraw-Hill.

Evans, P. (2008) 'Is an Alternative Globalization Possible?' *Politics & Society* 36: 271–305.

Eyerman, R. and A. Jamison (1991) *Social Movements: A Cognitive Approach*, University Park, PA: Pennsylvania State University Press.

Ford, L. H. (2003) 'Challenging Global Environmental Governance: Social Movement Agency and Global Civil Society', *Global Environmental Politics* 3: 120–34.

Foster, J. (2010) 'Why Ecological Revolution?' *Monthly Review* 61: 1–18.

Fraser, N. (2005) 'Reframing Justice in a Globalizing World', *New Left Review* 36: 69–88.

Fraser, N. (2010) 'Who Counts? Dilemmas of Justice in a Postwestphalian World', *Antipode* 41: 281–97.

Germinio, D. L. (1990) *Antonio Gramsci: Architect of a New Politics*, Baton Rouge: Louisiana State University.

Gill, S. (1990) *American Hegemony and the Trilateral Commission*, Cambridge: Cambridge University Press.

Gill, S. (1995a) 'Globalisation, Market Civilization and Disciplinary Neoliberalism', *Journal of International Studies* 24: 399–423.

Gill, S. (1995b) 'Theorizing the Interregnum: The Double Movement of Global Politics in the 1990s', in B. Hettne (ed.) *International Political Economy: Understanding Global Disorder*, Halifax: Fernwood Books.

Gill, S. (2000) 'Toward a Postmodern prince? The Battle in Seattle as a Moment in the new Politics of Globalisation', *Millennium* 29: 131–40.

Gill, S. (2012a) 'Introduction: Global Crises and the Crisis of Global Leadership', in S. Gill (ed.) *Global Crises and the Crisis of Global Leadership*, Cambridge: Cambridge University Press.

Gill, S. (2012b) 'Leaders and Led in an Era of Global Crises', in S. Gill (ed.) *Global Crises and the Crisis of Global Leadership*, Cambridge: Cambridge University Press.

Gill, S. (2012c) 'Organic Crisis, Global Leadership and Progressive Alternatives', in S. Gill (ed.) *Global Crises and the Crisis of Global Leadership*, Cambridge: Cambridge University Press.

Glasius, M., M. Kaldor, and H. Anheier (eds) (2006) *Global Civil Society 2005/6*, London: Sage.

Glassman, J. (2002) 'From Seattle (and Ubon) to Bangkok: the Scales of Resistance to Corporate Globalization', *Environment and Planning D-Society & Space* 20: 513–33.

Gramsci, A. (1971) *Selections from the Prison Notebooks*, New York: International Publishers.

Hackett, R. A. and Y. Zhao (1999) *Sustaining Democracy? Journalism and the Politics of Objectivity*, Toronto: University of Toronto Press.

Harvey, D. (2001) *Spaces of Capital: Towards a Critical Geography*, Edinburgh: Edinburgh University Press.

Harvey, D. (2003) *The New Imperialism*, New York: Oxford University Press.

Harvey, D. (2011) *The Enigma of Capital and the Crises of Capitalism*, New York: Oxford University Press.

von Hayek, F. A. (1976) *The Mirage of Social Justice*, Chicago: University of Chicago Press.

Hunt, C. S. and H. E. Aldrich (1998) 'The Second Ecology: Creation and Evolution of Organizational Communities', *Research in Organizational Behaviour* 20: 267–301.

Keane, J (2003) *Global Civil Society?* Cambridge: Cambridge University Press.

Macartney, H. (2008) 'Articulating Particularistic Interests: The Organic Organisers of Hegemony in Germany and France', *British Journal of Politics & International Relations* 10: 429–51.

Magdoff, F. and J. B. Foster (2010) 'What Every Environmentalist Needs To Know about Capitalism', *Monthly Review* 61(10). Available online: http://monthlyreview.org/100301magdofffoster.php. (accessed: 25 March 2013).

Markoff, J. (1996) *Waves of Democracy: Social Movements and Political Change,* Thousand Oaks, CA: Pine Forge Press.

Marx, K. (1844) 'Introduction to A Contribution to the Critique of Hegel's *Philosophy of Right'.* Available online: http://www.marxists.org/archive/marx/works/1843/critique-hpr/intro.htm. (accessed: 25 March 2013).

Marx, K. (1845) 'Theses on Feuerbach', Thesis X. Marx/Engels Internet Archive. Available online: http://www.marxists.org/archive/marx/works/1845/theses/theses.htm. (accessed: 10 July 2012).

McMichael, P. (2009) 'Global Citizenship and Multiple Sovereignties: Reconstituting Modernity', in Y. Atasoy (ed.) *Hegemonic Transitions, the State and Crisis in Neoliberal Capitalism,* London & New York: Routledge.

McNally, D. (2006) *Another World is Possible* Second Edition, Winnipeg: Arbeiter Ring.

McNally, D. (2011) *Global Slump,* Oakland, CA: PM Press.

Mirowski, P. and D. Plehwe (eds) (2009) *The Road from Mont Pèlerin: The Making of the Neoliberal Thought Collective,* Cambridge: Harvard University Press.

Molina, L. B. (2006) 'Centro Internacional Miranda', *MRZine* 15 September. Available online: http://mrzine.monthlyreview.org/2006/cim150906.html. (accessed: 23 October 2011).

Munck, R. (2006) 'Global Civil Society: Royal Road or Slippery Slop', *Voluntus* 17: 325–32.

Munck, R. (2010) 'Globalization, Crisis and Social Transformation: A View from the South', *Globalizations* 7: 235–46.

Nilsen, A. and L. Cox (2005) 'Why do activists need theory?' *Euromovements Newsletter.* Available online: http://eprints.nuim.ie/445/ (accessed: 3 October 2011).

Ollman, B. (2003) *Dance of the Dialectic: Steps in Marx's Method,* Urbana: University of Illinois Press.

St. Dennis, V. (2004) 'Community-Based Participatory Research: Aspects of the Concept Relevant for Practice', in W. K. Carroll (ed.) *Critical Strategies for Social Research,* Toronto: Canadian Scholars' Press Inc.

Smith, J. (2008) *Social Movements for Global Democracy,* Baltimore: Johns Hopkins University Press.

Smith, J. and D. Wiest (2012) *Social Movements in the World-System,* New York: Russell Sage Foundation.

Somers, M. R. and F. Block (2005) 'From Poverty to Perversity: Ideas, Markets, and Institutions over 200 years of Welfare Debate', *American Sociological Review* 70: 260–87.

Santos, B. de Sousa (2006) *The Rise of the Global Left: the World Social Forum and Beyond,* London: Zed Books.

Santos, B. de Sousa (2008) 'The World Social Forum and the Global Left', *Politics & Society* 36: 247–70.

Stephen, M. D. (2009) 'Alter-Globalism as Counter-Hegemony: Evaluating the "Postmodern Prince"', *Globalizations* 6: 483–98.

Stone, D. (2000) 'Think Tanks Transnationalization and Non-Profit Analysis and Advocacy', *Global Society* 14: 153–72.

Tarrow, S. (1994) *Power in Movement*, Cambridge: Cambridge University Press.

Teeple, G. (2000) *Globalization and the Decline of Social Reform: into the Twenty-first Century*, Aurora, Ontario: Garamond Press.

Van der Pijl, K. (1998) *Transnational Classes and International Relations*, London: Routledge.

Wallerstein, I. (1989). '1968, Revolution in the World-System', *Theory and Society* 18(4): 431–49.

Wallerstein, I. (2006) *European Universalism: The Rhetoric of Power*, New York: The New Press.

Williams, M. (2008) *The Roots of Participatory Democracy*, London: Palgrave Macmillan.

12
Conclusion: Rethinking the Politics of Diversity

Yıldız Atasoy

The human, social, and environmental costs of the current global financial crisis are often interpreted from a welfare-state perspective, with a focus on countries from the global North. Scholars in recent years have begun to examine the broader changes in state policy interventions designed to facilitate economic growth and consider the implications of these policies for social redistribution, climate change, and the politics of sustainability. The creation and use of financial markets for housing, health care, old-age security markets, and so on, has also begun to receive greater scholarly attention (Castles et al. 2010). Nevertheless, the consequences of climate change for social policy and the redistributive welfare-state remain largely unstudied (Gough and Therborn 2010: 716–8). It now appears that the state's involvement in the financialization of the economy is deeper than a 'retreat/evisceration of the welfare state' perspective would allow us to appreciate. Despite significant differences in European and American models in respect to social policy profiles and redistributive strategies (Castles 2010: 630–42), the welfare-capitalist states are deeply implicated in financial markets through market-creating, market-correcting, and market-compensating social policies (Schelkle 2012). Through these three social-policy roles, states are also implicated in the advent of the financial crisis, as Schelkle (2012) has revealed in his comparative examination of mortgage credit markets and the state social policy of promoting homeownership – especially among low-income earners in the United States and Europe. From this perspective, the ongoing, active state-policy interventions and wide-scale austerity measures adopted for the political management of the economic crisis in Europe cannot be described as leading to a crisis in the 'European model' of the welfare state and its historical dependence on economic growth. This is because the existing social policy model and programmes in Europe, as well as in the United States and Canada, have long been tied to financial markets, particularly since the shift towards free-market economics that began to spur growth in the 1970s (e.g. King et al. 2012). Moreover, the recent climate change debate has also been framed by the politics and ethics of *economization,* under the assumption that everything, including the environment, is commodifiable (Chapter 2 of this volume). The clear implication is that a value orientation towards endless growth will continue to frame social policy, despite the serious threats of climate change and economic crises for human well-being and the health of the biosphere.

Chapter 4 of this volume provides an empirical examination of the financialization of social programmes through the growing penetration of public-private partnerships (PPP) into the healthcare system in Canada. The PPP model has been presented as a management strategy for providing higher-quality services in a more cost-efficient manner. However, Whiteside shows that PPP-management design not only fails to deliver cost-effective healthcare services but serves to integrate the logic of 'economization' deeper into the normative framing of public welfare services, with an increasing depoliticized emphasis on 'value for money' and cost-pressure. Although this does not mean that the 'welfare state' is being dismantled in Canada, there is certainly a reversal in normative-valuational priorities concerning public social security and the overall sustainability of the public healthcare system. What is interesting about the partnership in public and private shares of health care spending is that it anchors the material base of the welfare state in the belief that a market economy model best serves economic growth and social programmes.

Despite crises, protest movements (as observed in Greece for example), and alternative models of experimentation with what has been described in the literature as 'post-neoliberalism' (as seen in Bolivia, Ecuador, and Venezuela) (Sader 2009), this book has shown that the prospects of a significant change from a market-oriented economic growth model in the world economy seem remote. In fact, for the countries studied in this book we have shown that in various ways, a neoliberal market-economy model has actually been deepening. For example, Chapter 3, on the neoliberalization process in Turkey and the specific case of water governance issues, is illustrative of historical explanations which tease out the specific and 'variegated' institutional and geographic character of neoliberalism. The authors trace the historical lineage of neoliberal reforms from the period of the Ottoman Empire and the Kemalist reform period of the early Republican era through to the imposition of policy related to EU accession. This not only provides a genealogical perspective on Turkish neoliberalization but sheds light on why neoliberal policies have succeeded and proliferated in modern-day Turkey. The chapter offers an important conclusion in directing our attention to the significance of tracing, across and within countries, the genealogies of market-oriented models through a global comparative-historical perspective. Such a research agenda will enhance our understanding of how market models persist over time and resonate with the policy choices of earlier periods. Through a comparative perspective we can learn much about the different 'logics' and meanings of neoliberalism grounded in cultural values, worldviews, and histories.

The Brazilian example considered by Cypher in Chapter 8 is also a cautionary reminder to those who would too readily generalize and universalize the history and working of 'neoliberalism' into a one-size-fits-all fashion. Cypher argues that a 'Washington-consensus type' of neoliberalism has never been firmly anchored in the socio-economic structure of Brazil, and that the growth path adopted by various governments to address poverty through redistributive policies is best understood as 'neo-developmentalism'. Cypher's description of the Brazilian 'modality' of an economic development project highlights the role of a more inclusionary, socially uplifting state redistributive policy in reducing poverty and inequality. This represents a model of 'growth with redistribution'. Although a focus on redistribution (for example, income redistribution) may be viewed as helping to broaden access to opportunities and upward mobility, Cypher shows that it is anchored within a general structural context of oligarchic landownership, wealth concentration, and educational inequality. However, it is not entirely clear from Cypher's chapter whether the making of a Brazilian modality of economic growth encompasses socially inclusive 'bottom-up' processes coupled with some degree of state autonomy, or represents a form that is imposed through top-down processes of policy intervention by neo-developmentalist state managers. Regardless, what this chapter makes clear is that growth-oriented developmentalism is deeply rooted in the history of Brazilian political economy, firmly centred on the idea that the state is responsible for responding to social inequalities. This is a 'negotiated' economic growth project, reflecting critical political attention to objective forms of inequality such as income and wealth mal-distribution, and lack of educational opportunities – all of which diminish opportunities for self-realization. This kind of a project allows us to raise important questions when considering whether new forms of civil society-based dialogue are emerging in the global political economy – not necessarily directed towards 'contesting development' (cf. McMichael 2010); but *in fact* directed towards expanding and deepening market models through compensatory, redistributive social policies. What is observed here are geo-historically varied trajectories of capitalism's transformation, but as aligned with the politics of redistribution.

The notion of 'development through redistribution', which might also be defined as 'left-developmentalism', seems to be grounded in the expectation that the state better manages development in ways that take inequalities into account, along with the sense of 'fairness' necessary for the effective functioning of the economy (e.g. Stiglitz 2012: 121–35). The deepening of neoliberal capitalism in the global South is consistent with redistributive politics and the expectation that the state will assume greater responsibility. In the case of Kerala, India, Gibson (2012) hypothesizes that redistributive policies can actually expand development if historically marginalized social groups directly participate in the selection and allocation of state benefits and public goods, such as public housing, latrines, and sanitation. Left-leaning political parties are also expected to play a role in the articulation and representation of the interests of the underprivileged at the state level. Cypher's work in this volume, as well as Gibson's elsewhere, may lead us to hypothesize the emergence of distinctive pathways of development through redistribution and a more politicized grassroots activism. Stiglitz (2012) is more concerned with governmental policies in relation to the socio-political consequences of economic growth *without* redistribution. In his 2012 book, *The Price of Inequality,* Stiglitz examines the effects of high economic inequality in the United States, emphasizing the potential threat it poses for social cohesion and stability, the future of democracy and national identity, as well as economic efficiency, productivity, and growth.

The African Union's new leader, Nkosazana Dlamini-Zuma, articulates her defence of development through redistribution in relation to the political implications of inequality. For her, the biggest challenges facing the African continent are underdevelopment, poverty and the inequitable distribution of wealth and income. She argues that 'development is not "nice to have," but it is essential for social peace and stability' (Jobson 2012: 58). Dlamini-Zuma's defence of economic development in order to realize peace and stability is a call for governments to play a greater role in responding to inequalities and attending to social distributive issues. It is a plea for a new kind of developmentalist politics, one which cultivates a sense of concern for inequality and mutual responsibility in terms of the *results* this inequality may generate, as observed, for example, in recent events during the so-called Arab Spring.

In assessing the *reasons* for desiring 'development via redistribution', it is important to take note of a full range of core issues concerning unjust inequalities. These issues involve the rethinking of a social episteme and normative commitments on how to define social and ecological survival value, reshape society, cultivate democratic citizenship, and initiate a more engaged civic life based on mutual respect. A core normative principle for mutual respect involves enhancing the capabilities of individuals and communities 'by the freedoms they actually enjoy to choose the lives that they have reason to value' (Sen 1992: 81), and allowing them to actively participate in the shaping of the conditions of their own care (Sennett 2003). Conceived in this way, 'autonomy', according to Sennett (2003: 120–6), is a powerful recipe for democratic citizenship. Much remains to be analysed here, and I will return to this topic later in the chapter.

Chapter 10 on Mexico shows that the 'negotiated' implementation of development does not always produce policy outcomes consistent with a certain model and in alignment with social redistribution in favour of the poor. Muñoz Martinez underscores the significance of classes and rival class fractions in the state mediation of distributional effects, generating contradictory outcomes for various groups. I would argue that state policy mediates conformity to an economic model through initiatives directed at reconciling the conflicting demands of various capital groups. The state's articulation of a policy framework is never a neutral, merely technical process. It is always embedded in, and contingent upon, the highly charged political relations of power struggles, contestation, and resistance. It is particularly noteworthy here that as state policy is subject to conflicting demands, negotiations, and reinterpretations by various societal groups, contrasting policy outcomes cannot be interpreted as an indicator of inconsistencies in the state's developmentalist role in bolstering a certain path of economic growth. The seeming inconsistencies insinuate the actual workings and context-dependency of the political economy as a historically negotiated process. This comes close to what Kohli (2009) calls the 'fragmented-multiclass' nature of the state in policy-making – a concept which helps us better understand the adaptive capacity and flexibility of neoliberalism as rooted in locally varied complexities. Although Muñoz Martinez's chapter reveals the complex, often conflictual relationship between various fractions of capital and the state, it nevertheless presents a picture of a 'cohesive-capitalist state', which Kohli (2009) defines in terms of being more responsive to the pressures induced by rival class fractions. I would further argue that in addition to class fractions, an empirically and theoretically complementary line of further research should also focus on the excluded and marginalized by examining state policy options that take into account citizen demands for equality. Such an inquiry must consider newly emerging social forces as political agents whose cultural and representational claims may enter into the reshaping of policy frameworks for redistribution. This research could help present a more balanced understanding of 'negotiation' which reflects on the interests of the marginalized in shaping public policy, as well as provide a theoretical foundation for the attractiveness of growth-oriented economic projects and associated processes of deepening neoliberal restructuring via redistribution.

Redistribution is generally understood as 'public social spending', mainly in terms of a percentage of economic activity or the adoption of major social programmes (Amenta and Hicks 2010). Recent literature also places an emphasis on the different mechanisms of redistribution provided through other forms of public intervention, including incentives and taxation, as well as different ways of providing social benefits including private spending on social provision efforts (Adema and Whiteford 2010). A focus on social spending – state and private – as a measurement of public goods provisioning often leads to a presentation of the effects of 'development' as delineating greater integration into the economy on the part of the poor and marginalized. However, this presentation lacks a much needed reflexivity which questions the value and meaning of the *materiality* of, and incorporation into, an economic model that is intricately bound up with a discursive logic privileging market competition and the economization of life. In contrast, democratic citizenship requires a recalibrated balance of power in which rights, equality, justice, and a politico-normative ethic of responsibility play a part in the making of socially inclusive politics (Somers 2008). We are then left with the question of how to make sense of a gap between a singular perspective on economic growth involving various forms of redistribution schemes designed to reintegrate the poor into the economy *and* the need to redefine the realm of the 'social' with a multi-perspectival approach to well-being that expresses different meanings of citizenship and the economy in a democratically inclusive way.

Although a market-oriented policy model has been adopted throughout much of the world, there is no single-policy convergence on its norms and practices. There are wide ranging space-specific variations in its content, meaning, and practices. Further, divergences in government policy in backing a market-driven neoliberal economy model suggest that the model has not followed a linear, prescribed path. Its enactment has been responsive to general citizen-based criticism, underlying power dynamics, historical lineages, and long-held discursive interpretive struggles. It is important to underscore that this book's emphasis on neoliberalism's 'flexibility' and 'adaptability' should not be seen as ignoring its commonly held knowledge claims and normative principles. There is a rather generalized 'anticipatory knowledge' (Schwegler 2008) structure of neoliberalism convened globally and embodied nationally by policy teams in devising a particular trajectory of change, albeit negotiated within the highly complicated field of political, cultural struggles and evolving political compromises.[1] That is to say, although the deepening of a market model is globally experienced, this book's emphasis on case-specificity and the flexibility of neoliberalism helps reveal that state-centric approaches are still hovering over the politics of restructuring through which conformity to economic growth is addressed, with an added emphasis on redistribution and, thus, the reintegration and disciplining of the poor.

Participation of marginalized groups in the workings of the economy, bundled with social provisioning, is often empirically observed in redistributive development schemes. But redistributive development must also be seen more generally from a particular social-change perspective that addresses the question of equality, justice, and democracy (Callinicos 2000; Sen 2009). A fundamental issue remains, compelling us to rethink what kind of 'value system' develops as the pursuit of redistribution becomes attached to a mode of knowledge which privileges market principles in the economy (cf. Atasoy 2013). A critical assessment of this connection is intertwined with an interpretive valuation of what it represents in forging a substantially more democratic, socially inclusive citizenship, and engaged civic life – one that addresses the generalized ontological condition of precarity for many in the world today. While a developmentalist emphasis on marginalized groups and their integration into the economy may aim to address the 'cumulative effects of poverty and discrimination' (Cameron and Palan 2003: 179), a rethinking of 'the deep structure' (Callinicos 2000: 87) and normative framework of the capitalist world economy is central to the critical reassessment of redistributive development. There is little dispute as to the historical role of liberalism in the global expansion and deepening of capitalism. As argued by Wallerstein (2011; 1995), liberalism (with its set of ideas, values, and norms) has been a 'political metastrategy' or programme that is integral to the historical deepening of the capitalist world economy and the promise of achieving a good society for many in the world.

Today, the term 'development through redistribution' is often used to address the demands and struggles of the poor, the dis-employed, the uncompetitive, the marginalized, and the excluded, whom, according to Cameron and Palan (2003), occupy the space of the 'anti-economy'. The anti-economy refers to a portion of the economy which is left out of national and global economies (Cameron and Palan 2003: 178). Although today's redistributive state is expected to address existential inequality and insecurity stemming from lived experiences in the anti-economy, it is not clear whether redistributive-development schemes can transform societies and economies from the bottom up. For the most part, as was the case with eighteenth-century liberalism, redistributive developmentalism is embedded in a singular policy category normatively preordained by the market logic of the competitive world economy, according to which 'people' must live. Rather than backing norms that sustain a redistributive vision directed towards substantive social change and inclusive democratic citizenship tied to social and environmental sustainability, the high levels of economic growth and export success achieved by the countries examined in this book are very much aligned with labour flexibilization, wage restraint, financialization, privatization of public goods, and economic incentive structures. These mechanisms and strategies are hypothesized into the choices and motivations of individuals which are assumed to rest on utilitarian considerations and a form of decision-making based on cost-benefit analysis measured in monetary terms.

Adopting a more optimistic tone, Gibson (2012) emphasizes 'redistributive direct democracy' (RDD) for the poor, who are seen to benefit from the development schemes undertaken by states. In the example of Kerala, India, RDD is devised and implemented with the help of left-leaning political parties which assist in the allocation of public goods to marginalized groups through direct citizen participation, especially the mass participation of women. With an empirical focus exclusively on the allocation of the *results* of development, Gibson takes the idea of 'development' itself for granted. Also, a redistributive scheme implemented through direct citizen participation is not only very rare but highly susceptible to manipulation and exploitation by state managers (Cook and Kothari 2000). What concerns me in Gibson's work is the possibility that the state may be capitalizing on conditions of poverty and marginalization for the discursive deepening of growth models, while keeping with a neoliberal policy orientation, which, in the case of India, was adopted in 1991. Further, there is a major issue here which remains unstudied: the effects of this type of 'redistributive development' on livelihoods, the right to participate in income-generating activities, and the overall normative condition and cultural meaning of socially inclusive citizenship. Nevertheless, according to Gibson, RDD institutions in large countries of the global South such as India, Brazil, and Indonesia can purposefully enlist the marginalized to allocate public goods such as housing and latrines. For Gibson, the participation of historically marginalized groups can expand the redistributive outcomes of development for civil repair that matter to households. No doubt this seems a powerful narrative, but it may also help to 'disguise' the relations of political economy as the state actually administers the existential inequalities, hence taming the dangerous classes and their popular outrage. If institutionalized, well-bounded organizations for the articulation and expression of political discontent in public politics are either absent or weak, the possibility of often spontaneous, transgressive contention arising from popular outrage may be quite high, with huge political ramifications, as observed in Arab Spring events. Possibilities for state-led 'containment' should not be dismissed in discussions on the various political means utilized for the allocation of the *results* of development. While RDD institutions may very well be part of the 'contentious democratization' process (McAdam et al. 2001: 264–304), it is important to be clear about the substantive changes this may bring to the quality of human life rather than drawing conclusions based on procedural processes about participation in decision-making.

The fundamental issue is not whether the results of development should be distributed to the poor. Rather, it is how to set the terms of value concerning social and ecological reconstitution and sustainability that attend demands for egalitarian justice and context-specific rights of individuals and communities in pursuit of self-definition and self-rule (cf. Patel 2009). This approach helps to shift the epistemological frame towards a different meaning and value orientation for embodying the connections between egalitarian justice and an engaged civic life – one which incorporates democratic social change and the language of rights mobilized by marginalized groups. This is a value orientation which requires critical engagement with growth-oriented narratives. It clashes with a singular orientation to the economic gains from such projects and compels us to interrogate certain solutions that connect the question of value to the provisioning of 'incentives', often by the state. Such 'solutions' are devised on the road to greater intensification of profit-driven thinking, which Adaman and Madra (in Chapter 2 of this volume) have examined through the notion of 'economization'.

As the dominant episteme of today, economization reduces the concept of citizenship to an ideal-typical understanding of individuals and groups exercising their preferences and choices in a manner circumscribed and delineated by 'incentives' based on calculating consequences (cf. Becker 1991; Bell 1979; 1960). A citizenship ethics based on incentive-provisioning describes the general criterion for citizenship common to liberalism; individuals are 'rational', motivated to maximize their returns, responding to a utilitarian cost and benefit analysis through calculative measurement (Sandel 2009: 31–57). This perspective raises far-reaching concerns about historical subjectivities and citizenship, the political domain of the social, and modes of valuation, in terms of the effects of the profit-driven, market-oriented restructuring of societies on social and ecological wellbeing. The more pertinent political question involves a different understanding of citizenship as a multi-layered concept. It is historically variable and contingent, and bears on a set of issues prescribed by a plurality of normative influences, cultural narratives, political struggles, and critical-interpretive positions. These issues attend a more comprehensive understanding of democracy and the democratization process (e.g. Atasoy 2011; Marshall 1963; Sassen 2006; Somers 2008; Tilly 2007; 2004; Yuval-Davis 2003). This broader understanding of citizenship does not evade the question of a political economy which unequally endows societal groups and further reinforces categorical, durable inequalities (cf. Tilly 1998), while also damaging ecological sustainability. It critically engages with it.

It is an error to suggest on the basis of redistributive development schemes pursued by some states that governments are actually retracting from their support of market-driven economic models and moving in the direction of a 'post-neoliberal' order. The existence of wide ranging space-specific variations in the content, meaning, and practices of market-oriented models, as well as governments' attentiveness to social redistributive issues, points to the crucial significance for research of rethinking the articulation between critical social analysis and a normative position on the question of equality and redistributive justice (cf. Callinicos 2000; Fraser 1995; Sandel 2009; Wright 2013). There is a global expansion of social redistributive policies and social welfare programmes pursued by many of the strong states from the global South, including Brazil, China, India, Indonesia, Mexico, South Africa, and Turkey (e.g. Castles et al. 2010; Haggard and Kaufman 2008). These policies do not represent an emergent narrative of 'convergence' with the socio-economic standards of countries from the global North. Countries of the global South do not share the post-war Keynesian legacy of welfare-state building with countries of the global North. They have followed a different trajectory, which McMichael (2012) has defined as 'developmentalist'. Given the widespread presence of the informal sector and the precarious labour of the wageless and dis-employed in countries of the global South, for example, government attentiveness to social issues cannot be understood through the prism of the twentieth-century welfare-state definition of the 'social'. The twentieth-century understanding of the social was associated with the concept of citizen-state, where the wage-earning class of organized labour was the main player together with capital (cf. Ferguson 2009; Polanyi 1944). Today, we observe a fundamentally different socio-political domain with complicated existential issues, marginalization, and survival strategies. Thus, a comparative-empirical exploration concerning public provisioning has to address diverse social-political agendas, multiple ways of negotiation, and political compromise which further muddle the question of how to articulate critical social analysis and a normative position on justice, equality, and redistribution.

Yörük (2012) argues that the current expansion of social welfare programmes and relief for the poor in countries of the global South may have become a common government strategy to contain various forms of political tension arising from increasing urban inequality and poverty. Similarly, Reis (2006) describes government support for the agrarian reform movement in Brazil as an inequality-reducing measure, one largely motivated to reduce urban violence, crime, and insecurity – social problems perceived by the political elite as the main negative effects of poverty. This strategy is not designed to promote a significant change in the prevailing patterns of redistribution. My purpose here is not to question whether these social welfare policies are beneficial for their recipients. I am interested in their deployment as policies politically aligned with a certain modality of development, however stable this alignment might be (cf. Collier 2005). In those approaches which defend 'development through redistribution', there seems to be something lacking – a broadly shared normative, cultural position on, and substantive moral engagement with, inequality and injustice, in terms of what needs to be 'valued' and respected in a rethinking of social and ecological sustainability (Sennett 2003). There is considerable evidence to suggest that redistributive policies are increasingly tied to a 'utilitarian' concern with poverty and inequality, a form of 'calculating' their social consequences (in a cost-benefit analysis) for economic growth and social stability rather than a commitment to egalitarian justice for its own sake (Sandel 2009: 31–57). The calculative spirit of much 'development via redistribution' fails to respect human dignity and ecological integrity, as Chapter 2 argues.

In the global South the pervasiveness of 'wageless labour' in the informal economy and the general precariousness of existence remain distinct from what Standing (2011) has described for those who live in the former welfare states of the global North in the context of lost job security following the economic crises of the 1970s and early 1980s. Rather than leading to the emergence of a new and dangerous global 'class', the 'precariat' in the global South utilizes a broad range of experimental strategies to survive on a day-to-day basis. According to Millar (2012), in her study of the urban poor in Rio de Janeiro who live by reclaiming recyclables from the city's garbage dumps, the poor continually refashion their existence as a means of 'evasion' rather than an act of resistance or critique. They must constantly negotiate their ontological condition of precarity as a survival strategy. Although it is not the focus of Millar's study, existing research shows that moving from 'survival' to 'transformation' requires active civic, political engagement with the context of vulnerability which continually generates vital injuries and perpetual ontological crises of persistent poverty (e.g. Datta et al. 2007; Eriksen and Silva 2009; Hutchinson 2012). Active engagement and the interrelated processes of remaking it (both locally and globally) also include negotiating the terms of living, vertically and horizontally, with and without directly targeting the state (cf. Houtzager and Acharya 2011). This perspective requires a fundamental shift in the normative attachment of social analysis to the notions of justice and equality – away from an emphasis on the calculative episteme dominant in market-driven societies. In this regard, our book's emphasis on geo-historical diversity and context specificity is crucial for rethinking the ontological condition of the social *through* place. Such an approach may allow us to better understand the context of vulnerability in the intersection of global-local processes that produce vital, existential inequalities and experiences.

The countries examined in this book continue to achieve high levels of economic growth. According to a report published in *The Economist* magazine (2012), this is also now true for Mexico, though it was hit hard by the 2007 global financial crisis compared to other large countries from the global South. A recent cover story in *the Guardian Weekly* (4–10 January 2013) was titled 'Meet the World's New Boomers'. According to the author, it is not the famed BRIC countries (Brazil, Russia, India, and China) but a second wave of up-coming countries, including Turkey, Mexico, and Indonesia that will soon dominate the global economy, largely because of their investment in infrastructure and education, as well as their ability to generate strong domestic demand. Hawksworth, chief economist at PricewaterhouseCoopers, expects that by 2050 Turkey's economy will be larger than Italy's and one of the largest in Europe, while Indonesia and Mexico are expected to outstrip Germany and the United Kingdom (Elliott 2013). The present book has shown that despite high levels of economic growth, ecological issues, existential injuries, and other vulnerabilities continue to constraint the life chances for many in the world. The policies of redistributive growth adopted by countries in the global South frequently appear to be more consistent with increasing commodification and the deepening of capitalism, rather than part of a general political process moving towards a more democratic and socially inclusive citizenship.

The other aspect of rethinking 'development via redistribution' concerns employment and skills, and the interrelated issues of economic and labour-market security. Invernizzi takes this up in Chapter 5 of this volume. Without delving into the general scientific and intellectual developments of nano-research in the context of science and technology studies, Invernizzi raises important research concerns in regard to the processes of industrial adoption and diffusion, and the labour-market implications of nanotechnology development for trade unions. The global nanotechnology labour market is still relatively small, employing workers mostly in the highly specialized scientific field of research and development. Only a small number of countries, transnational corporations, and nano-dedicated smaller companies are involved in the advancement of research to the level of production of nanotechnology-enabled products. Invernizzi's research provides important insights into the link between technological development and labour markets, suggesting that the implications of this technology are becoming instrumental for the competitiveness-enhancement strategies of many countries in the global economy. She argues that with the increasing diffusion of nanotechnology, industrial sectors and skill distribution may be reconfigured, with many low-skilled and labour-intensive jobs becoming redundant. At the same time, current global labour-force trends are likely to be reinforced in relation to outsourcing, displacement, and global industrial specialization, as well as the deepening bifurcation of work between highly skilled technology specialists and less skilled workers. Nanotechnology substitution of raw materials used in agriculture and the mining industry may also have a negative effect on employment patterns in emerging economies. Given the potential impact of nanotechnology on labour markets, Invernizzi explores the policy perspectives advanced by trade unions in the European Union, Canada, the United States, Latin America, and Australia, through an analysis based on published position statements and interviews. Although nanotechnology-related policy concerns range from social-ethical issues to health and workplace safety, trade unions have just begun to consider the implications of nanotechnology on employments and skills. In addition to the rather diminished role they currently play in influencing working conditions and redistribution, trade unions also lack the much-needed technical information and expertise necessary to fully appreciate the possible changes and challenges introduced by the new technology. This weakened position makes it very difficult for unions to articulate a social policy position which can advance social and industrial citizenship rights in the face of technology-induced labour market risks – risks that may be further intensified by the ongoing economic downturn.

'Social transformation' is a difficult and multifaceted concept involving highly charged, complicated, and protracted processes. It entails the reconstitution of societies, capital and social classes, the reconfiguring of states and political alliances, the remaking of institutions, and ultimately the re-definition of historical subjectivities and citizenship. There are now significant studies which aim to bring 'critical struggles for social change' into contemporary social analysis (cf. McMichael 2010). However, with the exception of Chapter 11, our book's empirical focus is not on the question of social struggle for transformation. Rather, the contributors examine social-change projects through an emphasis on the complicity of states in re-aligning policy with a strong attachment to the idea of economic growth, exports, and deepening commodification. Accurate observation of the world-wide strengthening of neoliberal capitalist relations is important if we are to avoid hastily constructed arguments on social-change activism confronting and/or contesting neoliberalism via various political means including 'participatory democracy', 'digitally enabled social-change activism', or 'global networked activism' (e.g. Baiocchi 2005; Earl and Kimport 2011; Juris 2008; Shirky 2009). Without minimizing the value of studies which advance the ways in which activist movements advocate new pathways for thinking about and carrying out social change (e.g. McMichael 2010), we observe that market-oriented programmes have been expanding worldwide through state social policy intervention under the current conditions of economic crisis. Our analysis of the complex connections between domestic and global dynamics across diverse cases spread over four different regions of the world indicates that neoliberal market-economy models, albeit contextually varied, are going to be with us for the foreseeable future, with all the attendant injuries they inflict. Therefore, as argued by Bowles in Chapter 9 of this volume, it is important to pay closer empirical and theoretical attention to the question of how the domestic particularities of national trajectories and the specific features of political compromises interact with the overall regularities in the global market economy. This is necessary to politically contextualize the global expansion of market models. In my opinion, it is through such efforts that we may be able to think of transformative politics *through* place, not through an imaginary polar divide between oppositional movements against global neoliberalism on one side and activism directed at state-centric policy schemes on the other.

Chapter 9 discusses the prospects of a structural change in China's economic growth path by taking into account a state-led perspective on the redistributive consequences of political realignments in the economy. As China's export-oriented growth has often been seen as contributing to global imbalances, some expect China to rebalance its economic development with a shift from an export to a domestic-demand orientation. A domestic consumption-driven growth path is deemed to be achievable in China mainly through income redistribution and social welfare policies, as well as accelerated urbanization and employment. For Bowles, this shift is not confined to a technical policy issue of channelling resources in order to resolve contradictions in the global economy for longer term global economic recovery. It may lead to a political collision of conflicting interests between export-led pro-growth and wage-led pro-redistribution policies.

The question of agency interpenetrating with forms of structure is central to an understanding of the primacy of the state in growth-oriented policy shifts. A concern with the consequences of wages, income inequality, and redistribution for economic growth, and the implications of this for market-correction, rests on a type of citizenship politics and discursive logic that connects the new patterns of economic growth to the capacities for deliberation, judgement, and reflective choice on the part of social actors acting in contexts which can be both constraining and enabling (cf. Emirbayar and Mische 1998). The logic of economization elaborated by Adaman and Madra in Chapter 2 of this volume reduces individuals and groups to the status of rational, calculating goal-seekers responding to incentives in their decisions and judgements. This conception of human agency draws attention to the incorporation of a greater number of individuals into the workings of the market economy through deliberative/reflective choice-making based on incentives. In determining value, rights in general and the limits of public goods allocation are tied to a calculative framework based on cost-benefit analysis. However, the elevation of a market-based normative value to epistemically dominant status is historically contingent upon the world-historical circumstances of the global economic crisis and the deepening of neoliberalism. Nevertheless, the connections between a changing economic structure and human agency, including transformative resistance and democratic citizen politics, are complex (e.g. Atasoy 2009; Campbell 2009; Emirbayar and Mische 1998; Gill 2007).

This complexity becomes even greater in relation to the issue of social reproduction, as seen in Chapter 7, on the growing privatization of care and the intensification of gender exploitation in China. A gradual shift in China's childcare policy from an emphasis on public provisioning to privatization has complicated the discursive meaning of 'relative gender neutrality' in the market economy when it comes to women's labour market participation. Ultimately, the ongoing state-led social reorganization of childcare through privatization shifts the material representation of gender relations towards one of inequality and exploitation, tying responsibilities of care to changes in the family that interpenetrate with the background structure of social class.

The channelling of resources into a wage-led growth model in China and elsewhere through redistributive policies, with the goal of correcting markets, can only reframe a value-orientation to emphasize the hierarchical rearrangement of states and political power, rather than opening a space for increased opportunities for democratic, socially inclusive citizenship. An 'ability to act independently of the constraining power of social structure' is defined by Campbell (2009: 407) as 'agentic power'. Sen (1992: 81) defines such power as the freedom-based assessment of justice – the capability of individuals to 'enjoy to choose the lives that they have reason to value'. Both conceptions have direct relevance to the social relations of political engagement for critically evaluating and recomposing the conditions of everyday life. As Chapters 6 and 7 show, a policy shift in China's economy would embody complications resulting from a concern with market-correction at the global level, thereby recalibrating capitalism's trajectory and further constraining the 'agentic power' of citizen groups in that trajectory. This has damaging consequences for the capability of individuals and communities to choose to 'lead one type of life or another' that 'they have reason to value' (Sen 1992: 40, 81).

Chapter 6 by Zhang demonstrates that in playing a constitutive role in the economy, the state in China encourages 'bidding wars' by local states to attract (typically) labour-intensive investment in manufacturing to rural areas. This policy has been implemented through the use of a 'floating population' of rural migrants which is available on a massive scale, initially migrating from poverty-stricken inlands to the booming coastal towns, and, more recently, making the 'long march' back inland from the eastern coastal regions. China's household registration system (*hukou*) has governed the movement of migrants back to the countryside, preventing them from settling permanently in cities. A new form of 'land enclosure' realized within the existing relations of China's socialist land-tenure system has displaced farmers from their lands, opening up massive space for industrial parks to flourish in the countryside. Zhang is clear that China's economic growth trajectory preys on the availability of cheap labour, the displacement of populations, and land grabbing mediated by the political manipulation of local state officials. The conclusions drawn in both Chapters 6 and 7 support Bowles' contention that economic growth in China will not translate into significantly different existential conditions for the poor, the vulnerable, and women. Therefore, China's prospects for adopting a wage-led growth path through redistribution appear rather slim.

Moreover, both the local-born and 'floating' populations of China appear to be accommodating changes in state-led perspectives on economic growth. While Zhang does not examine the tension resulting from such accommodation in the relations between state and citizens, this is a valuable subject for future research. The study of citizen politics and associated critical issues relating to the articulation of rights more generally in China, and elsewhere for that matter, would allow us to interrogate the extent to which state-policy manipulations constitute a single-focussed, top-down imposition of policy prescriptions. Zhang exposes the role of 'promotion tournaments' orchestrated by the central state in mobilizing the GDP-maximizing efforts of local officials, while pointing out that the financial burden of infrastructural investments lies within the jurisdiction of local governments. This opens yet another opportunity for future research, by problematizing the role of 'state-bureaucratic cohesiveness' in initiating and implementing large changes, and questioning the nature of the relationship between state officials and the conflictual situations in which bureaucratic cadres (local, provincial, and state) may find themselves (cf. Chibber 2002). It is also important in enabling us to critically assess the capacity of citizens and citizens groups to actively engage with the structuring contexts promoted by the state within which they lead their lives. Historical comparative research focusing on countries in the global economy which continue to achieve high levels of economic growth would, therefore, allow us to better understand the role of what Cypher calls the 'neo-developmentalist' state in the expansion and deepening of a neoliberal economy worldwide (Chapter 8).

Between 2008 and 2010, the British Broadcasting Corporation (BBC) broadcast a six-part television special which covered the transformation of White Horse village in western China from a verdant valley in Wuxi County into a modern urban industrial park. The show exposes the contingent practice of politics played out between citizens and state policy agencies. The BBC story concerns the disintegration of rural communities and the 'disappearance' of subsistence-based villagers into the newly created city as labourers and marginals, while manufacturing industries relocate to rural areas (Gracie 2010). The villagers express serious doubts about the safety and durability of new apartment buildings and are suspicious that developers have cut corners on construction materials by forging opportunistic political connections. They complain loudly that public safety has been compromised, and therefore refuse to move into their allocated apartments. Local state officials are seen to be important agents in reaching a 'consensus' – part of a government technique to urbanize the countryside and 'manage' the rural populations with the promise of prosperity, improvement in living standards, and greater educational opportunities for children. However, this consensus is also tied to the question of accountability on the part of the state, as embodied in the promises made by local officials. Although villagers believe that 'defiance is only temporary' and that 'the authorities win all battles in the end', it appears that the prospect of resistance, non-compliance, and criticism strategically underpins ongoing ambiguities in the relations between the state and citizens. Insight into the complexities of state-policy implementation through an understanding of the tensions and ambiguities of citizen politics is important for revealing the relations and context through which states exert control over their populations. It also allows us to recast social analysis by paying attention to what Abrams (1982: x) calls the 'puzzle of human agency', with its many digressions, confrontations, disputes, mistrusts, and conflicts – all contingently built on the process of restructuring context.

Bringing the contingent processes of a two-dimensional politics (structure and citizenship) into an analysis of the structuring of context is an important aspect of understanding large-scale changes *through* place (cf. Pigg 1992). 'Economic efficiency' and 'cost-benefit trade-off', which belong to the logic of economization, may very well define the epistemological criteria for determining value and the body of rules in orienting the localized, everyday practices of people within the world-wide discourses of market rule. This orientation may have important consequences for citizenship politics (Somers 1999). At the heart of the issue is the historical possibility of a process of reasoning which subjects a given criterion in determining value to the test of democratic accountability. This occurs in relation to long-held beliefs, a particular set of local/national circumstances, various globalized schemes, and world-historical conditions. Framing *contingency* in this way poses a methodological challenge to the historical possibility and location of the *public sphere* in which transformative politics is embedded – a topic taken up by Carroll in this volume.

As Chapter 11 indicates, transformative politics is typically slow and fraught with difficulties, yet still possible. Carroll places his hope in the transnational alternative policy groups (TAPGs) involved in producing counter-hegemonic projects at the global level. This type of transnational mobilization is an emergent component of 'global civil society' that is producing normative positions and knowledge structures which confront the global policy-making context of neoliberalism and advance democratic alternatives. Such an analysis accepts 'global civil society' as the public sphere of both global hegemonic and counter-hegemonic politics, based on conceptual recognition that the state-territorial political sphere is increasingly unable to meet the challenges of neoliberal globalization. Carroll's TAPGs are highly diverse in terms of policy orientation, organizational form, and spatial location. They face the possibility of absorption or cooption into left-alternative nationalist movements, with or without internationalist entanglements, or of becoming irrelevant to the localized social and political geography of citizen politics.

Although it does not pose the question of 'global civil society' in terms of a singular space of political power, Carroll's approach is premised on the *relocation* of power sources away from the state. This is significant when considering how to rethink the empirical and conceptual meaning of place-specific diversity within existing global policy contexts for defining value. By operating in an 'open space' for dialogue and engaging directly with capitalist and state power, according to Carroll, the political geography of TAPGs' global justice politics is not situated in nationally bound civil societies. I would suggest that this approach positions the politics of embeddedness in a polarized fashion between state-centred, nationally bound civil societies, on the one hand, and the global, on the other. Spatial polarization here is rooted in the fear that neoliberal globalization has eviscerated the public sphere of society where the language of rights, citizen politics, and claims of democracy might be organized. It seems to me that we need not oscillate between these polarities to define the social terrain of public politics. We have only to consider Polanyi's *The Great Transformation* (1944), which forwards the concept of 'protective counter movements', politically articulated in response to the destructive effects of the market economy on society and nature. Polanyi's discussion is historical and based on three variants of state-centred experimentation with social redistribution implemented during the Great Depression of the 1930s. From this intellectual legacy, we have inherited an appreciation for a historically specific understanding of the spatial domain of embeddedness in framing redistributive politics. This allows us to view today's fundamentally different socio-political domain from a perspective that need not be confined to epistemologically binary hierarchies of state-centred versus global. Perhaps, our historical task in this particular period of time is to address the multiple ways and places involved in the practices of citizenship politics – ways that question the uniformity expected from a global expansion of the discursive logic of economization.

Note

1. My own earlier work on the role of Islamic politics in the neoliberalization process in Turkey offers further illustration of a perspective for rethinking the politics of neoliberal restructuring in a theoretically different way. *Islam's Marriage with Neoliberalism* (Atasoy 2009) explores the political reworking of a neoliberal market-economy model in Turkey, which cannot be described as an instance of nationally specific implementation of a closed system of neoliberalism, nor as an 'Islamic' version of building a welfare-state regime. Rather, the book provides an explanation through a study of various societal groups which have been affected by deep class- and region-based inequalities. It also examines the social-cultural injustice of state-led developmentalism during the previous era (1930s–70s) of Turkish politics. Groups studied include newly emerging Muslim capitalists from smaller cities in Anatolia, Muslim women with concerns over the headscarf ban, and those involved in the Kurdish movement. Holding class-, region-, and culture-based grievances against statist developmentalism, these groups view themselves as victims of social injustice, marginalization, and exclusion. They are mobilized in repositioning themselves within history through a process of restoring rights, political and economic entitlements, and cultural recognition in the context of Turkey's EU membership bid, rights which they believe were eviscerated by the earlier statist model of developmentalism. The Islamic reworking of a market model thus includes the political and pedagogical shaping of a general normative position in the articulation of Islamic ethical principles of human dignity and justice combined with neoliberal cultural ideals. It is also frequently supplemented by the liberal-democratic concepts of individual human rights and freedoms. In short, a belief in the ontological primacy of a market-economy model in opposition to state-led developmentalism has been an ethical reference point for various Muslim groups in their normative appeal to social justice. Here, I observe a different kind of relationship being imagined and forged between the state, social policy, and the national political–economic domain, all within the general world-historical complexities of the capitalist economy.

References

Abrams, P. (1982) *Historical Sociology*, Somerset: Open Books.
Adema, W. and P. Whiteford (2010) 'Public and Private Social Welfare', in F.G. Castles, S. Leibfried, J. Lewis., H. Obinger, and C. Pierson (eds) (2010) *The Oxford Handbook of the Welfare State*, Oxford: Oxford University Press.
Amenta, E. and A. Hicks (2010) 'Research Methods', in F.G. Castles, S. Leibfried, J. Lewis, H. Obinger, and C. Pierson (eds) *The Oxford Handbook of the Welfare State*, Oxford: Oxford University Press.
Atasoy, Y. (2009) *Islam's Marriage with Neoliberalism: State Transformation in Turkey*, London & New York: Palgrave Macmillan.
Atasoy, Y. (2011) 'Two Imaginaries of Citizenship in Turkey: The Republican and "Ethical" Models', *International Journal of Politics, Culture, and Society* 24(3–4): 105–23.
Atasoy, Y. (2013) 'Supermarket Expansion in Turkey: Shifting Relations of Food Provisioning', *Journal of Agrarian Change* 13(4): 547–70.
Baiocchi, G. (2005) *Militants and Citizens: The Politics of Participatory Democracy in Porto Allegre*, Stanford, CA: Stanford University Press.
Becker, G. (1991) *A Treatise on the Family*, Cambridge: Harvard University Press.
Bell, D. (1960) *The End of Ideology*, Cambridge: Harvard University Press.
Bell, D. (1979) *The Cultural Contradictions of Capitalism*, New York: Basic Books.
Callinicos, A. (2000) *Equality*, Cambridge: Polity.
Cameron, A. and R. Palan (2003) 'The Imagined Economy', in N. Brenner, B. Jessop, M. Jones, and G. Macleod (eds) *State/Space*, Malden, MA: Blackwell Publishing.
Campbell, C. (2009) 'Distinguishing the Power of Agency from Agentic Power', *Sociological Theory* 27(4): 407–18.
Castles, F.G. (2010) 'The English-Speaking Countries', in F.G. Castles, S. Leibfried, J. Lewis, H. Obinger, and C. Pierson (eds) *The Oxford Handbook of the Welfare State*, Oxford: Oxford University Press.
Castles, F.G., S. Leibfried, J. Lewis, H. Obinger, and C. Pierson (eds) (2010) *The Oxford Handbook of the Welfare State*, Oxford: Oxford University Press.
Chibber, V. (2002) 'Bureaucratic Rationality and the Developmental State', *American Journal of Sociology* 107(4): 951–89.
Collier, S. (2005) 'The Spatial Forms and Social Norms of "Actually Existing Neoliberalism": Toward a Substantive Analytics', International Affairs Working Paper 2005–4.
Cook, B. and U. Kothari (2000) 'The Case for Participation as Tyranny', in B. Cook and U. Kothari (eds) *Participation: The New Tyranny?* London: Zed.
Datta, K., C. McIlwaine, Y. Evans, J. Herbert, J. May, and J. Wills (2007) 'From Coping Strategies to Tactics: London's Low Pay Economy and Migrant Labour', *British Journal of Industrial Relations* 45(2): 404–32.
Earl, J. and K. Kimport (2011) *Digitally Enabled Social Change: Activism in the Internet Age*, Cambridge, MA: MIT Press.
The Economist (2012) 'Special Report, Mexico: Going up in the World', 24 November.
Elliott, L. (2013) 'Meet the World's New Boomers', *The Guardian Weekly* (4–10 January).
Emirbayar, M. and A. Mische (1998) 'What is Agency?' *American Journal of Sociology* 103(4): 962–1023.
Eriksen, S. and J.A. Silva (2009) 'The Vulnerability Context of a Savanna Area in Mozambique: Household Drought Coping Strategies and Responses to Economic Change', *Environmental Science & Policy* 12: 33–52.

Ferguson, J. (2009) 'The Uses of Neoliberalism', *Antipode* 41(S1): 165–84.

Fraser, N. (1995) 'From Redistribution to Recognition? Dilemmas of Justice in a "post-Socialist Age" ', *New Left Review* 212(1): 68–93.

Gibson, C. (2012) 'Making Redistributive Direct Democracy Matter: Development and Women's Participation in the Gram Sabhas of Kerala, India', *American Sociological Review* 77(3): 409–34.

Gill, S. (2007) 'The Globalization of Party Politics', in K. Sehm-Patomaki and M. Ulvila (eds) *Global Political Parties*, London & New York: Zed Books.

Gough, I. and G. Therborn (2010) 'The Global Futures of Welfare States', in F.G. Castles, S. Leibfried, J. Lewis, H. Obinger, and C. Pierson (eds) *The Oxford Handbook of the Welfare State*, Oxford: Oxford University Press.

Gracie, C. (2010) 'A Portrait in Miniature of China's Transformation', BBC News Asia-Pacific, 29 November.

Haggard, S. and R.R. Kaufman (2008) *Development, Democracy, and Welfare States: Latin America, East Asia, and Eastern Europe*, Cambridge: Cambridge University Press.

Houtzager, P.P. and A.K. Acharya (2011) 'Associations, Active Citizenship, and the Quality of Democracy in Brazil and Mexico', *Theory and Society* 40: 1–36.

Hutchinson, J.A. (2012) 'Surviving, Coping or Thriving? Understanding Coping and Its Impact on Social Well-Being in Mozambique', *British Journal of Social Work*. DOI:10.1093/bjsw/bcs167.

Jobson, E. (2012) 'Development Is Essential for Peace', *The Guardian Weekly* (21 December–3 January).

Juris, S.J. (2008) *Networking Futures: The Movements against Corporate Globalization*, Durham, NC: Duke University Press.

King, L., M. Kitson, S. Konzelmann, and F. Wilkinson (2012) 'Making the Same Mistake Again – Or Is It *This Time* Different?' *Cambridge Journal of Economics* 36(1): 1–5.

Kohli, A. (2009) 'States and Economic Development', *Revista de Economia Politica* 29(2), April/June.

Marshall, T.H. (1963) 'Citizenship and Social Class', in T.H. Marshall (ed.) *Sociology at the Crossroads*, London: Heinemann.

McAdam, D., S. Tarrow, and C. Tilly (2001) *Dynamics of Contention*, Cambridge: Cambridge University Press.

McMichael, P. (ed.) (2010) *Contesting Development*, New York & London: Routledge.

McMichael, P. (2012) *Development and Social Change: A Global Perspective*, Los Angeles: Pine Forge Press.

Millar, M.K. (2012) 'The Precarious Present: Wageless Labor and Disrupted Life in Rio de Janeiro, Brazil', Unpublished Paper.

Patel, R. (2009) *The Value of Nothing*, New York: Picador.

Pigg, S.L. (1992) 'Inventing Social Categories through Place: Social Representations and Development in Nepal', *Comparative Studies in Society and History* 34(3): 491–513.

Polanyi, K. (1944) *The Great Transformation*, Boston: Beacon Press.

Reis, P.E. (2006) 'Inequality in Brazil: Facts and Perceptions', in G. Therborn (ed.) *Inequalities of the World*, London & New York: Verso, 193–219.

Sader, E. (2009) 'Postneoliberalism in Latin America', *Development Dialogue: Postneoliberalism – A Beginning Debate*, (51): 171–80. Available online: http://rosalux-europa.info/userfiles/file/DD51.pdf#page=173. (accessed: 3 August 2012).

Sandel, M.J. (2009) *Justice: What's the Right Thing To Do?* New York: Farrar, Straus & Giroux.

Sassen, S. (2006) *Territory, Authority, Rights*, Princeton: Princeton University Press.
Schelkle, W. (2012) 'A Crisis of What? Mortgage Markets and the Social Policy of Promoting Homeownership in the United States and in Europe', *Politics & Society* 40(1): 59–80.
Schwegler, A.T. (2008) 'Take It from the Top (Down)? Rethinking Neoliberalism and Political Hierarchy in Mexico', *American Ethnologist* 35(4): 682–70.
Sen, A.K. (1992) *Inequality Reexamined*, Cambridge: Harvard University Press.
Sen, A.K. (2009) *The Idea of Justice*, London: Allen Lane.
Sennett, R. (2003) *Respect in a World of Inequality*, New York: Norton.
Shirky, C. (2009) *Here Comes Everybody: The Power of Organizing without Organizations*, New York, NY: Penguin.
Somers, M.R. (1999) 'The Privatization of Citizenship', in V.E. Bonnell and L. Hunt (eds) *Beyond the Cultural Turn*, Berkeley: University of California Press.
Somers, M.R. (2008) *Genealogies of Citizenship*, Cambridge: Cambridge University Press.
Stiglitz, J.E. (2012) *The Price of Inequality*, New York & London: W.W. Norton & Company.
Tilly, C. (1998) *Durable Inequality*, Berkeley, Los Angeles, London: University of California Press.
Tilly, C. (2004) 'Trust and Rule', *Theory and Society* 33(1): 1–30.
Tilly, C. (2007) *Democracy*, Cambridge: Cambridge University Press.
Yörük, E. (2012) 'Welfare Provision as Political Containment: The Politics of Social Assistance and the Kurdish Conflict in Turkey', *Politics & Society* 40(4): 517–47.
Yuval-Davis, N. (2003) 'Citizenship, Territoriality and Difference', in N. Brenner, B. Jessop, M. Jones, and G. Macleod (eds) *State/Space: A Reader*, Malden: Blackwell Publishing.
Wallerstein, I. (1995) *After Liberalism*, New York: The New Press.
Wallerstein, I. (2011) *The Modern World-System IV: Centrist Liberalism Triumphant, 1789–1914*, Berkeley, Los Angeles, London: University of California Press.
Wright, E.O. (2013) '2012 Presidential Address: Transforming Capitalism through Real Utopias', *American Sociological Review* 78(1): 1–25.

Index

Note: Locators with '*f*' denote figures; '*n*' denotes notes; '*t*' denotes tables.

GPSR Compliance
The European Union's (EU) General Product Safety Regulation (GPSR) is a set of rules that requires consumer products to be safe and our obligations to ensure this.

If you have any concerns about our products, you can contact us on

ProductSafety@springernature.com

In case Publisher is established outside the EU, the EU authorized representative is:

Springer Nature Customer Service Center GmbH
Europaplatz 3
69115 Heidelberg, Germany

www.ingramcontent.com/pod-product-compliance
Lightning Source LLC
Chambersburg PA
CBHW060750150926
51501CB00004B/139

9781137293671